Helrunar
A Manual of
Rune Magick
by Jan Fries

Mandrake of Oxford

Overleaf: Stone from Smiss, Gotland

© Jan Fries and Mandrake of Oxford, 1993. 2002, 2006
PO Box 250, Oxford, OX1 1AP
ISBN: 1869928-903

Third edition

Other books by the author:
Visual Magick: Manual of Freestyle Shamanism
Seidways: Shaking, Swaying and Serpent mysteries
Living Midnight: Three Movements of the Tao
Cauldron of the Gods: a Manual of Celtic Magick

Contents

Skulda

Acknowledgments

To Frank and Volkert, in memory of our first experiments with rune stance and song. To Joe C. of NAPZ, who back in '82ev, asked whether I could compile some of my experiences in rune magick in a little book. To KG who responding kindly to the resulting thirty page manuscript made me dearly wish to improve it. To Maggie/Nema, by the same mouth for thirteen years of encouragement, bizarre ideas, new practices and lots of wild humour. To Julia, Claudia, Christiane and Manfred, all of whom kindly posed for the rune-posture drawings. To Volkert, for endless discussion on rune-lore, which showed much to our surprise, that we had independently arrived at a lot of very similar results. To Gavin and Mouse for years of fun in information-exchange -remember the wild boars! To Astrid for lots of practical experiments in rune magick, hypnosis and seething trances. To Mogg and Ruth of Mandrake of Oxford, for working their way cheerfully through a manuscript full of odd words in spidery writing. To Julia for love and laughter and the patience it takes to live with the obsessed. And finally to all of you who dare to go beyond book reading into the wild and wonderful world of practice, enthusiasm and personal experience: thank you!

Preface

The magical revival, begun around the opening of the twentieth century by various Victorian-era occultists, is alive and well near the end of the century .In turbulent times, humans tend to seek stability and comfort from truths and realities that transcend the turbulence. When familiar institutions fail, we look to the strange and mysterious. An increasing number of people are choosing to assume responsibility for their own spiritual growth through the twin ways of Mysticism and Magick. In this last decade of the century, there are occult bookshops in any medium-sized city in the 'western ' world; individuals and groups are publishing a growing number of occult magazines; there is an international community of occultists, with subgroups of wiccans neo-pagans, shamans, druids, ceremonial magicians, thelemites, Maat magicians, rune-workers, chaos magicians and others. There are Psychick youth, new-agers,

tantrics, and various self-realization groups that also publish copiously. Much of the available information is either micro-focused on a particular point of interest or a particular system or philosophy, or speaks in terms too broad and vague to be of practical use. Much of the material is either too complex or too simplistic, which isn't surprising, giving the range of levels of understanding among authors and audience. In *Helrunar*, Jan Fries presents a complete Magical system based on the runes, written in plain language that beginners can understand. Experienced Magicians will find it of interest also, since it contains the author's practical field experiences and informed theory. I find it both interesting and praiseworthy that Helrunar doesn't mention grades and degrees of initiation, even though the practices presented in it will provide numerous initiatory opportunities. Jan and I are long-term correspondents who finally met in England in

July 1990. We began with a link in the Maat current, a link which I came to value highly and to enjoy profoundly over the years. Jan writes about what he knows from experience, personal experiments, and happy survival. ('That which does not kill us makes us strong.') His graphic genius illuminates -not merely illustrates -the text. He's travelled extensively to draw numerous petroglyphs from life; those who are familiar with astral imagery will recognize that he draws from life in that realm also. His scholarship is trustworthy, and provides a solid background on the probable history of the runes. The best part of *Helrunar*, in my opinion, lies in the practices, in the definite actions and activities prescribed. The Sioux Medicine Chief, Black Elk, speaks about experiencing a mighty vision concerning the survival of his tribe. Rather than filtering his vision through words to communicate its import to the tribe, Black Elk taught the tribe a dance that he learned from the spirits in his vision. As they danced this sacred dance, the people of the tribe shared Black Elk's vision directly, without a mediator. So it is with *Helrunar*. If you work with the system Jan presents, persevering through obstruction and difficulties, you will be personally transformed. The term 'work' means exactly that: physical effort intelligently applied. Reading *Helrunar* won't transform you, but doing the practices will. Doing the practices means moving about physically, making (sometimes) loud sounds, and overcoming the embarrassment of acting like a fool in private. For the reader who has been working with runes for a while, *Helrunar* offers a fresh point of view. I'm sure Jan

would welcome your point of view as well. What he lacks in solemnity is more than made up for by an irreverent sense of humour and an artist's eye for the absurd. Magick changes with the needs of the time. Although there are a number of Orders, Covens, other groups and individuals who hold that traditions are to be kept unchanged, as a means of preserving them, still others extend the traditions from the past, to the present and on through to the future. The truth that underlies all valid systems of initiation is eternal and changeless. The manifestations of that Truth are changing constantly; each generation needs to interpret and speak the Truth in the language of the times. Our times are seeing the 'global Village' predicted by Marshall McLuhan rapidly linking itself in electronic communications. To balance this burgeoning unity, ethnic/traditional diversity should be encouraged and cherished. The only guarantee of continuity in a particular system is its evolutionary response to -and anticipation of - world changes. *Helrunar* speaks to this situation, encouraging an attitude of fluidity in approach to the runes along with respect for their traditional power and meaning. In my opinion, Jan is one of the most profoundly competent initiates in print today. He fulfils his ethical obligation to the international community of initiates by making the fruits of his experiences available in *Helrunar* and other works. Magicians don't proselytise, coerce, or spoon feed. Here is the material; the rest is up to you.

Nema

Newark,
Ohio USA

Introduction

Do what thou wilt shall be the whole of the Law
Hello! The book you are about to enjoy is a manual. It is meant for practicing magicians of various creeds and currents, for people who enjoy to experiment, to do exercises, to find their own unique interpretation of pagan nature religion. On the surface, the book deals with runes. As you may know already, the runes are an alphabetical system of writing which was popular in northern Europe before the Christian church inflicted the Roman alphabet on the population. Now the meaning of the rune signs went far beyond their use as a system of writing.

As with most ancient alphabets, the runes were considered a sacred system of cosmology, and for many centuries their use was restricted to members of the priesthood, who used them to write, to divine, to bind spells, to work magick, to construct sigils and talismans and to explore body and energy consciousness in various physical and mental exercises. To these priests, each of the rune signs connected with a very specific state of energy and consciousness.

The runes are not a single system but several. What we call the rune alphabets or the futhorc rows nowadays, are collections of sacred symbols which contain the mysteries of many pagan cultures. Some of those rune signs have seen magical use for some 30,000 years or so, which may give you an idea why I consider rune magick not so much as a Germanic or Nordic tradition but as a conglomeration of religious signs containing religious beliefs that began in the Neanderthal periods, were developed by our ancestors, the Cro-Magnon people, and put to magical use by many of the later cultures that made their way across Europe. These points will be dealt with in detail. I simply mention them here so you will get some idea on the scope of things you will encounter in these pages.

What does the word 'rune' mean?

Old English: 'runian' = to whisper.

'leodrunan' = song-runes

Old High German: 'rune' = secret, mystery.

Modern German: 'zu rauen' = to hiss or whisper secrets.

Old Irish: 'run' = secret.

Old Norse: 'runar' = mysteries.

Old Skaldic Icelandic: 'runi' = friend, companion, adviser.

'runnr' = woodland.

Middle Welsh: 'rhin' = magic charm.

Finnish: 'runo' = song, chant, incantation.

No doubt you know that runes can be used for divination, much like the tarot or the Chinese I-Ching. There are plenty of books on this theme, where you can teach yourself how to cast the runes and what they are supposed to mean. The more costly ones may even include a full set of runes, all tastefully done on little bits of plastic, so the result hungry will not have to crawl through trees and bogs looking for wood, but can enjoy the pleasure of instant divination in the comfort of well heated living room. Well, you will not find this sort thing in these pages. Though I do give the traditional meaning of the runes, as quoted from the various rune poems, in the last part of this volume, the emphasis is on practice. This means that I do expect you to enjoy nature contacts (such as trees and bogs), and if you don't, you should better give this book to someone who is better suited to the job than you are.

This is a book of discovery. You are invited to think and experiment for yourself, to do independent research, to explore the rune signs from within and to arrive at your own unique interpretation of the symbols. How can you do this? Lets look at the structure of the whole. The book is divided into three parts. These three sections are named after the Norns - Urda, Werdandi and Skulda, who refer to the flow of development (past, present, future) and to the three levels of the world tree: roots, stem, branches.

In the **Urda** part you will find plenty of material on the history and ethnology of rune magick and European nature religion. This is the soil out of which the system developed. The Urda part also includes chapters on nature experience, cosmology, Qabalah, shamanic practices and the baleful influence on nature religion of National Socialism.

The **Werdandi** part is concerned with practice. The runes are much more than ideas and theory. Each of the rune signs can be imitated by the body, i.e. the symbol form can be assumed in posture, ritual gesture, dance and hand sign. Using certain methods of breathing, chanting and imagination, the power of each rune can be conveyed through body, which leads to highly interesting experiences. Rune energy can be directly experienced this way and used to improve health and energy levels, it can also be used for various magical purposes and for group rituals. Other methods given in the Werdandi section detail divination practices, sigil making and the use of energy for ritual and shamanism.

The last part, **Skulda**, gives the material for the working. Here you will find the genuine old rune poems and various interpretations of the signs and words, plus a few comments I could not resist making. Apart from this dictionary, you will find a detailed description of trance practice and astral projection. These methods will help you to discover your own vision of the runes, i.e. the secret meaning they have to your deep mind. It is this knowledge, which comes from direct experience, that makes your rune magick valid and vital. Using these materials, you are free to develop your own system of rune magick. Let us consider rune magick a field of creative development. This may not look quite as impressive as all those books which promise to reveal 'the genuine old secrets of the holy tradition.' but then I do not believe in any tradition except 'find out for yourself!' This book does not offer the usual 'look up the answer' material so typical of trashy esoteric publications. It does offer methods for the direct experience of each rune. It may take time and effort to master these methods, but then this may help to evolve an understanding of the runes which is specifically suited to your nature, meaning that you have your own genuine experience of each sign and are free to put it to use as suits your will and being.

Instead of asking you to believe in my interpretations, I ask you to examine them critically. I do not want you to adhere to my dogma (which I may or may not believe as suits the occasion) but to explore with an open mind in the joy of self discovery. What works for me need not be suitable for you, do not trust me but find out for yourself.

In these pages you will find some curious metaphors to describe specific aspects of the self. I do not use them quite the way they are applied in the various schools of psychology, and so perhaps I should clear them up straight away. In exploring awareness, we encounter a division of consciousness, which is often classified as the 'conscious' and 'unconscious self'. In this book I will use the term 'conscious self' to describe those aspects of awareness which you experience consciously at any given time. Right now you are conscious of these words for example, and of the ideas, visions, feelings, inner comments which they trigger. You are probably not conscious of your hormone production, or the rhythms of your heart and lungs, or of the things which happened at work the other day. The conscious self is usually a very small field of awareness, which is conveniently considered as an identity, personality, or ego and which consists of various habits, skills, names, labels, achievements, neurotic strains and a deep-rooted belief in its own 'reality'. The 'unconscious self' is not unconscious, it is simply outside of our limited conscious self. The unconscious self, which is often referred to as the deep mind in these pages, does hundreds of fantastic things for us all of the time, and usually we do not even notice or appreciate them. It perceives much more than we consciously do, stores all memories, keeps our bodies healthy and in function, provides dreams and inspiration, keeps our habits automatic, works our thought processes, allows us to learn and forget, keeps our identity continuous and does a myriad of things for us which would utterly overwhelm the conscious self. When speaking in a general context I like to use the metaphor of the deep mind while in certain chapters the metaphor of the 'gods' and 'spirits' seems more efficient. If we consider the 'parts' of the deep mind as distinct entities, such as 'gods', 'angels', 'spirits', 'ghosts', etc., we may find it easier to contact them and establish communication. I do not claim that these beings actually exist. If we want to make contact, which is the essence of Helruning we will find that these models and beliefs are useful. In one sense, the model is true, and the experience real. In another sense, the model is not the reality but a representation of it. We need not believe that any model is real, it is enough to use it to achieve specific effects. What I write here is a book of lies and dead names. You will make use of these dead names, fill them with your experience, and make a system come alive which is specifically you. For this purpose, you should feel free to use any model which produces results.

There are deeper levels to this book, which deal, not so much with the runes but with the art and practice of achieving contact, communication and cooperation with the deep mind. What I write here makes sense to the deep mind, which probably understands much better than you do. Perhaps I ought to speak directly to your deep mind, whether you call it your 'inner self', 'gods', 'spirits', 'holy guardian angel' or 'flygia', and ask the whole of you to make the practices of this book a journey or self-discovery.

Perhaps you should also speak to your deep mind. More so, you ought to watch out for its answers. To make the most out of this book, you could perhaps establish the following habit. At the end of each chapter close your eyes for a moment and turn your attention inwards. Ask your deep mind if it has any comments, hints or improvements upon what your have just read. This will combine the words of these pages with the helpful advise of a genuine and living teacher, whom you may discover within yourself.

Another virtue which may be useful is patience. Some of the practices of this book will require repeated experiment before they begin to work. This means work, often hard work. Sometimes it will be easy and you will get good results, but often it will be difficult and you will need to perservere. Part of this book will be directed at your ego, your identity and at the nature of the reality you believe in. Often the ego with its clear beliefs and firm limitations is the greatest obstacle in the evolution of the whole self.

You will change yourself, and this essentially is what the magick is all about. Your deep mind will help you in this, the 'Great Work'. It has evolved ego in the first place and knows that personality is fluid and can be changed. It is in an excellent position to change you from within and to make you the healthy, life embracing person your whole self wills you to be.

Perhaps you're asking yourself what background this book developed out of. Though I practice and write about nature religion, I do not belong to any of the schools of Wicca or Odinism. This book stems from experience of the ancient ones, but also the modern current of Thelemic magick and its earthing in the Maatian network. These magical systems are all fairly abstract, and their mythology, which is strongly Egyptian/ Hebrew/Sumerian, comes from climes and landscapes which are alien to central Europe. To effect a solid earthing of Thelemic and Maatian consciousness I found it useful to adapt these energy currents to local conditions, to the mountains and forests, to the gods of nature, the rhythm of the seasons, the spirits of the land. *Helrunar* is a way of giving thanks to the spirits of the wild wood, to the natural heritage of pagan Europe. In another sense, *Helrunar* offers more than just another field of magical tradition.

If you go beyond the specific details of any magical tradition, you will notice that, though the beliefs, symbols and contents differ, the functions and structures of magick are international and timeless, and possibly, built into the structure of our brains. I offer this book by the same mouth to you, to me, to us, to all of us. With love and laughter, let us develop something new.

Now, apart from asking you to plunge into practice and fresh experience, I also ask you to get yourself two books. One of them is quite brief and very amusing; *Germania* by Tacitus, the famous Roman historian. The other volume is the *Edda* which is a collection of poems, songs and prose legends dealing with the various Nordic deities and beliefs. The prose parts of the Edda go back to a handbook for Skalds (Nordic bards), composed and collected by Snorri Sturluson around 1200AD in Iceland, while the poems and songs are several centuries older and can be traced to various Scandinavian and Middle European sources. I would not claim that the Scandinavian or Icelandic representation is an adequate description of the older Middle European beliefs. However, so much material was violently destroyed by the church, that these few manuscripts, hidden in Iceland at the northern rim of the world, are the only coherent descriptions of Germanic religion which have come to us. I will refer to these titles very frequently, so get yourself good translations and start to study them. Other works of interest can be looked up in the bibliography.

Love is the Law, Love under Will.
Jan Fries 1993

Preface to the third edition

When I went to school, my history teacher told us about the old Germani. In her opinion, the Taunus mountains were populated by a bunch of brawny brawlers who wore horned helmets and small pieces of pelt. They lived in hilltop settlements which were fortified by ringwalls. Barely able to manage agriculture, they had to rely on hunting to fill their stomachs. They lived in shabby huts with mud-plastered walls and when the Romans came, they fought the invaders with crude swords, pointy sticks and by hurling rocks at them. Those were the days…

Nowadays, the ringwalls of the Taunus are known as the work of La Tène time Celts, who lived on the heights in well organised cities. The largest of them housed as many as 20,000 inhabitants. The fertile Wetterau below the heights is recognised as one of the earliest agricultural districts in central Europe where people began to work the soil around 5,600BCE.

Quite a difference. But it will change again. When I completed the first (hand-written) version of Helrunar in 1989, I had no idea how much history would change over the next decade. I just knew that my history chapters were not good enough. The printed version allowed me to make a few amendments, to add a few much needed bits here and there, and to delete some gross inaccuracies. By the time the book appeared, the history section was already getting out of date. A few years later a new version was to appear. I wanted to rewrite the history stuff, but then my editor, always a cheerful soul when it comes to thinking practically, suggested that an appendix would be less trouble. 'Is there a demon of incompleteness?' he asked, a question I have pondered quite a bit over the last years. It catches up with me each time a manuscript reaches critical mass. The situation was still far from making me happy. So I was delighted to hear that a new edition was being planned, and that I could make some innovations. As a result, the first chapter (on stone age artists and their first symbolic output), the sixth chapter (a genealogy of magick from the stone ages to the iron age) and the appendix were fused into a single unit. Much of the text was rewritten, updated, edited and turned upside down. A large section on the bronze ages, the Celts, Germani and the later Vikings was added. It was a special pleasure to elaborate the theme of Wodan and Helja, and to detail worship in pagan Scandinavia. The chapter on magical rune inscriptions is now twice its original size. The chapter on Seiðr/seething

trances was rewritten, the bibliography was updated and twelve pages of new illustrations added. This does not mean that the job is complete. Archaeology is bound to provide further surprises. Dating of artefacts is still far from satisfactory and certain periods of prehistory are still very badly explored. What you can find in the new chapters is an attempt to catch up with rapid developments. By the time you read this, new data will have appeared. There is nothing more short lived than scientific model-making nowadays.

I hope that my efforts will contribute to your own research. More than ever, the modern pagan has a responsibility to look out for new developments and to do independent research. Don't simply trust me. You have a brain in your cauldron of knowledge that longs for action and entertainment.

The rewriting of so many items lead to some uneven spots and some tough breaks in style. Sorry folks, while it might have been fun to rewrite the whole (damn) book to get an aesthetically pleasing presentation, I find it much more fun to devote my time to new topics. Let me end this introduction by giving thanks to those who supported work on the new sections. Ronald Hutton for use of a paper on the modern goddess. Joe Revill for linguistic advice regarding the word *Helrunar*.

Most of all, I wish to thank Anad for all the joy in rune practice, forest walks and long hours of exploring prehistory.

Thank you!

Jan Fries 2005

1 How did it all begin?

The runes, as the system of cosmology and writing that we know today, were not developed all at once. Many of the signs appeared in earlier periods. The custom of marking abstract ideas by carving, scratching or painting signs is as old as humanity. As you will see in this chapter, it began before our own species appeared on planet earth. There are signs that look much like runes in many prehistoric cultures, in Europe and elsewhere, and some of these signs are so basic and common that they are almost an international phenomena. Points, lines, strokes, crosses, tridents, tree-shapes, arrows, waves, zig-zag, meanders and the like appear early in the Palaeolithic, and to this day they continue to fascinate. A lot of signs looking like runes appeared in stone age cave art (see the selection of symbols from Lascaux).

some examples

ᛁᛏ᙭ ᚤᚠᛈᚠᛘ ᛁᛐᚠᛉᛃᛝᚨ ᛄᚩᛈᚻ ᚦᚢ

This is not to say that 'the runes' as we know them today originated in the Palaeolithic. The runes are an alphabet. Our cave-artists did not use their signs as letters, they did not record sounds or words but ideas. We cannot be sure what these ideas were (though there are loads of interpretations and yours are specifically invited!) but we can learn from them nevertheless. There is something timeless about the language of symbols. You can gaze into a sign, you can visualise it in your meditation, and if you are experienced, you can even travel into it in your imagination. It takes a bit of training but it's worth it. There is much you can learn when you allow the signs to speak to you. A sign can be a visual bridge spanning millennia. All of this is happily subjective. Your inspiration may be miles away from what our cave-artists thought. Nevertheless, you may have learned something useful.

The modern runes, as used by various

Germanic people since (roughly) two-thousand years ago, were both a pictographic script (each sign is a picture with one or more meanings) and a phonetic device: each sign is one or more sounds, so that a meaning can be spelled that is not related to the pictures. The rune writers of the Germanic people used their script in both ways. They wrote words, just as we do, but they also wrote single runes, when they wanted to communicate the literal meaning of a symbol. Some of these meanings are a bit obscure, and consequently there are lots of rune inscriptions that cannot be read nowadays. The same applies to magick. Some sorcerers carved single runes for their symbolic value. The rune Nauthiz for help in need, the rune Thorn for curses and the Tir rune to give strength in battle.

What the stone-age artists thought or intended when they drew similar shapes on cave walls is a riddle that may never be conclusively answered. However, some signs are so simple and direct that their meanings may overlap with later interpretations. Possibly the people who developed the futhark alphabet made use of sacred signs that were part of their cultural heritage. For this reason, our journey to the roots of runes (and Central European religion and magick in general) begins not in the Iron age but a long, long time earlier. In the first version of *Helrunar*, I traced the use of abstract signs to the late Neanderthal people, whom I assumed to be the first humans into religion and ritual. This view is now out of date: nowadays Homo erectus is the candidate for the job. We find evidence for abstract signs and religion in periods that predate the beginning of our species by several hundred thousand years. It is, however, not enough to give a few snippets of information on the odd symbol, burial or excavation. To understand a given belief or custom you also have to know the context in which it developed. If you care to discover the runes, you should also learn about the folks who used them. Their religions developed from earlier faiths, so when we start with Urda's section, we should begin at the root.

Homo erectus

When writing the first edition of *Helrunar*, I assumed, like most researchers, that the first evidence for ritual activity and abstract signs in ancient Europe came from the age of the Neanderthal people. To begin our journey through the pagan past, we have to set our time machines to the first developed hominids. These are loosely called Homo erectus, meaning the erect human being. The term is misleading, as nowadays we know of earlier hominids walking on two legs. However, Homo erectus was allowed to retain the name. Mind you, it is by no means easy to decide who belongs to Homo erectus and who doesn't. There is no such thing as a scholarly consensus and classification differs from country to country. Homo erectus was not such a complicated character, but we still know so very little about these early ancestors and their relation to each other. Depending on the system of classification, we can locate the earliest specimen of Homo erectus in Africa some 2 million years ago. Java supplies a skull fragment dated around 1.6 million years and recently two skulls were found in Georgia, Russia, that seem to be 1.8 million years old Chinese specimen, the so called Peking man, are dated around 400,000 while the earliest known specimen from Europe, Homo heidelbergiensis, supplied a 600,000 year old jaw bone. In Homo erectus, we are facing the first human beings who are definitely past the animal stage. To begin with, a brain capacity of more than 1000 ccm far exceeded the size of earlier hominid skulls. At this stage, the early humans were not only adept at crafting a number of specialised stone tools. Excavations of the last years indicate that fire was used in their culture, at least in those branches of Homo erectus that favoured colder climes. This does not necessarily mean that erectus knew how to make fire. Fire also occurs in nature, as in lightning flashes or forest fires, and it is possible that mankind learned to collect and maintain fire long before they had the knack of making it. The Peking people, for instance, had huge fire pits where they guarded the bright element for years, possibly generations. Guarding their fires, our ancestors gazed dreamily into the flickering flames and naturally developed trance states. In Europe, we have Homo erectus evidence from several warm and at least one colder period that alternated during the ice ages. Each time the climate became warm enough, Homo erectus moved north into the fertile savannah country of what is now central Europe. In the process, the European form of Homo erectus acquired a number of unique characteristics. Consequently, experts cannot agree whether erectus should be classed as a single species or whether the highly developed European form, called Homo heidelbergiensis, should be a species by itself. Without fire and considerable advances in technology, survival in Europe would have been next to impossible: it was simply too cold. Where only a few decades ago, the erecti were seen as furry savages barely able to wield a stone tool, the present state of research hints at a far more developed society.

We are exceptionally lucky to have evidence from several hunting camps. This is a new development. Up to the 1930s, many scholars favoured the theory that early humans used to settle in caves. Indeed caves supplied some very early stone tools, both inside and outside the cave entrance. A cave, so it was believed, is almost as good as a house. It has walls, a rain-proof roof and affords a constant (if cold) temperature all through the year. This produced the popular image of the 'cave man', generally a hairy savage wielding a big club and dragging women around by the hair. By now this notion is totally out of fashion. It turned out that, though caves do contain some evidence of early humanity, such a stone tools and a bit of rubbish, these amount to very little material. Any cave settled for more than a few winters should be brimming full of rubbish, but this is evidently not the case. We know that caves were visited on occasion, but what these occasions were remains an open guess. The main problem with caves is that they are stationary. In tropical countries, Homo erectus prospered on a largely vegetarian diet, which was available all through the year. In central Europe, the climate was slightly warmer than today, but winters were a real problem.

Consequently, the northern branches of the species adapted to a diet that included lots of meat.

In Schöningen, Niedersachsen, Germany, the oldest known hunting spears, dating c.400,000BCE were discovered. Six spruce and one pine spear came up, carefully balanced to permit throwing, which were used to hunt the small and shy horses of the time. Spears designed for stabbing large game, such as young forest elephants and rhino, appeared in Bilzingleben, Bad Cannstadt, Klärlich and Clacton-on-Sea. So there were already two different types of spears around.

We can say goodbye to the club wielding savages, in fact, not a single club has ever come up in excavations. The evidence points at organised group hunts. Now a group hunt is a complicated effort involving planning, organisation, timing, division of work and above all, a reliable language or system of signals. If you are after a young forest-elephant, it makes sense to divert the older ones first. As erectus survived using such methods for millennia, we have to grant that they were certainly not as primitive as previously assumed. Hunters have to adapt to the game they are after. In the European bush-land, with its hot summers and cold winters, the beasts migrated. Homo erectus had to do the same in order to survive. For this way of life, a cave is unsuitable. We have to imagine camp sites where the hunter communities used to settle on their regular circuits across the land. Evidence for shelters constructed out of organic material and stone survives at several places, such as Presletice, Czech, c.600,000 BCE

and Nice, France, c.400,000BCE. Luckily, at Bilzingsleben, Germany, c.300,000BCE, a Homo erectus camp site was perfectly preserved (Kuckenburg, 2000, 15 - 29). The site, on the shore of a lake, was visited over a number of years. Eventually it was flooded by the rising water level and the human debris conserved by a thick layer of river chalk. Now, after decades of careful excavation, it is certain that the erecti settling at this spot used to live in tent-like huts made of leather, branches or plant fibre (missing) supported by poles (those made of mammoth tusks survive) and held in place by a rim of rocks and large bones.

Also, Homo erectus wore some sort of clothing and footwear to make the winters more bearable. Next to the shelters were small places that seem to have served as workshops. Each had a large stone 'anvil' in the centre, surrounded by various tools and rubbish. Excavator D. Mania proposes that each of them was used to work a specific material, such as flint, ivory, bone etc. This implies a division of work.

Even more surprising is an enigmatic circular space with a diameter of nine meters, which was mostly free of tools or traces of work. The circle was set apart from the rest of the camp by its surface, which consisted of a solid layer of stones and bones, pounded into the ground to produce a sort of pavement. Many of the bones show signs of strong pressure and pose the question whether they may have been danced into the soil. Around the circle appear a large number of Homo erectus bones, all of them skulls and

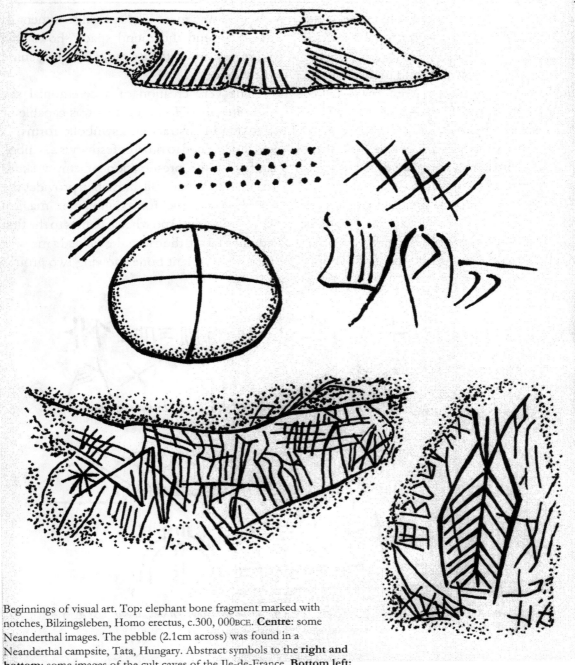

Beginnings of visual art. Top: elephant bone fragment marked with
notches, Bilzingsleben, Homo erectus, c.300, 000BCE. **Centre**: some
Neanderthal images. The pebble (2.1cm across) was found in a
Neanderthal campsite, Tata, Hungary. Abstract symbols to the **right and
bottom**: some images of the cult caves of the Ile-de-France. **Bottom left**:
Grotte-aux-Fees, Milly-la-Foret (simplifed); **bottom right**: Larchant.
Whether the 'letters' to the left of the main symbol are fecent additions is
an open question: the soft stone invites visitors to leave their own graffiti.

teeth. What had happened to the rest of the skeletons? The skulls had been forcibly opened to extract the brains. This seemed pretty sinister to the excavators and more so to the media, who are always keen for a bit of cannibalism to liven up a dry story. Nevertheless, brain extraction is not always a sign of cannibalism. Head worship, preservation of trophies, several phase burials and other explanations are just as possible. Several Homo erectus communities seem to have practised brain extraction (there is excellent evidence from Beijing). I find it doubtful that erectus opened the skulls simply for a yummy meal. The special treatment of skulls around the round space shows that there was more than simple hunger behind the event.

The very creation of a ceremonial site indicates that Homo erectus was capable of thinking in abstract and symbolic forms. A circle dedicated to ritual or festivity is a symbol, and so is the preservation of empty skulls around it. Perhaps Bilzingsleben provides the earliest evidence for religious or magical practises so far. And when it comes to the first attempts at art, the camp site yielded a massive piece of elephant bone showing two groups

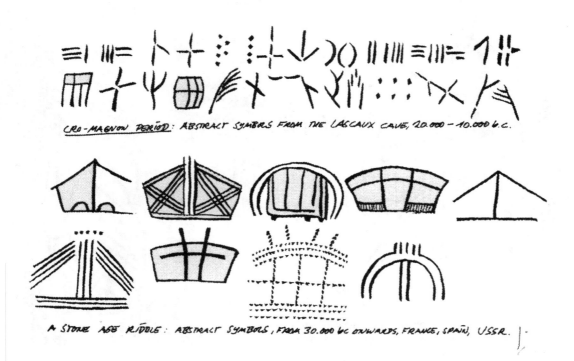

Cro Magnon period. Abstract symbols from the Lascaux cave, c. 20 000 -10 000 BCE.
Below. A stone-age riddle. Abstract symbols, from c. 30 000 BCE onwards, France, Spain, Russia.

of 14 and 7 carefully executed notches on one side. We can only guess at the meaning behind them. Someone was marking and counting something. Are we observing the first attempts at graphic symbolism?

Neanderthal people

With the evolution of the Neanderthal people (named after a valley near Düsseldorf, Germany) we come upon more evidence for religion and ritual. First, a word on terminology. When the Neanderthal people were discovered, they were given the name Homo Neanderthalensis, meaning the Human of the Neander-valley. At that point, they were considered furry savages and quite a long way from our own species, which has the gall to call itself Homo sapiens, the 'Thinking Human'. Over the last few years, the evidence for intelligent Neanderthal people has grown so much that they were also granted the title 'sapiens', so that their correct name is Homo sapiens neanderthalensis. Our species, deriving from the Cro Magnon type, is now called Homo sapiens sapiens, against all better judgment.

To begin with, the point where Homo erectus became Homo sapiens neanderthalensis is a matter of guesswork. What some call a young erectus is classed by others as an old Neanderthal, the period between 180,000 and 120,000 being especially disputed. As is the genealogy of the Neanderthal people, and their precise classification. Be that as it may, we have the first evidence for the classical Neanderthal type around 120,000BCE.

Neanderthal people pose a problem right from the start. You would imagine that Homo erectus gradually evolved a larger brain, which eventually turned the species into Neanderthalensis , but if this were the case, the earliest Neanderthal skulls should have been smaller than the later ones. Some of them are. However, from this early period we also have a surprising number of huge skulls, some of them housing 1700ccm of brain. By comparison, the skull of the average classical Neanderthal (100,000 - 30,000BCE) contained 1450ccm, more than the average brain size of our own species (1400ccm). Neanderthal people emerge from the unknown with a much bigger brain than can be accounted for. They obviously made good use of it as they invented some of the most crucial characteristics of humanity.

Up to the 1970s, the image of Neanderthal people as half naked, hairy, club wielding brutes was immensely popular. Neanderthal people were thought to be closer to the apes than modern humans. Based on the anatomy of a well preserved Neanderthal skeleton from La Chapelle, scholars created a reconstruction showing the poor guy standing in a crouch, with bent legs, a stupid, hairy face, clad in a small piece of pelt and equipped with the obligatory club. This Neanderthal, as everyone could see, was not even able to stand erect. He could not run properly nor could he cast anything in an overhead throw. As it turned out, the skeleton from La Chapelle is by no means typical. The Neanderthal was an old fellow crippled by chronic, bone-bending arthritis. Modern reconstructions are closer to the truth and show Neanderthals who walked (and ran) just as upright as we do.

Or consider the face. Neanderthal skulls differ from the skulls of our species in that they are flatter but longer. The eye ridges are more prominent, the nose is wider and the chin is underdeveloped. Early reconstructions favoured extreme eye ridges and hairy, brutish faces. But how did a face look in reality? If you only have a skull, you have no means of knowing how much flesh and tissue covered it. If you 'reconstruct' it with little flesh, the eye ridges are more prominent, if you decide on more flesh, you'll get a head that comes much closer to our type. Skin colour is completely hypothetical, as is the amount of facial hair. All of this is plain guesswork. It doesn't show reality but gives a perfect reflection of scholarly belief.

American images of Neanderthal people still tend towards the crude and primitive, European images tend to produce faces you could see on a street without noticing. In America, scholars prefer a more primitive form, and this is not going to change soon. There is too much popular literature featuring primitive Neanderthal folk. Just look at the enormously popular books by Jean Auel, where Neanderthals are chauvinist, sexist and given to violence and rape. Their inferiority to our ancestors is clearly indicated, in fact, they are such a primitive bunch that they seem to deserve extinction. Or the BBC production *Walking with Beasts* featuring Neanderthals clad in a heap of loosely connected pelts, with dirty, long hair, getting run over by woolly rhino and barely able to hunt by scaring a mammoth with fire. By contrast, the Cro Magnon type of Homo sapiens, our own ancestors, appear well organised in perfectly tailored clothes, clean, smart, with a proper haircut. This is not science, it's 'Master-race' mythology. If the Neanderthals were still alive, they might sue the BBC for racial discrimination.

It is absurd to imagine that Neanderthal folk did not have refined clothing, they survived under arctic conditions for more than 100,000 years. It is also absurd to believe that Cro Magnon people, if they really migrated into northern Europe as scholars of the 'Out of Africa' school propose, were so perfectly equipped for cold weather. Technologically, Neanderthal folk had the advantage. However, people like the idea of a savage 'elder cousin', as its always nice to have someone to look down upon. While some American scholars persistently adhere to this notion, most European researchers agree that the Neanderthal people were a lot more developed than is generally known. When you imagine the Neanderthal people, you have to envision a culture that builds huts, shelters and tents, wears functional clothes and footwear and has a system of work division within society. There were younger Neanderthal folk who went gathering and hunting and older people who seem to have spent much of their time preparing animal hides, possibly by chewing. Old people were cared for in Neanderthal society. Technologically, there is evidence for stone tools set in wood or bone, the same seems to apply to stone tipped hunting spears. Setting a spear-head into a wooden (usually yew) spear is a highly skilled task. Neanderthal

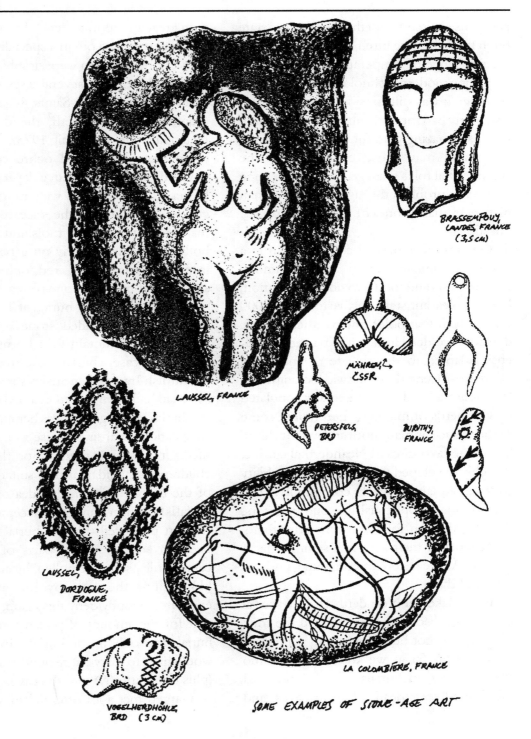

BRASSEMPOUY, LANDES, FRANCE (3,5 CM)

LAUSSEL, FRANCE

MÄHREN, ČSSR

PETERSFELS, BRD

BURNTHY, FRANCE

LAUSSEL, DORDOGNE, FRANCE

LA COLOMBIERE, FRANCE

VOGELHERDHÖHLE, BRD (3 CM)

SOME EXAMPLES OF STONE-AGE ART

people used birch-tar for this job. You generate birch tar by heating birch in an oven at a very specific range of temperatures. This is fairly easy using modern technology, but a hundred years ago it was still considered difficult. It is also pretty bad for the health, as making birch tar, that amazingly useful glue, damages the lungs and may cause cancer. How the Neanderthal folks managed to do something that was a problem through most of human history remains one of those unpopular questions.

Classical Neanderthal culture began in a period of almost tropical warmth, among fertile forests and food-providing vegetation, but this pleasant state only lasted for 10,000 years. From that point, the weather became drastically colder. Homo sapiens neanderthalensis adapted to the climate of snow and permafrost. Central Europe was looking much like the arctic tundra today and was populated by vast herds of migrating herbivores, some of them, such as mammoth and woolly rhino, becoming favourites of Neanderthal cuisine. A highly developed technology and mobility were essential for each community. The Neanderthal people, just like our ancestors, the Cro Magnon folk that came after them, spent most of their lives in a semi-nomadic fashion. As the herbivores migrated, humans followed them.

What makes the Neanderthal folk so special is that they discovered or invented the soul. Monkeys do not bury their dead, neither do apes, and (as far as we know) even Homo erectus knew no burials. The Neanderthal folk buried their dead, often in caves, and with great attention to detail. In most burials the dead were laid out in a specially prepared grave. Some of them were simply hollows in the cave floor, but in several cases, such as the caves La-Chapelle-aux-Saints, Régourdou and Quafzeh near Nazareth, the dead lay in rectangular graves (König 1973). They were often treated with red ochre colour and covered with a protective layer of stone. Better still, there was a wide range of grave goods inhumed with the deceased, such as mammoth ivory, stone tools and food. The body of La-Chapelle lay on a bed of flint, jasper, quartzite and red ochre, it was surrounded by large stone plates.

The grave of a boy buried at Teshik-Tash in central Asia yielded stone tools and a selection of mountain ibex horns. In one spectacular case, a burial in the Shanidar cave in Kurdish Iraq, pollen analysis revealed that the dead had been buried in a bed of flowers and herbs. Among them was hemp, leading to speculation regarding its use as a drug. The media immediately pounced on the 'flower-children of Shanidar' as they suited the spirit of the time. However, the idea of a flower burial is no longer universally accepted. Robert Gargett proposed that the burial may have been an accident when parts of the cave ceiling collapsed. The pollen, he argued, was blown into the cave by the wind. The excavators stoutly deny this claim, and insist that for the amount of pollen found in the burial (and only in the burial) freak winds would have to carry entire bundles of flowers (plus one butterfly) into the cave.

Gargett met a lot of criticism, which did

not stop him from declaring a good many other burials to be coincidences and accidents. This sort of thing is not research, it is arguing about ideology. Prehistoric research and speculation say very little about the way of life in the past, but they reveal a lot about what modern people consider possible or believe to be true. Every interpretation of the past is also a mirror of present day thought. Need I add that we have no idea what cannabis might effect on Neanderthal brains, which were certainly shaped differently from ours? If they consumed drugs we would still be ignorant how they affected them. Drug-consumption was occasionally proposed regarding tinder mushrooms and birch fungi in Neanderthal graves.

The Shanidar caves also provided bones of four Neanderthal people who had suffered from massive injury, and recovered. Possibly this indicates a crude form of medical treatment, certainly it shows that Neanderthal people cared for their sick and disabled. In La Ferassie, Dordone, France, excavators discovered the burials of two adults and four children. They also found nine earth mounds, one of them covering a child burial. Whatever the case may be, Homo neanderthalensis seems to have developed some sort of belief in a state beyond death. Funerals of such refinement have a lot of spiritual speculation behind them. We should keep in mind, however, that we are far from a common religion here. Burials show a fascinating originality. Some dead were buried intact, others only in part. Several burials of the period only preserved the skull, which was

generally buried in a bed of red ochre. In the Veternice cave near Zagreb the excavators came upon three skulls buried under a stone plate. The Grotta Guattari near Mont Cicero yielded what may have been a sacred district: a round chamber in the centre of which, between a few boulders, was the carefully placed skull of an adult. As you entered the cave it first appeared like a perfect sphere. This points the question whether the Neanderthal people, or at least some of them, thought spheres something special. There is a surprising amount of rarely discussed evidence for this. Several Neanderthal period caves have yielded stones that had been polished to spherical shape. In La Quina, Charente, a skull was buried together with a stone-sphere. El Guettar in north Africa provided 60 polished chalk-stone spheres which had been deposited next to a spring. A dozen spheres made from chalk-stone were discovered by Leroi-Gourhan in an inner chamber of a hyena cave at Arcy-sur-Cure, Yonne. Were the spheres symbolic of the human skull? Should we search for a head cult?

What seems basic to most burials is the use of red ochre, i.e. reddish earth, or earth burned to make it reddish. It can also be traced in settlements. Corpses were reddened, bones were placed in a bed of the substance. In all likeliness living people also made use of it to paint their bodies or items of daily life. Here we are on the trace of earliest art, much of it taking place on the body of the artist. And we encounter another innovation. The late Neanderthal people evidently wore ornaments. Items found in the Grotte du

Renne include five pendants made of carefully notched carnivore teeth. In their company was a polished bone needle, c. 12 cm long, with a notched head, and two fragments of what looks like crude rings drilled and carved out of mammoth ivory. Whether they graced fingers or costume remains uncertain. The important issue is that the late Neanderthal people wore symbolic items for non-practical reason. If we see them as ornaments, we have to wonder about the self definition of the species. It takes individuals to develop a desire to beautify themselves. As making bone and ivory ornaments is a lot of work, we also have to consider non-provable but more easily accessible ways of improving appearance. What did they do with their hair, how did they cut their fur clothes? But we could also postulate that these ornaments served a magical function, maybe as talismans, power objects or signs of status.

Did Neanderthal folks have a system of magic or religion? There was considerable discussion regarding what may or may not have been an altar. It was discovered in the Drachenloch, an extremely inaccessible cave high in the Alps. Here, a group of cave bear skulls was found in a curious arrangement. They were placed side by side within a strange stone box, one of the skulls, so it was claimed, having a bone sticking in its eye. This was taken as the earliest altar of mankind and certain evidence for a cult of the cave bear. More recent studies tend to doubt this interpretation. Cave bears hibernated in Alpine caves, and as this sort of thing happened continuously over many centuries, the caves accumulated the bones of those bears who died during the winter. What used to be an altar may also be a chance accumulation of skulls under a layer of stones that may have fallen from the cave roof. We will probably never be certain in this matter, as the excavation, like most of those of the 19th and early 20th century, was a sloppy and careless job.

A similar problem comes up in the excavation of the Krapina caves near Zagreb. Here a Neanderthal settlement was suspected. The excavators found the skeletons of 14 women and men, bone and stone tools and diverse foodstuff. All of them were in a terrible state. None of the skeletons was intact. Splintered human bone fragments, some of them scorched, lay carelessly mixed with all sorts of rubbish. Dragutin Goranovic immediately proposed cannibalism, and this idea was greeted with enthusiasm. For several decades, Krapina was paraded as firm evidence that Homo neanderthalensis happened to be a nasty savage. More recent studies on the site and its surviving bones have radically altered the picture. The dismal state of the cave turned out to be all too understandable, as the researchers had used dynamite instead of shovels for the excavation. A revaluation by Erik Trinkaus puts an end to the cannibalistic Neanderthal folk. The sorry state of the bones is simply due to the way they were unearthed. Before being blown up in the name of archaeology, Krapina may have been one of the earliest and best preserved cemeteries in the world.

With regard to symbolism, there are some

Two images from Lascaux cave. **Top:** Giant deer; **bottom:** bird-headed 'shaman' with dying European buffalo & woolly rhino, above a chasm in the most inaccessible part of the cave.

items of the Neanderthal period that show the first cautious experiments in graphic art. Some bone tools seem to be decorated with carefully made notches, which may have had practical (improving the grip) or spiritual purpose. There are stones decorated with arrangements of dots and lines, there are a few arrangements of straight lines, criss-crossed with each other. A piece of mammoth ivory found at Wyhlen in Baden shows rows of single lines and a cross. A polished circular stone disk, engraved with a cross, came up in Tata, Hungary. This makes the circle and the cross one of the earliest abstract symbols of humanity. Then there is the hollow. A triangular stone block covered the skull of a child in La Ferraissie, Dordogne. Its underside was decorated with a number of small hollows, drilled into the stone, four of them forming something like a square. Stones with hollows also appear in the rituals of several later cultures. During the bronze age they are especially popular. The bizarre stones at the Île-de-France near Paris also seem to have attracted Neanderthal folk (as well as Homo sapiens sapiens). There are numerous caves there, ranging from holes barely big enough to contain a single human to much larger grottoes. Many of these caves show bizarre and enigmatic graphical signs. The people of the Mousterien carved lines into the walls. Not side by side but often in wild patterns across each other. To this day, the place has not attracted the attention it deserves. The trouble with these images is that they are so completely abstract, if not random, that interpretation is impossible. Yet when you imagine seeing them in the flickering light of a torch, you will find that the designs come to life, that the lines begin to move and pulse in the rhythm of the fire.

Finally, a thought about music. Early accounts of Neanderthal people proposed that these poor primitives did not even have a language. This was amended gradually, and it was grudgingly admitted that people with specialised hunting techniques do need a bit of communication once in a while. The crucial question was the tongue bone. This extremely small and fragile bone cannot be found in apes, but it appears in humans, allowing us to shape sounds that other simians cannot produce. Neanderthal people were considered too primitive for a refined language, and there were scholars debating whether the Neanderthal mouth could produce more than two vowels and a number of grunts. Then, by a stroke of luck, a Neanderthal skull was found with the tongue-bone intact. Where it came to speech, Neanderthal folk may have been as chatty as we are.

And what of music? A questionable 'bull-roarer' appeared in the Pin Hole cave in Britain, but as it turned out, the bone had received its numerous holes in the digestive tract of a hyena. Flutes are the earliest instruments we know of. Two flute fragments (bird bones, complete length between 15 - 20cm, up to four holes), more than 30,000 years old, were unearthed in a cave in Southern Germany (Geißenklösterlehöhle near Ulm) and attributed to our ancestors. Much earlier is a bone fragment with holes from Haua Fteah cave in Libya, dated c.45,000 years. It was considered a flute or pipe and dated in the tricky period between Neanderthal folk and Homo sapiens sapiens. 1995 the Slovenian archaeologist Ivan Turk unearthed a flute fragment, made of bear bone, in a cave in former Yugoslavia (Kuckenburg 1999, 324-326). It comes from geological strata dated between 43,000 to 67,000 years. There are no signs of Homo sapiens sapiens activity in this location at the time, so whether they like it or not, the item has to be attributed to Neanderthal folk. When we imagine flute playing Neanderthals, we are a long way from the primitives imagined by early European scholars (and a few modern American academics). Music may be older than our species.

Tales of Two Species

Around 40,000BCE, Europe enters into the old stone age. The Neanderthal people had largely inhabited a period called Mousterien, now we are watching the emergence of a radically new period, the early Aurignacien. What strikes the observer as amazing is the sudden appearance of several innovations. Stone-working techniques improve, a range of new and better tools develop. At the same time, we observe an increase in all the characteristics that seem to define humanity. The style of building camp sites evolves, we find larger and more developed shelters, new tools, refined clothes and a lot of ornament. These changes were thought too extreme to be explained by Neanderthal evolution. Instead, they were attributed to our direct ancestors, the Cro Magnon type of Homo sapiens sapiens, who appear in central Europe around 35,000BCE.

It would be nice if I could tell you more

regarding the origin of our species. At the time being there are several conflicting theories attempting to explain this enigmatic process. Each of them suffers from several fatal flaws. Let me give you a brief synopsis with the proviso that the question is far from resolved and that I look forward to rewriting this passage in a few years. The traditional theory pointed at the fact that the bones and artefacts of our earliest direct ancestors all appear in Europe, mainly in a horizontal axis between northern Spain and the Carpathians. According to this theory, which was popular well into the 1980s, modern mankind developed in a cold Europe.

Next came the 'Black Eve' hypothesis (1987), otherwise known as Out of Africa I. A group of enterprising scientists led by Allan C. Wilson took samples of mitochondrial DNA from 147 women all over the world and analysed it with the amazing computer program PAUP (Phylogenetic Analysis Using Parsimony). PAUP is a program that compares data and produces possible lines of descent, which it analyses according to probability. Mitochondria are the cell's 'batteries'. They have a simpler code than the main DNA and are only passed on along the female line. Unlike cellular DNA, mitochondria have a mere 16,500 units of information, which makes them easy to analyse. After producing an array of possible pedigrees, the researchers stopped the calculation and declared that all mankind originated from a single woman who lived in Africa some 200,000 years ago! This hypothesis became immensely popular and was widely publicised by the media, especially in the United States. They did not bother to popularise the fact that 'Black Eve' became questionable within a few months. By 1992 it was thoroughly invalidated. Research by Alan R. Templeton showed that the same data and the same computer program could be made to show that mankind originated in Asia (and many other places), a theory few researchers were happy with. Excavations in most Asian countries are a lot more problematic than in East Africa, where you have open country, accessible geological strata, relatively stable politics and cheap labour. It turned out that the Wilson team had done their research in a fast and sloppy fashion. They stopped their computer calculation at an early point and did not bother to do several trial runs. Given such a vast amount of data, several estimates would have been the minimum. Templeton did the job more thoroughly and came up with a hundred lines of descent that were 'more probable' and did not originate in Africa. David R. Maddison proceeded to do 4,500 trial runs of PAUP, so by now we have more than 10,000 genealogies that are more probable than the original Black Eve. They lead to pretty much anywhere on this bonny earth. Reluctantly, Black Eve was sent into retirement. This did not make the media happy, as a dark (?) ancestress of mankind seemed so politically correct. You still find her alive and well in books by people who do not care to do much research. The Out of Africa fraction had suffered a terrible setback and European Origin was again looking good.

With the discovery of a Homo sapiens sapiens skull in Africa, dated 100,000BCE, and a number of similar finds in the near East (around 90,000BCE), European origin was discarded again and Out of Africa II appeared. The bones from Africa and Palestine show that anatomically modern Homo sapiens sapiens developed long before her/his first emergence in Europe. We are talking anatomy here. Technologically, there is still a vast gap between the African and European forms. Proponents of the African theory immediately proposed that humanity emerged in Africa 100,000BCE, moved to the Near East 90,000BCE and from there into Europe 35,000BCE. In the process, so it was stipulated, the more advanced (a rather meaningless term) Homo sapiens sapiens 'replaced' (exterminated?) the earlier Neanderthal people, who disappeared in central Europe c. 35,000BCE and in Spain 27,000BCE.

How and why this happened is still an open question, and it was not the only one. Out of Africa II came in one package with a number of nasty little ideas. One of them is the idea that our type of Homo sapiens sapiens is a natural killer. This idea was and is encouraged by a good many American (and some British) scientists, and it certainly fits modern politics. If it could be proved that our ancestors destroyed the Neanderthal people, this would strengthen the position of those who claim that war is natural and inevitable, and that inferior races had better get in line or die out. Typical for this ideology is the constant repetition that the Neanderthal people were 'inferior', 'incapable to adapt' or 'not creative enough to cope with the climate'. None of these terms really mean anything when you think about them. It turned out that the

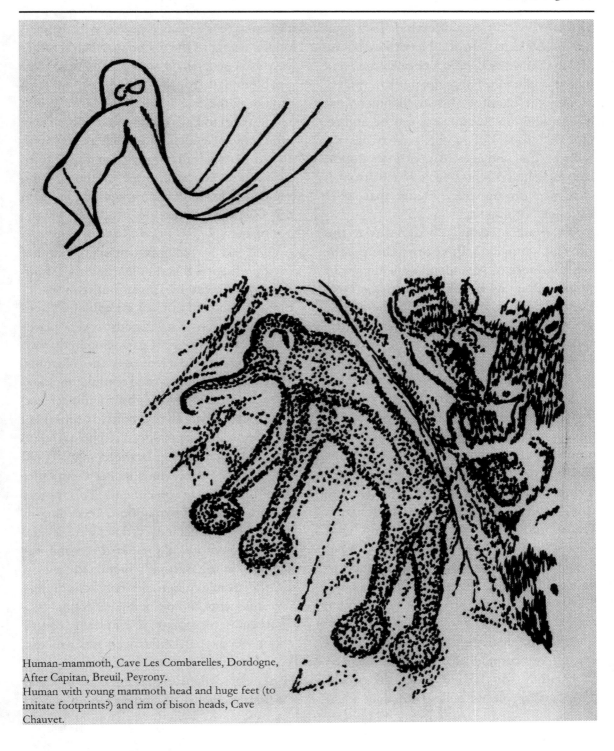

Human-mammoth, Cave Les Combarelles, Dordogne,
After Capitan, Breuil, Peyrony.
Human with young mammoth head and huge feet (to
imitate footprints?) and rim of bison heads, Cave
Chauvet.

'inferiority' of Neanderthal folk was remarkably hard to prove. Nevertheless, Out of Africa II is still the most popular theory of human evolution. This is not due to any facts, as with the handful of bone fragments we have, pretty much anything can be argued. Out of Africa II is a theory that has the support of a good many American (and some British) scholars who have a much stronger influence on the mass-media than their European colleagues.

There are a few snags with regard to this simple scenario. For one thing, the disappearance of Neanderthals is not such a simple matter as was assumed by the Neo-Darwinist fringe. In Palestine, Homo sapiens sapiens and Homo neanderthalensis coexisted, apparently peacefully, for a span of 60,000 years. Whether there was breeding between the species remains a difficult question, but there was certainly cultural exchange.

While Neanderthal folk and Homo sapiens sapiens approached the art of making stone tools with radically different methods, the Neanderthal communities settling in Palestine turned out refined tools that can't be told from the Homo sapiens sapiens artefacts. Perhaps in Europe a similar process took place. This is far from resolved, as all authorities seem to follow their very own preferences in dating the material (*Archäologie in Deutschland*, 2,1998 gives several different articles on the topic).

In some theories, the two species co-existed in central Europe, and influenced each other for 10,000 years, in others Neanderthal folk were almost extinct when Homo sapiens sapiens appeared. A lot depends on the dating of the material, which is not as easy as is generally assumed. The next huge problem confronting the Out-of-Africa faction is the fact that, though a migration from Africa to Palestine is conceivable, there is no shred of evidence for a further migration to Europe. Instead of moving gradually from Palestine to central Europe, we find Homo sapiens sapiens emerging in central Europe in 35,000BCE and moving gradually to the periphery.

This led to the formulation of another exciting theory, this one labelled the Multi-Regional Theory of Evolution. It proposes that mankind did not originate in one places but simultaneously developed in several places when communities of early hominids met, interacted and separated over the millennia. Here we have Neanderthal communities and Homo sapiens sapiens groups mixing and possibly breeding. Excavations in China (Dali and Jinniushan) produced archaic Homo sapiens sapiens dating between the 250,000 and 100,000 years, which makes them older than the African specimens. This points towards a parallel evolution. According to the Multi-Regional theory, there were several groups of anatomically modern humans, but it was left to the European branch to develop into the specific Aurignacien culture, including art, ornaments and refined technology.

It begins to appear that Neanderthal people may have strongly influenced this process. You probably noticed that between the beginning of the Aurignacien 40,000BCE and the first emergence of modern Homo sapiens

sapiens in 35,000 there exists a gap of 5,000 years, if we can trust the dating. During this period someone was inventing lots of fantastic things. It used to be assumed that only our species could have done so, leading to the conclusion that they must have been around in 40,000BCE to start the Aurignacien, no matter that they left no anatomical evidence. Then in 1979 a team of excavators was amazed to discover a Neanderthal burial in the middle of what used to be thought a Homo sapiens sapiens site at St. Césaire. Over the next years, the experts grudgingly began to accept that a number of Aurignacien innovations, such as mass produced stone tools and early art, were evidently not made by enterprising Homo sapiens sapiens but by the dear old Neanderthal folk.

We cannot, at this stage of research, be certain how far the Neanderthal contribution to the Aurgnacien went. This is very much a question of belief and scholarly interpretation. All we can be sure of is that our ancestors, Homo sapiens sapiens formed the middle and late Aurignacien. Who began the Aurignacien is more uncertain than ever. In these matters, question marks abound. Just when did our ancestors appear in ancient Europe? And just when did the Neanderthal people disappear? Dating this process is more enigmatic than ever. Just consider that nowadays we are happy to have bones, sometimes whole skeletons, of c.200 Neanderthal people. This is not much, when you consider that these bones come from a range of 100,000 years. Drawing maps and time-charts based on so little hard evidence may be good fun but hardly produces significant results. Then there remains, as ever, the question why the Neanderthals disappeared. The idea of an intelligent Homo sapiens sapiens replacing the strong but stupid Neanderthal folk through technological superiority can safely be discarded. When the two species met in Europe, both had similar brain size, similar intelligence, similar technology and as to superiority, the Neanderthal folk had already shown their ability to thrive in a cold environment for a 100,000 years.

If Homo sapiens sapiens originated in Africa and appeared in frosty Europe as a newcomer, they would have done well to learn from the older inhabitants. Mythologically, this may also have been a fascinating period. Old myths abound with beings of the past and eldritch races that prospered and disappeared. In the *Eddas*, the modern gods have to content with the much older race, the frost giants, who are deemed primitive but wise in the ways of elder lore. In a similar fashion, Greek gods battled the earlier Titans, the Irish gods fought the Fomors (a race of giants and monsters from under the sea) and so on. Or take the myth of the small races, the dwarves and elves, craftsmen and spell-casters of an earlier stage of evolution. Over the last century, a number of researchers (including Gerald Gardner) have suggested that such legends may well contain a vague memory of contact between our ancestors, the Homo sapiens sapiens of the Cro Magnon type, and the earlier Neanderthal people. The matter becomes even more uncertain when we attempt to work out whether Homo sapiens sapiens and Neanderthal people bred. A few highly celebrated tests of mitochondrial DNA seem to show that there is less genetic similarity between the two than used to be assumed. Such things get into the headlines. It soon turned out that only a tiny amount of the available genetic material had been compared. Comparing other sections of mitochondrial DNA produced entirely different results. How come those genetic wizards are always in such a hurry to publish their 'results'? I am sure that DNA analysis will contribute to our knowledge of prehistory eventually, in a few decades it may even become a proper science. More important may be the burial of a child in the Lapedo valley in Portugal. Some 25,000 years ago, this four year old had been buried on a bed of red ochre and burnt plant material, with deer bone amulets and a shell from the sea. It would be an easy matter to class the burial as one of the Homo sapiens sapiens type if the anatomy of the child were not so unusual. This child showed elements of both types, such as a weak chin and considerably shortened leg bones. Again, the meaning of this burial is highly disputed. A similar case was the Neanderthal skull found at Hahnöfersand near Hamburg, who exhibited a similarity to both types. Was he a link between the species? We'll, get to him in the next section.

Making History

Unlike what the media proclaim, the dating of prehistoric items is a lot more difficult than is generally assumed. Early archaeology had real problems in this regard. All the excavators could do was give a relative estimate (i.e. guess). Items were dated according to geological strata, which is not very precise. Unless a datable object was part of the find, things remained uncertain. Then there was typology. For instance, if you have a good date for a specific sort of pottery, and find a pot of the same type, it is likely that they may come from the same period. This is called 'relative chronology', in that it produces indications but no precise results. Nowadays there are several methods of dating available, but as it turns out, each of them has its drawbacks. Possibly the most precise is dendrochronology, which is based on comparing the year-rings in wood. The weather is different each year and so are the rings grown by the trees. By comparing thousands of preserved pieces of wood, it has been possible to produce tree-ring calendars for America and Europe. This method is almost precise to the year, provided the wood is well preserved. Such wood abounds in swamp settlements and lake-shore villages (many houses on the shores of the Swiss lakes can be dated with amazing precision), it comes up occasionally when Celtic mounds or ringwalls are excavated, but when there is only a small amount of wood in an excavation, dendrochronology is useless. You need a substantial chunk for dating, preferably with some of the outside intact. As wood rots, it is rare to find a well preserved piece. A few years ago, the only wood that could be dated was material that could be sawed into convenient slices. Nowadays, x-ray photography can give

Human with bison-head at the end of Cave Gabillou,
Dordone. Female(?) figure with head of a cave-lioness
and hooves, mammoth ivory, c30cm, Cave Hohlenstein-
Stadel, Asselfingen, Baden-Württemberg, c30,000BCE.

accurate pictures of year-rings in artefacts that are too valuable to be cut.

Pollen analysis is useful for swamp excavations, as each year, a new layer of plant life grows and decays. These layers can be counted. Pollen can also be analysed when it does not come from swamps, as it gives a good idea of the plant life and the climate. Thermo-luminescence is a new method. Sadly, it is such a new technique that nobody can be sure whether its results are accurate or not. It works best with ceramics. Then there is dating according to DNA analysis. This method has produced the most amazing figures you can imagine. Most of them are still waiting for any sort of confirmation. Maybe this approach will become a reliable guide in a few decades.

What most excavators have to rely on is still the dear old C-14 test. To freshen up your memory: our atmosphere is constantly bombarded by cosmic radiation. This radiation produces neutrons which interact with nitrogen, producing a specific amount of radioactive C-14. This isotope is constantly present in the atmosphere, it is absorbed by plants, and when the plants are eaten by beasts or humans, the isotope appears in their bones. The basic idea in C-14 dating is that a given plant, animal or human absorbs a certain amount of C-14 isotopes during life. After death, the absorption stops. Now decay sets in. It takes c.5600 years and half of the isotopes have disappeared. Another 5600 years, only a quarter remain. Using a lot of expensive technology, it is possible to count the amount of C-14 within a given sample. This allows a calculation of its age. Not that this is easy, a

good C-14 test is expensive and can take weeks. For his discovery, Willard F. Libby received a Nobel-prize and the praise of his colleagues, who assumed that using C-14 counting, any piece of organic material is datable. It did not take long for the flaws to appear. C-14 dating was based on the assumption that the influx of cosmic radiation was constant through the ages. This is not the case, radiation varies from time to time and place to place. Consequently, a specimen of a period rich in radiation contains more C-14 isotopes and seems younger than a specimen from a period (or place) with less radiation. Also, there are some organic materials, such as fresh-water shells, that are extremely hard to date. Soil chemistry can also influence the count. As a result, C-14 dates have to be calibrated, a process that can mean adding or subtracting hundreds or thousands of years. I should add that C-14 remains moderately accurate when done with recent artefacts: the older the material gets, the more unreliable the dates.

Then there are technical problems. Apart from contamination of samples, which happens easily and can upset the whole dating (even a few bacteria can ruin the job), counting requires a certain amount of sample material (not always available) and produces several possible dates. As a result, no two C-14 laboratories ever come up with exactly the same results. Usually a single test produces several results. These dates are given to the excavators, who have the job of deciding which date seems the likeliest to them. In other words, if the dating produces unusual results, these are generally disregarded, as the scholars on the job tend to prefer what seems probable to them. A purely subjective decision depending on scientific intuition and the opinion of the scholarly mainstream. Need I add that people tend to find what they are looking for? Given so many sources of error, a good many excavators doubt C-14 results on principle, and only accept them when they can be confirmed by other dating methods. Estimation by typology of similar excavations that can be dated by dendrochronology, for example, is still more reliable than C-14 on its own. For a good account of problems in C-14 dating, see Ginenthal 1995, 192-195. When dealing with specimens older than 20 000 years, C-14 becomes highly unreliable. It does, however, have its uses when used as supporting evidence.

Now for the news. Let me introduce you to professor R. Protsch von Zieten. The following account is based on *Der Spiegel*, 34 / 2004. From 1973, professor Protsch ran the Frankfurt Anthropological Institute and was influential in dating many of the most important specimen of early prehistory. Then, in 1984, Michael Mehlman complained (*Journal of Human Evolution*) that Protsch was supposedly dealing in sloppy fashion with facts, and occasionally bending them. The university heads ignored the 14 page report, and Protsch remained in office. They also ignored complaints by members of the institute, who were not happy about Protsch's dating methods. Dr. Protsch remained in office till 2004, even after it turned out that one of his titles wasn't genuine. Everything

collapsed summer 2004, when Protsch tried to sell 280 chimpanzee skulls he had acquired in 1975. He claimed that the collection belonged to him, the university that it belonged to them. The ensuing quarrel led the university to close and seal his office and the matter is being investigated by the police.

How wrong were the estimates? It now happened that a pair of archaeologists, Thomas Terberger (Greifswald) and Martin Street, (Neuwied), toured museums and collections and collected samples from a number of human specimen supposed to originate in the crucial period between the end of Homo sapiens neanderthalensis and the early period of our own type of Homo sapiens sapiens. As Terberger and Street insist, they were only doing a routine check of a number of hominid fossils, some of which had never been properly dated at all. These samples were submitted to the C-14 laboratories in Oxford. As it turned out, a good many of the items seemed a lot younger than had been expected. Especially off-the-mark were a number of important bones dated by Protsch. Terberger and Street declared that it had not been their intention to discredit Protsch, who sees the whole thing as an intrigue against him. Of course the Oxford results were not identical with Protsch's estimations, which nobody expected anyway. Some examples:

-the Neanderthal from Hahnöfersand. Protsch: 36,300 years, Oxford: 7,500 years. If the Oxford date is even moderately correct, the poor guy was not a Neanderthal man. Suddenly, it is not very surprising that he shows modern Homo sapiens sapiens characteristics. Amazing that nobody noticed.

-Man of Paderborn-Sande. Protsch: 27,400 years, Oxford: 240 years. The Oxford date was confirmed by another C-14 test (at Groningen). The skull is so new that it stank when it was cut.

-Woman of Binshof-Speyer. Protsch: 21,300 years, Oxford: 3,090 years.

This is a bit too much even for C-14 inaccuracy. Protsch claims that the Oxford tests were contaminated by the shellac coating the specimen. Possibly both estimates are off, so how about a few more? Before we can be sure about anything, several new tests of each item may be needed. Things became even more perplexing when the best preserved skull of the early Cro-Magnon period was to be tested. This is the celebrated woman of Kelsterbach (Frankfurt M.), dated by Protsch 31,200 years. The priceless item is kept in the safe of the Anthropological Institute of Frankfurt. Terberger and Street had asked earlier to date the venerable relic, and Protsch had refused. According to the *Spiegel*, the university authorities asked Protsch to open that safe, Protsch said no, and so the authorities had the safe opened by force. It turned out that the Kelsterbach skull is gone, and so are two other skulls. Will we ever see them again?

The Protsch affair is speedily becoming a serious problem for the study of prehistory. In leading his institute for 30 years, Protsch managed to date a wide range of famous items, not only of the last Ice-age but also of the early Neolithic, the Hallstatt time and even the mummy of a Catholic Saint. Over those thirty years, his dates, for what they are worth, have also influenced the estimates of a good many items which were not specifically dated by him. Remember that when a C-14 test produces several possible dates, as is usually the case, the excavators have to decide which seems most likely to them. Worse yet, we are not only dealing with items from central European prehistory. According to the *Spiegel* he was also influential in dating material from South Africa and, what a surprise, items from Tanzania. Considering on how little material evidence all those wonderful theories are based, even a few wrong dates can upset the whole picture. There are numerous scholars who can say goodbye to the work of decades, as all their efforts were based on questionable dates. Worse yet, when Terberger and Street took samples of early European hominids, they also received unexpected results for items that had only been dated by relative chronology.

-the skull from the Vogelherd-cave. It was found in company of the oldest works of art we know: the celebrated ivory carvings showing mammoth, cave lion and horse, usually dated 33,000 BCE. Earlier scholars assumed that the figurines and the skull belonged to the same period, and that we might have the head of the earliest human artist. According to the Oxford test, the skull is much younger than the statuettes, and has a maximum age of 5,000 years. This makes the guy a farmer of the middle Neolithic when mammoth and cave-lion were long extinct. If the ivory figurines are as old as they were supposed to be, they need not be the work of

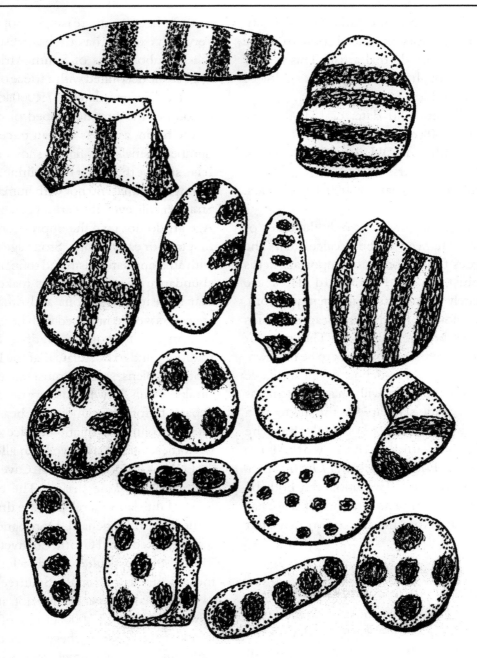

Numbers or symbols? **Top**: three pebbles from the cult cave of Birseck-Ermitage, near Basel, Swiss, late Palaeolithic between 12,000 and 10,000BCE, painted in red ochre, not to scale. **Bottom**: Mesolithic pebbles from the cave of Mas d'Azil, red ochre. A selection, not to scale. The 'dice' bottom left is interesting, it shows the numbers 5, 2 and a line on a third surface. Counters, talismans or lots for divination?

our ancestors. Could the 'earliest works of art' that 'our ancestors' produced come from the hands of a Neanderthal artist? This is now possible, though it certainly makes a lot of scholars shudder.

-Emsdetten. Old date: c. 15,000 BCE. Oxford: 2,460 years.

-Weißenthurm. Old date: 13,000 years. Oxford: 1 945 years.

-Urdhöhle. Old date: 30,000-10,000 years. Oxford: 8,470 years.

Consequently, it is not only the dates of Protsch that need to be recalculated. The same goes for a good many important items of prehistory. If the Oxford dates are moderately accurate (still an open question), a large amount of early European hominids have just been invalidated. The map of European prehistory may have to be redrawn, after a thorough re-dating of all available items. Whether this will happen remains doubtful. Some scholars see the matter as a minor problem, others feel that the foundations under their work have disappeared. For the time being, Out of Africa and Multi-Regional Evolution can both be put on ice. An immense amount of work has to be done before the discussion may start again.

Sorceries of stone-age migrants.

Homo sapiens sapiens, the Cro-Magnon type or simply our closest ancestors, continued a number of customs that had begun in Neanderthal times. Among them are the use of red ochre for funerals, the occasional special treatment of skulls. Ornaments (or proto runes?) become increasingly popular (one very early example has just been discovered in the Blombos caves of South Africa. It is a large stone decorated with a frieze of carefully engraved X signs, dated c. 75,000BCE) and we encounter the first developed pieces of art. These begin, as far as we can trace it, with a number of small ivory figures showing animals. It is a strange thing that Palaeolithic art should start with animal and not with human images. Stranger still, even the earliest pieces of Stone Age art do not give the impression of being first tries or early efforts. Stone age art begins with amazing naturalism and refinement. The abundance of animal images makes it likely that the earliest religions and rituals of our ancestors were concerned with beasts. It is an easy matter to point at various Shamanic traditions and to postulate that the European Homo sapiens sapiens must have thought similarly. This, however, is very much open to debate. Before we can discuss beast cults of the Palaeolithic it might be nice to define what these cults may have been all about.

Let's take a look at cave art. Cave drawings appear over a long period. The earliest of these, if the dating is reliable, are drawings of cattle in Abri Blanchard, Dordogne, and the recently discovered Grotte Chauvet, dating c. 31,000BCE. Most cult caves are a lot younger, the majority date from the Solutréen (21,000 to 18,000BCE). Cave art did not stop then, however. Around 17,000BCE one of the most famous caves, Lascaux, began to be decorated with hundreds of animal images. We have cave art all the way to the Neolithic, when the first farmers of southern France and Spain drew images of domestic animals. What is strange about cave art is the fact that it emerges almost perfectly developed.

Cave art offers a wealth of brilliantly drawn naturalistic animal images. Just as in earlier periods, Homo sapiens did not settle in caves. As far as we know, the caves were used for religious or magical purposes. Some of them were regularly visited, and new drawings were added, layer upon layer, over a span of several thousand years. Others seem to have been visited only once, for the explicit purpose of drawing pictures and practising who knows what rituals. Where early interpreters suggested that caves were the churches or temples of the Palaeolithic, the evidence paints another picture. Many of these caves were difficult to enter and a lot of drawings are hidden in inaccessible places. This suits a magical interpretation. Communal worship or congregations can be assumed in a number of cases, as when we have footprints in the cave floor, but by and large they are an exception.

The pictures can be interpreted in many ways. The story began in 1879, when Don Marcelino de Sautuolas explored a cave on his property. This was Altamira, a name that has since become famous. While he was pondering some stone tools near the entrance, his daughter wandered in with a torch. Shouting 'Look at the bulls!' she returned to her dad. The cave turned out to house a vast gallery of finely drawn bovines. This was not only unusual, it was unique. Up to this point, only a number of small, portable works of stone-age art had been known. That our ancestors

were fantastic graphical artists was a new discovery which was met with instant disapproval. Don Marcelino invited the leading lights of the Academy of Science to his country retreat, and found that none of the experts was willing to waste time and energy on a forgery. In all politeness, Don Marcelino was informed that he, as an amateur, obviously meant no harm, but was the victim of a hoax. When Marcelino had some of the paintings copied, the experts were even more amused. They decided that such drawings were much too good to be the work of ice age people. All of this took place without a single scholar bothering to take a look at the originals. This sorry situation continued over several decades. From time to time new caves full of original artwork were discovered, but none of the academics bothered to visit them. It wasn't until 1901 that an expert on Ice age art, E. Carthailhac, journeyed to study the suspect material. Seeing the bulls of Altamira he changed his mind, as well as that of the scientific community.

All of a sudden cave art became a topic of popular interest, and the concept of the primitive ape man was exchanged for the image of the Ice Age genius. Yet how could the magnificent pictures be explained? The first theories proposed that the animals were drawn for hunting magic, i.e. that the hungry cave man drew the sort of beast he would like for dinner. Some drawings show wounded animals bristling with spears and arrows. Several animal-drawings had been stabbed with sharp pointed weapons; ritual stabbing of a bear effigy was assumed for a cave near

Montespan, France. Such evidence points at sympathetic magic, i.e. the belief that if you hunt a picture, you will be equally successful in hunting the beast it shows. This theory was fashionable for a while. With the discovery of further caves it became increasingly doubtful.

I shall make use of the statistical survey published by André Leroi-Gourhan (1980). While it is true that 25% of the animal images found in the Pyrenees show marks of wounding, and thereby give evidence for hunting magic, the full total of wounded animals in all caves amounts to 4%. Also, not all animals which show wounds make a good meal, while on the other hand, beasts that were often hunted and eaten, such as boar, small mammals and waterfowl, appear very rarely in cave art. Even the reindeer, staple food source of our ancestors for millennia, is not as common as it ought to be. Leroi-Gourhan's statistics give an interesting insight into the frequency with which the beasts were portrayed. Most common are horses, they amount to 30% of the total sum. Another 30% consist of wild cattle, aurox and European bison. 11% are deer and giant deer images. Mammoth yield about 9% and capricorns or mountain ibex 8%. Reindeer are only evident in about 4% of the pictures. Finally there are bears (1.6%), large cats (1.3%), woolly rhino (0.7%), while the rest of the images consists of monstrous creatures, unusual animals and humanoid entities. Also, the beasts are not evenly distributed, as there are caves that emphasise some species and neglect others. Of the humanoid figures, 75 of which were known in 1980, 32% are classed as definitely

male, 18% as definitely female, and 50% are neutral or defy interpretation.

Such data called for new interpretations. Leroi-Gourhan, under the impression that *almost all 'cults' are in some way based on fertility*, proposed that the arrangement of animals was based on a principle of polarity. In his opinion, the two largest groups, horses and cattle, are representation of the male and female principle. This suggestion was embraced by a number of scholars who agreed in general, but could not agree when it came to deciding which group was supposed to represent what gender. Another theory was formulated that claimed that the beasts were drawn to ensure their fertility. It makes a measure of sense that a hunter society works magic to ensure the continuance of the beasts it depends upon, or atones its feelings of guilt by a rite of placation. It makes very little sense when we consider the large cats, who were anything but easy to live with.

Why should a hunter bother to ensure the fertility of sabre tooth tigers and cave lions? The discovery of cave Chauvet and cave Cosquer complicated the issue. Cave Chauvet contains 36 drawings of cave lions and panthers, more than the entire amount known so far. Why so many of them in a single place? And why so early? If the dating can be trusted, Chauvet is one of the earliest sites of Ice-Age art. Paradoxically, its images are classed among the most highly developed. The cave contains drawings of horses shown frontally, thereby demolishing the claim that the stone age artist knew only how to draw in profile. It also showed two cases of what may be called

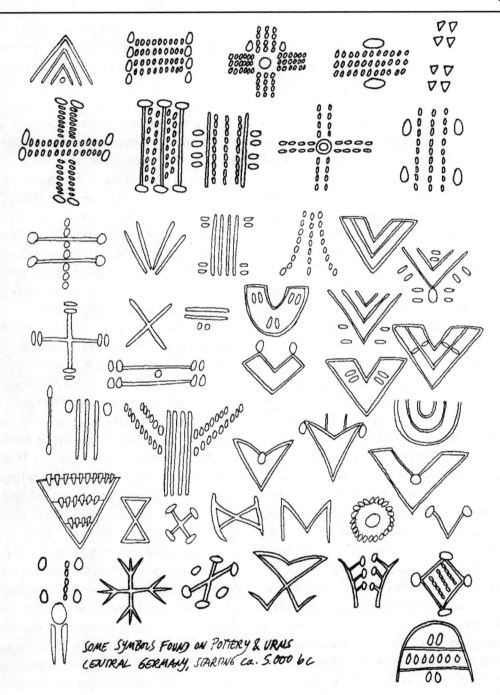

SOME SYMBOLS FOUND ON POTTERY & URNS
CENTRAL GERMANY, STARTING ca. 5.000 bc

Symbols in use in just one location, Central Hessen, Germany,
decide for yourself whether they are simply pretty or have hidden meaning

shape shifting: a bison head on top of human legs, and a weird mammoth with a surprisingly human anatomy and strange round feet. All in all, each newly discovered cave poses more questions than it solves, and reminds us to keep an open mind.

Another attempt at interpretation tried to establish which types of animals appears in which part of caves. Leroi-Gourhan classed all caves as female symbols, other authorities attempt to distinguish between male and female parts of caves, or speculate that there may have been public and private parts, dedicated to specific rites and visited only by select members of a priesthood. Such systems may be fine when applied to a single cave, but when they are used for generalisations, they tend to fall apart.

So far, there have been plenty of exceptions to any rule that has been proposed. Likewise, modern researchers are not quite as obsessed with fertility as the older generation. Anthropological research has shown that hunter-gatherer communities are not as crazy for fertility as was once assumed. Under agricultural circumstances, fertility means more farmers, who cultivate more land. To the migrants of the cold European tundra, overpopulation meant starvation. Hunter-gatherer groups go to considerable lengths to keep their population below a certain threshold, including abortion and infanticide. This may seem cruel, but it is not half as cruel as what happens when the size of a community exceeds its natural resources. We can be certain that fertility was not considered an absolute blessing in those days.

Likewise, early researchers believed that the Ice age people were primitive, meaning that they spent their days battling and copulating. If this were the case, we should come upon more drawings showing sex, be it among animals or humans. This is definitely not the case. Human copulation is very rarely shown, the same goes for the mating of animals. Then we have a number of sexist theories regarding gender roles. Very few of them based on any sort of hard evidence. Indeed, if the stone-age people had been half as keen on gender and sexual roles as the scholars who wrote about them, we would find more nudes. How come so many human images show no certain gender?

Another problem comes from the frequency in which some beasts are shown. Why are there so many horses, for instance? And how shall we explain the species of which only a few, isolated drawings are known, such as owl, spider, boar, salmon or cave hyena? There is a large cave hyena drawn next to a tiny panther in cave Chauvet. Is the size a measure of importance? And why are so many animals, such as wolverines, lynx, fox, otter, beaver and so many small mammals and birds entirely absent? If we simply interpret the animals as totemic, or as power-beasts, this exclusion seems rather unusual. Many early cultures admired wolves and boars, identified with them and used them as totem images. Why did the artists of the younger Palaeolithic choose to draw them so rarely?

One of the vital questions regarding cave art is why so few humans are shown. Most caves have no human images at all. And when they do, these are often in a strange state of transformation. Cave art shows several excellent images of people who are partly changed into animal form. Take the 'sorcerer' from Lascaux. His image is in the deepest and most inaccessibly part of the cave, directly above a chasm. The scene shows a woolly rhino to the left, its tail lifted, walking away after excreting manure. To the right there is a dying bison, its belly torn open, the guts spilling over the ground. Between this strange pair lies a man with erect penis and a bird head. Beside him a staff topped by a bird and a few rough lines that may or may not be broken hunting spears. Cave Trois Frères provides two horned shape-changers. One is a bison headed dancer, holding what is possibly a music bow.

The other appears in most books on shamanism, in the famous rendering made by early cave art explorer, Abbé Breuil. It seems to show a masked or owl faced dancer with deer antlers and fox-tail. The drawing is a lot more fascinating than the original. Few books show photographs of the cave painting, and those that do disappoint their readers. Either the original drawing faded enormously over the last decades or the good abbé used his imagination to provide a fantastic reconstruction. It has become a common fashion to identify this image as the 'horned god'; a deity of modern Wicca, and to assume that it is the earliest form of male divinity, a horned god for a cult of hunters. This charming idea has a number of flaws. We have no way of knowing whether the shape-changers in cave art are shamans, mask dancers,

camouflaged hunters, spirits, ancestors, legendary entities, tribal totems or deities. All we can be certain about is that in Palaeolithic art, the transformation of humans into animals was an essential element. Also, not all shape-changers wear horns or relate to a cult of horned beasts. You may recall the mammoth-human from Grotte Chauvet, the cat-headed nude woman and man engraved on pebbles of La Madeleine, the bear-man from Mas d'Azil and the bird headed trancer from Lascaux. And with regard to 'male divinity', it should be noted that a good many shape-changers exhibit no sign of gender at all. The divine couple of modern Wicca, 'Horned God' and 'Great Goddess', can only be considered the earliest gods of mankind if we ignore a lot of evidence. Horned gods appear in the Palaeolithic, but they are a lot more popular during the Iron Age. This is not necessarily a male cult either. Many horned gods of ancient Europe are not typically male deities but appear sexless, and several of them are definitely female.

We run into similar problems when we search for a meaning of the numerous abstract symbols that abound in cave art. In Lascaux, and a number of other caves, there are hundreds of abstract signs defying interpretation. We can be reasonably certain that these signs served as symbols, not as letters, and that we are not dealing with the earliest alphabet in the world. Nevertheless, these signs were part of a varied and original symbolic language. It is hardly surprising that there are many signs looking like runes among them. We have no idea of their meaning to the artist-sorcerers. Nor can we be certain that a symbol, which appears around 30,000BCE, still has its original meaning in another cave 10,000 years later. Then there are arrangements of dots which may or may not mean numbers, and several caves where hand prints, positive and negative, serve as decoration. Some of these hand prints, showing some distortion, were taken as evidence that the hunters of the Ice Age practised cruel amputation rites when they were not thinking about fertility. Less dramatic interpretations attempt to explain missing fingers as a hunter's sign language. Thus, while we can be certain that there is a lot of magic and religion in cave art, the question 'what magic would that be?' remains as mysterious as before.

The other major item of religious activity which always comes up in discussions on Stone-Age art and magic is the human figurines. Here we run into a topic that is fascinating as it says not only something of the beliefs of the younger Palaeolithic but even more of the scholars of the 19th and 20th century. As you may know, there are a number of human figurines dating in the middle of the younger Palaeolithic. Several of these statuettes look like an obese faceless women. It has been a common fashion to class these so called 'Venus statuettes' as images of a mysterious 'Great Goddess' and to explain them as fertility symbols. This interpretation is very much the product of the last two centuries. It was often claimed, and still is by the sort of folk who avoid new research, that the younger Palaeolithic (or any other early period we know little about) was a

peaceful time characterised by belief in a single great mother goddess who was in charge of fertility. Hand in glove with this assumption comes the theory that mankind was matriarchal. This idea is not the product of the Stone Ages. To begin with, the human statuettes do not come from all periods of the younger Palaeolithic but from a relatively short period. As far as they can be dated, most of them seem to come from the period between 25,000 and 23,000BCE (Hutton 1991). This turns them into a relatively minor development of a specific period. The next issue is the character of the goddess. The first scholars who wrote on the topic assumed that fertility was the major obsession of the Stone Age migrants. When they discovered a few figures of fat, faceless women, they immediately assumed they had evidence for the worship of a mother goddess. Few are aware that there are a lot more statuettes than generally appear in the popular books.

W.G.Haensch published an interesting study that illustrated the 100 statuettes (and fragments) known in 1982. Of these, I can only class 36 as definitely female. 3 are male, one seems to be a hermaphrodite. The rest shows no sign of gender or is so damaged that sexual identification is impossible. It turns out that round statuettes tend to endure the millennia much better than figures with thin limbs (which tend to break). Even in the female group there are numerous figures that cannot be explained as fertility objects. Several statuettes have small breasts or lack a pregnant belly. While there is certainly a bias towards pregnant females, it would go too far to call

Images of the Irish
Megalithic, starting
c.4900BCE. Top: a
selection of common
symbols.
Bottom: chamber stone 8
of satellite 2, Knowth,
after Brennan.

them all images of a fertility goddess. The same goes for other human images of the younger Palaeolithic. A considerable amount of them is definitely male, some are half-human and half-beast (shape shifting shamans?) and several are so monstrous that we can't be sure we are dealing with humans at all. This upsets the once-popular gospel that the Ice-Age hunters only portrayed faceless pregnant women. Several figurines show faces, so the face-taboo theory can also be discarded. It also raises the question whether these images were actually worshipped. They seem rather small for group worship, larger images made from plant material would be a better solution. Were the statuettes idols, talismans or pin-ups? The scholars of the 19th and early 20th century were certainly fond of classing any inexplicable object as an 'idol', and there are numerous 'idols' exhibited in museums which may have been children's toys or practical jokes.

Let us take a look at the myth of the Great Goddess. For a start, it ought to be mentioned that she is based on monotheism. In 19th century thought, a single great god was simply taken for granted. This was usually the patriarchal god of the Judao-Christian religion. When thinking of prehistory, and looking at these statuettes, it seemed natural to assume a similar monotheistic deity for our distant past. Now there is absolutely no evidence for early monotheism. All pagan cultures we know of venerated a range of deities who were in charge of various aspects of life. Among them were numerous female deities. We meet them as patronesses of cities, districts, countries,

arts, professions, crafts, war, technology, love, the family, justice, sacred spaces, hunting, science, fortune and so on. A few of them were in charge of nature (these are arguably goddesses associated with specific parts of the landscape, such as rivers or mountains) and none of them functioned as an all-inclusive mother goddess. The identification of a single goddess with nature and with several distinct goddesses appears to have been made only once in antiquity, we find it in Apuleius' *Golden Ass* (c.175CE) where it is attributed to the Isis of the Romano-Greek mystery cults.

With the advent of Christianity, goddesses of all sorts had a difficult time. This changed somewhat during the Renaissance, when the odd Greek deity appeared in art and literature as a poetic metaphor. It is only with the advent of industrialisation that romantic poets began to praise the beauty of nature, and to identify nature with a number of Greek or Roman goddesses. Here we are at the beginning of a new interpretation. Over the years, a new role model postulated that male gods were in charge of technology and progress, whereas female goddesses were praised for chastity, fertility and a general motherly care for all living creatures. Mother Nature is an invention of the industrial period. According to Ronald Hutton's fascinating *The Discovery of the Modern Goddess* (much of it incorporated in *The Triumph of the Moon*, 1999), Eduard Gerhard, in 1849, was the first author to propose a single goddess behind all those of antiquity. This theory soon received a lot of support. Whenever scholars came upon images of ancient goddesses (or strange females) they immediately classed them as images of the Great Goddess. Monotheism seemed so natural to them. This concept led to the idea of matriarchal society.

Several important scholars adopted this attitude, such as Sir Arthur Evans, to whom we owe a matriarchal Goddess-centred Minoan culture of Crete. Cretan museums are full of male statuettes that could easily be classed as gods. Somehow they never make it into the popular books. Simultaneously, several scholars selected a range of symbols which, as they believed, once represented the Great Goddess. Goddess images were all items showing holes, circles, clefts or spirals. Such interpretations say more about the scholars of the 19th century than about the beliefs of so called primitive people. The theory of the Great Goddess was further developed and gradually invaded the Feminist and the New Age movement. The Goddess became a sign of female emancipation. The Great Goddess personified Mother Nature pure and simple. Ancient goddesses used to represent trades, skills, crafts, activities and aspects of civilisation. The modern Great Goddess was simply venerated for her ability to bear and raise children.

This trend has changed over the last decades. Several feminists tried to oppose the cult of the Great Goddess, insisting that equal rights of women should not be derived from a highly questionable mythology. Research published by Peter Ucko and Andrew Fleming in the 1960s showed that the theory of Goddess-centred-matriarchy stood on a very shaky foundation. They did not disprove the

matter but simply pointed out that at the present state of knowledge, we cannot be certain of anything. Over the next decades, most scholars became extremely cautious with regard to the Goddess and her matriarchal society. Not so the Pagan movement, Wicca and the New Agers. In the triple Goddess of modern Wicca, an invention of Robert Graves, we encounter one of the most conservative images of female spirituality. Here the Goddess is defined by the purely biological functions of virgin, mother and crone.

The Goddess of Wicca is also interesting as she provides good evidence that a totally modern deity can function as well as any ancient one given enough belief. Wiccans tend to believe that their goddess is the earliest prototype of female divinity in the world, and often see themselves as perpetuators of 'the old religion'. To me, they offer a fascinating example that gods can be created anytime, and that a newly constructed Great Goddess may be as functional as any of the genuinely ancient deities. Anyone who has practised Wiccan rites will be aware that there is a definite reality to the Goddess, no matter that her origin is so recent. God-making happens more often than people know or dare to admit. In fact, it is much easier to find access to the Goddess than to a lot of really ancient deities. Waking an old and forgotten god is a laborious process that often requires years of dedicated trance work, intense emotionality and a lot of patience. Many of the elder deities are in a wretched state after millennia of oblivion. They have little or no energy, are badly out of touch with the times and require re-education to adapt to modern ways of thinking. I've met several who resented being woken, loathed modern humans and screamed for their usual offerings of blood and violence. A few of them made the transition and chose to wake to the new aeon, but this process was often slow and difficult.

Making a new 'old deity' is a lot easier. Wicca did this, but so did countless cults all the way through human history. Whenever a new deity is invented, its prophets go to great lengths to prove that it really happens to be old and venerable. This says a lot about the nature of the human mind.

It is not the intention of this text to annoy people who believe in the Great Goddess of the Palaeolithic or in matriarchal Ice Age societies. For all I know, such things are quite possible. The problem lies in proving them. We know next to nothing with regard to human religion and social organisation over a period of at least 30,000 years of (European) Homo sapiens sapiens. During such a long time, any sort of religion or social organisation may have existed. We have to admit that we know hardly anything and tend to generalise from very little factual evidence. If you really care about these cultures, keep an open mind.

The Forest Folk

Between, 10 000 and 8 000BCE, depending on location, the last ice age ended and the weather turned warmer. The huge ice shield of northern Europe and the glaciers extending from the Alps began to melt. With warmer weather, great changes occurred. Many of these had to do with water. The melting glaciers swelled the rivers and land that had hitherto been frozen for most of the year became a soggy morass. And the landscape itself transformed. With the melting of the glaciers, wide sections of land, freed from the enormous weight of the ice shield, began to rise. So did the ocean level, flooding wide ranges of coast-land, and eventually dividing Ireland and Britain from the Continent. On the central European mainland, the forest returned after a hundred thousand years of snow and ice. Birches were among the first trees to raise their branches to the warming skies. They had survived the cold as tiny shrubs, but soon enough they developed into bushy little trees. Rowan, a hardy survivor on stony ground, made its reappearance from sheltered dells and valleys. Pine began to cover the hill- and mountainsides. And in the wetland at the riverside the willows, poplars and alders began to thrive, gradually turning the morass into firm earth.

To the Ice Age hunters, this vegetation was something amazingly new. So it was for the beasts, most of whom were well adapted to a frosty, snowy environment. As the weather turned warmer, many of the great animals became extinct or moved towards Russia, where the climate was still cold. Many hunter-communities followed these beasts, leaving central Europe with less inhabitants than ever. But strangely, some of the hunter groups chose to stay. This may seem a simple decision when seen from our point of view. To the tribes who accepted this change, it must have involved a complete reversion of the earlier order.

NEOLITHIC
SPAIN
4000 – 2000 bc

What happened to religion when so many power beasts died or moved away, never to be seen again? And what faiths replaced the earlier cults when the open tundra became gradually covered by a dense forest dominated by birch and pine? Where earlier generations observed the great beasts from miles away, the forest dwellers had to adapt to an environment where the horizon was rarely visible. While the Ice Age beasts had often migrated in great groups, the forests beasts, such as roe and red deer, boar, elk, bison lived in small groups and relatively stable territories. There was less game than ever and new hunting skills were urgently needed. Luckily, with the advent of warmer weather, the range of plant life improved. There was more food available, such as water-lily roots, berries, fruit, mushrooms and nuts, and as some of it could be prepared and stored, flesh became less important for survival. We are now well within the Mesolithic era.

Mesolithic means middle stone age, and is often defined by changes in tool production. With the return of the forests, wood became widely available and wood cutting required better axes. During this period, stone axes undergo a remarkable improvement. The same goes for small stone tools, such as harpoons with barbs and miniature tools, such as drills, saws etc. needed to work the wood properly. Keep in mind that during the Mesolithic, people were still migrating across the land. These movements were not random, but in an annual cycle based on the advantages of certain landscapes during certain seasons. In bush-land and forest, the bow became the dominant weapons, at rivers and lakes, fishers used harpoons, nets, hooks, and in some coastal areas (Denmark comes to mind) the sea provided such an abundance of food that generations survived on mussels and shellfish, leaving behind enormous amounts of rubbish.

Unlike the Ice Age cultures, the Mesolithic migrants left little evidence for their way of life. Where the earlier cultures made use of rocks, bones and ivory in building a campsite, the Mesolithic folk could use a wide range of organic materials which decayed without a trace. We can imagine tents and huts made of branches, foliage, grasses and reeds, and we can speculate about wooden carvings and astonishing objects of art, but in prosaic reality, none of them can be proved. The same goes for the religions, myths and sorceries of these people. Where earlier cultures had left enduring artwork in caves, as carved bones or ivory, the Mesolithic offers a few painted pebbles (see illustration). Cave art itself largely disappears, apart from a few caves in Spain. Unlike earlier cave art, the emphasis shifts from naturalistic animals to humans. The Mesolithic artists portrayed humans gathering plants and honey, dancing, feasting, hunting, and, with depressing regularity, shooting arrows at each other. Many of the abstract symbols that graced earlier art disappear. We have next to no burials from the time. What did those people do with their dead? What sort of afterlife - if any - did they believe in? A unique find at Star Carr in Yorkshire, c. 7,500BCE, provided several sets of deer antlers made to fit into human caps. Two similar items were unearthed at Bedburg in

Nordrhein-Westfalen. They consist of magnificent antlers and parts of the skull, with carefully drilled holes to permit attachment to the head. Were they part of the costume of some deer-cult shamans or simply head-wear used by hunters as camouflage?

The Neolithic Revolution

As the Mesolithic is defined as the period between the end of the Ice age and the beginning of agriculture, its length varies from place to place. Agriculture is one of those surprises. Only a few decades ago, it used to be assumed that the Mesolithic migrants invented agriculture c.3000BCE when they noticed that edible plants can be grown from seeds. Sowing, so it was thought, led to the development of the first primitive fields, and from there to the invention of solid houses and settlements is not such a wide step.

This theory has undergone a few changes. For a start, we find the central European Neolithic beginning much earlier than was assumed, as around 5,700BCE wide ranges of fertile land were being cultivated. At the time being, it seems that agriculture was invented in the Near East around 10,000BCE. The evidence shows that a number of plants were cultivated, such as two types of wild wheat and barley, as well as several domestic animals, such as pig, cow, goat and sheep. Most of these plants and animals are not native to central Europe. It started the Neolithic period, the new stone age, which is defined by agriculture, domesticated animals and plants, settlements and often by pottery. How agriculture spread into Europe remains a

riddle. It used to be assumed that the technology gradually spread from tribe to tribe, but this does not seem likely at the present state of research. Instead of a gradual evolution we find the first Neolithic settlers in central Europe with a surprisingly uniform and refined lifestyle. The typical early Neolithic house, for instance, is not a shaky hut or a mud hovel but a large house, 25-40m long, 5-8m broad, erected on five rows of massive poles. It is generally divided into three sections, one with reinforced walls for sleep, one with a second storey for the storage of grains, straw, hay and a centre with widely spaced pillars providing room for work, daily life or festivity. Around these buildings are large subterranean storage pits and paddocks for animals. Apart from these standard long houses there is evidence for a few shortened versions, leading to much speculation with regard who lived in special buildings.

The first farmers cut and burned down stretches of forest to win space for cultivation. Another outdated theory, based on Gordon Childe's observation of jungle farmers of India, claimed that the first farmers used to exhaust their fields so fast that the settlement had to be shifted every few years. This theory, entitled *shifting cultivation*, turned out to be wrong. The first farmers always chose the extremely fertile loess earth close to rivers for their settlements, they cultivated several plants which enriched the soil (peas and lentils) and made use of manure. Far from living as travelling farmers their settlements endured for decades or even centuries. Indeed the central European Neolithic starts with so much technical refinement that we have to assume that it was introduced by migrants coming from somewhere in the south-east. How they blended with the Mesolithic migrants remains unknown. Perhaps we should imagine several centuries during which the two ways of life coexisted, and developed a system of trade and cultural exchange.

For quite a while, the early Neolithic has been paraded as an egalitarian society. Burials are plain and pretty similar, cemeteries of several hundred graves showing hardly any difference with regard to wealth or social status. We find earthenware goods, food, simple ornaments and a few tools for whatever life-after-death these people believed in. However, these cemeteries only contained a small section of society. Most early farmers were buried without traces, provided they were buried at all. And so we are left to wonder whether the 'plain egalitarian society' may already constitute a social or religious elite.

With regard to religion, we have very little evidence. The early farmers must have had a religion that differed from what the Mesolithic migrants believed. To a hunting and gathering society, the gods are the providers of game, plants, foodstuff, and survival depends to a large degree on the rituals and sorceries that make the journeys easy and the food supply steady. To the farmers, mobility was a thing of the past. The new gods were in charge of the weather. Rain and sunshine are a lot more important to a farmer than to a hunter. In a sense, the farmers committed themselves to thrive by their own efforts. Perhaps such new

ideas as ownership and inheritance of arable ground were developed in this time. And look at what happened to the shape of society! Where the Ice Age hunters often migrated in groups of less than 30 individuals, the farmers started a population explosion. There were (at best) 10,000 people in central Ice Age Europe, in the early Neolithic this number soars into the hundred thousands. This means larger settlements and consequently a society where more laws and regulations are needed. The first settlements were basically a few long houses with some distance between them. They did not look like villages and, as far as the archaeologists can tell, they were not fortified. A farmer's society tends to produce a surplus of food which can be stored, traded or used to support a number of 'professionals', such as craftspeople, traders or a regular priesthood.

I often wonder how religion and cosmology transformed in this time. What made hunting migrants decide that it is better to build houses and to till the fields? Using the most primitive ploughs imaginable, the farmers worked much harder than most hunter-gatherers do, and paid a heavy price in terms of damaged backs. Among the most popular plants cultivated at the time was sleeping poppy, so maybe the farmers did not only make oil of the seeds but used opium for anaesthesia and entertainment. But all this remains speculation. What were the religions, the dances, myths and arts of the early farmers? Did they invent the spirits of the fields, such as the corn wolf, the grain hag, the corn king, did they celebrate the cutting of the last sheaf?

SANDSTONE MENHIR
ST. SERNIN-SUR-RANCE,
AVEYRON, FRANCE
BELOW: STELE IN
THE DOLMEN MANÉ
ER H'ROÊCK,
LOCMARIAQUER,
BRETAGNE.

Things were confusing enough in the early period, when agricultural societies were so similar. After c.700 years, the farmers and migrants had fused to such an extent that numerous new agricultural cultures developed. Soon enough the fertile loess country was occupied and settlers moved into less hospitable districts. It took almost a thousand years before farming had spread from central to northern Germany, and during the fifth millennium BCE it reached Britain. In the next centuries we encounter numerous more or less original Neolithic cultures, each of them developing its own style and way of living.

While farming produced more wealth than before, the ever increasing communities led to an increase of diseases and warfare. The Neolithic period was not a peaceful time and the communities soon developed ways of fortifying their settlements. Evidence for mass murder appears at Talheim, Baden-Württemberg, Germany, where a group burial of more than 30 people was unearthed. All of them had been executed by knocking their heads in with stone axes. We also find evidence for ecological disasters. When the first farmers cleared the forests of southern England, they were not aware that the layer of humus covering the chalk was thin and vulnerable. Soon enough the rains had washed the fertile soil into the valleys, leaving much of the country incapable of supporting woodland. With regard to the religion and magic of the early farmers, we are very much in the dark. Most of their legacy consists of earthenware pots. Luckily, they used to ornament their ceramics with a wide range of symbols. In the illustration you can see symbols in use in just one location, central Hessen, Germany, and decide for yourself whether they are simply pretty or have hidden meaning.

Farmers and Astronomers

Around the year 5000BCE we find the first evidence for large earthworks in central Europe. Our early farmers had developed into several more or less distinct cultures. Some of these were keenly interested in astronomy. To the farmer, the calculation of seasons is a lot more important than to the migrating hunter-gatherer. Fields have to be prepared and crops sown long before it looks as if the weather would ever improve and time keeping is useful to organise this. Wrong timing can ruin a harvest and endanger the entire community. So around 5,000BCE we encounter the first observatories. This is a recent discovery, for which we can thank aerial surveillance. Under certain conditions of light, especially at dawn and dusk, the sun throws long shadows and earthworks may appear where the land looks flat to the person on the ground.

One such discovery is the massive earthwork of Goseck, Sachsen-Anhalt, c.30 km south of Halle. Imagine a circular space at the centre. Surround it by two palisades made of stout tree-trunks, but leave small gaps at certain key points. Surround the outer palisade with an embankment, and dig a ditch around it. Enclose the ditch with another, higher embankment and cut three entrances through it. This gives you a round structure with several rings. For decoration, put up a lot of cattle heads near the gates in the palisades.

The result is a remarkable astronomical observatory. When the first light of the rising sun, or the last rays of the setting sun where shining through the gates in the embankment and the gaps in the palisades, it was possible to estimate the exact days of the summer and winter solstices. Also, the south eastern gate was also pointing to the stars of Taurus at the winter solstice when the structure was built, c.4,800BCE. There were two shallow pits, one of them outside the outer palisade, the other outside of the outer embankment. One contained bones of a right and left arm and a right leg of an adult, the other parts of a hand. This made the excavators and the media holler 'human sacrifice!', while more sober-minded scholars observe that bones can also come from corpses. That Neolithic ditches sometimes contain corpses or parts of them is well attested from southern Britain. Another possibility is the sacrifice of a person to ensure the safety of a building, a 'foundation burial'. This sort of thing can be unearthed occasionally, just think of Maiden Castle in southern England. On the whole the custom seems to have continued well into the Roman occupation, and you can still find traces of it in medieval myth (the tale of Merlin). Now Goseck is not unique. The 'Schalkenburg' near Quenstedt, Sachsen-Anhalt, shows a lot of similarities. Here we have five circular palisades with three entrances. It seems to be built c.4800-4400. A similar construction of circular palisades was uncovered in Svodin, 50 km south/east of Nitra, Slovakia, dating c. 4700BCE and at Künzing-Unternberg, Bavaria, also c. 4700BCE (*Opferplatz und Heiligtum*, 2000).

Similar earthworks, usually circular and consisting of various circles of ditches and embankments, have been found from Hungary to Britain. They co-exist with the Megalith period and some of them continue well into the bronze age. Perhaps we should consider them as part of the megalith culture, as the astronomical purpose is similar to that of certain stone arrangements. Whatever the early farmers had in mind, apart from keeping a precise calendar, their astronomical observations continued for several thousand years.

Cults of the Stones

Megalith culture is one of those things that get a lot of attention. When people erect huge stones, be it as single, standing stones, in circular arrangements, as avenues or use them to build chambers, the result is not only impressive, it also tends to last. Historians began to wonder about the megaliths (mega = large, lithos = stone) long before they knew anything about the earlier cultures, and invented a wide range of explanations for them. Sites such as Stonehenge were identified as Roman, Saxon, Viking and Celtic by passionate antiquarians, long before any sort of dating was possible. This resulted in the common fable that the Celts used to build megalith structures, and though there is not a shred of evidence, it remains alive and well in popular opinion. For country folk, standing stones were simply the result of supernatural activity. There is a wide range of tales that explains standing stones as missiles hurled by angry giants at each other. Then there are the dolmen (Bretonic : table stone), chambers made of huge rocks with a flat stone on top, usually covered by a thick layer of earth, which were thought to house dwarves and beings from deep-below-the-surface. Most dolmen have rather low ceilings, you have to stoop to enter them, and this suits small folk of great cunning, wise in sorcery. Today many dolmen have lost their protective earth cover. The rocks stand free under a wide sky, and the room-like character of the interior is lost as the wind blows steadily through the gaps. When these structures were raised, they looked like mounds. Here we may have the first hollow hills of European prehistory.

Megalith structures were not only popular, they also appear over wide parts of Europe. At the time being, the earliest seem to be Irish, where complicated passage 'graves' were used for astronomical observations. These structures have been dated to c. 4,900BCE. A little younger are the Bretonic megaliths, some of which go back to c. 4,500BCE, Then there are stone arrangements, circles and barrows in wide ranges of the British isles, along the coast of the North Sea, Denmark is crammed full of them and so is southern Scandinavia. Northern Germany has plenty of megalith barrows, in central Germany the custom was less popular (though remnants of a few stone circles and standing stones survive), in France we find stone arrangements all along the coasts and the same goes for Spain, Portugal, North Africa, the Mediterranean islands and Italy.

It does not stop in Europe, however. Megaliths were popular in lots of countries, at one time or another, and this includes China, Korea, South East Asia, India and other locations. What amazed the first serious researchers is the fact that megaliths appear over such vast parts of Europe with such speed and also with a certain uniformity. At first, the scholars proposed that the megaliths were crude attempts to copy Egyptian pyramids, Near Eastern temples or tombs. This notion went out of fashion when new dating methods proved that the megaliths were older. Then followed the theory that the megaliths were the last visible signs of a pan-European religion. It was proposed that megaliths were erected as a result of considerable missionary activity, and that the cult spread along the coastlines. This may have something going for it, as indeed the majority of great stone arrangements are fairly close to the sea. Stone circles were thought to mark places of festivity while dolmen and barrows were considered graves chambers. A good many barrows contained burials or traces of them. It was hard to be sure, though, as many barrows had been plundered long before academics became interested. In Germany, the majority was blown up during the 19th century, when farmers decided that the rock could be sold for good money. Some used dynamite rather than having a bunch of scholars messing up their fields and getting in the way of the harvest.

So what is the secret of the great stones? Things turned out to be a lot more complicated than expected. For a start, Megalith culture is not a unified, single phenomena. Megaliths were used for all sorts of purposes over a range of several millennia, and while the basic

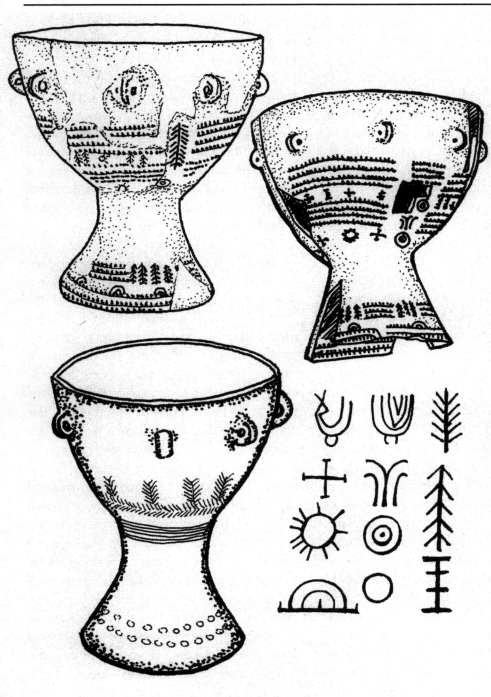

Earthenware drums, Megalith period. **Top**: Hornsömmern, brown drum with white ornaments including crosses, circles, spruce trees, height 25cm, diam. 21 cm. **Top left**: the reconstructed version, top right showing the reverse side, before reconstruction, after Kossina 1936. Bottom: Ebendorf, Wolmirstedt, c. 3000BCE, height 26cm, diam. 17cm, design shows twelve spruce twigs, seven holes to bind the skin, from stone-chamber tomb. **Bottom right**: a selection of symbols from drums.

structures, the standing stones and the stone chambers, remained popular, the actual construction and use varied enormously. We could imagine that standing stones might be a representation of a phallic sky deity and that the barrows and chambers represent the womb of a subterranean earth goddess. I like this idea, but have to admit that it is remarkably hard to prove. Historians soon decided that stone arrangements and barrows appear in various shapes and sizes, and that there were differences regarding their construction, distribution, age and use. This has turned out to be more complicated.

Only a few decades ago, leading experts were proud to classify half a dozen types of basic megalith structures. Recent research has left a good many theories in tatters, and will continue to do so. For every rule that was paraded in the seventies and early eighties, there are so many exceptions that we can confidently forget about generalisations.

Consider the dolmen, or barrow grave. Though there are lots of them scattered all over Europe and northern Africa, their structure and contents are far from uniform. Some dolmen contained burials, but as it turns out, this may have been a late development. The early Irish dolmen, particularly in the Boyne valley, were built to calculate the seasons of the year (see Brennan, 1994). On certain dates, rays of the rising or setting sun entered the dark passages and illuminated rocks, or symbols on them. Newgrange and Dowth are aligned with the winter solstice, Loughcrew and Sess Kilgreen are aligned with the summer solstice, the

equinoxes can be calculated at cairn T, Loughcrew and at Knowth. Quarter days can be measured at cairn L and H, Loughcrew (8th of November) and cairn F on the 6th of May. Cairn S is useful to observe the quarter days of the 6th of May and the 8th of August, cairn L shows the quarter days of 8th November and the 6th of February. Let me add that these are the astronomical quarter days. They are not the same thing as the rural quarter days that make up the Gaelic year, and the ceremonial calendar of many modern pagans.

The Boyne observatories are still functional, after so many thousand years, unless they were messed up by thoughtless academics during the reconstruction of the barrows. I should add that, while the position of the stars (as seen from earth) changes steadily over the millennia, the position of sunrises is relatively constant, as the sun is so close to the earth. You can calculate the passage of the seasons by setting up a few poles or standing stones. All you need is a single pole called the pointer, and a few poles to mark where the pointer's shadow falls at sunrise or sunset on equinoxes, solstices and quarter days. Measuring shadows is all well and good, but any pole or stone throws a broad shadow. This may be fine for the calculation of the equinoxes. Earth circles the sun in an oval, not a circular course. Around the equinoxes, the length of days and the motion of the sun are easy to estimate, but at the solstices, the daily change is slight and difficult to measure. If you want a really precise calculation, it is much better to build a subterranean structure where rays of light come through an entrance and extend through a long, dark passage, to illuminate a large rock, marked with all sorts of symbols, at the very end. Better still, when the sunrise (or sunset) is obscured by clouds or bad weather, you can measure where the rays are falling on the next day, or the day after.

Good dolmen provide symbols on specific rocks that allow the astronomer to keep the calendar up to date. This was done in the early Irish cairns, and the same goes for many of the early Bretonic ones. Nevertheless, we cannot say that *all* early dolmen were calendaric devices. Some were built without any relation to specific dates, and indeed, it seems as if the early meaning of the structure was forgotten at some point. While I am fairly sure that the Bretonic and British dolmens I enjoyed functioned as ritual spaces, there are loads that may have been sites of ritual at first, but were used by much later generations to bury their dead.

Some dolmens were used for the burial of one person. Some only for the burial of certain parts of the body. Some contained groups of people. Some contained entire corpses, others ashes, urns or bones. Sometimes the bones were bleached or burned, sometimes we find them arranged neatly, piled up in heaps or simply tossed into the chamber without consideration. Human bones were occasionally mixed with animal bones, several species appear, but we cannot be sure if they represent food for the dead or functioned as power-beasts or place guardians. Some corpses were buried in much older dolmens. Some were first buried in earth,

unearthed after a while, and then put inside a barrow. Some dolmen contained groups of people of one or both sexes, or of specific age groups. Some were opened only once, for a specific burial, others repeatedly, and occasionally bones were taken out again. Several dolmen did not contain their dead in the central chamber but behind the rocks, within an earth mound. If the dead went into the space outside of the stone chamber, just what was the chamber used for? A ritual space between the living and dead? For more detail, consult Ronald Hutton's brilliant *Pagan Religions of the Ancient British Isles*.

To propose a 'single megalith religion' on the basis of so much variation seems rather naïve. Burial customs differed immensely from district to district and time to time, as did the way of constructing the dolmen. Even the theories that attempted to show linear progressions, fashions or developments of types have been invalidated by countless exceptions to each rule. Then there is the question just who was buried in the barrows. Most of the people who built megalith structures were not buried in them. It takes hundreds to thousands of workers, plus lots of time, to erect a dolmen or a stone alignment. Just think of the effort involved in transporting and shaping the stones! You need a surplus of labour and food, this implies relatively large communities and a climate that is warmer than today, allowing for better harvests. Who was buried within a dolmen? Certainly not the workers. Yet it is not necessarily the members of an aristocracy or priesthood who came to rest beneath the hollow hills. We could imagine the dolmen as a luxurious grave for important people, but we could also imagine that the dolmen was a religious site, and that the corpses within were sacrifices or place guardians. Such a wealth of possibilities has not made the archaeologists profession an easy one.

The same problems occur in the study of stone circles and alignments (i.e. 'avenues' etc.). The idea that stone circles are astronomical observatories was proposed fairly early. A. Thom examined numerous circles and came up with the 'megalithic yard', a measure which was supposed to be used by all megalith people. It still exists in some popular books, in the real world it has long been disproven. In fact, professor Thom was allegedly caught distorting maps and shifting boulders. Likewise, the early attempts to relate all stone circles to astronomy didn't make anybody happy. You can't just say 'this is the rock showing the rise of a certain star' when you don't know when that rock has been set up. Without a good date for the building of a given circle, we cannot estimate its astronomical meaning. Such dates are not always available, and they certainly did not exist in Thom's days.

More so, why build a circle at all? To set up a device to measure the equinoxes, solstices and quarter days, you need only six stones or poles (see illustration). A complete circle is a lot of extra work. Also, the circles have not always been in the same shape. Some of them were rebuilt repeatedly during the megalith period, just look at the different stages of erecting Stonehenge. Others were messed up by treasure hunters or fanatic Christians. Occasionally, stones were toppled and buried by the locals, this seems to have been the case at Avebury, where a number of hidden boulders have been discovered under the soil. And what of the enthusiastic excavators of the 19th century? Some of them took great liberties with fallen rocks when they attempted to re-erect them according to their fancy.

Then there are circles that were built in valleys or places that prevent good astronomical observations. As a result, we know that some circles were aligned with the calendar while others were not. Some may have had several functions over the millennia. I should add that megalithic astronomy used to be unpopular among academics over the last decades. After the initial enthusiasm, when any stone circle was classed as astronomical, scholars became very reluctant about the possibility and shied away from it whenever possible. The trend is changing now, at the beginning of the 21st century, as more and more astronomical earthworks are being discovered. To sum things up, we know less of the megalith culture in general, and more of it in particular, than ever. The very idea of a single megalith culture misleads, and blinds us to numerous local and temporal possibilities.

And what of the stones themselves? Just because stones last they tend to appear as the main thing in megalith religion. As it turns out over the last decades, there also existed a number of structures which did not make use of stone but of wood. Woodhenge is one such example, another is Seahenge (c.2000 BCE), a circle of 55 tree-trunks surrounding a central oak which had been set up, roots to the sky, in the centre of the circle. Wood is hard to trace in excavations as it usually rots. At Seahenge it survived as the slime and sand of the seaside covered the structure, and effectively prevented decay. It's difficult to estimate nowadays, but maybe there were more wooden alignments and circles than those made of stone. A wooden circle needs regular maintenance every few generations, but then it can be built with less effort than a circle of stone. And what should we make of the other enigmas of the megalith period, such as the artificial chalk hills, Silbury and Marlborough?

With regard to runes, there are a number of megaliths which show signs and symbols. Most of them date from the earliest period of megalith culture and can be seen in Ireland and Brittany. In Brittany, I sketched several images, but as you can see in the illustrations, the signs do not show the angular shape found in most runes. Instead, they tend to be rounded. The Irish evidence is much better than the Bretonic. Martin Brennan, in his excellent *The Stones of Time* has worked out the basic vocabulary of signs appearing in Ireland, where they are closely connected with astronomy. I include a few drawings and recommend that you get his book and enjoy it. It's a good idea to meditate on the signs and to enter them by journeys in the imagination.

Finally, an innovation of the megalith period is ritual drumming. More than a dozen small earthenware drums, dated around 3,000BCE, have been unearthed in tombs of the Walternienburg-Bernburg culture (see illustration). Several are ornamented with symbols not unlike runes. One of the favourites is the signs of an evergreen branch: it appears not only on the drums but also on the stone plates sealing the tomb chamber. Evergreen trees may have been chosen as a symbol of life after death. These drums are typical for the burial of privileged people of both sexes. I should add that the drums, though rather small (usually less than 30cm), show considerable refinement. They have a similar form as the oriental darabukas, the Egyptian tablas and the fairly recent west-African djembes. The special shape allows the player to produce a wide range of sounds, from a high pitched slap near the edge to a deep, dynamic bass in the centre of the skin. Scandinavia also provides a few small earthenware drums just prior to the bronze age, but most I have seen are simple and plain cylinders with a broad rim. Not much to drum with, but the ideal shape for friction drums, a principle found in the humming-pot and in the Brasilian cuica.

In Search of the Indo-Europeans

One of the more fantastic denizens of the archaeologist's world are the Indo-Europeans. These people are happy and alive in linguistic research, but so far they elude the excavator in an utterly frustrating way. The Indo-Europeans cannot be located on a map. They are a hypothetical culture and what we know of their language is a reconstruction.

For a start let us look at their discovery. In the 19th century, a number of linguists began to wonder about the close similarity of several languages. The word 'mother', for example, is Mâta in Sanskrit, Mater or Meter in Old Greek, Mater in Latin, Mothe or Muti in Old Prussian, Mathir in Old Irish, Mati in Old Slavian and Matar in Tocharian. 'Sister' is Schwester in German, Soeur in French, Soror in Latin, OHG: Swester, Gothic: Swistar, Old Slavic: Sestra, Old India: Svasâ. 'Brother' is Bruder in German, Old Indian: Bhrâtâ, Old Persian: Brâtar, Lithunian: Broter. Such similarities show relations between languages.

When we find that in certain languages the oldest words are related, we can assume that these languages developed from a common origin. This is not always the case, as sometimes new technology is imported together with its (foreign) name, or conquest makes a new language the official one, but when the similarities abound, a certain relationship is likely. Our scholars decided that there is a group of languages that seems to have a common origin sometimes in prehistory. They called it Indo-Germanic, not because the culture came from India or Germany, but as the representative names of the most eastern and western languages of the group. In the 1930s, the term was thoroughly abused by German scholars, so that modern linguists prefer the more neutral Indo-European. One of the things that appeared fairly soon is that the huge complex of Indo-European languages consists of two distinct branches. To differentiate them, they were called after the word for 'hundred' which is Kentum in one branch and Satem in the other. Kentum languages are Celtic, Germanic, Venetian, Illyrian, Talic, Greek, Latin, Hethitic, Luvian and Tocharic. Satem languages are Balto-Slavic, Albanian, Thracian, Phrygian, Armenian and Indic. The two branches developed from a common root. It has been proposed (Kilian, 1983) that the two branches may have separated before 3000BCE. But what sort of common culture was the origin of such a wealth of languages? To answer this question, linguists began to seek for old words that are shared by most of the languages. The Indo-Europeans had agriculture before they separated into two branches and dozens of sub-branches, as can be deduced by the presence of very similar words for ploughs and agricultural tools. And this was just the beginning. Common to most Indo-European languages are similar terms for many old ideas, such as words that describe family relationships, social structures, everyday items and numbers. Collecting similar word-roots, Herman Hirt made a long catalogue of concepts which he believed were common to the early Indo-Europeans. Here are some samples.

Climate and Landscape: ice, hail, snow, mountains, plains, rivers, lakes. Whether the ocean was known is still open to debate.

Tools: quern, spade, plough, sickle, sieve, wagon, axle, wheel, yoke, ship.

Beasts: dog, cow, cattle, goat, pig, horse, sheep, eel, blackbird, aurox, bear, beaver, bee, finch, squirrel, elk, duck, otter, goose, fox, jay, hen, hare, herring (?), weasel, deer, crow, hedgehog, crane, lynx, louse, mouse, raven, sparrow, sturgeon, wolf.

Trees: birch, yew, oak, alder, ash, fir,

MEGALITH PERIOD ART

ROSSEIRONE, GARD

STELE DE LAURIS VAUCLUSE

ALMEIRA

ESTRAMADOURE

LUNIGIANA ITALIA

SAINT BENEZET, GARD

GENNA ARRELE, SARDINIA

hazel, lime, elm, willow. Beech is still under discussion.

From such studies, it was hoped to discover the homeland of the Indo-Europeans. This was more difficult than expected. We are reasonably sure that Kentum languages developed in countries that were covered by forests, by people who lived on cattle breeding, agriculture and fishing, while Satem languages were developed in dry, plains country, by people who bred cattle and sheep, moved around in a semi-nomadic fashion and practised little agriculture. Looks easy, doesn't it? You can be sure there are plenty of exceptions.

Lothar Kilian proposed that the origin of the Indo-European languages may go back to the end of the last ice age. At the time, the North and Central Europeans were severely restricted in their mobility. To the north was the vast ice shield that covered so much of Scandinavia, Britain and northern Germany, while to the south the Alps provided a huge, ice-covered barrier. In between these cold zones was a relatively warm corridor where plants grew and animals moved, often in vast herds. People could move from east to west, but not from north to south, and the isolation may well have produced the light skin colour and the common language.

When the climate became warmer, some folks decided to search for new homes, beginning the migration of the Indo-European languages. But just where was the homeland of the Indo-Europeans? Elder books tend to locate them in Central Asia or around the Black Sea. From this (fictional) location, so

we read, the Indo-Europeans moved in great trecks, westward into Europe and eastwards into India. Complete with this hypothesis came the belief that the Indo-Europeans were a war-loving, aggressive and thoroughly patriarchal bunch of conquerors. None of this can be proved with any certainty.

A more recent hypothesis approached the problem from the linguistic point of view. Kilian cites research for the oldest place-names. In the land between central Russia, the Black Sea and the Rhine, Indo-European word roots are the oldest in evidence. If this is true, the Indo-Europeans did not invade Europe, but developed there. Another recent hypothesis points at central Anatolia, in Turkey, as a possible place of origin. Archaeology can contribute little to the problem, as language, unlike bones and grave goods, cannot be excavated. And just how certain can we be that the Indo-Europeans evolved in any single location? Some of them had a real penchant for travelling. The Indo-European Aryans who conquered India between 1500 and 1200BCE (the dates are still disputed) may have been close cousins of the Germanic people at one time. This seems unusual, as the Aryans spoke Satem languages and the Germans Kentum, but when you compare the *Vedas* with the *Eddas* you will discover some amazing similarities.

The common German wind and storm god Wodan, leader of the wild hunt and companion of ghosts and spirits, has an ancient relation in the Indian storm god Vâta, who is celebrated in two hymns of the *Rig Veda* (10,168 and 10,186). I have quoted the former in *Seidways*, where the god is celebrated as the driver of the wind-chariot across the stormy sky, attended by tempests like maidens coming to a rendezvous, eldest of the gods, embryo of the universe, king of all. Here is the other one, praising the god as the sustainer of life and keeper of the elixir of immortality:

> Filling our hearts with health and joy,
> may Vâta breathe his balm on us:
> may he prolong our days of life.
> Thou art our father, Vâta, yea, thou art
> a brother and a friend,
> so give us strength that we may live.
> The store of Amrita laid away yonder,
> O Vâta in thine home,-
> Give us thereof that we may live.
>   (trans. Ralph Griffith)

When the *Rig Veda* was compiled (1200 - 900 BCE), Vâta was already a minor god who soon faded into oblivion. His function as a wind god shifted to the wind god Vâyu, while the stormy, tempestuous side of the god became associated with dangerous Rudra, originally a dreaded god of the wilderness; healer, poisoner, killer and ascetic. Rudra is associated with ghosts and spirits just like Wodan is, and travels in the company of maddened phantoms and crazed women. He later transformed into Shiva.

Likewise, the black goddess Nirriti, in charge of doom, disorder, destruction and guardian of the darkest hells, has astonishing parallels to the Icelandic goddess Hel. The same goes for the dark goddess Kâlî, who appears briefly in the early *Upanishads*, maybe around 500 BCE. The Vedic Indra is a thunderbolt wielding, dragon/serpent fighting god whose heroic deeds closely resemble Thor's regular battles against the Midgard-serpent. Both serpents coil around the world, the Icelandic one being the brother or sister of Hel, while the Indian one is brother to the demon Vala. The names of Hel and Vala go back to the same root, meaning hollow, cave, hole etc.. Both of them share a subterranean location, the former as the goddess of death, hell and the underworlds, the latter as a demon who abducts sun, moon and dawn and locks them up in a cavern until Indra comes round for a fight to release them.

Or think of the Vedic obsession with such numbers as 432,000 (the years of the present age of corruption) or 4,320,000,000 years (a kalpa, or world cycle). *Prose Edda* (*Gylf.* 40) relates that Valhalla has more than 500 doors and four times ten, and 800 Einheriar warriors, Odin's elite troops, pass through each door when it is time to fight the wolf. 540 x 800= 432 000. Note that both sources are concerned with the topic of world ages. Vedic lore also connects with other European mythologies. Zeus was identified with Indra when the Greek attempted to invade India. The Vedic Varuna, god of space and vastness (later god of the oceans and waters) is a close relation of the Greek god Uranus. Maybe or maybe not Loki and Agni share more than a fiery nature. Ushas, radiant, red-breasted goddess of Dawn, riding in her chariot at the emergence of the sun, is not only the most popular Vedic goddess. She has European counterparts, goddesses associated with dawn, beginnings or springtime, such as Eos, Aurora and the Anglo-Saxon Eostre. The latter is associated with spring and the Easter festival (named after her), but alas, Bede recorded no details, and without his testimony, we wouldn't know she existed at all.

Then there is the enigma of the divine families or tribes. The Vedic Aryans were not a single culture but a number of tribes sharing a language. They did not invade India at once but arrived over several centuries, each new group having a somewhat different religious outlook. And they worshipped several divine families. The best known are the Devas, 'the Shining Ones', from the Indo-European root *deiw-, the (bright) sky. The Devas are the major group of deities in Hinduism, but in the earlier Vedic period this was not the case. We find relations to the word *deiw- in several European cultures. The Latin deus (god) comes from the same root, as does the Greek god Zeus, the old Germanic god Twisto and the later deities Tir, Tiwaz and Zis.

Another prominent group of gods are the Asuras, whose name may or may not be related to the Nordic Aesir, i.e. Odin's tribe. Could the Danavas of the Vedas connect with the British family of Don and the Irish family of Danann? With the advent of early Hinduism, the Asuras and the Danavas were turned into Demons. Several popular Asura gods of the *Rig Veda*, such as Agni, Varuna, Ushas, the Maruts, Soma, the Âdityas and Rudra were transformed into Devas to keep them popular. These examples should suffice to show that anyone interested in European paganism would do well to study Indo-European mythologies. Or even more exotic ones.

In the *Rig Veda* (10, 90), we learn that everything was created out of a primal being with a thousand heads, eyes and feet, called Purusha, or simply 'the man'. When Purusha was sacrificed, he became the seasons, the life forms, the animals of forest and village. The mind became moon, the eyes became sun. The gods Indra and Agni were born out of Purusha's mouth, Vâyu was created out of his breath, his head turned into heaven, the navel became the middle world, the feet turned into earth, the ears became the directions of space. Purusha was dismembered and the whole world was created out of him. This is really close to the myth of the primal giant Ymir given in *Prose Edda* (*Gylf.* 5-8). Better still, Ymir is nourished by a primal cow called Audhumla, who is close to a Vedic creation goddess, a cow called Aditi. The primal giant is not confined to Germanic and Indian myth. In early Chinese myth, the primal giant, origin of everything, is called Pan Gu. Now Chinese is definitely not a Indo-European language. However, one branch of the Indo-Europeans, the Tocharians, moved east and are recorded in Chinese history. In 170BCE they lived less than 500KM from Beijing. Some ideas certainly got around. With regard to European prehistory, it remains very hard to decide whether a given culture can be classed as Indo-European or not. Were the first farmers, the beaker folk, the megalith people or the bronze agers Indo-Europeans? Scholars have been debating this for more than a century and it doesn't look as if they would come to a

Water-bird headed dancer
from Val Camonca

consensus in a hurry. Last, a word on Indo-European itself. Our scholars did not stop at comparing words. They also tried to work out their earliest, and hopefully original form by drawing up complicated tables of origin. As a result, there is today a language called Indo-European which might come close to the original. Words in this language are always prefixed with a star, to show that they are hypothetical. You will find plenty of them lurking in the Rune Companion in part three. Lots of rune names acquire a deeper meaning when we explore their Indo-European roots.

Bronze age

Megalith culture was still prospering when people began to experiment with metals. First we have some experiments with copper, leading to the production of some pretty ornaments, but changing very little with regard to everyday life. Flint was still a much better cutting tool, in fact, a well made flint knife has an edge that is sharper than the best surgical scalpels we can make from steel. Metallurgy made a great leap forward when people discovered that a mixture of copper and 4-10% tin produces a metal that is a lot more durable than either of them on its own. It was the beginning of the bronze age. Now 'ages' of prehistory are not really ages at all. They are simply a modern way of ordering periods about which we know very little. People did not start by saying 'Hey, we got bronze now, a new age is here!'. Did people in the 20th century behave like that when they began to produce plastic? Of course not. New technologies take a while before they change things. In central Europe, people began to work with bronze around 2,200BCE. The discovery of bronze occurred during the last third of the megalith period. It did not end the megalith period. Stonehenge was built by folks who had bronze axes, and while it certainly constitutes an impressive effort, it is based on pretty much the same astronomy that people had used two thousand years earlier. What we can witness in the centuries after the discovery of bronze is a gradual decline of megalith structures.

The circle at Stonehenge is a fascinating mixture of elements that were made with enormous effort and care, and stones that were made in a slap-dash fashion. Some of the stones were set carelessly that experts wonder whether the whole thing was ever really complete or whether parts collapsed while it was still under construction. Similar observations apply to other structures. In northern Germany, for instance, barrows became increasingly smaller and more primitive. What had started out as refined astronomical observatories in Ireland and Britanny around 4,900BCE turned into small, primitive barrow graves with few extra chambers and no observable astronomical significance. It makes me wonder whether the original intent of these buildings had been forgotten. People still considered astronomy an important matter, but they seem to have changed the way they calculated the calendar. So gradually, the dolmen turned into barrow graves and ever smaller mounds. Likewise, stone circles seem to have become a rarity. This did not happen in all places at once. In Denmark and southern Scandinavia, some of the traditions of the megalith folk seem to have survived, if in a somewhat reduced form, almost to the Viking age. We are now approaching the full development of the Bronze Age, when bronze was not a costly luxury but a material that was used for hundreds of everyday purposes.

These ages are enigmatic, to say the least. Several cultures seem to have expanded across Europe, large scale horse breeding being an important innovation. People used bronze for tools and ornaments, but they also began to produce weapons that were specifically designed to kill other people. A sword is not a hunting weapon, a helmet is not a fancy hat. Horse breeding made warriors mobile, and before long we have evidence for organised warfare. This is not to say that earlier periods were less violent. It is just that a new technology allowed violent people to get better at it. Settlements changed. Warfare made fortification a matter of necessity, and we can observe a steady increase in well fortified hilltop settlements. A good many Celtic ringwalls were erected on earlier bronze age fortifications. In southern Germany, many people sought shelter and protection by building fortified villages at the shores of great lakes, or even some way out in the water. People moved about a good deal, be it voluntarily or by sheer need. The climate changed repeatedly, and so did the vegetation. We have a semi-warm period in the early bronze, a lot of confusing changes of climate in the middle bronze, and a drastic change to cold and wet weather at the end of the bronze age. It was an uneasy period about which we

know far too little. Nor do I feel confident in writing this chapter. The archaeological evidence for these periods is not very impressive and our knowledge is still full of gaps. May I ask you to keep an open mind and to do your own research? Some of the things in these pages will turn out to be wrong, and it is up to you to read up on new research. The bronze ages are bound to spring some surprises on us over the next decades.

When we try to understand the religions of the time, we are faced with a chronic lack of reliable evidence. The megalith people left us plenty of evidence in the form of durable stone buildings, including signs, symbols, offerings, burials and the like. When people stopped building in great stones, their beliefs became exceedingly hard to trace. Archaeology suddenly had to make do with very little evidence for anything. We have a lot of pottery, we have bronze grave goods and are able to trace the construction of buildings and settlements, but when it comes to religion, the score is very low. This is not to say that the bronze age cultures were not religious. Maybe a lot of their sacral art was made from perishable material. But what did it look like? And just what did the people believe in? A good many of the gods that we know from the later Celts and Germani were around during the bronze ages, if not in the megalith period. Tough luck that we don't know who worshipped them, or in what form, or even where it happened.

The Bronze Age of Scandinavia left us some great material. The cultures up north had access to a good many sites where huge

SCANDINAVIAN
ROCK-ART
2,500 bc-?

rocks had been polished by the motion of the glaciers thousand of years earlier. These rocks were an ideal surface for pictures. In places like Alta (Norway) or Bohuslän (Sweden), bronze age people engraved the smooth rock surfaces with thousands of images. We see boats and sledges, people playing lure-trumpets, dancers, acrobats, folks in bird costumes, huge warriors (or gods?) with spears and axes, abstract symbols and a wide range of animal life. The rendering is refined and aesthetic. It eventually disappeared under a protective layer of moss (where it survived to our age) but you can find some of the images on the ritual drums of the Sami.

A similar thing happened in the Alps. Sites like the Val Camonica preserve the rock art of several millennia. Again, we have well-polished slabs of rock, inviting passing migrants (c.7,000 BCE) to leave a picture. Graffiti is contagious, the images increased over the centuries, and by the time people decided to settle in the southern Alps, they had rocks in the neighbourhood showing images and symbols of many centuries. The fashion flourished, and during the bronze age, it became part of religion. This leaves us a wonderful insight into the bronze age ideologies of Scandinavia and the Alps, but when it comes to the countryside between them, we are still very much in the dark.

The same goes for the British isles, where religious imagery is notoriously scarce and hard to connect with specific people. With regard to central Europe, the bronze age cultures left so little pictorial evidence, be it images, pictures or statues, that many historians proposed that representations of deities, humans and animals were highly restricted, if not completely taboo. This is not the case with all bronze agers between the Alps and Scandinavia, but all in all, the amount of good religious art is very small. We observe a similar tendency among the early Celts of the Hallstatt period, most of whom seem to have been shy about human and divine representations. There are a few crude images, such as standing stones with primitive faces, which pose the question why a people with great artistic and technical skills preferred a primitive image to a well-developed one?

So things are pretty cryptic in central Europe. We have a few odd works of art that seem related to religion, not that we know what they were good for. As our topic is mainly the central European cultures out of which the Celts and Germani developed, I shall now explore a few matters from continental Europe. Writing about other regions is a great temptation but goes far beyond the scope of this essay. Nor can I give a complete description. Let me just list a few crucial components.

During the Bronze Age, sacrifice became increasingly important. We have large deposits of offerings, such as the daggers, shields (fragmentary or entirely made of bronze), ornamental disks, wheels, helmets, trumpets, swords, sickles and axes. Most of these items were cast into rivers or swamps. However, they are not evenly distributed. A short 14 km section of the Rhine near Mainz provided some 250 bronze offerings, by comparison the entire river Main yielded only 110 objects, widely distributed over 500KM (Kubach, 1994). Evidently some people thought sacrifice a must while others did not bother. Should we assume that there were several distinct cultures, with distinct religious customs, living in close proximity? Similar deposits have been uncovered in rivers such as the Danube, the Neckar, the Elbe and a lot of smaller streams, but in each case the deposits differed. When we compare them to river and swamp offerings from Britain, Ireland or southern Scandinavia we can achieve a trance of perfect confusion. Some people of the bronze age shared a custom of sacrificing valuables, but what they offered and where was widely different. Nor are the water offerings made for the same purpose. An offering at an estuary may have a different meaning than one close to dangerous rocks and cliffs. Different periods favoured different offerings.

Similar but just as enigmatic are the swamp sacrifices. In southern Germany, swamps tend to contain more ornate needles and less swords and axes. The ornate needles were part of female costume, as appears from burials, so we may guess that women sacrificed in swamps while men preferred rivers. Not that things are so easy. Many a woman was found wearing ornate needles in her burial costume that were so long (up to 50CM) and dangerous that I wonder whether they were ever worn in daily life. Some of them must have been a threat to anybody nearby, and to the lady who wore them, too. If you look at reconstructions you may wonder how many women accidentally died from hiccups. Or maybe the really long ones were meant to bind dangerous women

to their graves (see *Cauldron of the Gods* on the dangerous dead). The ornate needles, by the way, are one of the few items that may have had a talismanic function. Some types have circles at the upper end that look suspiciously like religious symbols. While few look like runes, they certainly have their place in the occult imagery of ancient Europe.

Offerings were not constant during the bronze ages. During the early bronze we have plenty, the middle bronze may have been more peaceful and there are fewer sacrifices, while the late Bronze Age, a time of warfare and cold weather, provides large sacrifices. In the late bronze, there are not only some of the most magnificent depositions of weapons, there is also something systematic in them. Kehmstadt in Thüringen provided a deposit of seven expensive swords and a long lance-head, all of them pointing in the same direction.

But bronze goods were not the only sacrifices. In the Middle Bronze Age, the people at the Danube began to sacrifice by fire. Thick layers of ashes and rubbish reveal sacrifices of animals and earthenware vessels. These appear with some regularity on hilltops or near cliffs and pinnacles, and sometimes we have shards of sacrificed vessels that continue all the way to the Iron Age. Several popular sacrificial sites of the bronze age people continued to be in use all through the early Celtic Hallstatt period. Some bronze age people liked to offer earthenware vessels full of food. In several places, such vessels were left on clifftops or rock pinnacles, at others they were smashed or buried. And while foodstuff is the major offering, there are

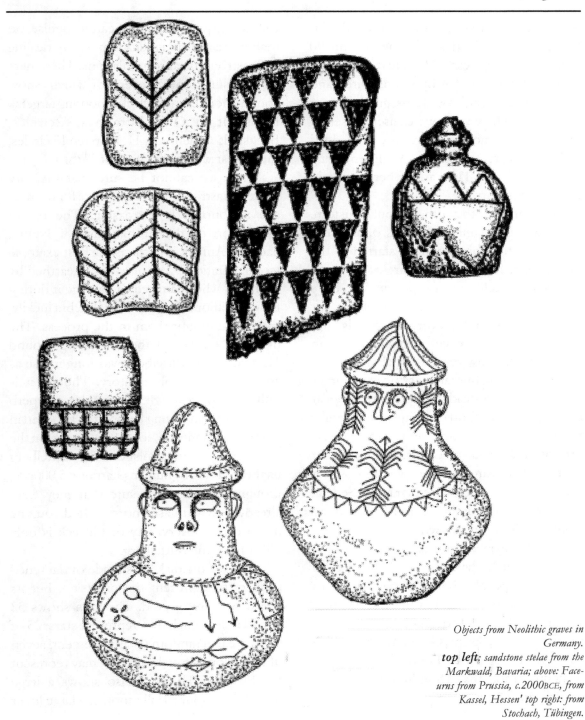

Objects from Neolithic graves in Germany.
top left: *sandstone stelae from the Markwald, Bavaria; above: Face-urns from Prussia, c.2000BCE, from Kassel, Hessen' top right: from Stochach, Tübingen.*

some weird exceptions. A dry well near Berlin-Lichterfelde received an offering of some 90 ceramic drinking vessels. Unlike the majority, these contained linden-blossoms, birch-and willow catkins, mugwort, ferns, grains, honey and spices. The vessels were carefully set up on a wooden structure, they were even padded with grass to prevent damage. A cult venerating trees and plants? The earliest herbal teas in European history?

Wells bring us to another popular custom. The fashion of digging cultshafts, or using dry wells for offerings may have started in the bronze age. Likewise, there are some caves that served religious purposes. We have evidence for plant and animal offerings, for articles of clothing, everyday goods and ornaments. Some caves contained human remnants, leading to the usual discussion whether they are humans sacrifices or burials of the dangerous dead. Human bones appear in company with food offerings, occasionally the bones are damaged, and some experts proposed cannibalism. Don't ask me whether it's true. There are always experts proposing cannibalism, it's such a popular topic. Several caves show a predominance of bones coming from children, young women and youths. Most of the Bronze Age was not very peaceful.

Images of humans and gods are rare in central Europe. Northern Germany provides a few images on rocks, but these are a rarity and distinct from Scandinavian rock art. Most Bronze Age rocks of Germany show little cups and hollows. There are dozens, sometimes more than a hundred little hollows drilled into the stone. Usually, they do not follow any pattern that we can recognise, no matter the charming idea that we are dealing with astronomical constellations. Then there are the 'sun-stones': several of which show concentric circles (much like shooting targets). Hapstedt in Oldenburg has 12 circles, Beckstedt, Oldenburg 11, Horsten 17 circles, the largest with a diameter of 77cm.

While we cannot be sure that they are related to astronomy, the evidence for bronze-age astronomy is increasing. The recent excavation of the bronze disk of Nebra, Sachsen-Anhalt, is perhaps the best example (see illustration). The disk was unearthed by amateurs who managed to damage it during the excavation. They tried to sell it, but luckily, the police caught them in the process. The disk was buried on the Mittelberg around 1,600BCE. The Mittelberg was long in use as an astronomical observatory. Though it is only 252 metres high, it provides a superb view of the sun setting behind the Brocken in the Harz-mountains, some 80km away, on the eve of the summer solstice. The Mittelberg has been visited by humans starting c.5,000BCE, though we cannot be sure that they were already busy with astronomy. Mind you, the much older observatory of Goseck is only 25km from the Mittelberg.

Now for the disk. It is made of darkened bronze (to represent the nightsky), but its ornaments are of gold. The item shows 32 small circles which may represent stars. 25 of them are in a random (?) arrangement, seven of them come in a cluster that may represent the Pleiades. The disk also shows a large round circle (Sun? Full moon?), a large lunar disk and a large curve that can be interpreted in many ways.

Archaeologists proposed that it's a ship, or a solar bark, as the bronze age has several representations of solar barks, especially in the later periods. Astronomers prefer to reverse the disk and propose that the upside down 'bark' is a symbolic representation of the milky way. Be that as it may, the crucial items of the disc are the two round bows at the very edges. They describe an angle of 82 degrees, the exact measurement of the solar course in Sachsen-Anhalt. It has been proposed that the Pleiades were a crucial part of the calendar. Their last appearance on the 9th of March may have given the time for sowing. Of course there is a great deal of speculation on other angles and dates.

The disk was modified several times over two centuries. The curves at the sides were added at some time, then the ship symbol, finally, a series of holes were cut into the rim. The purpose of the holes remains a riddle, just like the question why the disk was buried, together with some swords, spiral bracelets and axe-heads. The composition of the metals is still under discussion. Some of the gold seems to have come from the northern Rumania, which is surprising, as gold was available in the neighbourhood. The copper may have come from Austria. All in all, the disk of Nebra will provide entertainment for many generations of scholars.

Possibly related to astronomy are a number of peculiar gold - 'hats' that were unearthed in a variety of places, such as Avanton, Dép. Vienne; Ezelsdorf in Bavaria and Schifferstadt, Rheinland-Pfalz. They are dated in the late bronze between 1.400 and 1.000BCE. These 'hats' are conical tubes of very thin ornamental goldfoil, some have a slight rim. The ornaments show an amazing variety of abstract symbols, most of them defy interpretation. At the time being, it has become popular to associate the astronomers of the bronze age with these 'hats'. Museums exhibit pictures of bronze age astronomer-shamans prancing around with golden tubes on their heads. That they were really hats is very much under discussion. The item from Ezelsdorf is almost 90 cm tall and the gold has an average thickness of 0.75mm. If you pull it over your skull tightly, the foil breaks, and if you wear it lightly, it is bound to topple. It would not have survived a few falls without destroying the elaborate ornamentation. More likely is the idea that the 'hats', if they were hats at all and not vessels for sacrifices, or ornaments gracing the top of poles, were fixed securely on statues.

And while we are speaking of gold, it is interesting to note that much of the gold used in Germany came from Ireland. There was plenty of trade between the British Isles and northern Germany in the megalith and bronze period, which may account for the similarity of astronomical earthworks or the presence of an alpine corpse right next to Stonehenge.

By now we have come to the final cultures of the Bronze Age. The central European Urnfield culture appears as a distinct culture, it may well have been one of the major ancestors of the later Celts. At long last we are seeing some advances in art. Typical are ornamental cauldrons, often adorned with waterfowl images, items that were definitely religious artefacts. Cauldrons were probably sacred to earlier cultures as well, but here we have several that go beyond practical cooking. These cauldrons are often on wheels, thereby combining the ideas of the solar chariot with the waterfowl design. Such combinations are not unusual and can be found from the Balkans to Scandinavia, they continued well into the Celtic Hallstatt period. Then there are a range of bronze rattles, sistrums and jingling items that seem to have played a part in ritual. Some of them look a little like stylised humans, a great advance for cultures that feel shy about pictures. We also observe an increase in ceramic figures of cattle, pigs and birds. Some of them were hollow, they contained tiny pebbles and were used as rattles. Whether they were regular instruments is a difficult question. Most of them appeared in burials and seem to have been played only once (at the funeral?).

The end of the bronze ages overlaps with the gradual refinement of ironworking technology. This was a more complicated process requiring greater skill, effort and fiercer heat, but it had the advantage that iron was more common than bronze. Low quality iron is available in many places, while copper and tin often had to be imported. The first iron produced in central Europe was not of a very good quality, indeed, some of it was inferior to bronze.

The earliest iron in Germany comes from the 11TH. - 10TH century BCE (small items such as needles, chisels, rings), but it took a while until it replaced bronze. For some mysterious reason, the end of the bronze age is characterised by a lack of copper and tin. For unknown reason, the distribution ceased at some point (Jockenhövel 1994). Some made do by experimenting with copper and lead, others said goodbye to the past and went for iron.

Appeal for Cataclysms

The middle and late bronze ages were a time of great changes. Many of these were influenced by the climate, which changed a lot and became increasingly nastier. At the same time, we can watch a lot of cultures on the move. We witness the disappearance of several great civilisations and the end of many flourishing cities and settlements. Many of these were destroyed by fire, and the fire, so it was thought, could be blamed on great armies of marauding Indo-Europeans fighting their way into Europe. Nowadays we know that some of the Indo-Europeans developed in Europe, and that the evidence for devastating fire is not restricted to settlements but can also be seen in uninhabited places, on high mountains and in desolate swamps. Around the Mediterranean, great floods surge over coasts and plains. The volcano of Santorini explodes, Minoan culture is drowned by a vast wave, the Hittite culture disappears and hordes of unspecified 'northern people' move south by sea and land. As the inscriptions of Medinet Hapu record: 'Their forests and fields are scorched by fire…the heat of Sekhmet has burned their countries'. The texts of Sethos II (c.1215 - 1210BCE) state: 'Sekhmet was a rotating star that spread its

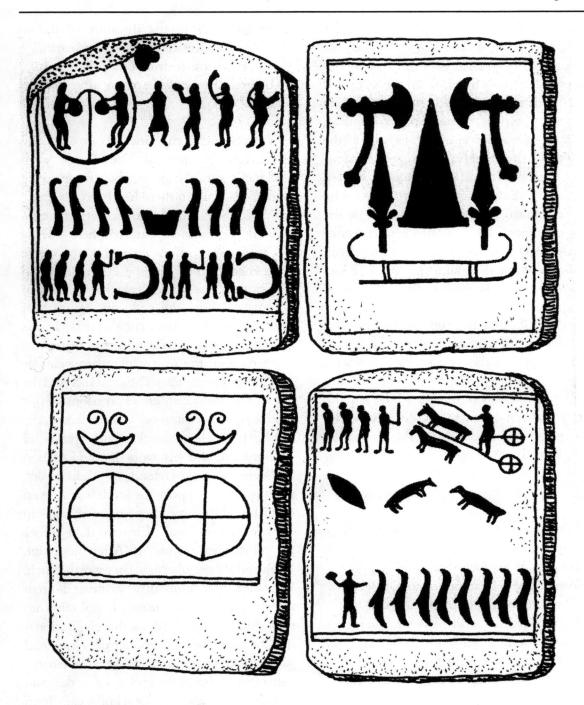

Images from a stone-chamber tomb, Kivik, Schonen, height of the stones c. 120cm. A sacrificial ceremony?

fire in flames, a torch of fire in the storm'(Spanuth, 1976, 224-284). Temple inscriptions from Ugarit-Ras-Shamra record the star Anat which 'fell from the skies and murdered the people of Syria' sometime in the 13th century BCE. The northern migrants appear under a variety of names such as the Dorians, the Heraclides, Deni, Sakar, Prst (Philistines), and Atlanteans in written history. They conquer most of the Mediterranean but are finally beaten by the fleet of Ramses III. Egyptian priests record the Atlantis tale, as given by Plato, from prisoners of war. All in all, a time of confusion, war and chaos. Just what happened in those days?

In the 1940s, the anthropologist and psychologist Immanuel Velikovsky began to collect legends of the great flood. Such myths, describing one or more cataclysms, are common, not only in the Near East and the Mediterranean but also in more than 200 cultures all over the world. In Plato's *Timeaus* (22-23) an Egyptian priest is quoted saying that many catastrophes have befallen humanity:

'The greatest through fire and water, lesser ones through a thousand different reasons. What they say among you (the Athenians) of Phaeton, the son of Helios (the sun god), who once mounted his father's chariot and who destroyed the surface of the Earth by fire, as he could not keep the path of his father. This may be related in the form of a myth, but it is true and comes from irregularities in the motions of the celestial bodies that circle around earth, and from the destruction of the Earth by great fires as it happens after long ages.'

Patronisingly, the priest compared the Athenian's historical knowledge with 'children's stories', mocking them for speaking of one flood when there had been several.

Velikovsky, who unearthed an immense amount of data on catastrophes, swiftly became unpopular with the scientific fundamentalists of his time. After all, he did not stop at researching cataclysms, he also speculated about the collective traumas of humanity arising from such events. In his opinion, modern civilisation tries to repress the terrors of the past while unconsciously seeking to repeat them. The arms race and the use of nuclear energy are expressions of this madness, and Velikovsky was an outspoken critic of both. He was blacklisted, his publisher blackmailed, and his work ignored. Albert Einstein, a close friend of Velikovsky, attempted to support his studies and even contributed to some chapters on changes in earth's rotation, Sadly, Einstein died before the project really took off. After this point, Velikovsky's reputation wasn't worth much. The idea that humanity witnessed great catastrophes in early history is still taboo to many, suggesting, as it does, that civilisation is not the singular end product of a long and weary road to progress, but that it existed many times between cycles of order and barbarism. Consider the best know cataclysm

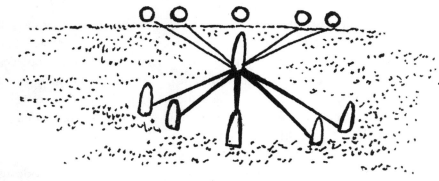

Top: how to build your own Megalithic calendar. Central is the marker stone, its shadow indicates the time of year. The position of the sunrise is shown from left to right: summer solstice; quarter days 6th of May and 8th of August; equinoxes; quarter days 8th of November and 4th of February; winter solstice. To measure the days by sunset another five standing stones (markers) are needed. After Brennan, not to scale.

Bottom: the disk of Nebra, c. 1600BCE, showing two golden edge pieces (giving the 82 degrees of between summer and winter solstice, one of the pieces is missing today), a full and a half moon, the Pleiads, diverse stars (random arrangement?) and a curve that may be interpreted as a solar bark or as a symbol for the Milky Way. The holes in the edges (a later addition) were omitted for this drawing. The golden images are inlaid on a disk of darkened bronze.

scenario of the Christian culture: the exodus of the Israelites fleeing Egyptian 'slavery'. We read that the Lord in his wrath visited several plagues on Egypt, including perpetual darkness, locusts and a rain of blood. The Egyptian papyrus *Ipuwer* describes the same episode. Here, as in the *Bible*, we read of a rain of blood (volcanic ash?) that fell from the skies, turning all waters red, killing the fish, and forcing the people to dig water-holes near the stream.

'All the waters of the stream were transformed into blood,' wrote Ipuwer, 'plague is all over the country, blood is everywhere.'

Both *Ipuwer* and *Exodus* relate how the beasts died in the fields, as did all humans who couldn't hide in houses. Velikovsky found references to the same blood-rain in Tartar mythology and the *Orphic Hymns*. It is also mentioned in the *Kalevala*, that enchanting collection of Finnish spells and sagas. Sadly, we cannot make much use of this epic, as its compiler Lönnrot was too creative in his arrangement of the song material. *Ipuwer* and *Exodus* agree that after the blood-rain, sand, pebbles, dust, rocks and stones came falling from the skies, and that all trees, plants and the whole harvest were destroyed. Earthquakes, volcanic eruptions, floods and the like followed, and the skies became dark for years. This sort of tale appears again and again. Sometimes the order of events is changed and always, a different explanation is given. Just look into *The Siege of Knocklong (Forbhais Droma Damhghaire)* for an Irish version, or into the *Mahâbhârata* regarding the birth of Garuda. Parallels abound in the *Eddas*.

In the *Hrafngaldr Odins* the four dwarves who support the earth and skies lose their strength: the heavens topple into the gaping void, earth and sun lose their places and the sinking sun is pulled up again, much like the episode in *Joshua* 9,10 that relates how the sun stopped on its course, and its parallel in Maya myth, where time stops and the night continues endlessly.

Think of Herodotus, who was told by Egyptian priests that there have been many changes in the motions of the sun, and that in two ages, the sun used to rise from the west. The magical *Harris Papyrus* refers to a cosmic battle of fire and water, during which earth topples, south becoming north. *Ipuwer* wrote that the earth fell over, and rotated like clay on a potter's wheel. This is close to Navaho mythology, which relates that one of the world-ages ended when the deity of the earth-axis left its place (Zolbrod 1984). And to the *Eddas* (*Grottasongr*) relating how the golden age of peace and plenty ended when the two giant ladies Fenja and Menja ceased turning the huge world quern.

The *Eddas* are full of such items. Nine worlds appear frequently, which may be a geographical or a cosmological model. It could also be a model of history, as many old mythologies describe world-ages and aeons as 'worlds'. As in other mythologies, the end of a world or age was usually marked by a catastrophe. The *Eddas* hint at several such worlds that ended in a cataclysm. Like Noah in the *Bible*, the giant Bergelmir escapes a great flood in a boat, while all other giants are drowned by the waves. Another cataclysm

Bronze age:
'Sistrum' type bronze rattle,
Hochborn, Rheinland-Pfalz,
33,5 cm.
Bronze razor with ship/
sledge/dragon image and
triskel, Harsefeld,
Niedersachsen, 15cm.
Bronze razor with two
ships/dragons and two
fantastic beasts, Emsbürgen-
Nattenberg, Niedersachsen,
10,2 cm.

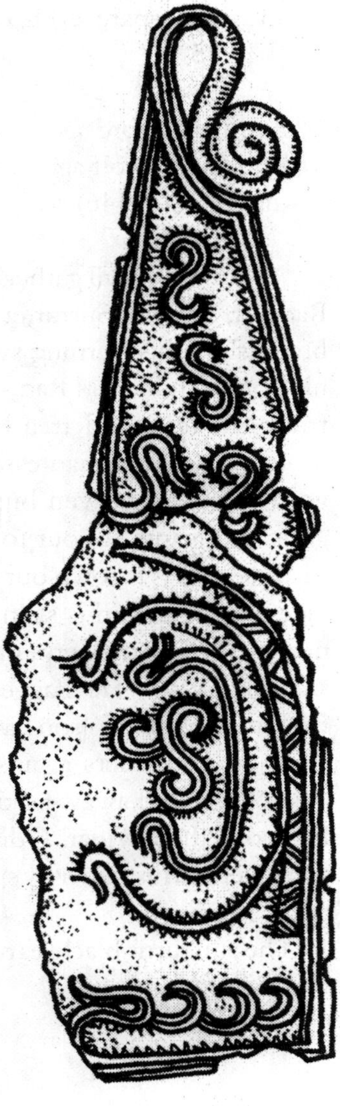

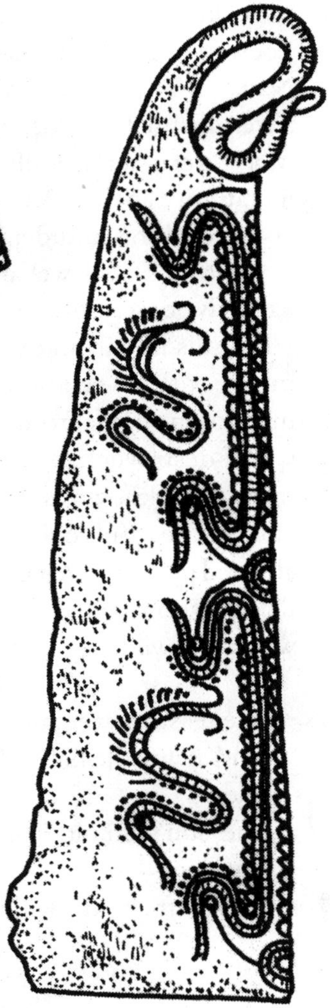

took place when the all-inclusive giant Ymir was slain by Odin and his brothers, who proceeded to build a new world out of the giant's body. The *Eddas* do not stop there. Odin collects the greatest heroes in Valhalla as he needs warriors to fight the wolf, the fire giants and assorted evil from under the sea when the world-age ends. The end is not final, however. After fire and water have devastated the world and most of the gods and giants have killed each other, a new cycle begins.

Such world cycles can be found in many old cultures. Some, such as the classical Greek, knew of four worlds, as did the Hopi and the Navaho. The Maya of Mesoamerica counted seven distinct worlds, as does the *Visuddhi-Magga*, a classical Buddhist text, and the *Avesta* literature of ancient Persia agrees. The Chinese go beyond this and detail ten ages.

In the *Eddas*, we are treated to a very extensive description of the end of the world. Here, it is not an angry and jealous god who meets out universal punishment to liberate his chosen people from Egyptian slavery. The world-destroyer has several shapes in Nordic myth. Best known is the Fenris wolf, one of Loki's dreadful children, who had been chained up to prevent the worst. At the end of the age, however, the chain breaks and the wolf runs wild.

> He feasts on the marrow of fallen men
> and stains the halls of the blessed with blood
> the sun's shining darkens in coming summers
> all weathers are wild: you know what

this means? (*Vol.*33)

Are the blood stains synonymous with the blood-rain? When the wolf breaks its chains, the 'Twilight of the Regents' begins. Sun and moon are devoured by the beast and the Fimbulwinter sets in, a winter that lasts for years.

> The earth screams, evil Disir fly
> and men spare each other no more
> (*Vol.* 45)

> Axe ages, sword ages when shields split
> Wind ages, wolf ages, before the earth
> tumbles (*Vol.* 46)

All forces of evil gather for the final fight. Radiant, flaming Surtur, a fire giant, comes brandishing his burning sword, Loki breaks his bonds and steers Ran's ship Naglfar, the trunk of the world tree bursts into flame, mountains shatter, giantesses stumble, heroes go to Hel and heaven bursts apart. As the gods and giants set out to meet their wyrd, earth herself is thrown out of her path. Odin faces the wolf, and is slain. Thor battles the noxious Midgard-serpent and delivers a smashing blow. He staggers for nine steps, falls and dies, the poison having finished him. Freyr wields antlers against Beli, as he had given his sword away. Loki struggles against Heimdal; then Widar, Odin's one-night old son revenges his father by splitting the wolf in two.

The sun turns black, earth falls into the sea

the heavens hide the joyous stars
Geysers churn round the all-feeding
world tree
the heat of the flames licks to the height.
(*Vol.* 56)

Well, we can't top this performance and so, in the next line, a devastating flood surges over the world. Most gods have met their doom, most giants did likewise, and we can be glad to hear that after the flood ebbs, a fresh new earth arises from the deep and grass begins to grow. *Vafthrudnismal* 45 says that two humans survived the cataclysm. Their names are Lif (Life) and Lifthrasir (Life-spark) and they hid in Hoddmimir's wood, feeding on morning dew just as the Israelites fed on Manna falling from heaven.

What is the physical background of such events? Velikovsky speculated a great deal about this and changed his mind a few times. Was it meteorites, planets out of their path or passing comets? I wouldn't dream of voicing an opinion. The sky is full of dragons, one way or another, and some destroy while others beget new life. A direct hit by a large meteorite might easily cause earthquakes, volcanic eruption, floods, tornadoes and produce a cloud of dust that darkens the skies and lowers temperature for years. This causes massive destruction of species, but on the other hand, such influences might increase cosmic radiation afterwards, affecting the mutation rate and promoting the appearance of new species.

So did it happen? Will it happen again? Popular opinion on such topics is gradually changing. In Velikovsky's days, science was not ready to admit that even a single great cataclysm had happened. Theories of evolution that involved catastrophes were popular in post-revolution France, but in England, the founding fathers of geology had decided that all change happens so slowly that nobody ever notices. Darwin subscribed to this notion, and consequently, evolution in his book takes ages of steady, unnoticeable plodding. Sudden leaps were not just dangerous in politics, they were also abhorred by science. Today, the scholarly establishment is gradually admitting to a few select catastrophes, such as the meteorite that may have finished the dinosaurs. They still object to the idea that humanity ever witnessed such things. Small, local catastrophes are undeniable, but great, global disasters remain unpopular. Real or imaginary cataclysms certainly play a major part in most mythologies. Maybe they derive from historical events and maybe they describe an archetypal fear deep within our racial memory. Whatever the truth of the matter may be, belief in such cataclysms is one of the essentials in early pagan mythology.

The big catastrophe of *Ipuwer* and *Exodus* is dated around 1300-1200BCE by Spanuth, whose researches on cataclysms and the Atlantis tale are well worth reading, and around 1500BCE by Velikovsky, who used another (and highly idiosyncratic) time scale. Another, lesser catastrophe seems to have occurred c.50 years later, and still another smaller one, according to Velikovsky, happened around 800BCE. Surprisingly, not long after this date a good many new cultures appeared. We find the Etruscans moving to Italy, Rome founded, the Celtic Hallstatt period beginning and so on. Perhaps the Celts had such catastrophes in mind when they told Alexander that they fear nothing, except that heaven might fall on them.

Celts and Germans

After the end of the Urnfield time, a number of new cultures appear in central and northern Europe. When I say new, this is to say that we cannot simply class them as direct descendants of the earlier ones. However, we should keep in mind that the new cultures are not totally new. Every culture builds on the memories of its ancestors, even when it develops entirely new ways of living. What was new was the increasing use of iron, and the consequent military superiority conferred by better weapons. We have now come to the European Iron Age. In the process, a lot of tribes moved around. How the people of central Europe developed into the two groups called 'Celt' or 'German' is still an uncertain question. It has been proposed that the so called Celts developed in the countries directly north of the Alps and the Germani close to the north sea and the Baltic. This view, though popular, has its shortcomings. Let us look at the written record.

The first European reference to Germani comes from the pen of Poseidonios (135 - 51BCE) in whose (sadly lost) writings the Germani are compared with the people of Gaul. Poseidonios tells us that the Germani are similar to the Gauls in nature, social institutions, appearance, customs and life style, only that the Germani are a little wilder, taller and have fairer hair. At the time, most Romans saw little reason to make a difference between what seemed like very similar barbarians to them. Dionysios of Halikarnassos wrote that the land of the Celts is divided in its centre by the Rhine, the western part being called Gaul, the eastern Germania. Diodorus Siculus informs us that the people on both sides of the Rhine are Galatians (i.e. Celts).

The Romans had their first contact with the barbarians from beyond the Alps in 387BCE when several Celtic tribes under the control of Brennus (the Raven) moved into northern Italy with the intent to stay. The weather was nice, the soil fertile and winters were short and mild. Sadly, the land was already well populated and there was little space for the newcomers. The locals were by no means happy about this unexpected invasion. Roman ambassadors, pretending to take a neutral position, offered to mediate. In the process they physically attacked a Celtic spokesman, which brought the conference to a sudden halt. Instead of continuing to parley with the north Italians, the Celts packed their gear and moved towards Rome with such swiftness that the 'eternal city' had no time to defend itself. Brennus had Rome plundered, the survivors fled to the Capitol and paid a heavy ransom for the freedom of their city. This was the first direct contact of Rome with the northern barbarians, it turned out to be a national trauma.

Next, let us look at the situation 121BCE. By the time, the city state Rome was expanding,

Horned god
from Val
Camonica

Roman soldiers had successfully occupied most of northern Italy and were spreading into the dark and cold countryside north of the Alps. Simultaneously, the climate turned to the worse. The weather got colder, rainfall increased and the harvests became more miserable each year. Around this time, and unknown to the Romans, a fantastic migration was beginning. In the lands around the north sea coast and the Baltic, many tribes were faced with starvation. Not only had the harvest been a failure. Terrible storms had destroyed vast stretches of fertile coast-land, the hungry sea surging over pastures and fields, and the local tribes were faced with absolute destruction. So the Cimbri (or Cimmerians), the Teutones, the Ambrones, the Tigurini and a number of their neighbours decided to move south. In Gaul, so they had heard, the climate was kind, the earth fertile, there was wine and olives and sunshine for everyone. Rather than stay at home, these tribes chose to risk everything. How they proceeded in their migration is something we don't know. They appear in history in 113BCE when their cattle-drawn wagons reached the northern rim of the Alps, and thereby the attention of the Romans. By the time, the original migrants had been joined by numerous tribes from Central Germany, and their total number was estimated between several million and (more realistically) 300,000 people.

When the huge migration encountered the first Roman outposts at Noreia, just north of the Alps, the Romans were by no means certain whether they were dealing with Celts or Germani. Nor did they care much. The one thing they knew was that a horde of 300,000 barbarians on the move constituted a threat to Roman security. In their eyes, the barbarians were terrifying giants. The 'Germani' of the time, if you measure swamp corpses and skeletons, had an average height of 172 cm while the average Roman soldier measured only 155 cm. Even the women tended to be taller than the legionaries. And these women were quite as terrifying as the men. If we can trust Strabo (7,2), the Cimbri had a number of aged, grey haired priestesses who wore white robes, iron girdles, swords and walked barefoot. Occasionally they selected some suitable candidates among the prisoners, crowned them with floral wreaths and led them to a huge cauldron. There they cut their victims throats and watched the spurts of blood gushing into the vessel. Others disembowelled their sacrifices and interpreted the death agony, much as was later claimed of the Druids of Gaul. From this, so Strabo wrote, they divined the future.

It is hardly surprising that the Romans were scared out of their wits. But not only fear made Roman historians describe the Cimbri and Teutones as savages. You have to recall that the tribes who had joined the migration left most of their property at home. When you have to reduce your standard of living to the bare essentials that can be packed into a cattle drawn wagon, you are bound to appear a lot more primitive than you really are. It came as a great relief that the Cimbri and Teutones, to call them after their largest tribal units, were not intent on warfare. When they encountered the Romans, they sent messengers who asked

Small items from the Bronze age

Top left: pendants, Berlin-Spindlersfeld.

Top right: earthenware object with nine prongs and five holes, possibly a calendar (?), length 18,5 cm, Mainz-Hechtheim.

Middle left: anthropomorphic pendant from Offenbach, Hessen, bronze-wire flattened with hammer strokes, height c. 4 cm, late Urnfield-period.

Middle left: 'comb' and pendant, Hüfingen, Baden-Württemberg, pendant height c. 4,8 cm.

Bottom right: three ornate pins, bronze, Huttenheim, Rheinsheim, Stettfeld (Baden-Württemberg), c.1600 - 1200BCE

Bottom centre: ornate pin from Bleckmar, Niedersachsen.

Bottom left: pins, ritual offering, cult cave of Bad Frankenhausen, Thüringen, c. 1500 - 1300BCE. The pin with the 'tree-symbol' is from Darmstadt, Hessen.

in all humility whether there were any land available for them. The Roman officers, terrified by the tall barbarians, swore oaths of friendship and lead them into ambush as fast as possible. This worked well, as the barbarians trusted Romans vows and promises, only that the ambush failed miserably. The well organised Roman army found itself crushed by a lot of ill-equipped savages, among whom, to their surprise, even the women fought. This was the first encounter, but similar ones were soon to follow. For several years the tribes moved more or less randomly across central Europe. Occasionally they encountered and beat Roman armies, but on the whole they did not care for victories but sought a place to live. This was a real problem, as Europe was densely populated in those days. At some point they quarrelled and divided into separate units, and this turned out to be their downfall.

The Teutones and Ambrones were slaughtered in 102BCE, the Cimbri a year later, just as they were about to move into Italy. It says a lot about their mentality that to the last battle, these 'barbarians' trusted the Romans to keep their vows, to fight honourably and without trickery. A broken vow was unthinkable, and success in battle a gift of the gods, granted for honourable conduct and superior virtue. They had a religious mentality, which the Romans neither understood nor respected. In their eyes, the tall barbarians were simple minded and naïve. This only made it easier for the Romans under Marius to cheat them. The battles of 102 and 101BCE put a stop to the barbarian migration. Velleius

speaks of 150,000 slain Teutones, Plutarch, more cautious, records 100,000 slain or enslaved. Of the horde moving with the Cimbri, Florus tells us that 65,000 died, Plutarch proposes almost twice that many, and both only agree when it comes to the 60,000 prisoners who were sold into slavery. How many survivors fled from the battlefield and where did they go? Over the next decades we learn nothing regarding conditions north of the Alps. The Romans preferred to leave the barbarians well alone.

Things changed somewhat once Gaius Julius Caesar enters the scene. Caesar was a brilliant and ambitious strategist who came from a noble but impoverished family. In those days, the easiest way to become rich was to govern a province of the Roman empire, and to impose a lot of new taxes for personal profit. Caesar bribed his way and managed to win control of the province Gallia Inferior. From there, and without permission from the senate, he tricked and fought his way into Gaul, which had hitherto been a free and independent country.

It was thanks to Julius Caesar that a fundamental difference between 'Gauls' and 'Germans' was postulated. Caesar wrote his annual reports about the war he was waging in Gaul. These reports were widely read in Rome, especially by members of the senate, many of whom felt wary of the megalomaniac who wrote them. In Caesar's account, Gaul was a rich and fertile country, well worth conquering and a certain boon to the growing Roman empire. By contrast, across the Rhine, the 'Germani' were living in a bleak and dismal land full of dark forests and dreary swamps. They were a poor and primitive people, so Caesar claimed, who had no proper deities, priests (he speaks of Druids) nor zeal for sacrifices. They practically dedicated their life to warfare, lived in muck and mud, wore no clothes (apart from small pieces of fur) and were forbidden by law to settle or cultivate land for more than a year. Wine, so Caesar declared, was prohibited and trade was only allowable to dispose of war-won valuables.

None of this is true, if you look at the archaeological record. In Caesar's oversimplified geography, anybody living east of the Rhine was automatically a German, everybody west of it, a Gaul. This was easy to understand but posed some problems when it came to tribes who did not fit into the pattern. Consequently, Caesar allowed for exceptions, but in general he classed a lot of Celtic people as Germani simply due to the fact that he found them living on the wrong side of the river. The 'German' tribes Usipeti, Ubii, Vangioni, Nemeti, Triboci, Sugambri, Tencteri, Treveri, Cheruski, Chatti, Marcomani and Suebi all happen to have Celtic names. The Germani he knew best and whom he parades as shining examples of barbarous savagery were that agglomeration of tribes called Suebi. We do not know what language the Suebi spoke, but linguistic research shows that several of these tribes, such as the Triboci and Nemeti, spoke Celtic languages.

The 'king' of the Suebi, Caesar's arch-enemy Ariovist, had a 'name' which turns out to be a Celtic title for 'War-leader' and has its closest parallel in Old Irish. When Caesar carelessly labelled the tribes as Gaulish or Germanic he was not making anthropological studies but inventing a geography that had very little to do with reality. His questionable approach had the purpose to legitimise his violent conquest of Gaul, while supplying good reasons for leaving Germania alone. Caesar had to give a lot of reasons for waging a constant war against so many people in what was, evidently, not even a Roman province. Warfare required the permission of the senate, and Julius Caesar, lacking this permission, had to make up good reasons for attacking and slaughtering one tribe after another. Consequently, his *Gallic War* is full of emergencies which leave the poor dear no choice but to continue with the fighting. In Gaul he could always claim that a revolt was being planned. How a free people in their own country could 'revolt' against a bunch of Roman invaders is an open question. Likewise, the Germani were called a threat to the Roman people, when most hardly knew of Rome, and cared even less. Caesar proposed that the Germani were planning to occupy all of Gaul and then to march towards Rome via southern France. He did not mention that a number of Germanic-speaking people were already living in Gaul, just as a number of Celtic-speaking people could be found living and prospering in Germania.

When you read Caesar's account, you may well be enchanted by the charming and cultivated style of its author. Caesar was good at making up excuses for atrocities and massacres. He often mentions that cruel deeds are much against his nature and hardly ever hints at the amount of money he made when he sold thousands of people into Roman slavery. It takes the account of other writers to look behind the scenes. Frontinus wrote that Caesar committed crimes against humanity when he had people slaughtered who had been promised a free and unmolested return to their homeland. Cassius Dio reported that Caesar's troops were on the verge of mutiny, complaining that Caesar's war was neither just nor legitimised by senate or the people of Rome. After Caesar had massacred a Germanic tribe that was already pleading for peace, Cato demanded before the senate that Caesar ought to be delivered to the barbarians (the survivors of the blood-bath, most of whom had fled across the Rhine). In his opinion, Caesar's war crimes were bound to bring divine retribution on the people of Rome unless they made up for the damage and punished the culprit. Caesar, having become rather wealthy in the meantime, bribed a few senators and escaped his just punishment. All of which goes to show that his contemporaries did not trust the successful strategist and treated his war tales with suspicion. Even the convenient classification of Germani and Gauls was not accepted by all. When Caesar reported having built a bridge across the Rhine to carry fire and sword to the Germani, Diodorus insisted on calling them Galatians. Even after Caesar's death and deification some historians, such as Appian and Cassius Dio, continued to call the 'Germani' Gauls.

This situation changed with the gradual occupation of the country to the right of the Rhine. The Romans made use of Caesar's artificial classification and coined the name Germania for a province that was home to dozens of tribes, none of whom called themselves by such a name. Even the name 'Germani' remains a mystery. One theory claims that it is the shortened form of a tribal name, the Tungeri, whose warriors, the Tungermen, gradually became known as Germani. Another theory purports that the word comes from Ger, meaning a spear, or from Gerste, meaning barley. To complicate this further, there was a Celtic speaking tribe in Gaul and Belgia that called itself Germani.

Next we come to the famous historian Tacitus (55-119?), who wrote a monograph on the Germani, the invaluable *Germania*. This was an amazingly new idea, as it constituted the first ethnographic account of a country and culture ever written. Tacitus wrote about the Germani, who, in his opinion, were simply all people living in the Roman provinces Germania superior and inferior. In this matter he accepted Caesar's definition without a trace of doubt. We should not criticise him too harshly for this error, as he had probably never been to the country he described so eloquently, and obtained much of his information from other people's tales. Between themselves, Caesar and Tacitus practically defined (or invented) Celts and Germani as distinct cultures. The main difference between them is that Caesar's Germani are rude barbarians, whereas Tacitus' Germani are noble savages, whose moral virtues contrast with the common vices of

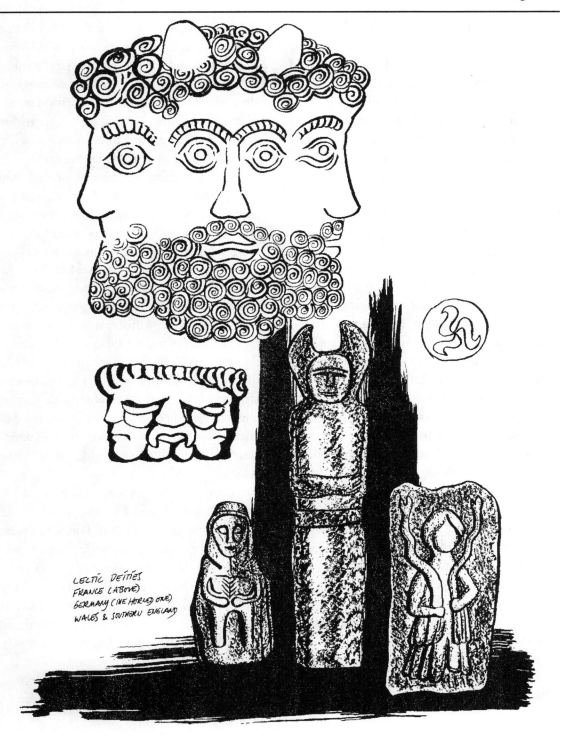

CELTIC DEITIES
FRANCE (ABOVE)
GERMANY (THE HORNED ONE)
WALES & SOUTHERN ENGLAND

Roman civilisation.

To this day the *Germania* is one of the best sources on the pagan past. It is a short and highly amusing work that has enchanted its readers for centuries. Nevertheless, it cannot be entirely trusted. Tacitus idealised his barbarians, as he imagined them to be ethically superior to his contemporaries. In consequence, the *Germania* contains a lot of remarks on the ethical superiority of the Germani which have very little to do with historical reality. This trend continued for a while. There were a number of Roman literati who copied the notion of dark and dismal Germania peopled by war-hungry savages, and some of them elaborated the theme. Most writers had never been north of the Alps. Even those who were in Germania did not always improve the picture. Pliny the Elder saw military service in Gaul and Germania and wrote twenty volumes on the Germanic wars (sadly lost). Nevertheless he relates that the German islands house people who have hooves instead of feet, and mentions another race that walk nude in any weather, wrapping themselves up in their gigantic ears. What fascinated many literati were the Germanic warriors, who were so keen on war that they despised fixed abodes, proper agriculture and generally wore tiny pieces of pelt or tree-bark instead of clothing. They are an invention of Julius Caesar, who possibly confused mobile warrior bands with the proper inhabitants (whose houses, agriculture and clothing were quite developed).

Tacitus was much read in Rome but seems to have disappeared after the Christianisation.

The Christians considered Tacitus an enemy of Christ, as he had written unkind things about their cult. It was an amazing stroke of luck that a few copies of the *Germania* survived, the earliest being discovered in a monastery in Hersfeld in the 15th century. Historians, antiquarians and a few humanists made it the foundation of their national dream.

Things became more complicated in the 19th and early 20th century. At the time, a good many European nations were thinking in terms just as imperialistic as any en vogue in Rome. Caesar was considered an invaluable author on war strategy, and what the power mad warmonger said regarding prehistorical anthropology was taken as gospel. After all, Caesar had a very modern way of thinking. His ambitions were practically the same as those of all European nations. The scholars of the 19th century admired the victorious strategist so much that his remarks on land and people were accepted without doubt or criticism. At the time, most European nations were desperately discovering or inventing their supposed ancestors.

German scholars eagerly pounced on Tacitus' claim that the Germani are so plain and primitive that they could only be a purely aboriginal people. This made Tacitus' work an invaluable propaganda tool for the nationalist movements of the 19th and early 20th century. The demagogues treated the *Germania* as if it were the absolute truth, and used it to define a German super-race that has little in common with the living reality.

At the same time, many French scholars were busy proving that all Celtic culture was a product of France. In their gospel, French culture was totally Gaulish, and influences from across the river, such as the Frankish kings who constituted the royal house, could safely be ignored. Britain, with her characteristic mixture of British and Anglo-Saxon people, saw the enmity between the two power blocks as a conflict between Germani and Celts. This was not just a harmless illusion but a political statement. In the official scholarly interpretation of the time, which leaned heavily on Caesar and Tacitus, the Celtic people of Britain were thought to be an unruly agglomerate of quarrelsome tribes with wild ideas and very little discipline. Everybody assumed the Celts to be mystical, enigmatic, poetic but generally incapable of organising their own lives. By contrast the Germanic people were thought to be rational, logical, disciplined, materialist and down to earth. Borrowing a couple of distorted ideas from Darwinism, the outcome was a racial theory that proved once and for all that the Scots, Welsh and Irish were incapable of governing themselves and could be happy to be ruled by clear and sober-minded thinkers in England. In those days the myth of the romantic and magical Celt was invented and contrasted with the equally idiotic myth of the practical, rational German. None of this had anything to do with real prehistory, but it was useful to keep the Irish on their knees. Scholars thought in terms of fixed countries (ignoring the fact that prehistory is full of people migrating over wide distances) and in terms of pure races and nations, when in plain truth most of prehistoric Europe was

populated by tribes that were none too friendly with their neighbours.

All of this boils down to the insight that the division of tribes into German and Celt, though still fashionable in popular literature, is a lot more complicated than was previously assumed. Even if we look at the problem from the linguistic point of view, where the Germanic and Celtic languages can be shown as related but distinct tongues, we run into many difficulties.

The scholars of the 19th century favoured the idea that the Cimbri, Teutones, Allobrogi et al were Germanic. Consequently, we find them in lots of books on Germans but hardly ever in a book on Celts. Modern linguistic research has shown that the Teutones were an agglomerate of tribes, many of whom must have spoken Celtic, as the group name Teutones is a Celtic word meaning *the Tribes*. Likewise the Cimbri or Cimmerians were ruled by a Celtic nobility. Already the Grimm brothers were wondering why supposedly Germanic nobles would have Celtic names like Boiorix, Teutobod, Lugius etc. As it seems unlikely that a handful of Celtic nobles would rule a tribe consisting of more than 100,000 'Germanic' people, the logical conclusion is that the Cimbri were a Celtic speaking mixture of tribes. This is not exactly good news to the proponents of the theory that postulates a Celtic south and a Germanic north of Germany.

After the united Cimbri, Teutones and company had moved across central Europe in a vast and devastating treck, not much of the earlier tribal organisation will have remained. When confronted by such a horde of hungry migrants, many local tribes saw little choice but to join the migration. 'There goes the harvest' they may have said 'let's pack our stuff and move!' Consequently, during the migration years we find a number of flourishing Celtic oppida of central Germany falling into disuse, mainly as there was not enough population left to keep the fortification intact. The Teutones and Cimbri, if we can trust the Roman historians, originated at the coast of the north sea, where, according to general belief, no Celts should have lived. Some scholars tried to get around this problem by postulating that the Teutones were an isolated enclave of north-Celts, whatever that may mean. Or take the culture of the Chatti, a 'German' tribe settling in northern Hessen. Drusus led five legions against them (as much as Caesar needed to conquer all of Gaul), destroyed their stronghold and assumed the title 'Germanicus' to celebrate the victory. We can reconstruct his march through the Wetterau and we know that at the time, the only inhabited oppidum was on the Dünsberg in northern Hessen. Excavation at the Dünsberg in 1999 did not only bring up a lot of Roman projectile weapons but also firm evidence that the inhabitants were Celts, and had been since the Hallstatt period. Perhaps the time has come to abandon the popular concept of Germani and Celts. It makes sense to speak of north Germans (the Scandinavians) or the Island Celts as cultural and linguistic groups, but in central Europe the situation was and is confusing. Some people evidently spoke what we would call Celtic or Germanic

languages (plus several languages that disappeared in the meantime) but this does not mean that they saw themselves as members of any larger cultural or linguistic group. The people of prehistory did not think in terms of nations, as we do nowadays. And with regard to the popular illusion that Celts and Germani were arch-enemies, any student of prehistory can assure you that the real enemy of each tribe usually happened to be its closest neighbour.

If you asked me to generalise what the so-called Celts and Germani of central Europe had in common, a lot of ideas come to mind. Both linguistic groups practised agriculture and bred cattle. They had stratified societies with several 'classes', such as farmers, traders, craftspeople, warriors, priests and nobility, but the actual way in which each tribe was governed is usually unknown, or shows a wide degree of variation. Some Germani and Celts venerated sacred trees and plants and a number of animal totems, such as wolf, boar, bear, serpent, swan, falcon, eagle, raven, plus domesticated animals such as cattle, horse, and dog. All known central European tribes believed in polytheistic cults, as well as ancestors and a wide scope of house and nature spirits, many of them malign. Sacrifices of animals, weapons, treasures, foodstuff and occasionally humans were a common matter. Cult places were often sites of natural beauty, such as springs, rivers, lakes, swamps, islands, mountaintops, great rocks or sacred groves, and these locations were visited for ritual, sacrifice, oath-taking, feasting and to exhibit

Some Celtic
coins, France and
Germany,
400-100BC

war trophies. Among the most important religious symbols are heads (or skulls), cauldrons, pillars or trees reaching to the skies, triskels, swastikas and anything that can be sorted in units of three and nine. People wore talismanic jewellery, such as ornate brooches, necklaces, amber, and bundles of magical plants.

All of this is oversimplified. It is not that all Celts or all Germani adhered to such customs. The scope of different beliefs within each 'group' is wide. You might say that *some* Celts and *some* Germani shared a given custom, but when you consider how faint the evidence usually is, it would be wrong to assume that all Celts and all Germani did so all of the time. Regarding most Celts and Germani, we know very little at all.

Such generalisations might produce the impression that 'the Celts' and 'Germans' were not two different but a single culture. I prefer to propose that there was a vast amount of tribes, many of them sharing characteristics with each other, but just as we have similarities, there was also a wide field of individual development. The Germani are not a single culture, and neither are the many people classed as Celts. Telling the difference can be very difficult when we look at what is today central Germany along the Rhine, i.e. the part of Germania the Romans were familiar with. If you move your attention to the north east, however, you begin to find evidence that the Germanic speaking people had a much lower standard of technology and art. The Germani living towards Denmark and at the shores of the Baltic had a lifestyle that varied widely from the familiar flowering of Celtic culture in Gaul. Now Gaul is not representative for all the Celtic people.

In Gaul, people used to settle in mountain- and hill-top cities, many of them housing more than ten-thousand people. Such cities promoted the development of specialists. A Druidic theocracy, for example, and the development of various specialised professions were only possible thanks to the surplus wealth that such cities generate. You can only have professions when there are enough people around to make it worthwhile. In Germania beyond the river Elbe, the settlements become smaller. The Germani of the north-east tended to live in isolated farms, in villages or at best in small towns. As a result, their technology remained rather simple. There were still people in those parts who were ignorant of the potter's wheel after the Gaulish Celts had been using it for centuries. Some of the Germani even invited Roman artisans into their districts, where the treasured specialists erected high-tech ovens that could produce 70-80,000 earthenware vessels a year (Haarhausen, 3-4th century). With regard to houses, there are several types. One of them is similar to the typical Bronze Age longhouse. The roof was supported by two rows of pillars and parts of the house were stables. This type was especially popular in places of awful weather, such as the islands of the North-sea, where the cattle provided much needed extra heat. Further inland, there are farms that have distinct stables set at a distance from the main building. A third type is the ground-house, a building that was largely subterranean. These structures were often used for spinning and housework, as can be seen from the typical rubbish inside. As the Germani were fond of small settlements and tiny villages, they did not usually have a professional priesthood. Instead, the people of the household had to do much of the ritual for themselves. Contact to any sort of 'official' religion was only common during field processions during the warm season, when a group of priests took a wagon with an idol for a journey through the countryside. Such processions could last for weeks. They were often an occasion for the collection of offerings and, just as important, of taxes imposed by the local rulers. We have evidence for processions that remained popular as events of merrymaking, feasting, drinking, love-making and general happiness even under Christian rule, much to the disgust of the clergy. When you look at the cults and faiths of Scandinavia, you should keep in mind that most of the Vikings lived in a setting that is similar to the Germani of the north-east. Rural communities, independent worship and no central dogma and authority. Sounds much like modern paganism, doesn't it?

Sources of Germanic mythology

Our knowledge of pagan deities comes from several sources. Most prominent among them are two Icelandic works, the *Poetic Edda*, a collection of songs relating the deeds of Nordic gods and heroes, and the *Prose Edda*, a work composed by the brilliant statesman Snorri Sturluson (1179-1241). I hope that you have read both of these works, as they are simply essential to an understanding of pagan Germanic religion. The material of the poetic *Edda* can be dated between 800 and 1200, i.e. the Viking period of Scandinavia. While some elements in the songs arguably come from a much earlier age, the form in which they were preserved is definitely medieval. The skalds who composed the songs may have been pagans, but they were aware of Christianity and Islam, which may or may not have influenced the tales. There is a great difference between the medieval, far-travelling Vikings and the simple minded folk that fought against the Roman conquest a thousand years earlier. If you imagine that the Vikings subscribed to exactly the same mythology as the central European Germans a thousand years before, you also have to imagine a society that is completely reactionary in its unchanging adherence to 'old values'. That this is not the case is obvious from the countless subtle differences between Germanic myths. Good evidence that the *Eddas* reflect late Icelandic beliefs rather than 'Pan-Germanic' mythology. For people who insist that the German people shared a common, and unchanging religion, such details are unpleasant news. For those who really care to learn of, and from the deities of the pagan past, they show that religion in pre-historic Europe was not a static, unchanging tradition but a wide field of beliefs, customs and creative innovations.

It may be of interest to compare the *Poetic Edda* with other pieces of mythological literature. What strikes me as pretty unique is the fact that the poems, while describing the gods and their deeds, do not contain a single eulogy, praise hymn or (complete) invocation.

Unlike so many other pieces of holy writ, the *Eddas* give no commandments, prohibitions or catalogues of sins. Even the *Havamal* (the Song of the High One, i.e. Odin) is a work of common sense advice. When Odin tells folks how to order their lives, he gives hints and warnings, but he leaves the full responsibility of choice to the audience. Where it comes to the deeds of the gods, we encounter dry narrative and humour.

The later *Prose Edda*, composed by Snorri Sturluson, is a not-quite-trustworthy summary of pagan beliefs. The *Prose Edda* is a handbook for skalds. Most of it is comparatively unknown, as it is concerned with the complicated methods used to compose poetry. Snorri gives several dozen styles of working with alliteration and metre which make for very dry reading. To liven up the theory, he included samples of old tales, and these passages are the parts of the *Prose Edda* you are likely to find in a bookshop. Now in Snorri's time, the old tales were mainly pagan myths. To introduce them to a Christian audience, Snorri prefaced them with a text which is not generally found in books on pagan mythology. It claims that the Aesir were not gods but a family of deified humans who had come to Scandinavia from Asia (this explains the name) and that Odin in particular was no deity but a skilful sorcerer. This interpretation was composed for a Christian audience. After all, Snorri was not only a passionate poet but also (at least nominally) a Christian and a nobleman deeply involved in politics. He was one of the richest men of Iceland, held the office of the Law-Speaker at the Icelandic All-ting (major

assembly of all people) on several occasions and opposed a political union with Norway so strongly that his enemies assassinated him.

When he composed the *Prose Edda*, Iceland had been Christian for more than 200 years and doubtlessly a lot of old pagan lore had been forgotten. As Mogk points out (Dumézil 1959, 54), Iceland of Snorri's time had a bishop's seat, Benedictine cloisters and several thriving schools. The Icelandic literati were well acquainted with Christian literature, such as the works of Origines, Eusebius, Gelasius and Bede. Of the classical authors, we can be sure they read Pliny, Horace, Ovid, Sallust, Jordanes and Paulus Diaconus. In other words, they were at least as well informed regarding classical mythology and history as with their own ancestral lore. So we cannot take Snorri as a witness of a living tradition. The funny thing, however, is that while Snorri makes it clear that he is a Christian, he also included a line (*Gylf.* 6) stating his belief that Odin and his brothers rule heaven and earth. Thus, it is far from clear if we are dealing with a Christian, a pagan or a pagan-Christian author.

However, even if Snorri was a pagan in disguise, he was still a refined and sophisticated intellectual, well acquainted with the *Bible* and several classical authors, who was recording a mythology that was rapidly fading into oblivion. This is not the same thing as the numerous faiths of the central European Germani prior to the Roman occupation. Snorri's work is at best a reconstruction.

I ask your pardon if I over-emphasise this issue, but I am mightily fed up with all the neo-Germanic faiths that treat the *Eddas* as

Celtic fibula of
Oberwittighausen
500-300BC; Tarasque,
300BC, statue from
Noves;
Skull ornament, 200BC,
Temple of Entremont.

'the word of god' and try to erect a stubborn fundamentalism on such shaky foundations. If we imagine a single pagan dogma we are excluding a wealth of creative possibilities. There was not one Germanic pantheon but many, the beliefs of one tribe were necessarily different from its neighbours and the myths changed and transformed to suit various times and conditions. This is exactly what we encounter when we draw together the snippets of information that come from other parts of Germanic culture. On the continent and in Britain the power of the church was much greater than in rural Scandinavia. As a result, an enormous amount of mythology was deliberately destroyed, together with the people who believed in it. Nevertheless, the odd bit of elder lore emerges here and there. The Scandinavian Sagas, Rune poems, the spells from Merseburg, the Anglo-Saxon spells and field-blessings, the Christian catalogues of prohibitions, and odd items hidden in songs and folk tales give good evidence that Germanic religion never constituted a unified whole. This, in itself, may turn out to be a blessing for the pagan community. Gods and myths change to adapt to different times and circumstances. There are differences between the primal forms of Wodan as a storm god and the refined form of Odin gathering slain heroes in Valhalla. Religions change to suit the worshippers. What is the next step? The Odin you encounter in your rituals may be more genuinely suited to your time and culture than the warrior deity of the sagas. The traditional form may be obsolete in our days, but what you experience is the living reality.

Perhaps future myths will have Odin consulting a computer called Mimir. The gods have a right to go with the times. I hope that you understand the freedom and responsibility inherent in this concept. Your union of today shapes the reality of tomorrow.

German Religion before and during the Conquest

The most important event in the social life of the early Germani was the Thing, meaning the assembly. The word appears as Old High German: Thing, Ding, Swedish: Ting, English: thing. It means the assembly, parliament or court, but is closely related to the 'matter, object' that is to be decided, i.e. the 'things' under discussion. To avoid the confusion of the assembly with things (as material objects), I shall use the term Ting for this text, even though it is not precise.

There were several sorts of Ting assemblies, ranging from small meetings for a few villages to large scale Tings attended by the folks of several districts. Tacitus records the importance of this event, when whole communities, if not tribes assembled. Thanks to the Sagas, we are pretty well informed about the Ting of the Vikings, whereas the earlier common Germanic Ting has to be reconstructed from Roman hearsay. It seems that the Germani had an early form of democracy. Communities had leaders, and these leaders were elected. Kings were elected from noble families while war-leaders were chosen for their ability (*Germania*. 7). Routine decisions were made by the chosen leaders while important decisions required the consent of the whole community (*G.* 11). Tacitus tells us that the kings had no absolute power and that the war-leaders kept their authority by giving a good example, and by fighting in the vanguard.

Only the priests, so we are told, had the power to punish, to bind and to order an execution. As the people of a tribe lived in widely separate districts, they were allowed several days to journey to the sacred Ting-place. Here the entire community assembled in arms. At the Ting, court was held, judgements were made, there were sacrifices, elections, political speeches and doubtlessly a lot of ritual. Just as important were trade, courtship and communal drinking. Ambassadors were received, treaties were made, young men sought for teams of enterprising warriors and so on. During much of the official part, the priesthood demanded silence and meted out punishment. A good Ting was a peaceful assembly. Just how peaceful appears from an incident in Drusus' 'Germanicus' career (Tacitus, *Annales* 1, 50-51).

Drusus had been informed that the Marsi were about to celebrate a feast at the sacred grove of the goddess Tanfana. It was late in autumn of the year 14CE, the weather was dry and the skies clear. His legionaries attacked in the middle of the night, when most Marsi were drunk beyond comprehension. The troops slaughtered without regard for age or sex, and devastated the sanctuary. It says a lot that the Marsi had not even bothered to post sentries. They believed in the sacred peace of the occasion and paid bitterly for their innocence.

And while we are dealing with the grove of Tanfana, you might wonder whether the goddess was venerated in a physical form. Was there a statue of the deity?

In the Bronze Age cultures of Germany, the use of idols, statues and pictures of deities is such a rare matter that several scholars have proposed that these people had a taboo against such things. The lack continues in the early Hallstatt period, where images of people (or deities) are indeed rare. Some obviously existed, but nothing comparable to the wealth of divine images popular in the late La Tène period and during the Roman occupation.

Among the early Germani, things look similar. Caesar declared that 'the Germani' have no temples or statues, and Tacitus repeats and elaborates this claim. Mind you, he contradicts himself when he speaks of the image of the Nerthus cult, and of the insignia of the gods, which were carried into battle. Generations of scholars reinforced this belief, until, what a miracle, a number of swamps yielded wooden statues that had been preserved from decay by the chemistry of the water. The earliest statues date around 400BCE, the majority were made and worshipped during the first centuries CE. Just a few examples (after Much, updated by Jankuhn; and Ralf Busch). Possendorf in Thüringen: wooden statue with one 'arm' held up, c.90cm. Close to it a patched up bronze cauldron, seven ceramic vessels, a human skeleton. Brodenbjerg, Jütland: a phallic figure, 88cm, surrounded by numerous broken ceramic vessels. Oberdorla, Thüringen: at least four wooden statues with widely different appearance. One female figure, bovine bones and parts of a human skull in a ceramic vessel. One smashed female figure amidst ceramic vessels, broken animal bones and the scattered bones of a young girl. A pair of statues made from forked branches. Rebild, Jütland: female figure, 105cm, and remnants of woollen textiles (perhaps the statue used to wear clothes). Braak, Holstein: female and male figures, almost 3m tall, with sockets for the attachment of arms. Plus ashes, scorched stones and ceramic vessels. Wittemoor, Wesermarsch: Five abstract humanoid wooden images set up on both sides of a wooden path leading across the swamp. The figures lack faces and details, maybe they were originally painted. So there have been statues, if primitive ones, and we can only guess how many of them, as in most places there was no convenient swamp to preserve them for millennia. Its worth considering that many of the wooden statues have well developed genitalia that might remind you of Adam of Bremen (4,26) who compared the image of Freyr in Uppsala with Priapus. The statues have been interpreted in numerous ways, be it as ancestors, swamp guardians, community spirits and more. As they received sacrificial offerings we can be sure they were more than crude decoration.

We have more evidence of sacrificial customs. Like the late Bronze Age folk and the Celts, the Germanic people were fond of making elaborate sacrifices. Religious activity involved sacrifice, as did the swearing of vows and the congregation of the community. There seem to have been a lot of household sacrifices as well, but as you can imagine, a sacrifice of a bit of food, flowers or a small animal is not important enough to be mentioned by the Roman literati (for whom such sacrifices were self evident), not does it leave much to cheer up the excavator. Such sacrifices were common to most prehistorical people in ancient Europe.

What the Roman historians generally emphasise is human sacrifices. This may be propaganda, as the Romans who occupied Germania had abolished the custom in their homeland and condemned it with the severity of fresh converts. Sure, during and after the second Punic war they were still busy at it, and certainly they had no qualms about watching gladiators slaughter each other on circus days, but then, the games were civilised entertainment, in contrast to human sacrifice, which was barbaric and detestable. So how much truth is there to the Roman accounts? That human sacrifices happened is fairly obvious, the problem lies in deciding the frequency. Sometimes prisoners of war were sacrificed, and occasionally whole enemy armies were dedicated to the gods, maybe as keeping and caring for prisoners is not always easy for an army on the move. According to Tacitus' *Annales*, 13, 57, the Chatti and Hermunduri fought each other for the ownership of a sacred river. The stream was in disputed frontier territory and rich in salt, hence a source of wealth and, so Tacitus says, a place where the tribes believe that they are close to the gods. The victorious Hermunduri had dedicated their enemies to Mercurius (Wodan) and Mars (Tiu, Zis). After the battle they proceeded to slaughter captives and horses, much to the delight of the Romans.

In peacetime, there seem to have been regular occasions when humans were sacrificed, but again, the question remains just how often such events took place. In the much later sagas of the Viking age we have most evidence for the custom. Are they representative for the beliefs and ceremonies of the continental Germani several centuries earlier? Swamp corpses are sometimes considered human sacrifices. When you dig up a corpse that has been bound and killed in some ingenious way, the issue may be decided by blaming religion. In Tacitus *Germania* we encounter the remark that certain criminals, cowards and 'debased' folk (whatever that may mean) ended in swamps. So a swamp corpse may be a sacrifice, it may be a condemned criminal and in some cases it may be both. As far as we know, the Germanic people preferred to sacrifice criminals (just like the Gaulish Druids did), which makes the whole affair a mixture of religion and rough justice.

The matter is complicated by the fact that some swamp corpses seem to have been treated respectfully. The two young men of Hunteburg, Osnabrück, were placed close to each other. Each was clad in a costly, high quality blanket. Their large size (1.85m and 1.90m), carefully trimmed beards and fingernails indicated that we are dealing with high status people. When it comes to ordinary sacrifices, we sometimes find them where wells, lakes or rivers are dredged. All three sites were considered sacred (by most of the prehistoric cultures), they were places where the gods were close to humanity, where offerings could be given to the otherworld and where serious vows could be made.

Swamp excavations produced considerable evidence for offerings. Lundtoft, Jütland: 20 to 30 ceramic vessels containing sheep bones and the bones of lambs with carefully split skulls. Bukkerup, Fünen: leg bones of oxen, a pig bone and two leg bones of a horse. Barsbek, Plön: a large amount of dog bones, a dog skull, several horse-skulls. The major sacrificial animals were bovines, sheep, horse and dogs. In some rare cases, it was vessels filled with butter , fat, or hazelnuts.

Treasures were also popular, for example the four neckrings (torques) of the swamp at Wahnbeck, Ammerland (early Iron Age), the crown-shaped torque of Emmendorf, Uelzen, the torque of Debstedt, Cuxhaven and so on.

Most famous of the sacrificial sites is the Thorsberg near Süderbrarup in Angeln. On a space of only a few square metres a vast treasure was excavated: fibula, ornaments, ceramic vessels, gold, Roman coins, parts of wagons, shield-buckles, riding equipment, saddles, tools, weapons (Germanic and Roman) and, as a special boon, some well preserved textiles, among them a magnificent blue cloak. These put an end to the myth of the primitive, fur wearing Germani.

It turned out that during the century before the common era, the main offering was foodstuff in vessels. By the second century, weapons appear, and by the third century, it's almost exclusively swords and fibula. (Capelle in Busch, 2000).

Not only swamps received sacrifices: springs and wells are among the most popular sites for offerings. Take the Rhumespring, a spring beneath a lake measuring c. 30 x 40 metres, district Göttingen, close to the Harz. Large amounts of sediment were excavated between 1998/1999. They yielded sacrificial offerings beginning c.5300BCE and continuing to the last century before the beginning of the common era, plus medieval stuff and some modern items that may be 'sacrifices' or, more likely, rubbish. The goods include ceramic vessels, a perfectly executed, unused flint axe-head, fractions of fibulae (large ornamental safety pins to hold the cloak together) and a number of coins. Tossing coins into the lake has continued for the last two thousand years.

A well at Bad Pyrmont produced goods that were deposited during the first centuries. Most of them are fibulae, including some ornamented with boars and other animals, plus coins and an extremely rare gold ladle, maybe an import from Britain. Ralf Busch speculates that the types of offerings point to female as well as male sacrificers. The Bullenteich near Braunschweig-Hagen, in use during the first centuries CE, yielded coins, fibulae, ornaments, amber and glass-beads, loom-weights and a few Roman tools, such as pincers and a tiny spoon to clean ears. Unlike other sites, no weapons were found, and again, it was suspected that a large number of the offerings were made by women.

The Priesthood

We have next to no information on the nature of the Germanic priesthood before the Romans came and conquered. Tacitus refers to priests, but never bothers to give much detail. If we trust his account, we have to imagine priests who had a dual function. On one hand they were the custodians of religious lore, on the other they were experts on law and occasionally judges. These two offices are distinct to our modern way of thinking. To the pagans of old, they were inseparable. Law was the result of divine order, the êwa (eternal law) being the domain of the êwart, an old term for priest that was later applied to Christian priests. Likewise terms like Old Saxon: êosago, OHG: ésago and old Frisian: âsega meant those priests who spoke or declared the eternal law. The priests officiated at the Ting assembly and were the only people entitled to give judgement or mete out punishment to offenders. They performed the great public sacrifices, but where it came to small-scale worship, it seems that the people of each farm did their own sacrificing. A regular priesthood is only convenient in those parts of the country where many people live together. When people settle at some distance, as in northern Germany, each homestead has to do some ritual without professional help.

Priests fetched the insignia of the gods from sacred groves and carried them to war and they accompanied sacred wagons on processions through fields and country. Field processions were immensely popular. The wagons housed the gods (images or obsessed mediums?) and people accompanied them with much festivity. Whether the pristhood was an organised caste, similar to the Gaulish Druids, remains an open question. Among the Germani of the early medieval time, several names were in use to describe priests. Wulfila mentions 'gudja', other surviving terms are *godi* and *cotinc*, if the priests were named after their contact to the gods (gud). Sacrificial priests were called blôstreis and pluostrari, while harugari and parawari were the guardians of temples or groves.

These terms have an uncertain etymology. Also, they give the impression that there was some organisation to the priesthood in old Germania. This may be an error. In most districts we have no idea what people performed the job, how they were organised and just what they thought they were doing. The few bits we have regarding the appearance of priests are just as enigmatic. *Germania.* 43, discussing the little known people of the east, proposes that the priest of the Naharvali worshipped twin gods called Alcis in a sacred grove. He wore female costume; we do not know whether he did it all of the time or only for ritual. This is not as unusual as it may seem. Shamanic transvestites are well attested among a good many north Eurasian cultures, where the officiating priest assumed the ritual dress of her/his helping spirit or deity when officiating. The Naharvali priests seem to have worn their hair long, and so did the Hasdingi and the Hartunge (Mullenhoff in Much). By contrast, Jordanes wrote that the Gothic priests, the pileati, were named 'hat bearers'. They wore white clothes and a special hat during ceremony, while the rest of the population bared their heads. There is also some evidence that priests generally came from noble families.

With regard to temples, we have very little archaeological evidence. Tacitus, always ready to praise the noble savage, suggested that it was against Germanic belief to confine gods in temples. Worship in the seclusion of a sacred grove seemed more impressive to him, and considering what a dirty and noisy place Rome had become in his days, we can't really blame him. Imagine narrow streets, houses with up to ten floors, more than a million inhabitants, smoke, dirt, dust, excrement, and maybe you can sympathise with him. Tacitus was an early romantic.

Sacred groves or even forests can be found in place-names, such as Heiligenforst near Strassburg, Heiligeloo in Holland, Heiligenholtz near Zwifalten and Halahtre in Westfalia. Golther further mentions bishop Unwin of Bremen, who ordered his congregation in the 11th century to destroy all sacrificial forests. In 779 a Saxon chieftain, direly wounded after a battle against the Franks, had himself carried to a sacred forest to meet his end amidst his gods. Sacred groves and forests are a standard item in the sermons of Christian missionaries, who generally went hopping mad about them.

Nevertheless, the odd temple building crops up here and there in Tacitus' account. As most of these buildings seem to have been small wooden huts, it comes as no surprise that the archaeologists have a tough time unearthing any. The same went for Anglo-Saxon temple buildings, of which Blair (1977) declares that none have so far been discovered. Or maybe we simply can't identify them…it is very hard to tell the difference between a small temple and a small hut unless you find some further evidence, such as sacred objects, a special and secluded location and soil that shows the regular shedding of blood. What we know from elder literature is that the gods (and their cults) often owned considerable wealth. Many temples had treasure and some of them were part of a larger sacred district. The entire island of Helgoland was once the property of the Frisian god Forsites, who owned the meadows, the buildings, the cattle, the springs and took ten percent of everything gained by the local pirate industry. This state of things continued well into the Christian era, the last reference is from the eleventh century.

Little is known about the fate of the priests during the Roman occupation. We do not read that any cults were specifically prohibited. Unlike the Druids of Gaul, who were restricted, prohibited and finally exterminated, the Germanic priests seem to have adapted to the new rulers. This seems simple but it isn't. We haven't got the faintest idea how it happened. Keep in mind that the Romans did not occupy all of what constitutes Germany today. They occupied the south up to the Taunus mountains, but encountered too much resistance to push much further. Instead, they built a frontier wall, the Limes, which spanned some 500KM from Rhine to Danube. In some parts, this wall was a solid structure, reinforced to repel regular attacks. Other sections were more loosely built. Here, the Limes worked as a symbolic frontier and as a means to convey information, from watchtower to watchtower, to the nearest troops.

The Roman territory did not stop at the wall. A defence that allows enemies to approach to the very frontiers is not very practical. Some cunning politicians granted much land beyond the wall to retiring veterans, who were free to built large farms and cultivate the soil. Such veterans made good fighters, and as they fought for their own ground, did not require payment. In consequence, the Roman influence extended beyond the frontier. Likewise, a good many chieftains of 'free Germania' became economically indebted to the Romans. Those chieftains were sorely tempted by the luxurious import goods so freely available on the Roman side of the wall, but at the same time they found their own economy suffering. The Romans introduced so many technical innovations that the folks outside the empire found it hard to compete. Southern Germany, as mentioned before, was peopled not only by 'Germani' but by a good many Celtic tribes. No Druids are mentioned among them, nor do we know much about their priesthood. It seems that they got along with Roman religions. This was not a difficult matter. The Roman empire permitted any religion, no matter how exotic, that accepted a few simple rules. One of them was the worship of the guardian angel of the emperor. This spirit was not just the personified divinity of the ruling Caesar, it was also the spirit of the empire itself. Human sacrifice was strictly forbidden and religious tolerance was a must. In consequence, there were countless religions in the Roman empire, in the legions and ultimately in Rome herself. Some of them were imports from all parts of the empire, others were freshly made up. Anyone could found a new religion, all it needed was a very few worshippers, one or several deities and a permission from the government, which was easy to get. For all its drawbacks, there was more religious tolerance in the Roman empire than at any other period of European history.

Now the Roman occupation was relatively tolerant regarding native faiths, but it certainly changed the religious outlook of the occupied. Where earlier, the tribes had known only their own gods and maybe a couple from their neighbours, the introduction of completely exotic religions must have broadened their minds. There were dozens of cults active in the Roman legions. Legionaries were recruited in any conquered province, and wherever these soldiers went, they took along the gods of their homeland. Frontier cities became the meeting points of gods from Europe, Africa and Asia. For example in Nida (Frankfurt), people worshipped Juppiter, Mars, Candida, Kybele, Mercurius, Mercurius Germanicus, Hercules and Fortuna (patron deities of the XXII legion), Astarte, Mithras, Isis, Epona, Serapis and various local genii. While some Germani may have remained true to their gods, they couldn't help learning from the other cults.

The other section of Germany occupied by Romans was in the north of the country. Here the Romans conquered the shores and islands making their way inland along the Rhine or other rivers. The result were two provinces, Germania superior (the south German 'highlands') and Germania inferior (the flat northern countryside). To the east and in between existed a broad section that remained nominally free. What happened in these parts is anybody's guess. I suspect that those tribes that chose independence found themselves cut off from most of their neighbours and faced economic crisis and poverty. The whole structure saw frequent attacks, especially between 222 to 235CE, and disintegrated in 260CE when a conglomerate of tribes, calling themselves the Alamanni (All-People) broke through the Limes and devastated the land.

We know very little about the next centuries. The 'barbarians' were a simple people who preferred to live in isolated villages. Soon enough, most of the great cities of the Celtic and Roman age were plundered and became ruins. While some Germani managed to occupy Rome and set up an emperor of their choice, the majority were busy devastating what remained of urban civilisation. Tribes joined under successful warlords and went plundering. Goths, Vandals, Alamanni, Franks…even the Huns got involved.

The centuries after the fall of the Roman empire remain among the least known periods of human history. People went for large scale migrations and almost continuous warfare, with a few plagues thrown in for good measure. Just look at a few migration routes (largely simplified). The Goths seem to have started out near the Baltic around the year 150. They travelled south-east until they reached the Black Sea. Then the West-Goths went marauding through Greece and up the Balkan and from there to Rome. Some went to southern Italy, some to southern France, then to Spain. The East-Goths chose a shorter route, the left out Greece and plundered their way through the Balkan, Austria and then to Rome, where they arrived eighty years after their cousins.

Their close relations, the Vandals, swept from the Baltic through Germany and northern France, then south into Spain, across the ocean at Gibraltar, then through North Africa to Carthage, where they split and sailed to Rome (arriving between the West- and East Goths), Sicily, and several Mediterranean islands. The Franks, coming from northern Germany, fought their way into rich Gaul where they established themselves as rulers. The Angles, Saxons, Jutes and similar minded folk decided to have a go at Britain. In between these migrations, hordes of Huns came sweeping all the way from China. The result was simply a mess. Most of the new tribes were happily illiterate. They destroyed much of what the Romans had developed and when it came to recording history, they preferred songs to writing. For several centuries, our knowledge of history and custom is restricted to the comments of a handful of usually Christian authors, most of whom had better things to do than write about the barbarians who were touring Europe. It was only after the church gained a solid foothold in northern Europe that we get the odd bit of information regarding the

pagan past. Most churchmen were not sympathetic with paganism, nor were they interested in recording pagan beliefs. However, we have some correspondences between missionaries and several catalogues of sinful activities that allow a vague and distorted view on pagan religion. More on this further on.

The Sanctity of Women

Let's have a look at women in Germanic religion and society. This topic is hard to research as so many scholars have over-done it during the 20th century. Good old Tacitus recorded that, to his surprise, the Germans believe that there is something sacred to women. In Caesar's *Gaulish War* (1,50) we learn that the 'mothers of the family' of the Suebi used to perform divination by lots that actively influenced war strategy. Well I wont argue whether that conglomerate of tribes, the Suebi, should be considered 'Germanic' as Caesar pretended, or are at least partly Celtic, as modern linguistics demonstrate. There are a number of Germanic seeresses who actively made politics by their prophecies, the best known example being the famous Veleda, who was the spiritual power behind the devastating uprising in the year 69CE. Officially, the revolt was led by a Batavian called Civilis, who wore his hair long and red because of some oath, but behind the scenes it was Veleda whose prophecies roused the tribes to revolt.

Veleda is not a name but a title based on German *velêt-, which is closely related to old Irish filid (seer, prophet, poet) and middle Cymric gwelet, to see. Tacitus tells her story, starting with *Histories* 4, 61 where she is described as a noble virgin of the Bructeri 'who ruled widely according to the ancient belief of the Germani, that many women are prophetesses and, with increasing superstition, that they are held to be goddesses.' Her predictions regarding the total defeat of the Romans made her popular. During a dispute between the Agrippinensi (the people of Cologne) and the Tencteri, she was honoured with the task of being one of the two judges to mediate the case. In this function she received numerous presents, but, as Tacitus notes, (*Hist.* 4, 65), nobody was permitted to see her or approach her save a close relation. To keep her apart and secure, she was housed in a tower close to the river.

In *Hist.* 5, 22, the 'Germani' make her a present of the freshly captured flagship of the Roman admiral Cerialis. The latter barely escaped being captured. When swimming elite warriors of the Batavi took the ship in the middle of the night, the Roman admiral wasn't aboard but on the shore, making love with a girl called Claudia Sacrata. In the meantime, things began to look bad for the tribes. They won numerous battles but could not win the war. The Romans were just as exhausted from the constant depletion of their troops. Tacitus' account ends as Veldeda is approached by messengers of Cerialis, asking her to consider the numerous defeats of her people and whether she wouldn't do something kind for the Romans. This is good evidence that Cerialis appreciated Veleda as a politician, not an occult authority. As the rest of the *Histories* are lost, we know little about the end of the tale.

Some sort of peace was made, and possibly Veleda was part of a delegation to Rome. The peace treaty was unusual, as it absolved the tribes from guilt and punishment.

However, there are signs that things did not go well for her. As Fischer Fabian (1975) records, a minor Roman poet refers to 'the pleas of the captured Veleda'. The fragment of an inscription unearthed in 1926 at Ardea, south of Rome, refers to 'the Veleda of the drinkers of Rhine-water' (a metaphor for the Germani). The text is badly damaged, but parts of it remain readable. One addresses emperor Vespasian that Veleda should sweep the floor and tend the lamps of a temple, the other points out that the oracular arts can only work when money is paid for prophecy. It seems that she was betrayed, sold into slavery and finally became a professional oracle in a Roman temple.

Tacitus mentions another famous seeress, called Albruna 'She who is advised by the Elves', or, if the name is derived from *ga-rûnô: 'Close Friend of the Elves'. Sadly, he gives no details whatsoever. Then there are a few mad women who appear here and there in Roman histories to prophecy doom. One of them approached Drusus and scared him away from the river Elbe, see Suetonius (*Claudius*). Dion (67, 5, 3) mentions a virgin named Ganna who, after Veleda, was prophetess 'among the Celts'. In his book, all Germans are Celts, so we don't know what culture we are dealing with. She seems to have visited Rome in the company of a king of the Semnoni. Emperor Vitellius frequently consulted a seeress of the Chatti, who told him he wouldn't

Northern Europe: **Top left** and anticlockwise: saddle ornament in eagle shape, Gotland, Sweden; Small disks, Mecklenburg, Germany (c800AD) Rune text on the 'rosetten fibel' Seeland, (3-4th century); Fibula from southern Sweden (with runes); ornament from Skara, West Gotland; Odin and Freki, detail from the Thorwald Cross, Isle of Man, 10thcentury.

get anywhere as long as his mother remained alive. Soon the old lady died of poison, the only question being whether she took it voluntarily (Suetonius, *Vitellius*).

Add to them the priestesses of the Cimbri (Strabo) and you can see that, in old Germania, a number of women held priestly functions and were highly respected (if not feared). Just how many is a difficult question. So is the question whether all women were considered as imbued with a sacredness or whether this role only applied to nobility. I am sure you have your own guess here, so have I, but then, so has every scholar, and none of us can prove much to clear up the issue. During the Nazi period, Tacitus' passages on Germanic morals and virtues were celebrated to show the spiritual superiority of the Germans. Likewise the 'sacredness of women' was turned into propaganda material. Tacitus was thinking of frenzied priestesses. The Nazis preferred the 'sacredness of motherhood' and proposed that German women were sacred due to their ability to bear strong boys (that make good soldiers). The whole thing ceased to be a question of research and became a matter of ideology and faith. After the war, the new generation of scholars shied away from anything popular among the Nazis, and proposed that Germanic women were never respected for any sort of sacredness. Those scholars were shy of sacredness in all its forms and where the Nazis saw evidence for religion everywhere, they preferred to imagine common sense farmers and materialistic folk who didn't care much for the gods. It is only in recent decades that German scholars are beginning to explore religion. We can expect to be entertained by more fashionable interpretations. Regarding women, this may turn out to be interesting. We have evidence that young noble women were occasionally offered as hostages (for instance Tacitus *Hist.* 4,79, where the wife and the sister of Civilis get the job), indicating that some women were highly honoured. Likewise, we have some evidence for fighting women. Not only the raging wives of the Cimbri and Teutones (Plutarch, *Marius*), whose effort might be classed as self-defence. Dion 71,3,2 writes that there were women in arms among the slain of the Markomanni-wars and Vopiscus, *Vit. Aureliani* 34 records that female Gothic warriors in full armour ended in Roman captivity.

Pomponius Mela (*De Chorographia*) describes not only Germani who are incredibly primitive and war-loving, he also describes young women who join the men in warfare. 'Bending bows, riding, hunting are occupations for maidens, to slay an enemy is the fee demanded from the adult; not having killed an enemy is thought dishonourable and is punished by eternal virginity...' He also adds that the women burn off their right breast to develop a better, and unimpeded punch, but this is obviously cheap journalism based on Heredotus' Amazons. While it is extremely unlikely that this sort of thing was practised by young women in general, it remains possible that some women joined war-bands and went marauding, like so many young men did. Such professional fighters may be the root of the later Nordic tradition of the Valkyre. A Valkyrie is more than a warrior, in many texts she also functions as a sorceress. Some fought on the battlefield, others fought while trancing, by sending their spirit and a host of raging animal spirits against the enemy. In later, Nordic literature we find more evidence for fierce fighting-women, unscrupulous queens and a whole host of seeresses and women wise in sorcery (see *Seidways* for details).

Rudolf Much, whose research in these matters is invaluable, also refers to numerous female Germanic names, many of them directly related to warfare. What seems hard to prove is the claim that women had a right to vote at the Ting assembly. It does not appear in Nordic literature and cannot be shown in earlier common Germanic customs. That some woman were deeply into politics is obvious, but we cannot be sure whether simple farmer's wives shared the same political responsibilities as their husbands.

Deities of Height and Depth

Who were the gods of the Germanic people? We can answer this question in several ways. The easy way, appearing in countless popular books on the topic, is to pretend that the Icelandic pantheon, well known from the *Eddas*, was also known and venerated in Germany and England. As pointed out earlier, this is definitely not the case. We can be sure that there were wide differences between the faiths of the people before the Roman occupation and the beliefs of the medieval, widely travelled Vikings. Let's take a look at a few deities. I wont even try to discuss all of them, but then a brief look at a few important ones may be useful.

Closely related to the topic of this book is Odin (Óðinn). Let's start with the elder form. According to Tacitus, the main gods venerated by the Germani were Mercury, Mars and Hercules. The former is easily identified with Wodan. Like Mercurius, Wodan is a guide of the dead, a traveller, who holds a spear (Mercury a staff), both wear broad hats, both are inventors, tricksters and both are related to speech, words, spell-craft and eventually, writing. The Roman Mercurius has a lot of attributes that do not appear in Wodan's cult, but then, the Romans chose to describe foreign gods by identifying them with similar deities of their own religion, they did not pretend that these deities are actually the same. Like the Germani, the Gaulish people venerated Mercurius as their major god (Caesar). An unusual choice, as apart from the Thracians, all other old European pagans preferred chief deities who were wielders of lightning, bringers of fertility, and destroyers of enemies, i.e. gods who could be identified with the Greek Zeus and the Roman Jupiter. Germani, Celts and Thracians chose an intellectual god as the head of their religion.

The Roman Mars is easily identified as one of the numerous war gods. In Scandinavian myth he appears as the one-handed god Tyr, who lost his hand when the Fenris wolf was bound. In common Germanic myth, we find a similar god called *Tiw-, OHG: Zio, AGS: Tiw, Tig, Goth: Tyz, Tius. Closely related is the Saxon god Saxnôt. These gods derive their name from the ancient Indo-European root *deiw-, the bright sky. They may well be related to the Gaulish god Teutates. In Tacitus *Ger.* 2, we read that the Germani celebrate the earth born god Tuisto and his son Mannus as the ancestors of their people. Tuisto may be the earliest rendering of this god. The name is not only related to the sky, and to a wide range of similar Indo-European sky gods. It also means 'double, twinned, two-sexual'. The eldest deity of the Germani was androgyne, both male and female (Herrmann, 1996: 371). Mannus is not only the first single-sexed being, it is also mankind itself. The name derives from a root that means 'thinking, mindful, remembering', more on this in the chapter on the M rune. While the original Tuisto did not make it into mythological literature, there are a large number of deities with closely related names.

The branch of war-gods has been mentioned, the other branch is gods that relate to weather, fertility and justice. Here we come to Hercules. No, the Germani did not believe in the semi-divine Greek hero. However, the Romans saw images and heard tales of a god who could best be compared to rough Hercules. These are the gods *Thunaraz, the OHG: Donar (Thunder), AGS: Thunor, ON: Thor (þórr). They have parallels in other cultures, such as the Gaulish Tanaris, Taranis, the Welsh *taran* (thunder) and the Greek Zeus. Like Hercules, the common Germanic thunder-god wields a club or hammer. Both travel frequently, fight giants and monsters, both are a bit rough, great eaters and drinkers, and have an appeal to farmers and artisans. When we identify the main gods cited by Tacitus as Wodan/Odin, Tiu/Tyr and Donar/

Thor we arrive at a combination that can be found in the oath sworn by Anglo-Saxons at their baptism: they had to denounce Thuner, Woden and Saxnôt.

Are these three the main Germanic gods? How about some local variation? Think of Adam of Bremen, who recorded that the major gods worshipped at the temple of Uppsala were Thor, Woden and Fricco (Freyr). The latter is a god of rural fertility, associated with phallic symbols, who was enormously popular in old Sweden. He was the chief god of the old Swedes before invading tribes introduced the cult of Wodan. In the process, Wodan lost the initial W and became Odin, while Freyr lost much of his importance. Though a few Swedish kings bore his name (they appear as Frodhi or Frodo and are associated with a golden age of peace and plenty) it seems that before long, Freyr became a minor farmer's god, while the nobility sacrificed to Odin. Freyr is related to such words as 'freedom' and the German: Freude (joy).

The names Wodan and Odin have a fascinating etymology. Wodan, in the elder form, has several shamanic functions. He is associated with the dead and the slain, he appears as a wild rider, a god of storm and gale, a leader of the wild hunt who features prominently in common Germanic myths. The name Wodan comes from OHG: wuot (insane), GOTH: wods (angry, obsessed), OE: wod (raving), OICE: odr (raving), OENG: wod (sound, voice, poetry), OICE: odr (poetry). You can find the modern German 'Wut' in his name, meaning anger, rage, fury, wrath, but in the elder form, the concept included the ideas of madness, obsession, and ecstatic frenzy. The name 'Wodan' is not the only one. Folklore retains a lot of variations, such as Wode, Wotan, Woide, Wods, Wuotes, Muotes, Guotes, Godes and Uodan. Paulus Diaconus records the name as Gwodan, it might be related to the British Gwydyon who appears prominently in the *Mabinogi* and several poems of the *Book of Taliesin*. As John Matthews points out, the Welsh gwydd means tree, while gwyddon means magician, and gwyddor is science. While Gwydyon is a super human sorcerer and Gwodan a god, the two share a lot of traits, such as bardic skills, cunning, spell-craft, sorcery, shape-shifting and an unreliable trickster nature.

Now the Germanic Wodan is not a chief of the gods, as Odin is. The continental god leads the wild hunt, a fierce and devastating cavalcade of spirits, elves, the dead, the unborn and uncanny creatures of all descriptions who come howling through the autumn skies, stripping leaves from branches, damaging homesteads, spreading panic and madness in their path. The wild hunt is also associated with music. Several tales state that the ghostly army is accompanied by the most wonderful, unearthly music, and there are even a few tales relating that musicians can gain exceptional skill from meeting them. If you are good, wild Wode will press your fingers against your instrument, so hard that blood squirts, and when they have healed, you'll have learned more than most.

Now the legends of the wild hunt show a wide range of variations. Quite often, local heroes take Wodan's place, so you can find tales where Barbarossa or King Arthur lead the ghostly cavalcade. Even goddesses do the job from time to time, one of them being Lady Holle, riding a three legged horse (a triskel). Wodan as a god of rage and ecstasy was not only popular among the priests and sorcerers. He was also a god who made warriors battle-mad, who turned his chosen into wolves and bears, who granted protection from iron and made enemy weapons brittle like twigs. In this function, he became the favourite god of a number of warlike tribes. These tribes invaded Scandinavia at some time. They conquered the land and installed their major god as chief deity, king of the gods, father of all. This was the birth of the Scandinavian Odin, whose tales you can enjoy in the *Eddas*. It is also the way Wodan got into the genealogy of the Anglo-Saxon kings, who saw him as their primal ancestor, as did many kings of Scandinavia.

Odin is a god with many titles. As chief of Valhalla, he is called Aldafaðir (All-Father); Aldagautr (All-God); Haptaguð (Head of the Gods); Har (the High), Jafnhár (Equally High) and Thridi (the Third). As a god of war, we encounter Odin as Hertýr (God of the Army); Herblindi (Blinder of Armies); Hjálmberi (Helmetbearer); as the Father of Victory and Valgautr (God of the Battle-slain). More shamanic are such titles as Hrafnaguð (Ravengod); Drauga Dróttinn (Lord of Ghosts); Hangaguð (God of the Hanged); Ari (Eagle); Arnhofdi (Eagle Head); Ofnir and Swafnir (names of Odin that appear in the catalogue of worms and serpents of *Grimn*.

34); Grimnir (the Masked one); Gondlir (Bearer of the Magic Staff?); Blindr (the Blind One); Báleygr (Flame Eye); Bileygr (Mild Eye); Vakr (Wakeful); Njótr (the Enjoyer) refers to the god when he receives sacrifices. Wind and storm appear in Viðrir (the Weatherer), Váfudr (Floating); Svipall (Mobile); Thundr (the Sweller); Ómi (Shouter); Geigudr (the Terrible Storm) and Yggr (the Terrible). In the latter, widely popular form, Odin 'rides' the world-tree. Odin as a traveller appears as Vegtamr (Used to Ways); Víðforull (Wide travelling); as a god of wisdom he is called Fjolsviðr (Much Knowledge); Glapsviðr (Deceptive Knowledge); Skollvaldr (Custodian of Deception); Sadr (True); Sanngetal (Sensing Truth); Oski (Granter of Desires). This is just a short selection of translations by Golther, there remains a wide range of names that defy our comprehension. Just how many independent local gods were integrated in the cult of Odin?

Odin retains some of the elder characteristics in those songs and myths that show him travelling anonymously, having riddle contests with wise giants, stealing the mead of inspiration and raising dead seeresses from the hollow hills. He is a powerful shamanic figure. His companions (helping spirits) are two wolves, Geri (Greed) and Freki (Devourer), and two ravens, Hugin (Thought) and Munin (Memory). You will observe that these animals are closely related to the idea of death: they carry the slain to the otherworlds. Odin is also noted for his transformations into animal form. At the same time, he was identified as the father of most gods, which produced some difficult genealogies, and installed as the serene regent who gathers slain heroes for the final fight at the end of the age. This was an innovation. The elder, Germanic form is associated with dead folk and spirits, but there is no evidence for a warrior heaven, such as Valhalla, on the continent (the sole exception seem to be the Erulians and some Celto-Iberians, see *Cauldron of the Gods*). In common Germanic myth, the dead go into mountains and hills (or mounds, if you like), from where they may re-emerge on occasion (a hint at rebirth?), be it as humans or in the shape of birds, mice, serpents, butterflies or various small animals. A heroic death on the battlefield is not required. You can see traces of this in Scandinavian legend, which is full of contradictions on the topic.

Closely associated with Odin is the figure of Loki, a fiery god of questionable manners, who happens to be Odin's blood brother. The two get on like wind and fire. Loki as a trickster and deceiver is well known from the *Eddas*. He was a well known deity in Scandinavia, where he made it into numerous folk legends. He also appears in Britain, here in a healing spell from Lincolnshire (Dumézil 1959 : 49). To make it work, three horseshoes were fixed to the bed of the patient and tapped with a hammer:

Feyther, Son and Holy Ghoast
naale the divil to this poast;
throice I smoites with Holy Crok
with this mall Oi throice dew knock

one for God an' one for Wod an' one for Lok!

Loki is bright and brilliant, but he is also a cheat, a deceiver, a satirist, and a god who objects when things become too rigid. As the 'Father of Lies' he is the great illusionist, but when you read the magnificent *Lokasenna* you may find him as the voice of truth. Strange as it seems, the honourable gods need a jester, trickster and clown from time to time. This is the case for all teams: when you have a bunch of similar people working together, their worldviews tend to confirm each other. This leads to habitual stagnation and dull-mindedness. Just look at the groups, organisations and cults you know from experience! Loki's contribution to such groups is ridicule, criticism and unexpected deeds. As a result, we find Loki involved in a good many uneasy situations.

One of his acts is the assassination of Balder, another is the beginning of the end of the world. This has led some modern pagans to propose that Loki is a force of evil. Such explanations are misleading. There is no such thing as evil-in-itself in Germanic myth. Perhaps the killing of Balder wasn't nice, but then, the gods' attempt to make Balder immortal and invulnerable may also have been an error. In a changing universe, eternal and unchanging things get in the way of innovation. As to the end of the world, well, in Germanic myth (just like in real life) it happens repeatedly.

Then there is theft. Loki stole loads of things. We have some of these tales in the *Prose Edda*, other stories only exist in fragmentary or distorted form. Loki is a highly ambiguous figure who may or may not be related to the Celtic gods (and semigods) Lugus, Lugh and Lleu. All of them are clever, bright, skilled in many crafts and not always trustworthy (but then, what god is?). At this point, Odin and Loki have a lot in common. An enigmatic verse from the *Edda* (*Fiolvinsmal* 26) mentions that Loki used runes to shape a lethal missile:

Laevateinn (Twig of Evil) she is named,
Loki made her from runes,
down in the deep, before the gate of the dead
in Saegiarn's (Laegiarn: Greedy for Doom) shrine, she rests near Sinmara (?)
protected by nine locks.
 (translation after Neckel in Dumézil).

As a rune-maker, Loki is of special importance for this book. When you use the runes for divination you will soon learn that some of the answers are anything but serious. Someone out (or in) there is enjoying a good laugh. Hey, come on, is that really you? I should add that Loki is not just a 'Viking devil', as some claim. There is a folk-ballad (*Lokka-táttur*) collected by Olrik and given by Dumézil that relates how a farmer went dicing with a giant. The stake is the farmer's son, and when the giant wins, the father appeals to the gods to save his son. Odin hides the boy in a grain of wheat, but the giant finds him. Hoenir hides the boy in the feather of a swan, but he is discovered again. It is cunning Loki who hides the child in an egg inside the belly of a fish. Soon enough the giant goes fishing. Loki becomes the oarsman, and when the fish is caught he changes the boy to human shape and hides him behind his back. Reaching the shore, he tells the boy to run. The giant sees him fleeing, gives a yell of rage, and pursues as fast as possible. Now cunning Loki had made the farmer set up an iron pillar (a ritual post?) at the entrance of the farm. The boy rushes past the pillar, but the giant slams straight into it. What a good opportunity! says Loki and tears off the giant's leg. The leg re-grows, but Loki tears off the other as well, places a log between them, and goes indoors boasting that he has kept his word.

According to Dumézil, telling this tale was prohibited. Its existence proves that some people appealed to Loki for help just like they prayed to other deities. Loki is a god who gets things done, so beware.

Icelandic myth pairs Odin with a number of goddesses, the best known being wise Frigg, who knows the fate of all. This is another innovation. Among the Anglo-Saxons and the Langobards, Odin's wife is Frea, in most of Scandinavia it was Freya (The Beloved, the Dear one), the well known goddess of love. Freya appears prominently in *Eddic* myth, but as a popular love goddess she is not exactly a deity of chastity or marital faith. She has a mate, called Odr, who went missing shortly after the marriage, and apart from this, there are plenty of references to her loveplay with various gods, giants, several skilful dwarves and her own brother Freyr. Strong stuff in a culture noted for prudishness: in Iceland, even simple love poetry was prohibited. It was unthinkable to the Icelanders that their serene chief god has a mate noted for infidelity and incest, and so the goddess Frigg was introduced at a fairly late date.

Frigg keeps a marriage good, she is goddess of the household, but where it comes to popularity, she never came close to Freya. Freya is also associated with magic. In one song she raises a dead seeress from her mound to learn a bit of hidden lore. In the *Ynglingasaga* she learns the art of seiðr from Odin (see *Seidways* for details). We read that she rides the radiant boar Goldbristle, and in her care is a falcon costume for shape-changed flight. She receives half of the dead heroes who come to Valhalla after a tough day on the battlefield. Does this make her a death goddess? Or should we wonder whether half of the Viking warriors thought themselves dedicated to Freya? But Freya and Frigg are not the only goddesses associated with Odin. As god of poetry, the Father of Songs drinks wine with the goddess Saga, the personified essence of storytelling. A north Scandinavian Legend mates Odin with the mountain giantess Skadi, their offspring were the Sami people (*Seidways*).

Then there is a common Germanic tradition that couples Wodan with the goddess Helja. Her name comes from a common Indo-European root *uel-, to hide, hele, cover. Related is German: Höhle (cave) and English hollow.

In the Taunus mountains, Hessen, Germany, we encounter the storm giant Wode, who dwells on a mist-enshrouded mountaintop with Lady Holle (Verleger,

Taunussagen, and *Seidways*). The Holle or Helja of central Germany is usually a benign Goddess associated with mountains, caves, springs, death and rebirth. There is a mountain in northern Hessen, the Meissner (originally Weissner, the White One) where her cult seems to have survived for a long time. The Meissner is a volcanic mountain. Its slopes are studded with rocks, there are basalt pillars emerging from the earth and deep cracks in the ground release the sulphuric smell of smouldering coal. It is also a mountain that has suffered from excessive coal mining. There are roads going to the mountaintop, there are buildings, antennae and altogether too many tourists. Close to the top is the 'Frau Holle Lake', a 'bottomless' lake fed by underwater springs. Only a few centuries ago, local women used to climb to the lake, where they sacrificed and prayed to have children, and occasionally tossed a changeling into the deep, black waters. Frau Holle was known as a benevolent goddess with a rough sense of humour. She is renowned for turning drunkards into oxen by ringing her magical bell, and in wintertime, when she has covered the scenery under a veil of pure white, she walks through villages and homesteads blessing those who work and cursing those who laze.

In a valley close to the mountaintop is the Kitzkammer, a tiny cave of volcanic rock. 'Cave' is not the proper word. Imagine a vertical gap in the basalt, barely large enough to stand upright and to lie full length, with a thin stone roof threatening to fall in. According to legend, Lady Holle had a heart for homeless girls and women, those who had lost their relations and those who had been kicked out for getting pregnant. There was an invisible palace on the mountaintop (or under the lake) where these woman could dwell. One day, Lady Holle was out for a walk in the mist, and our girls began to quarrel. When Holle came home, she found them screaming and hitting each other. So she rang her magical bell and transformed them. The girls became Kitze, a term that might mean cats (Katzen), small owls (Käuze) or young roe deer (Kitze). In this shape they were confined to the Kitz-chamber. Is this a vague memory of a pagan priesthood? Were initiates of Lady Holle's cult located on the Meissner? I have been inside the Kitzkammer. It has exactly the right shape for an initiation-cave and a magnificent view across a slope to a rock that looks a bit like a human head with long hair. You can see a photo on the back cover of this book. The Meissner also offers access to a vast cave, the Hilgershäuser Höhle, known as Hessen's biggest cult cave. The youths of Hilgershausen (a nearby village) used to walk to this cave on Easter morn keeping strict silence. They entered the cave, offered a few flowers, and collected sacred water at a subterranean spring. Nowadays the place looks like a rubbish heap. I had hoped to trance a bit, but as it turned out I spent several hours collecting rubbish left by tourists, alcoholics, would-be-Satanists and irresponsible pagans. Holle appears in several folk tales of central Germany, the best known one is 'Frau Holle' in Grimm's fairy tales. The English translation has turned her name into 'Mother Hulda'. Again, the goddess is associated with an underworld that can be entered through a well, and her myth is full of references to the passage of the seasons. She has terrifying teeth, but apart from this, is benign to the active and nasty to the lazy. The goddess has several names in Germanic tales, such as Hulda, Holla, Uolla and, as her earliest form, Helja. Local variations appear as Lady Wolle and Lady Rolle, as Lady Ellhorn, Irle, and Rough Else. A close relation of hers appears in Norwegian myth, where she is called Huldra. From the front she looks like a beautiful nude lady. Seen from behind, she reveals a gaping huge hole in her back, as she is completely hollow. Huldra is a goddess of forests and wild places. Her children are elves, fairies, trolls and other unchristian creatures.

In Icelandic myth her name is Hel, and she is described as a horrible underworldly death goddess, half black and half flesh coloured (or white). Her name is also the name of her abode, Hel being an early form of hell. The Christians stole the word hell, and made it a place of heat. The Icelandic hell is a place underneath a root of the world tree. It is a cold, foggy place where the dark dragon Nidhöggur sucks the souls, where the 'roaring cauldron' swirls and the eagle/giant Hräswelgr devours the carcasses of dead belief and hope. In Niflhel (Fog-Hell) the dreams and delusions of life fade. All who go there appear as shadows, they walk through gloom and murk, and dwell in halls made of twisting serpents. What a metaphor for the coiling DNA within each living cell! This is the place to forget identity. After death, sinners go to Hel, so the sagas state, first of all criminals, oath-breakers, adulterers, blasphemers, cowards and those who died of disease (the shameful 'straw-death') instead of fighting. Looks like a place of punishment, doesn't it? However, the tales include the occasional contradiction. The dying dragon/giant Fafnir tells young Sigurd that all men go to Hel eventually. Heroes go to Hel (*Waf.* 43), no matter how bravely they died, and the same goes for all the gods of Asgard (*Hraf.* 11). Even young, innocent Balder, son of Odin and Frigg and a shining example of every virtue you can think of, ends up in Hel's foggy halls. So does his assassin, blind Hödr (strangely, this is a form of Odin). In Skaldic poetry, both gods are called Hel's companions. Finally we learn that both re-emerge from Hel after the end of the world. The dark dragon Nidhöggur (*Völuspa,* 64) emerges from the Nida-mountains, carrying the souls of the deceased on his wings. Were they supposed to repopulate the earth at the beginning of the new age? These are not the only references to reincarnation in the *Eddas*. Odin's choice warriors are reborn every evening after a tough day of fighting, and the final line of *Helgakvida Hjörvardssonar* states that heroic Helgi and his beloved Swawa were reborn.

Now the Icelandic Hel is a dangerous figure. Nevertheless, Odin grants her power over nine worlds. This is one of those jokes. We learn that there are nine heavens, nine hells and nine worlds. It's a matter of perspective. Seen from heaven, all worlds are hells, and seen from hell, all worlds are heavens. Whatever it is, it is here, and whether this world appears as heaven or hell depends entirely on you. To confuse things further, I have to add that the common Germanic form is not always a nice goddess, let alone a mother-goddess, as some would have it. Helja can appear in a male form in continental folklore. He is called Hel, and he is death personified. Mr. Hel rides at times of pestilence. When the dogs howl in the middle of the night, Hel is among them. When pestilence breaks out, Hel has arrived, and when it ceases, Hel has departed. There are spells that can force Hel to move elsewhere. Those who recover from severe disease are known to 'have come to an agreement with Hel' or 'to have sacrificed to Hel'. There are local variations to the tales. Sometimes Hel is a headless black horse. Sometimes he is a black rider on a black horse, who peers into windows in the middle of the night. Whenever he gazes into a house, one of its inhabitants is doomed. The horse can also be white or grey, and sometimes it has only three legs. Another version combines the female form with the death-dealing occupation. Then we learn of an old lady, clad in black, riding a horse called Hel, carrying doom and death (Neckel, 1974:301). Not that this is the only case of sex-changing in Germanic myth. More on this topic in the chapter on Seiðr.

Where it comes to Celtic religion, we find a close relation of Helja in the Gaelic goddess Cailleach, who is associated with mountains, springs and wells. In some forms she is a winter goddess, striking the ground with her club until it is frozen solid, in another form she is the mate of the chosen high king. First she appears as a dreadful, dark giantess, raging mad with hunger, her huge mouth gaping, fangs gleaming, her body wretched with cold and hunger. Those who can bed her in this shape are admitted to kingship and may marry the land. After a good night of making love she transforms into a beautiful young lady who is love and generosity herself. This Cailleach has a winter and a summer side. She may be a companion of the king, but she is also a mate of the greatest poets and bards, people who enjoyed a similar status as royalty. You can find more data on her in *Seidways*, in Irish myth (the tale of Njall is worth exploring), in the ballad of Sir Gawain and Lady Ragnell and in the folk song of King Henry. Sometimes the Gaelic war-goddess Morrigan appears as the Cailleach, so get yourself some good books and do some research on your own, its certainly worth it. All of this might give the impression that Helja is the 'Great Goddess' of the Germanic people. This is certainly not the case. Helja/Hel were worshipped by some and dreaded by others. In wide districts, she seems to be completely unknown. Other goddesses abound, such as Lady Berchte and Lady Gode (a female form of Wodan?), Lady Freke, Lady Werra, Lady Gaue and Lady Fuik.

The Vikings also had some famous goddesses apart from the Eddic ones. One of the most remarkable is the fierce Thorgerd Hölgabrud, who was the patron deity of Jarl Hakon, the last pagan king of Norway, and his family. In her temple in Gudbrandsdal, she had a life size statue, adorned with a gold ring on her hand and a cloth over her head. Beside her stood images of Thor and Irpa, her sister

(*Njálssaga*, 88). During the sea-fight against the combined fleets of the Jomsvikings (987 or 988CE), Hakon realised that things were going badly. He had himself rowed to a wooded island where he kneed, facing north, and invoked Thorgerd for help. Thorgerd and Irpa remained silent. Hakon promised sacrifices of beasts and valuables. When no reply came, he knew the goddesses were angry with him and promised humans. This didn't work either, and the desperate jarl went to the limit. He promised any human sacrifice, except for himself and his sons Eirik and Svein. He had another son, Erling, who was but seven winters old. The goddesses chose Erling, and Hakon, returning to his ships, had Erling sacrificed.

Soon the battle resumed. The fleets faced each other, Hakon's ships close to the shore, the Jomsviking fleet coming from the open sea. The day began hot and bright, but suddenly black clouds came from the north. By afternoon, a raging thunderstorm was unleashing lightning and hail on the Jomsvikings. They had undressed earlier, and the frosty gales caught them in their underwear. Havard the Brawler and several visionary men gazed into the fleet of Hakon, and saw Hölgabrud moving between the warriors. Her hands were held high, each of her fingers shot forth arrows and every arrow slew a man. Around her were pale, ghostly figures unleashing evil, others saw a serpent in the flood. The Jomsvikings, despite the weather and their enemies, kept fighting. All of a sudden, the skies cleared and the storm began to abate. Hakon, in his frenzy, stood in his ship, calling on Thorgerd and Irpa to remember the sacrifice. Soon the skies became dark again, icy winds blew and snow fell. A blizzard enveloped the Jomsvikings, the storm blew into their faces and their arrows were repelled by the gale. Havard gazed again, and saw two huge women, where before there had only been one. He demanded that Sigvaldi should flee. Sigvaldi thought it a brilliant idea and began to turn, but the other chiefs did not agree. Moments later the whole fleet disintegrated. The leaders of the Jomsvikings leaped from ship to ship, swearing, quarrelling and killing each other and the storm devoured the survivors. A handful of ships made it to the shore, the last Jomsvikings spent a night in the freezing cold and by morning they were captured. Thanks to Hölgerd and Irpa, Hakon found himself victorious.

We have this tale in several versions, the most detailed being the *Jómsvikinga Saga,* 44. It even informs us that the Jomsvikings weighed the hail stones to measure Thorgerd and Irpa's power and each of them weighed an ounce. Well done. Another tale. Hakon once decided to have his revenge on the skald Thorleif, who had escaped to Iceland. He had a human figure made from a chunk of wood, and placed the heart of a sacrificed man within it. Invoking Thorgerd and Irpa, he made the figure stand, walk and speak. It received the name Thorgard (a misspelling of Thorgerd? Was it a figure of the goddess?). They sent this spirit to Iceland, where it impaled Thorleif with the very spear that Hakon had given him earlier, a spear that had stood in the temple of Thorgerd and Irpa. Let me end by asking why such a colourful pair of goddesses did not make it into the *Eddas*? Were the Icelanders so strongly opposed to Norway that they would not accept the goddesses of a noble Norwegian family in their religion?

Viking religion

How do we trace a religion? Most of the Vikings were not very literate. Religious lore was preserved by story-telling and annual festivities. It was a practical religion that was based mostly on deeds. Now among the Scandinavians, just like the Germani, the greatest times for religion and sacrifice were the annual rituals. Each blót (strengthening) was an opportunity to strengthen the tie between humans and gods. The gods needed sacrifice to be strong and powerful, so the Vikings believed, and the costlier a sacrifice, the more could be expected in return. There were several occasions for blót sacrifices, differing from culture to culture, but as a rule, the greatest blót offerings were connected with the religious year.

The annual festivities of the Vikings are much better attested than their common Germanic ancestors. The Scandinavians had three major festivals, occasions of sacrifice, festivity and general merrymaking. The *Ynglingasaga*, 6, tells us: 'One should sacrifice towards winter for a good year, at midwinter one should sacrifice for growth and the third time towards summer; this is the sacrifice for victory.' The younger *Olafsaga Helga*, 104, states: 'It is their custom to have a sacrifice in autumn to greet the coming of winter; they have another sacrifice in the middle of winter,

the third towards summer, when they greet summer.' Chapter 112 mentions one Sigurd Thorisson. When he was a pagan, he used to sacrifices three times during winter: one at the beginning, one in the middle and one at the coming of summer. After converting to Christianity, he remained true to this custom. He celebrated a meal with his friends in autumn, a Yule-feast in winter and a third at Easter, all of them attended by many guests. The Farmer Harekr gave three major feasts each year, a Yule-feast, a midwinter feast and one at Easter. The precise dates of these feasts remain uncertain. Thorgrim (*Gislasaga Surssonar*, 1, 27) celebrated a feast for the coming of winter in late autumn and sacrificed to Freyr. The beginning of winter was the start of the new year. Sometimes this date was close to the Gaelic Samhain at the end of October. In other instances, the proper season was the end of September. Widukind mentions a Saxon feast at the beginning of October when the dead were venerated for three days. The feast could take a while. The Breidfirdingas (*Eyrbyggjasaga*, 43) used to have ball-games at this date. All around the field, huts were erected and many people came to stay for half a month or more. Others celebrations were shorter. Thietmar of Merseburg has it that the Danes held Yule after the 6th of January. In Norway, Yule was in the month Thorri, and happened between the 9th and 16th of January. Among the Anglo-Saxons, the first and second month of Yule were January and February. Among the Goths, the first month of Yule was November. As Golther (where you can find more detail) mentions, it was King Hakon who decided that Yule should be celebrated at the same time as Xmas. The Yule-feast, no matter when it happened, usually involved games and present giving. The feast towards summer was celebrated early in spring. Even this date is occasionally called Yule; the *Hervararsaga*, 12, has Yule in February.

By contrast, feasts in midsummer are not recorded. There may have been a bit of neighbourly drinking and in some places, such as Iceland, the major Ting (assembly) met in June for sacrifice, feasting, assizes, games, elections and political decisions. Participation was a must, those who did not come were fined. Such midsummer feasts were exceptions. There is no reference in any saga to a celebration of May, the spring equinox is only mentioned once by Adam of Bremen, harvest feasts and the autumn equinox seem unknown. It is not that people wouldn't have liked a bit more festivity. However, in Scandinavia, the warm season does not last for long, and most of it consisted of farming, harvesting, fishing, travel, warfare, work and more work. Under such conditions, you may get drunk at home with a few friends, but it is not very practical for large communities to feast for days on end.

Priests of Scandinavia

Here our information improves a good deal. When the Vikings were christianised, they began to record much of their old lore, including pagan material. It also included a lot of fantastic elements, meaning that you can't trust anything you read. The sagas are a unique form of literature. Where the Irish and British storytellers of the period delighted in excessive use of adjectives, the Nordic literati tried to reduce their language to the barest essentials. The sagas are dry and often so terse that we have to guess what their author's were talking about. A typical example is the perplexing remark 'The kings took seats in the house, but their women warmed the gods near the fire.' (*Frithjofs Saga*). We learn nothing whatsoever regarding the meaning of this phrase. What's your guess?

Scandinavia had several forms of religion. The priest was generally called guði, goði, gudija, the priestess guðja, plural. gyðjur. These terms are close to the terms used by some elder, continental cultures, but whether the office was similar remains unknown. The people of Gaul, for instance, had a priest called gutuater, 'Father of the Voice' or 'One who raises his Voice'. One of them was executed by Julius Caesar (the voice said the wrong things), but whether the gutuater had anything to do with Druidry remains an open question.

To complicate things a lot, there are significant differences between the priests of Denmark, Norway and Iceland. Golther describes several forms of organisation. In Norway, the office of the goði was to build and maintain a temple, to perform regular worship and sacrifice. These events were attended by neighbours and relations, who had to pay a fee to make up the costs. The job had a high status but it required a certain amount of wealth. In consequence, it was often noble folk who became priests. They had a function in the community, but they still had the right to call the temple and its property their own.

Temples appear under several names in Nordic literature. The most common is simply hof or hov, a term that generally means a fenced space. In German it came to designate property, several buildings, a farm for instance, set apart by a fence. In old Norwegian and Anglo-Saxon, it also meant a temple. Nordic temples were often set apart with a real or symbolic barrier, be it a chain and a few posts, or a proper palisade with doors that could be locked. More common terms are goðahús (House of Gods) and blóthhús (House of Sacrifice).

Thorolf had a temple dedicated to Thor on the island Mostr in Norway. When he decided to move to Iceland, he had the temple dismantled and rebuilt in his new homeland. The new temple had several doors, the image of Thor was carved on the sacred pillars and 'Nails of the Gods' (reginnaglar) sticking in them. Don't ask me what these nails were, nobody seems to know. The temple had an altar with a large golden ring. The ring was held by the chief during ritual and vows were sworn on it. And there was a copper cauldron to collect the blood of animal sacrifices, and a twig to sprinkle blood over the pillars, the walls and the beer-brained congregation. (*Eyrbyggjasaga*, 3-4).

Cauldrons were an essential part of the blót, the sacrifice. Animals dedicated to the gods were never grilled or eaten raw. The proper way was to seethe them in a sacrificial cauldron. In Sweden, the assembly took their name from this act: the sudnautar are the 'seething-companions'. In general, the animal sacrifices were at least partly eaten by the worshippers. One of the favourites in Scandinavia was horse-flesh. The Christian church was utterly against this, and tried to outlaw it wherever possible. The Icelandic pagans made it a condition for their conversion that they were allowed to retain the custom of horse-eating. So there was nourishing food at the blót ceremony. Thorolf's temple also had an eternal flame and drinking equipment. Part of the ritual was regular toasts to the gods, in this case, to Odin, Njörd and Freyr.

Thorhadd the Old was priest in Märi near Trondheim. When he moved to Iceland, he took along the two sacred pillars that supported the roof near the high seat and the temple-earth. In Iceland, he had the temple rebuilt and gave the sanctity of the Märian land to his new home (*Landnáma*, 4, 6). Most of the Norwegian priests were owners of their own temples. They also functioned as judges and mediators. By contrast, the Danish priesthood was occasionally employed. Golther mentions rune stones with the names 'Ruulfr Nuraguþi' (Hrólfr Nóragoði: Hrolf, Priest of Nóri') and 'Ali Sauluaguþi' (Ali Solvagoði: Ali, Priest of Solva).

Rich and important people could own temples and employ other people to act as priests. Those who were employed as priests had a lower social status than those who officiated in their own temples. Whether they had much to say in matters of law is an open question. In Iceland, things were different. Iceland was populated by a lot of disgruntled Vikings, by people who had run into trouble with the Scandinavian kings, by landless sons,

Viking art. **Top**: top of a
memorial stone from
Tjängvide, Gotland, Sweden.
The image shows Odin on his
eight-legged horse. He is greeted by a
Valkyrie holding a drinking horn. The
image also appears on another stone
from Gotland. The hut is supposed to
be Valhalla, on the other stone it shows
three doors. The figures remain enigmatic.
Rune inscription (very faint) deleted.
Bottom left: woman with a horn, probably a
Valkyrie. Silver pendant, Birka, Sweden, 10th
century, female burial.
Bottom right: often identified as a Valkyrie,
but just as possibly a priestess bearing a staff

fugitives, enterprising souls, criminals and dropouts. When the first settlers arrived around 874 they simply chose a spot to call their home and began building. The early Icelanders had no common law nor constitution. They did as they liked, quarrelled a lot and often ended up killing each other. People built temples when and where they liked, and the better ones were soon attended by neighbours and friends. Each priest became the unofficial leader of a district, where he (or she?) officiated in sacrifices, assemblies and legal disputes.

The Icelandic priests became foci of spiritual and worldly law. As Iceland had no kings, the priesthood soon became the supreme power. Priests were rulers, and when the amount of priests and temples became a burden to the population, their number was restricted. This happened in 965, when the number of major temples and legal districts was limited to 39. No doubt there were more temples than this, as every person could build and own one.

There was never a religious monopoly in the Germanic world comparable to the Druidic monopoly on ritual practice in Gaul. Small rituals and offerings could be made by anyone. Larger offerings and a personal temple were available to those who could afford them. Official temples (hofudhof) were still larger and often had a political function beside the spiritual one: they served as congregation sites for whole districts. Adam of Bremen, hardly a sympathetic source, recorded what had been related to him by an unknown Christian. The main temple of Uppsala, close

to Sigtun, was built entirely of gold. Three deities were venerated as statues. Thor, the mightiest, sat in the centre, and to his right and left were Wodan and Fricco (Freyr). Nearby grew an ancient, evergreen tree of unknown species, and a spring was venerated, generally by drowning people in it. The entire temple was surrounded by a heavy golden chain. It might be a similar custom as the ropes that were used to mark the space for courts. Nearby in a sacred grove the trees were laden with sacrifices. According to Adam, the pagan Swedish used to sacrifice nine males of each species of animal (including humans) every ninth year, and left them dangling in the branches. The celebration lasted nine days around the spring equinox, (which is not too likely) and involved drinking, feasting and (dishonourable) sing-song.

The truth of this account is somewhat questionable. You find it repeated in many books on Nordic religion as if it came from a reliable witness, which pious Adam wasn't. Another, and even wilder account appears in the *Ragnars Saga Lodbrókar*. When king Eystein was ruler of Sweden, Uppsala was the greatest temple in the whole country. Eystein used to worship a goddess at the temple, she was a cow called Sibilja and received most of the sacrifices. In times of war, Eystein would coerce the cow to the battlefield (this took many sacrifices). Standing in the first line, Sibilja gave a terrible roar that confused the minds of the foes and made them attack each other. As a magical creature, she had to be slain in a magical way. Ivar the Boneless, weak but wise, had himself carried to the battlefield on a shield. He asked for a tree and made a bow out of it. He shot two arrows into Sibilja's eyes. Then he had his warriors lift him up. Making himself light as a feather, he was thrown at the cow, and making himself heavy like a mountain, he landed on her. He later founded London, believe it who may.

Large temples appear in most Scandinavian lands. Denmark seems to have at least four (Viborg in Jütland, Odense [Odins vé i.e. sanctuary], Ringsted-Hleidra and Lund.) The Frisians celebrated in Helgoland or in nearby (nowadays sunk) Forsitesland, the Saxons had one or several Irminsul pillars in sacred groves, cut down and destroyed courtesy of 'Saxonbutcher' Charlemagne. In Holland you have Walcheren, famed for numerous images of the sea-goddess Nehallenia. Even the Romans prayed to her before daring the journey to Britain. She may be a close relation to the Suebian goddess Nerthus, and the *Eddic* god of the oceans, rich Njörd, father of Freya and Freyr. Norway had a major temple in Gaular, another in Drontheim and in Vikin. These temples were so important that they were regularly attended by the nobility. Nearby, whole districts could gather for Ting assemblies. Such sites were too important for regular priests. It was often the highest nobles who performed the sacrifices.

Priestesses appear occasionally in the sagas. The *Fornmanna sögur* 2,73 refers to a priestess of Freyr. She was a beautiful young lady who was formally married to her god. Were male priests married to goddesses on occasion? As Joe Revill informed me, the Anglo-Saxon 'Helruna' can be translated as 'friend',

companion or even husband of Hel. *Fornaldarsögur* 3, 627 mentions 60 priestesses in a great temple in Biarmland. Maybe they were fantastic, as Golther proposes, but they do provide evidence that large communities of priestesses were not unthinkable to the medieval Vikings. Then there is a large number of women who were fortune tellers, seeresses, prophetesses (spákonur, volvur). They were not usually connected to any sort of established religion or temple and we cannot consider them part of a regular priesthood. As the topic of volvas and prophetic women has been treated in *Seidways*, forgive me for not repeating the matter here.

Christianization

When the Roman empire collapsed, it left behind a muddle of religions. Some citizens had joined the Christian cult, and tried hard to force others to participate. Others had belonged to the cults of the empire, or adhered to a blend of Celto-Germanic faith. At this time, the religions from before the conquest were hardly remembered. When the missionaries ranted against pagans, they were referring to any elder cult that did not happen to be Christian.

That the conversion involved violence is not only obvious from the practical execution of the job but also from the way the early missionaries thought. When the Bishop of Reims baptized the Frankish King Chlodwig in 496, he spoke the famous words: 'Bend your head in humility, proud Sigamber, worship what you used to burn, and burn what you used to worship.' The East-Frankish vow of baptism (7th C.) included the question 'Will you deny the demons?', to which a cheerful yes was expected, or else.

Things became really violent under the reign of Charlemagne, who is generally remembered as a glorious emperor who united the German countries under the banner of Christianity. In the process he had a number of bloody battles with an agglomerate of pagan tribes called Saxons, a term deriving from the short sword, or long knife, the sax, which they habitually carried. Charlemagne, a stout believer in the sort of violent Christ who grants victory in battle, soon acquired the name Saxonsbutcher. In a decree dating from c.787, he introduced some radical new laws. To begin with, he introduced the death penalty for the murder of priests (a financial penalty was not acceptable). He also introduced the death penalty for human sacrifice, for alliance with pagans, for those who plunder or destroy churches. Worse yet, adherence to pagan rites and refusal to be baptised were punishable with death, as was cremation of corpses and negligence in fasting.

We owe to Charlemagne the destruction of several major pagan sacred sites. At least one of them was equipped with an Irminsul (Irmin's pillar), a huge cult pole which was supposed to support the sky. Such pillars appear with some regularity in Eurasian belief, be at as trees of life or as symbols for the earth axis. Charlemagne had the largest Saxon Irminsul cut down in 772, amply demonstrating that he was not only a religious fanatic but also a cunning businessman. Around the pillar, so we learn, the Saxons had deposited considerable treasure in silver and gold. Charlemagne is also famous for inventing new methods of converting the heathens. Rather than dragging a screaming and fighting Saxon aristocrat to baptism, he found it more elegant to have the pagans beaten unconscious. In this state they could be baptised easily. Of course such a baptism did not show much efficiency once the pagans came to their senses again. However, if they complained it was acceptable to kill them, as after all, their eternal soul had been duly saved. When Charlemagne united his kingdom and destroyed the Saxon religion, the last pagan cultures of central Europe disappeared. His son, Ludwig the Pious, saw to it that the freshly converted people remained in line.

In the first version of *Helrunar*, I suggested that the violent conversion of the last pagans may have been the beginning of the witch hunt. The pagans, after all, were redefined as worshippers of idols, devils and demons. The Saxon vow of baptism (c.790) includes a line that the candidate had to forswear the worship of 'Donar, Wodan and Saxnot and all the demons who are their companions'. Nevertheless, it now seems to me that the former pagans were not simply redefined as 'witches' and 'devil worshippers'.

The idea that witches and sorcerers can harm other folk was widely popular in pre Christian pagan times. In Rome for instance, the attempt to murder a person by witchcraft was a punishable crime. The same goes for a number of pagan cultures of ancient Europe. Witches were not believed to be ecologically minded healers, cunning men or wise women, they were feared, despised and persecuted. Early Christianity introduced an entirely different idea. In their book, everything that happened was preordained by God. Witchcraft and sorcery as such were believed to be impossible, as without Gods will, no spell could ever function. This idea was highly attractive to superstitious Constantine, the first Roman emperor to accept Christianity. Mind you, privately he adhered to the cult of Sol Invictus, the invincible sun, which had, at the time, not been identified with Christ. Christianity insisted that believing in the power of magic equals doubting the omnipotence of God. Charlemagne agreed with this and proclaimed, in accord with the synod of Paderborn (785 and 786), that those who are blinded by the devil and believe in the manner of pagans that someone would be a nightwitch who devours other folk, and who burns this person or eats of the flesh, shall be punished by death. Good evidence that the nightwitch, presumably some sort of vampiric entity, was part of old Germanic belief. It also poses the question why anyone would bother to eat the flesh of this creature. A decree of 799 tells us that witches and sorcerers ought to be imprisoned, but their life shall not be harmed. An Irish council of the ninth century condemns all Christians who believe in the existence of witches and forces them to repent. This attitude comes certainly as a surprise when you look at the passionate witch hunt incited by church and state a few hundred years later.

Where it comes to the activities of pagans, we have to be thankful to all those enraged churchmen who wrote lengthy descriptions of them. The extensive list composed by Boniface is summarised in *Cauldron of the Gods*. An catalogue of similar length was given by Saint Eligius who raved against pagan superstitions in a lengthy sermon. Let's have a summary, the original amounts to five pages in Herrmann's *Deutsche Mythologie*. Eligius specifically prohibited divination, drawing lots, interpretation of signs, sorcery, prophecy, observation of omina (flight and song of birds, sneezing), belief in auspicious and dangerous days, belief in lunar cycles, new-year activities (making gifts, sacrifices, setting up a feast-table for spirits, watching the fire for signs, sitting on the roof to see visions), solstice fires (celebration, song, dances, processions), calling on demons or the names of Neptune, Orcus, Diana, Minerva and the Genius, May-time festivity, Thursday feasts, the 'day-feast of moths and mice' (?) and indeed all sacred days apart from Sunday, lighting lamps and swearing oaths at rocks, springs and trees, in groves and at the junction of three ways, wearing amulets or sacred texts around the neck, herb-spells, purification sacrifices, making fumes (incense?) go through hollow trees and earth-holes, invocation of Minerva and goddesses while spinning, wearing amber, calling on the moon during eclipses, being lazy at new moon, believing that the obsessed are influenced by the moon, worship and invocation of sun, moon, stars and the sky, belief in horoscopes and birth-hours, healing the sick with amulets, divination, trees, springs and worship of dead trees. Whew. He also ranted against the carnival feasts when bearded warriors walk around in girl's costume.

Among the Anglo-Saxons, we have some good accounts of pagan customs, as the church imposed penalties on them. The laws of 690 were less severe that the (later) laws of Charlemagne, the hardest being ten years of penance for major sacrifices to the demons. The text forbids eating, drinking and feasting at pagan shrines; sacrifices to the demons; consultation of diviners; self-made divination; augury; amulet-making; the practice of sorcery, enchantment and black magic; love- and abortion-potions; spells; sitting on a roof or in an oven for a cure; taking vows at trees, springs, stones, boundaries; going out in the hide of a cow, wearing the head of a horned beast or transforming into the likeness of a beast on New Year's day; changing the mind of a man by incantations to the devils; sending storms; observance of dreams; herb-spells; keeping Thursday sacred; shouting to aid the moon during an eclipse and fasting for the moon to effect a healing (Scott, 1979).

It would go too far to deal with the painful process of Christianization in all pagan cultures. In many countries, this process was often uneven. Between the first Christian emperor of Rome, paranoid and superstitious Constantine, and the thorough enforcement of the new religion was a hundred years of turmoil. Likewise, when you look into the works of Bede, you can observe that the conversion of the Anglo-Saxons was by no means easy. Saint Alban was executed by a pagan priest who also held the office of a judge. In Kent, Ethelbert was a good Christian

king, but his son Eadbald reintroduced pagan rites, married a former wife of his father and, so Bede tells us, 'had fits of insanity and was possessed by an evil spirit'. The east Saxons reverted to paganism after the death of King Sabert. Bede gives a touching episode where the three pagan sons of the king disrupt Mass and try to force bishop Mellitus to give them some white bread. When the bishop refuses to hand it to the unbelievers, the three drive him and his followers into exile.

King Edwin was converted by Paulinus. As he debated whether he should join the new religion, pagan chief priest Coifi supported this plan and told the assembly that the old gods are worthless. He argued that if the old gods were any good, they would surely have favoured himself, their most devout worshipper, before all men. As evidently the gods did not grant Coifi all success, honour and royal favour due to him, there is no truth in them. After due debate, the king agreed to favour the new religion. Coifi immediately asked for a spear and a stallion 'for hitherto it had not been lawful for the chief priest to carry arms or to ride anything but a mare'. He received the kings best stallion (evidently royal favour was easier to win under the new deity), rode to the temple like a madman, hurled the spear inside to desecrate the structure and ordered it burned down.

By contrast, king Redewald tried a policy of tolerance. He had a shrine set apart which housed both the Christian and the pagan gods, with a special section of the altar dedicated to human sacrifice. The church was not amused. In 640, King Earconbert of Kent began his forty year reign. He ordered and enforced the complete abandonment and destruction of idols and pagan shrines in his realm - the first English king to do so. In 665, plague swept large parts of Britain. The east Saxons, suffering badly from the devastation, lost faith in Christ. Their King Sighere ordered the rebuilding of pagan temples and the resumption of sacrifices to the pagan idols, until King Wulfhere sent Bishop Jarman to restore the faith.

Scandinavia was converted even later. The influence of the church was at first restricted to the courts of a number of high kings, many of whom only paid lip service to the new creed. Out in the country, worship of the old gods continued as ever. Scandinavia was christianised in stages. The conversion was gradual and by no means as violent as Charlemagne's efforts regarding the Saxons. Around 700, Willibrod visited the Danish king Agantyr. He did not manage to convert him, but received (or bought) thirty youths whom he took home to make good Christians. At the time, the Scandinavians were just becoming the scourge of Christian Europe. Ships full of armed warriors came raiding each summer, plundering coasts, sailing inland along the rivers, sacking cities or demanding tribute. They saw a bit of Christianity on those journeys, but it did not impress them much. In their eyes, Christ was a weak god who could not even protect his followers. It took a long time before the Christians learned how to defend themselves from Viking raids. This, eventually, changed the general estimation of the deity. Christ became more appealing when successful in war. It was, as usual, the nobility who encouraged the new religion. War is one aspect of the matter, but even more important is trade. All the early bishoprics were at rich trade-places and missionaries worked hard to establish Christian communities among the traders, who in turn controlled much of the wealth and cash-flow between Scandinavia and the continent. After raiding and plundering became increasingly difficult, the Scandinavian kings had to rely on trade to fill their coffers. Denmark assumed Christianity around 965, in the reign of Harald Blue-Tooth, after bishop Poppo had demonstrated his faith in Christ by walking around with a piece of red-hot iron in his hands. King Harald set up a rune stone showing a picture of Christ and an inscription that he had made the Danes Christian. Good show but not exactly true. Harald was an elected king, he had no absolute power, and if his nobles had not agreed, there would have been no conversion.

In Norway, Christianisation made a faltering start around 950 under King Athalsteinsfostri, who had grown up in Christian Britain. Southern Norway, close to the Christian south, co-operated, but the people of central Norway resisted violently. King Olaf Tryggvason almost crushed the pagan resistance around 995, then he died, and it wasn't until Olaf 'The Saintly' Haraldson that Christianity was imposed. Olaf fell at Stiklastad, fighting the pagans of central Norway, in 1030. The war may have had a religious reason, officially, but in reality, there were pagans and Christians fighting in both armies.

Though Olaf lost and died, pagan religion did not recover (Olsen in *Wikinger, Waräger, Normannen*). Sweden held out longer. We have few records on the matter, but it appears that the people around old Uppsala remained pagans until c.1100. There was considerable bloodshed on both sides. The people of Finland managed to evade Christianity until the 13th century, and the Sami (Lapps) made an even better effort and avoided Christianisation until the 17th century. What happened after the advent of Christ? People in far away districts continued much as before, happily mixing pagan customs with Christian dogma. The feasts continued, but their ceremonies changed. In the more civilised south, in cities and at important trading places, the church allied itself with the government and demanded strict obedience. Instead of common clan-law, written laws were introduced and the state became the protection of the individual. The power of the clans declined, elections became a thing of the past, church and king became more powerful. Women were shocked to find that under Christian law, they were supposed to be subservient to their husbands. This had not been the case in pagan times (Steinsland in *Wikinger, Waräger, Normannen*).

And finally Iceland. The frosty isle had no kings, its political leaders were chosen by democratic election, and consequently the church found it much harder to influence key-persons. There were some missionaries around, but they did not have much to say. Some Icelanders were Christians, but others had come to Iceland specifically to evade the conversion. It was even possible to believe in both Christ and the old gods, no matter how much this annoyed the church. Iceland is also the only country in Europe where Christianity was not inflicted on the population by fire and sword, but by a democratic election. In the year 1000, the All-Ting had a lengthy debate pro and contra the new cult. Tolerance was well and good, it was argued, but a single country should have a single faith. At the time, half of the population was pagan. When the pagans decided to offer two humans from each district as human sacrifices, the Christians declared they would dedicate the same number of men to the service of god. They successfully argued that the pagans offer the worst men to their gods (i.e. criminals and slaves) while the Christians offer the best of theirs to God (and dedicate them to a churchly life). So Iceland became Christian, a bishop seat was granted in 1056, but pagans were not persecuted. Their cult simply became unfashionable and gradually disappeared. We have to thank the Icelanders for this example of religious tolerance. In a more narrow-minded culture, the texts of the poetic and prose *Edda* would not have survived.

2 Where did the runes come from?

Rune type symbols can be found in most periods of history in almost any country. A few paleolithic examples have been given, here are some more.

Mas D'Azil: ᚦ᠆ᚤ ᚠ ᚭ ᛘ ᚷ

A bone from Rochbertier cave:

ᚷ ᚤ ᚤᛁ ᚤᚠᚴ ᚦ ᚤᚤ

And a more recent example of the late stone age: Alvâo, Portugal, c.4000 BC:

ᚷ ᛉᚤ ᚭᚴᚤᚤᚢ ᚤᚴᚺᛁᛁᚦᚠᚤ

The preference for this sort of 'easy to scratch' symbolism seems to be deeply ingrained in human consciousness. There is a considerable difference between an ideogram [an idea-picture] and an alphabetical letter, which expresses an abstract sound value. All early systems of writing began with ideograms and some, such as the Chinese, retain this ancient method.

The runes are both alphabetical script and ideograms—i.e. the various letters are also pictures. This a custom which may be found in some of the elder alphabets (such as Phoenician or Hebrew) but not in Roman script. All systems of writing began as a sacred and secret art which was usually restricted to members of the priesthood. Likewise, to the common people a written word was something magical, a device that contains an idea which cannot be deduced from the shape of the signs.

Very few samples of the early stages of

rune writing have survived. Those that have, as far as they can be deciphered, seem to deal with religious dedications. The oldest known rune texts come from the second century. There also exist a few proto-rune inscriptions which look like a mixture of the Alpine alphabets with the common twenty-four rune Futhorc, such as this inscription from 200BC:

ᛁᚢᛁᛁᚨ ᚥ ᛁᚥ ᛏ ᛁᛏᛋᚨᚤᛁᚲᚨᚻ

The text comes from a helmet found in Negau (Steiermark). It reads from right to left 'Harigasti Teiwa.' 'Teiwa/z' is one of the oldest Germanic deities and 'Harigast' (guest of the army) is one of the names of Wodan. The right to left direction is typical for early rune texts, though rather unusual for European alphabets. That rune type symbols have been in use for millennia is beyond question. Examples will be found in part III of this book, where each rune letter is shown complete with similar shapes from earlier periods. Probably these earlier shapes were ideograms, not letters. Just where did the use of the rune alphabet come from? This question has upset whole generations of scholars. There exist a number of more or less reasonable explanations which vary in accordance to the fashion of their time. I will try to give a short description of the more colourful theories, not to provide answers but to elaborate on the riddle. Create your own working theory if you feel like it and do not worry too much over the 'facts'- in a decade or two they will have changed, like everything we believe to know.

1. 'The Futhorc developed out of Roman Script.'

This is a classical theory which was fashionable during the last century. At that time nobody credited the German/Celtic people with any sort of culture, hence the stubborn belief that all civilized custom must have been imported. It was firmly believed that 'the light came from the east', meaning that the north Europeans were a herd of crude savages, barely domesticated by the refining influence of the Roman empire. Roman script and rune letters show a degree of similarity, such as ᚠ = F, ᚢ = U, ᚺ = H, ᚱ = R etc., which settled the matter for several decades. Then the flaws in the theory began to be noticed. Roman writing goes left to right while early rune texts move in the opposite direction. The order of the Roman alphabet is quite different, and there are several rune letters that have no parallels in Roman script. Also, the earliest rune writers were probably priests, and consequently on rather hostile terms with the Roman conquerors. It seems unlikely that they would have accepted a sacred system of writing from the occupation force.

Some authors continue to cling to a curious adventure story. They claim that the Cimmerian/Cimbri and Teutonic people learned the alphabet from the Romans or the Alpine tribes before getting massacred, and that the few survivors carried the new knowledge north on their hasty flight. On the whole, the 'Roman origin' theory is rarely voiced nowadays.

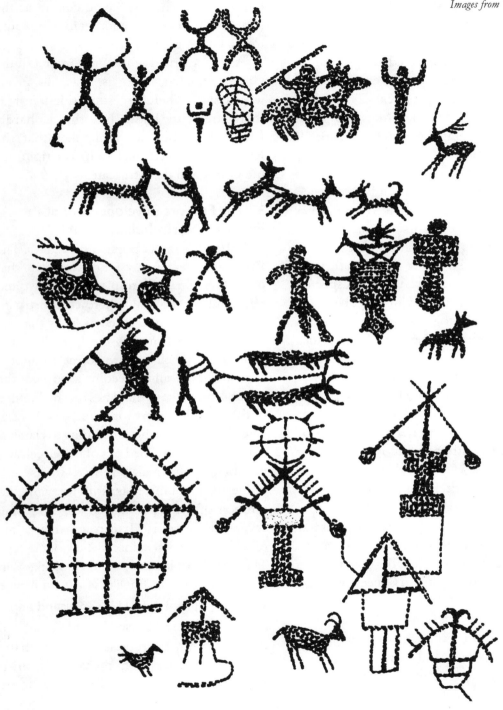

2. 'The Futhorc developed out of the Greek alphabet.'

This theory has several advantages. For one thing the Greek people did not appear to conquer but to trade, which makes cultural exchange much easier. Greek sailors had a trading colony at Massilia (Marseille) from where they operated a vast network of continental trade routes. They were on friendly terms with the Celts, who learned the art of coin making from them around 400BC, each tribe speedily developing its own distinct symbolism. Greek sailors travelled to the north sea and to Cornwall centuries before Rome acquired her characteristic megalomania. It has even been suspected that Homer's description of the Phaeacian islands parallels Plato's description of Atlantis (there is an amazing number of similarities well worth the research) Both of them thought to be in the North Sea, while the Kimbrians described by Homer (who lived in perpetual darkness in the far north of the world-ocean) are probably the Cimmerians/Cimbri of history. Other authors mention the meeting of Goth tribes with Greek traders at the Caspian sea (south Russia) around 600BC. There are some curious parallels in the mythology of the Celtic tribes and certain Greek cultures, which led Robert Graves to the assumption that the Celts did not originate in southern Germany but in Greece, and that their entire mythology can be explained in terms of Greek symbolism. We need not accept his historic fantasies to realize that the proto-Celtic tribes (Indo-Europeans) split up at some point of their migration, one branch becoming the Celtic culture at the springs of the Danube, another moving south to the Greek islands.

As to the origin of the Futhorc out of the Greek alphabet, there is, alas, no proof whatsoever. There are similarities, just as there are with Latin, but this is hardly remarkable when we remember that the Romans borrowed much of their script from the Greek and the Etruscans.

3. 'The Futhorc developed out of the Etruscan/North Italian script.'

This theory is rather popular nowadays. The Etruscans were a mysterious culture that came (presumably) from the near east and settled in northern Italy where it blended with the local population. It seems likely that the Etruscans came, just as the legends claim, from Troy. Their culture seems to appear around 700BC and speedily absorbed the cultural influence of the tribes that had settled in the southern Alps for some 6,000 years. The Etruscan alphabet, according to classical authors, was developed out of the Greek and its original Phoenician source. In its new homeland it got mixed up with the signs and symbols of the the Alpine tribes, producing several distinct north-Italian alphabets some of which come very close to Futhorc letters. The ᛝ rune for instance would look like V in Latin and Etruscan, but like ᚠ or ᚠ in Alpine script. ᚼ , ᚾ looks like H in Greek and Latin, like ᛒ , ᛒ in Etruscan and like ᚾ in Alpine letters. ᚱ, as a rune, is identical with the Alpine ᚱ but differs from the Greek, Roman and Etruscan ᛁ ᛁ ᛁ. These are some

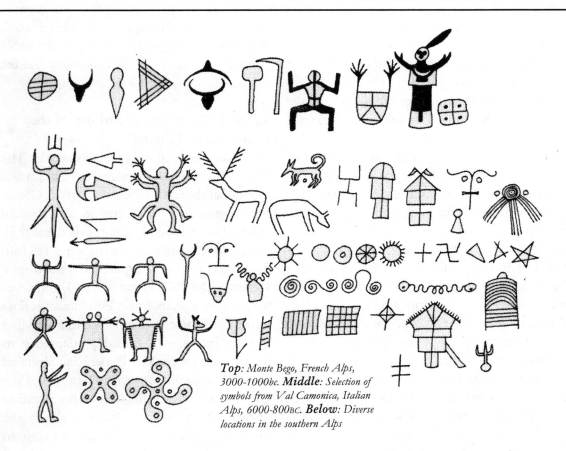

Top: *Monte Bego, French Alps, 3000-1000bc.* **Middle**: *Selection of symbols from Val Camonica, Italian Alps, 6000-800BC.* **Below**: *Diverse locations in the southern Alps*

similarities, nevertheless they do not explain everything.

It has long been thought that the Etruscans brought culture to their new country. This cultural chauvinism has long blinded scholars to the wealth of symbology left by the Alpine tribes. All over the Alps, but especially in their southern ranges, rock pictures have been found ranging from the nomadic periods when the Ice Age ceased (around 6000BC) over the development of agriculture, the taming of beasts to the confrontation with the Etruscans. In the famous Val Camonica [valley of the Camoni] in northern Italy, more than 30,000 rock engravings have been found. Similar numbers of carvings are known from Monte Bego and many other places. These pictures, symbols and ideograms cover the entire history of Alpine life up to the Roman occupation under Caesar Augustus when the local culture came to a swift and brutal end. Among these symbols are several rune-like forms which science considers 'badly written Etruscan in a local dialect,' meaning that they cannot read them. Here is an example I saw at Val Camonica:

The similarity of such signs with rune letters made certain Nazi scientists declare that the Camoni people were really 'migrated south Germans' in spite of the fact that they appear several millennia before the Germans did.

Where the Camoni and their fellow tribes originally came from is unknown. They traded with the people north and south of the Alps but on the whole they stayed in their secluded valley. Some examples of Alpine rock engravings are shown above. I give them not so much as traces for the rune signs but for the fun of it.

4. 'The Futhorc developed out of the Phoenician alphabet'

Here we really get into guesswork. The Phoenician alphabet, as was related by several classical authors, was the source of the Greek, not to mention the Etruscan and Roman script. The old Greek script, called linear-B, used syllables instead of letters and fell into disuse after some unspecified catastrophe around 1200BC. After several centuries without an alphabet, the Phoenician sailors introduced their twenty-two letter alphabet to the Greeks, who speedily adapted it to their sound range. The Phoenician alphabet has several similarities with Hebrew but the question of who influenced who is rather unclear. Very little is known about the Phoenicians, who were skillful enough to build the temple of Jerusalem for Solomon but left no literature. Their culture is connected with the sea. They were sailors and traders unequalled in courage, cunning and diplomacy. Where they came from is a difficult question. Apparently their culture began in Palestine where desert dwelling nomads got mixed with a sea faring culture coming from some unspecified 'northern country'. There are some theories that connect the migration raids of sea people with Plato's Atlantis tale. The sea-people were finally thrown back by Ramses III who got the essence of the Atlantis tale from prisoners of war. It is possible that these sea-people got mixed with the Canaanite nomads of the Lebanon, creating the Phoenician race. In this case it might well be that those sailors from 'beyond the pillars of Hercules' (Gibraltar) brought some of the letters of their alphabet with them. Some scholars make this idea the basis for a claim that certain 'northern proto-runes' were the origin for all European script. Of course there is little evidence to support such ideas. What is certain, however, is the fact that the Phoenicians, earlier than the Greek and Romans, travelled out of the Mediterranean, discovering wide parts of Africa and sailing to the north sea and to Britain for tin and amber.

5. 'The runes developed in the north of Europe.'

This theory was very popular among scholars who did not like Rome (and who could blame them?) Rune type symbols dating around 3,500BC have been found in northern Germany, and Scandinavian rock art from 2,500BC shows similar ornaments. Here are some samples:

These signs are symbols, not letters. Current thinking is that the elder twenty-four rune futhorc was introduced to Scandinavia around 400. Rune writing got popular at a much later date. The typical Scandinavian sixteen rune futhorc was developed during the Viking ages (800-1200) Now sixteen letters is a rather small number of sounds and certainly less efficient than the twenty-four rune system. The question 'why make an alphabet smaller?' has found no satisfactory answer so far. It should be noted that the Scandinavian sixteen rune 'younger futhorc' has a parallel in the sixteen rune futhorc of the St Gallen texts dated around 400.

6. 'The Futhorc came from Atlantis.'

Some scientists may shudder when they read something as fanciful as this. Rightly so, for very few occultists have bothered to read the original Atlantis texts (*Timaeus* & *Critias*), as

Top: Neolithic Germany;
Bottom: Scandinavian Rock Art

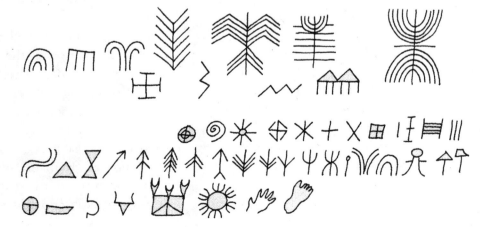

given by Plato. For a start you should forget all the surrealistic stuff written by Blavatsky, the Theosophists, Rudolf Steiner, Cayce, Fortune, Grant, not to mention all the fantasy authors. Their vision might speak of a psychic reality; probably not of a historical culture. The idea of a super-civilization with atomic power and space exploration has nothing to do with Plato's tale, which is largely ethnological.

Let's look at some evidence. Around 4,500BC the 'megalith' (big stone) culture began to spread all over Europe's coasts, leaving an overwhelming legacy of huge stone monuments, such as the dolmen of Morbihan, the stone avenues of Carnac, the barrows in Ireland and the stone circles of Stonehenge. They left hundreds of dolmens and barrow graves in northern Germany, Ring wall structures that were old when the first Celtic tribes stumbled upon them, and any amount of Menhirs (standing stones) on all Atlantic coasts as well as most coasts of the Mediterranean, and older than the Egyptian legacy. That megalith culture was spread over the sea is clear enough, where it came from is not. We do not even know whether they were Indo-Europeans.

Try to imagine how much trade, religious conversion, scientific knowledge and military might are required to make so many different people and cultures raise very similar stone sanctuaries. If we imagine some advanced island culture behind these developments this might answer some difficult questions. Plato's 'Atlanteans' fit this idea remarkably well. Their island 'Abalus', 'Basileia' may well be the source for the tale of Avalon, Lyonesse and Ys, to mention just a few sunken islands of mythology. Usually such islands get drowned 'for the sins of their priests.' Most north sea countries have tales of the enchanted glass castle ('glass' was an old word for 'amber') on a magick island. It is interesting to note that this island is usually described as an accursed place of great evil, which contrasts nicely with all the etheric spirituality attributed to Atlantis by esoteric idealists of the Zimmer-Bradley variety.

While it seems possible that Plato's Atlantis was an island on the Danish coast we need not insist that it was the only one of its kind. As to the origin of the runes in this place, or with the megalith culture, there is very little evidence. Whether the megalith people carved runes is hard to determine. I have been told that there are some rune-like signs in some Spanish dolmens. But in Brittany I only came upon symbols composed of curved lines. Below are some samples, dated between 4,000BC and 2,000BC

7. 'The runes developed out of the Vinca script.'

Where past generation of scholars thought of the Sumerian script as the oldest human writing extant, modern researches and new methods of dating have come to class the little known Vinca script as the oldest human writing known. The Vinca culture flourished c.5300 and 3500BC in the Balkans, reaching from Hungary, Rumania and the former Yugoslavia to the northern rim of Greece. Vinca, where the inscriptions were discovered, is about 14km from Belgrade. As far as we know, the Vinca script consisted of more than 200 signs, which makes it likely that it was based on syllables not letters. The signs were scratched into clay tablets. Apparently it was a sacred script, as all known inscription come from cult places and graves, far away from settlements, where not a single inscription was found. The Vinca people, as is believed today, were a cattle breeding farmer culture of non Indo-european origin.Some of their statuettes have been found, depicting either bulls or abstract female figures with wide hips. Male figures have not been found so far, indicating that the Vinca people were possibly matricentric. The signs of their script frequently resemble runes, which is hardly surprising when we consider how many signs Vinca script consisted of. This culture ended around 3500BC - there is much speculation whether they were crushed by marauding Indo-European tribes or scattered by some natural catastrophe - leaving the Balkans in a state of an-alphabetism. It might be interesting to consider that about a thousand years later, the earliest Cretan script (Linear A) appeared. Its sixty odd signs show some similarity with the Vinca script, so possibly some of the knowledge passed south. Surprisingly, for a (supposed) non Indo-European culture, Vinca signs included the swastika and the wolf hook.

Images in a
Breton
dolmen

WELL...
WHAT
DO YOU
BELIEVE ?

Scandinavian Rock Art c.2,500BC, rune signs are a more recent addition

3 The futhorc row

Futhorc is the common name for the rune alphabets. The word is made up out of the sounds of the first six rune signs: Fehu (ᚠ) Uruz (ᚢ) Thurisaz (ᚦ) Ansuz (ᚨ) Raido (ᚱ) Kenaz (ᚲ). These six runes are the only ones which occur in the same order in all rune alphabets. There have been several distinct systems of rune writing in Europe. According to scholarly belief, the original futhorc was invented north of the Alps in the first centuries A.D. This system called the 'common futhorc' consisted of twenty-four runes. As it spread through Europe, it was repeatedly modified. In Britain it was extended into up to thirty-three runes, in Scandinavia it was simplified to sixteen.

Academics like to treat the runes simply as a system of writing, and forget the sacred and magical meaning of the Futhorc. How many sound symbols are needed for a functional alphabet? Twenty-four symbols can easily describe most combinations of sounds. Alphabets with more than thirty characters include so many similar sounds that we find it hard to differentiate them nowadays. In a system of sixteen letters we have to assign more than one sound to each rune, such as Fehu = F,V (ᚠ), Ansuz = A, O (ᚨ), Beorc = B/P (ᛒ). Though inscriptions in such a system can still be deciphered, the text is far from easy reading.

In divination how many symbols are needed to describe the universe? As each rune corresponds to a specific type of energy/consciousness we may assume that the runes as a whole express the totality of the world. This is essential if we want to use them for divination. We have to be able to ask all questions and to receive all possible answers. How many possible answers are needed for a complete description of the world? The Chinese system of the I-Ching uses two forces (0 + 1), three levels (earth, man, heaven), eight 'atmospheric descriptions' (the Pa Qua or trigrams) and through their combination, sixty-four images. The tarot uses twenty-two trump cards and fifty-six lesser cards. The Hebrew Qabalah applies ten basic numbers/realities and twenty-two paths between them, which correspond to the tarot trumps. Geomantic divination deals with two states of energy and creates sixteen images from them. The sixteen is equally popular in the West African kauri shell oracle, which yields a fantastic range of 16 x 16 x 16 answers. Sixteen energy currents are classified in the tantrik system of the kalas (colours/energies/rays), if we double this number we get the thirty-two facets of the Qabalistic tree of life, and doubling these brings us to the 64 images of the I-Ching.

If the number were too small, we will have to overload the possible meanings in each symbol. This will reduce the precision of the answer. If the number is too great the system gets too complicated and the practitioner is required to carry around a small library! If we look at the sixteen rune futhorc systems we usually encounter theories claiming that the sixteen rune system is an adaptation of the twenty-four rune futhorc. This is true insofar as the sixteen rune row became popular in Scandinavia around the year 800, i.e. at a time when Christian power politics were busily exterminating rune writing in central Europe.

Now, why would a functional system of writing be reduced to a far less efficient one, if not for the reasons of magick and religion? The Scandinavian reduction is meaningless unless we emphasize the sacred meaning of each sign, and consider the alphabetical use as a side effect.

Things get even more complicated when we consider that the Scandinavian system was by no means the first futhorc to use sixteen signs. The monastery library of St Gallen, near Bodensee, Switzerland, contains a few manuscripts *Abecedarium Nordmannicum*, with mnemonic rune verse dating around 400, which makes them at least three hundred years older than those of Scandinavia. The oldest of the manuscripts features a system of sixteen runes and comes from the country near Fulda, Hessen. As the texts are little more than a mysterious list for memorization they never attained the popularity of the English, Norse and Icelandic rune poems.

ᚠ FEU FROMA (FIRST)
ᚢ UR ANMOT (?)
ᚦ THURS THRÍ STABA (THREE STAFFS)
ᚨ OS OBANA (UPMOST)
ᚱ RAT RÍNNÍT (RUNS)
ᚲ CAN CLÍUVÍT (CLEAVES)
ᚺ HAGAL HARDO (HARD)
ᚾ NAUT NAGAL (NAIL)
ᛁ IS ÍAR
ᛋ SOL SKÍNÍT (SHÍNES)
ᛏ TÍU B BIRKA BÍVÍT (TREMBLE, QUIVER)
ᛚ LAGU LEOHTO (LIGHT)
ᛗ MANNA MÍDDÍ (MIDDLE)
ᛉ YR AL (ALL)

OLDER VERSION, 400-500 a.?.

ᚠ FEU FORMAN (FIRST)
ᚢ UR AFTER
ᚦ THURÍS THRÍTTEN STABU (THREE STAFFS)
ᚨ OS IS THEMO OBORO (HIGHEST IN HEAVEN)
ᚱ RAD RÍTAN ENDOST (WRITTEN AT THE END)
ᚲ CHAON CLÍUT THANNE (GAPES/ADHERES TO)
ᚺ HAGAL HABET (HAS) ᚾ NAUT
ᛁ IS ÍAR ENDÍ (AND) ᛋ SOL
ᛏ TÍU B BRÍCA ENDÍ (AND) ᛗ MAN MÍDDÍ (MIDDLE)
ᛚ LAGU THE LEOHTO (THE LIGHT)
ᛉ YR AL BÍHABET (EMBRACES ALL)

NEW VERSION, 800-900 a.?.

ᚠ ᚢ ᚦ ᚨ ᚱ ᚲ

ᚺ ᚾ ᛁ ᛋ

ᛏ ᛒ ᛚ ᛗ ᛉ

Here we have two samples of a sixteen rune futhorc independent of the Scandinavian systems. These St Gallen alphabets show a lot of independence from the common twenty-four rune systems. Indeed they seem to be more closely related to those of Scandinavian, if we consider the shape of the runes. It seems hard to tell which of the systems was the root of the other.

The old or 'common' futhorc consists of 24 runes which are grouped in three 'families' or 'eights' (ON Aettir). Traditionally, the three Aettir are attributed to particular deities. The first aettir, starting with ᚠ, is connected with Frey and Freya, deities of life, growth, joy and abundance. The second aettir, which begins with ᚺ or ᚾ is attributed to Wodan in his aspect as 'Har' (the high) or 'Hödr' (the one with the hat/hood). Another valid link connects H with Helja, the veiled one of the underworld, or with the Hyndla, 'the wolfish one'. The second aettir is often believed to relate to shamanism and outdoor activity - notice the many nature phenomena, such as hail, snow, ice, fields, swamp, forest etc., in the series. Wodan as Hödr is a wanderer.

The third aettir begins with the ᛏ rune, which is attributed to the primal bisexual god Tiu, Tir, Twisto. There are several possible interpretations of the three aettir. One theory claims that the first aettir describes Asgard (the divine or ideal world), the second Midgard (the human or middle world) and the third describes Utgard (the primal or outer world). Another interesting theory claims that there is a circles of the year hidden in the Futhorc. If we project the three aettir as a circle, this produces interesting results (see illustration).

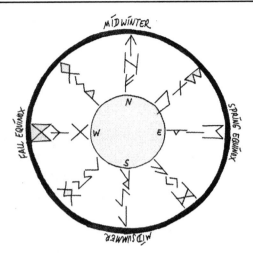

ONE POSSIBLE ARRANGEMENT OF
THE RUNES AS A 'WHEEL OF THE SEASONS'

Most of these examples come from the excellent *Runes* by R.W.V. Elliott. If you feel confused by the range of these rune alphabets, you should study the variations that may arise in a single district. The following table shows variations in rune writing between the years 900 - 1000AD in the district of Uppland, Sweden.

The only rune that has no variations is Isa. It should be emphasized that the rune variations listed above come mainly from memorial stones, and have little if no connection to the older forms of rune magick. By 800 rune writing had become a popular fashion in Scandinavia. The same diffusion that makes the rune signs so difficult to read happened to the names and sound values of each rune. We encounter Fehu (ᚠ) as 'feu' 'fehu' or 'fa' on the continent, in England the name was recorded as 'feoh', in Scandinavia as 'fehu', 'feu' or 'fe'. The local variations make the etymology of each rune name a difficult affair, especially when we consider that there may have been countless variations we do not know about. Obviously we cannot afford to insist dogmatically on one specific name or mode of writing. What, then, is the proper name of each rune, and by what word should its energy be roused? To search for the correct name is a waste of time and effort. All variations are right insofar as they express variations of the proper idea. Proficiency comes if you concentrate on the sound itself and practice all variations that come into your mind. With Fehu you might experiment with something like, 'fifefafofufeofaefuo..', i.e. you focus on the 'f' sound and allow a spontaneous flow of sound variations to grow around it. As rune magick is not a ready made system but the revival of a somewhat mysterious tradition (rune = mystery) feel free to make our own rules and experiment. 'Chaos song' exercises are vital for rune magick. The song/tune/chant that 'comes-to-be' should be powerful and rhythmic, playful and passionate as you weave sounds with no concern for meaning. Free improvisation is important exercise, especially for introverted or tongue-tied practitioners.

I would also like to mention the variety of futhorc most popular in Germany nowadays. The system consists of eighteen runes, namely:

Sometimes the nineteenth rune Othila (ᛟ) is integrated as a side aspect of Ansuz (ᚨ). This system lacks any historical verification. Indeed, we find that the symbolism repeats itself on occasion, as in the ᛜ and ᛄ runes, which are, historically speaking the same rune. The same sort of rudimentary thinking may be observed in the attempt to classify ᛉ as the 'male principle, reaching for the height' while ᛦ is supposed to be 'the rune of women, earth-bound and demonic.'

ᛤ, as a variation of ᛟ is popular folk sign. It may be considered a 'reduced swastika' resembling the ancient glyph of the 'wolf hook' which graced some peasant houses. The middle line, as some say, is meant to break the power of the wolf. The sign has a history of at least six thousand years and was quite popular in the megalith religion. Many of the rune names of the eighteen-rune system show considerable divergence from any historic rune names.

At the turn of the century, the occult ideologue Guido List suffered an eye disease that left him blind for several months. During this time, List 'received' a vision of the 'true

Some Futhorc Alphabets

ᚠᚢᚦᚩᚱᚳᚷᚹᚻᚾᛁᛄᛇᛈᛉᛋᛏᛒᛖᛗᛝᛞ
F U TH O R C G W H N I J E P X S T B E NG D

ᛚᛗᛟᚪᚫᛦ ᛠ
L M OE A AE y EA
SCRAMASAX SWORD, THAMES, 700-800

ᚠᚢᚦᚩᚱᚳᚷᚹᚻᚾᛁᛄᛇᛈᛉᛋᛏᛒᛖᛗᛚ
F U TH O R C G W H N I J E,C P X S T B E M L

ᛝᛞ ᛟᚪᚫᛠᛦ
NG D OE A AE EA y
VIENNA, AROUND 800

ᚠᚢᚦᚩᚱᚳᚷᚹᚻᚾᛁᛄᛇᛈᛉᛋᛏᛒᛖᛗ
F U TH O R C G W H N I J E/C P X S T B E M

ᛚᛝᛟᛞᚪᚫᛦ ᛠ ᛡ ᛣ ᛢ ᛥ
L NG OE D A AE y EA io K G Q ST
NORTHUMBRIA, ca. 800

ᚠᚢᚦᚩᚱᚳᚷᚹ ᚻᚾᛁᛄᛖᚩ ᛈᛉᛋ ᛏᛒᛖ
F U TH O R C G W H N I J EO P X S T B E

ᛗᛚᛝ ᛟᛞᚪᚫᛦ ᛡᛠᛢᛣᛥᚷ
M L NG OE D A AE y io EA Q K ST G
CODE OTHO BX
OLD ENGLISH RUNE POEM
ca. 900

ᚠᚢᚦᚭᚱᚴᚼᚾᛁᛅᛋᛏᛒᛘᛚᛦ
F U TH AO R CH N I A S T B M L R/z
ZEALAND, DENMARK, ca. 900

ᚠᚢᚦᚭᚱᛋ�†ᛁᛅᛋᛏᛒᛘᛚᚱ
F U TH A R CH N I A S T B M L R
ÖSTERGOTLAND, SWEDEN, 900-1000

ᚠᚢᚦᚮᚱᚴᚼᚾᛁᛅᚢᛛᛏᛒᛦᛚ
F U TH O R K H N I J y S T B M L
OLD NORSE RUNES, NORWAY

ᚠᚢᚦᚮᚱᚴᚼᚾᛁᛅᚢᛛᛒᛦᛚ
F U TH O R K H N I J y/R S T B M L
ORKNEY ISLANDS

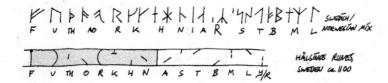

Top: Swedish/Norwegian mix
Bottom: Halsinge runes, Sweden ca.1100

and original runes', eighteen of them, together with appropriate new names. Considering these word roots as the original ancient language of the 'true Aryan', Guido List proceeded to take the German language apart, revealing all sorts of surprising new insights. After some surgery, List recovered his sight and became one the founders of National Socialism. Being a prolific writer, List provided dozens of huge volumes on Aryan speech, symbols, heraldry, customs and even Qabalah (he firmly believed the Qabalah to be a German mystical system stolen and abused by 'fiendish' Jews!). And if you bother to work your way through mountains of useless information, you may find the basic notions of the Nazi movement buried there. By 1904, Guido List had already predicted 'the solution of the Jewish question', i.e. slavery and homicide, decades before anyone heard of the Nazi movement. Later, List added a noble 'von' to his name and became one of the leaders of the notorious Thule Society.

After the war the system was 'rediscovered' by Karl Spiessberger, also known as 'Fr. Eratus' of the Fraternitas∴Saturni∴ Spiessberger tried to get the Nazi influence out of the system but failed miserably, as most of his sources were leading Nazi occultists. Spiessberger is perhaps the most popular author on runes in Germany today and directly responsible for the amazing confusion in rune symbolism that is common hereabouts. After he got thrown out Fraternitas Saturni he went the usual way, namely selling dubious information in costly workshops. Now I would not claim that an eighteen-rune system is useless. Some have inflicted this system on the rune song of the *Edda*, which has eighteen verses, and though I cannot quite agree with this interpretation, there are plenty of modern pagans who like it. Anyway, it gives a touch of eldritch mystery to an entirely modern artificial system.

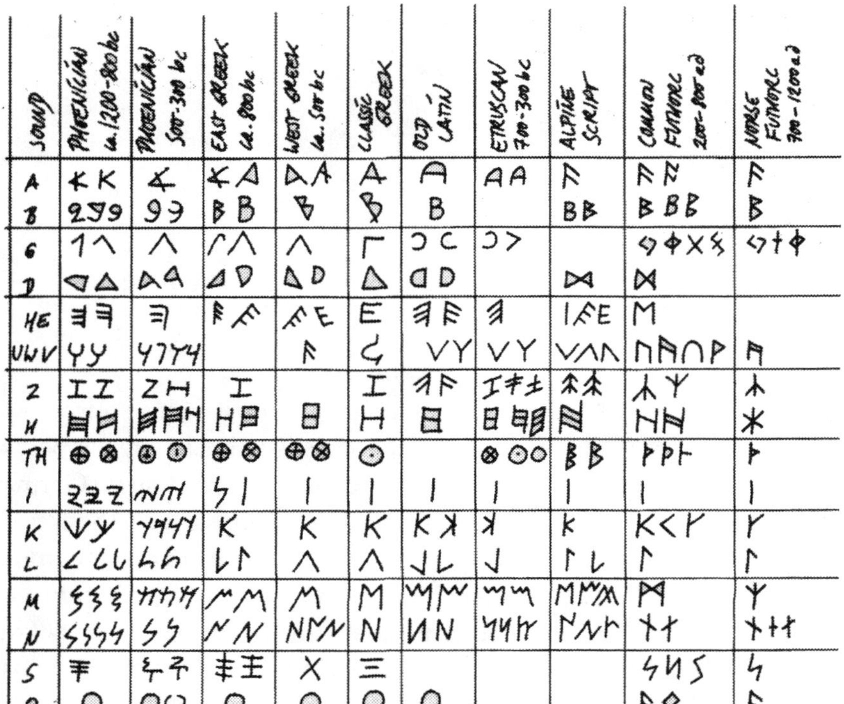

SOUND	PHOENICIAN (a.1200-800 bc)	PHOENICIAN 500-300 bc	EAST GREEK (a.800 bc)	WEST GREEK (a.500 bc)	CLASSIC GREEK	OLD LATIN	ETRUSCAN 700-300 bc	ALPINE SCRIPT	COMMON FUTHORC 200-800 ad	NORSE FUTHORC 700-1200 ad
A	ΚΚ	�ኀ	ΚΔ	ΔΑ	Α	Α	ΑΑ	⊬	⊬ⲃ	⊬
B	�
99	99	ΒΒ	Β	Β	Β		ΒΒ	ΒΒΒ	Β
G	↑∧	∧	↜∧	∧	Γ	ϽC	⊃>		◇ΦΧ◇	◇⇂Φ
D	◁△	△◁	△D	△D	△	⊏D		⋈	⋈	
HE	∃∃	∃	⊬⊬	⊬Ε	Ε	∃∃	⅃	ΙⅎΕ	Μ	
UVW	ΥΥ	⅄ⅅ⅄Υ		⋌	Ͼ		∨Υ	∨∧∧	∏∩∪Ρ	⊓
Z	ΙΙ	ΖΗ	Ι		Ι	⅂⊬	Ι⊤⊥	⋏⋏	⋏Υ	⋏
H	∄∄	∄∄∄	ΗΗ	⊟	ΙΗ	⊟	⊟⊟	⋙	⋈⋈	✳
TH	⊕⊕	⊕⊕	⊕⊗	⊕⊗	⊙		⊗ΟΟ	ΒΒ	⊳⊳⊢	⊳
I	⌇⌇⌇	⋏⋏⋏	⅂Ι	Ι	Ι	Ι	Ι	Ι	Ι	Ι
K	∨Υ	Υ𝟋Υ	Κ	Κ	Κ	ΚΚ	Κ	Κ	Κ◁Υ	Υ
L	∠⌐⌐	⌐⌐Ч	⌐⊦	∧	∧	⌐⌐	⅃	⌐⌐	Ρ	Ρ
M	⌇⌇⌇	⋀⋀⋀⋀	⋀⋀	⋀	Μ	⋀⋀⋀⋀	⋀⋀	⋀⋀⋀⋀	⋈	Υ
N	⌇⌇⌇⌇	⌇⌇	⋏⋏	⋏⋏⋏	Ν	⋃⋀	⋀⋀⊬	⋏∧⊬	⊬⊬	⊬⊬⊬
S	⊤	⊋⊋	⫶⫶	Χ	⩧				⊊⊓⊊	⊊
O	○	ΟΟ	Ο	Ο	Ο	Ο			⊬⊗	⊬
P	⌐⌐⌐	⌐	⌐⌐	⌐∏◁	⌐	⋏⊬	⅃	Β	⊊	
TS	⌇⌇	⌇⌇⌇			⋒⋍				⋎	⋏
Q	⊖⊖⊖	⊖⊖	⊖		⊊	⊖	⊖			
R	⊖⊖⊖	⊖⊖⊖	⊳⊳D	⊳⊳⊳	⊳	⊖⊳	◁	Ꭱ	ꓤꓤꓤ	ꓤ
SH	⫝⫝	⫝∨⫝	⊊⊋⊋	⊊⊋⊋	⊊	⊊	⊋	⊊⊋⊋	⊊⊓⊊	⊊
T	+Χ	⌐⊓⊳	⊤⋏	⊤	⊤	⊤	+Υ	Χ⋏	⋏⋏	⋏
F			⊖Φ	Φ	Φ	F	8	F	⊬⊳	⊬
ŘS							9		Υ	
Ç							ꝺ		⌡	
O/W	⅄⌐	∨	∨Υ	ΥⅣ∨	Υ				∏Ρ	
KS			Χ+	∨Υ	Χ					
PS			⅄Υ		Υ					
Ō			Ω		Ω			◇◇	⊬⊗	
Ē									⌡	
NG									Χ◇☐	

The Common Old Germanic Futhark Scripts

F U TH A R K G W H N I J P É Z S T B E

M L NG D O

THE KYLVER SCRIPT
24 RUNES

F U TH A R K G W H N I J É P T B E

M L Z O D

THE GRUMPAN SCRIPT
22 RUNES

F U TH A R K G W H N I J É P Z S

T E M

THE BREZA SCRIPT
19 RUNES

F U TH A R K G W H N I J É P Z S

T B E M L NG O

THE VADSTENA SCRIPT
23 RUNES

F U TH A R K G W H N I J É P

Z S T B E M

THE CHARNAY SCRIPT
20 RUNES

4 Magical rune inscriptions

Runes can be used for many purposes. While among the early inscriptions spell-crafting and talismanic runing are not unusual, the later inscriptions, especially in the Viking age, were often carved for practical, everyday purposes. By the time runes became really popular among the Vikings, they have almost ceased to be used on the continent. Also, the secret knowledge of writing had passed from priests to well-educated folk, then to traders, and soon enough all sorts of inscriptions were being made. Some of these still carried an aura of mystery. To the non-literate, all writing carries a touch of the occult, and possibly the people who had their name inscribed on some tool or ornament thought that this would bring good luck. This is the simplest possible use of runes: to indicate the ownership of some item. Some people simply inscribed a name on an object. This can be a bit confusing as we do not always know whether that name is of the object or the name of its owner. In the pagan north, people liked to name their weapons and believed that the item acquires a soul and a certain individuality. Just think of the ritual sword found in the river Thames. It bore the name 'scramasax' and showed a complete futhark on its blade, the runes being inlaid with silver, copper and bronze. Ownership could also be indicated by longer inscriptions. 'Domnall seal-head is owner of this sword' (leather strap with bronze ornament, Greenmouth, Ireland, c.1100) is a good example. Or the inscription could name the maker of the item: 'Thorfast made a good comb' (comb made of deer-horn, Lincoln, Britain, 10th century) is almost like a trademark.

Some craftspeople were certainly proud enough to sign their goods.

A fascinating early rune inscription comes from the tomb of a noble Alamannic lady of the 6th century, unearthed in Neudingen, Baden-Württemberg. The tomb contained a highly sophisticated loom, obviously an expensive item. One fragment of the loom bears an inscription that can be translated as 'Love Imuba Hamale Blithguth written' (for the original, see *Seidways*). This means that Hamale gave this loom as a present to a lady called Imuba, and that a woman called Blithguth runed (inscribed) the item. This is unique evidence. The dedication commemorates an act of giving. We do not know the occasion, but it must have been important. Good looms were expensive and people didn't just give each other items of furniture without a good reason. It shows that in the 6th century, rune writing was not restricted to males. Blithguth could read and write in a period when very few people could, and the act of *runing* was important enough that her name was included in the inscription. Here we are not exactly in the realm of profane inscriptions; the act of runing has a distinct magical quality (Fingerlin, 1981). The inscription 'leub' (love, beloved) also appears on a fibula from a female burial in Eggers, Rheinland-Pfalz.

An image of a deer or capricorn was discovered in the cave 'Kleines Schulerloch' near Altessing, close to the Danube in south east Germany, in 1937. It was briefly celebrated as the only example of German Ice-age art. However, a rune inscription right next to it

makes the image a bit more recent. The text is in elder futharc runes and reads 'birg:leu.b:seabrade'. It may or may not have anything to do with love (leub?) (Adam, 1978).

Inscriptions in the elder futhorc appear in several female graves. The fibula of Soest, Germany, 6th century, reads: 'rada dratha', both are female names, one of them probably the giver, the other the receiver of the ornament. A rune-cross gives the additional name Atano in code, this may be the writer of the inscription. The fibula of Friedberg, Hessen, 5-6th century, has the inscription 'thuruthhild'. It was found in a female grave, the name being a form of the female name Thrudhild, meaning 'strength of battle'. Was it the name of the deceased, the name of the brooch or the power that was supposed to reside in the item? Another female burial, Alamannic, early 7th century, Bülach, provides a fibula inscribed 'frifridil du ftmik' and two L runes, possibly for prosperity. The text is uncertain. Krause proposes 'fri-fridil (gives the fibula). You embrace (take) me.'

Let's take a look at a few inscriptions. We shall start with inscriptions in the elder futhark. My primary sources are Krause, Düwel and Arntz. Occasionally, I give them in transcribed form. Sometimes the letter R is written as a capital letter. This is to indicate that the rune in question is not the usual raido/rad but the rune eohl/algiz which may have been pronounced like an R or like Z or TZ, if only the experts could agree.

'Haduwolf set three staves; F F F'
Stone of Gummarp, Sweden, c.700.

Here the F rune is repeated thrice to mark a special and secret meaning or event. This is an indication that runes were not just used as letters. In several magical inscriptions, single rune signs are given for their symbolic value. By carving a single rune, an idea could be communicated. This custom appears in the *Edda* (*Sigrdrifumal*, 6-7) where you can read of victory runes that were carved into swords while calling on Tyr. Such inscriptions occasionally survived, they usually consist simply of the T rune. The valkyrie Sigrdrifa also mentions that doom can be averted by carving (or drawing) an N rune (need, necessity) on a nail. Many more examples appear in the subsequent verses which I won't quote, do yourself a favour and read it for yourself. It may be proposed that the three F runes refer to wealth, cattle and property, surely attractive to anyone in an agrarian society, but as we don't know, we can't be sure. What's your guess? If you want to understand the runes, you had better go slowly. Don't skim over the pages. Stop, pause, consider. You'll progress faster when you give yourself time.

Some rune inscriptions are exceptionally short. Others make use of certain words of power. There are several magical words on record, sadly, we cannot be entirely sure about their meaning. The best known is the word 'ALU'. Alu has seen a lot of interpretations. One claims that it is related to the concept 'all', but this is hard to prove. More certain is

'sanctuary, under divine protection'. This interpretation is founded on the fact that the word was sometimes used to deter evildoers. However, it could also mean 'magic'or 'sorcery'. We find the closest counterparts in other languages. The word 'ale' seems related, and the word 'hallucination', both of them referring to changes of awareness. The Hittite language preserves the word 'aluwanzatar', meaning 'sorcerer', and 'alwanzahh', 'to enchant'. Greek 'aluein' is 'to be beside oneself' and LITH: 'aliótis' is 'to rage, to do crazy things'.

ALU is often related to magical practice. It appears on several bracteats (LAT: bractea: thin disk), such as those from Slangerup and Kläggerod. Bracteats are beautiful thin disks of metal that generally bear a picture and sometimes an inscription. They were worn as ornaments or talismans. On the arrow shaft of Nydam alu appears as lua. When the *Sigrdrifumal*, 7, mentions ale-runes (olrúnar) the reference is not necessarily to alcoholic mysteries but to ALU runes, giving protection and magical skill. Another favourite term is the word AUJA which may mean 'hail' or 'blessing'. It appears on the bracteat of Skodborg:

'auja alawin auja alawin auja alawin J alawid'
'hail Alawin, hail Alawin, hail Alawin, J (good year) Alawid'.

A bracteat from Seeland shows a head, horse and spear. Next to the runes is a tree-rune: from the central stem, three branches point downwards on both sides. It reads:

'hariuhahaitika farauisa gibuauja ttt'
'Hariuha am I called, who knows dangerous (things). I give blessing.'

A spear shaft from Kragehul, Fynn, has the inscription:

'gibu auja'
'Give good luck'.

Words like EHWU, EHWE, AWE and AWA are worth contemplating. Variations occur in Denmark, Norway and Gotland. The word was sometimes spelled with the two runes E and H in combination (bound runes). It offers evidence that not all people who wrote it could actually read: when you write the runes E and H close together, you get a combination that can be confused with the runes L, T and I. This happened occasionally. The sacred term Eh, Ehwu etc. may go back to the Indo-European root *aiw-, meaning 'eternity, long duration, life-force'; the word is the root of our word 'aeon'. These primal beginnings were mutated among several languages.

In the Germanic culture, they appear prominently in the names of some priests, the éwart, i.e. the custodian of eternal law (éwa), the eosago and the asega, the speakers of eternal law (OHG: é). These priests had juridical functions, they were the keepers of the ancient legal lore, the 'eternal', god-given laws of antiquity. In those days, the sacral order of the world was also the foundation of its legislation; religion and state were not separate. The term also appears among some Celts. The Celto-Iberian inscription of Botoritta is a beautiful example (see *Cauldron of the Gods*). This text deals with the regulations and duties connected with land owned by a couple of obscure gods and used for diverse purposes by several communities. The inscription reads like a dry statement of obligations, fees and taxes, but the occasion when it was dedicated, in the presence of numerous witnesses (who signed the reverse side), was an 'aiuisás', a sacred cult feast.

However, there is also another option. The Germanic word for horse is ehwa. It is possible that the term connects with horses, or more specifically, sacred horses. Tacitus recorded a few details on horse cults. To some of his Germani, the horse was considered closer to the gods than the priesthood. This was more than just a veneration of a powerful (and beautiful) animal with very little brain. We encounter sacred horses and horse deities among some Celtic people, best known being Eqona/Epona, the goddess of horses, riding, journeys and the patroness of the Roman cavalry. She may have started as a popular goddess in the Rhineland, but as soon as the Rhineland Celts joined the legions, she got around all over the empire, and was soon venerated by elite riders from all parts of the classical world. Arguably she was more popular in the legions than she had ever been in her homeland. The other is the British Rhiannon, who is sometimes identified with Epona, and called a goddess, in spite of the fact that we cannot prove the first point and find her as a supernatural lady, but not as a goddess in medieval lore (*Mabinogi* 1 & 3).

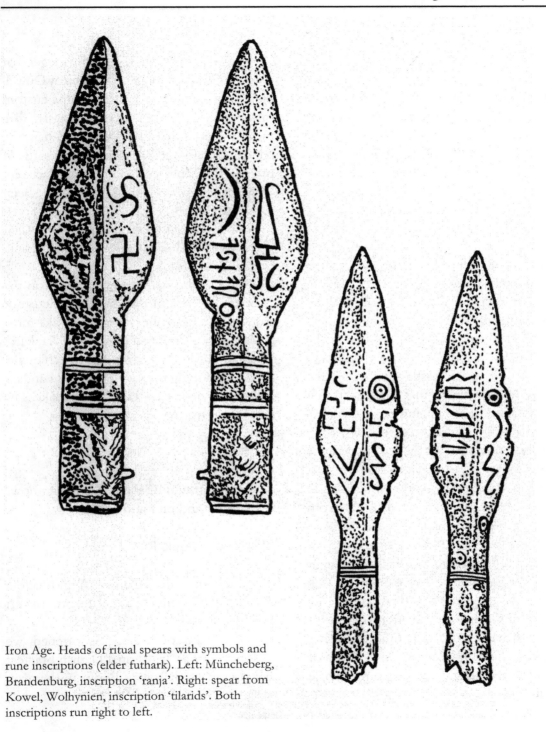

Iron Age. Heads of ritual spears with symbols and rune inscriptions (elder futhark). Left: Müncheberg, Brandenburg, inscription 'ranja'. Right: spear from Kowel, Wolhynien, inscription 'tilarids'. Both inscriptions run right to left.

Among the Germani, horses enjoyed a similar esteem. They were beautiful, a perfect dedication to the gods, and a popular meal for sacrificial feasts. This may be in contrast to the Celts of northern Gaul, who often sacrificed horses but rarely ate them during ritual (unlike in daily life, when they did). The *Eddas* mention several horses. Best known is Odin's eight legged horse Sleipnir. What do you make of the eight legs? A spider? Or a coffin and four bearers, as Fritz Leiber suggested so fittingly?

Another word with sacral meaning is laukaR. This is simply the leek plant (allium porrum) which enjoyed great esteem among several ancient people, such as the Welsh and the Scandinavians. To the vitamin-hungry north, leek was a blessing. It may also have been popular among healers, as the plant contains disinfecting essential oils. In the *Edda*, (Vol. 4) we learn that leek is the first plant that grew at the beginning of creation. Nobles gave a leek plant to their newly born offspring, a symbolic gift that ensured divine blessing (see *Helgak. Hundingsbana*, 1, 7). *Sigrdrifumal* 8 suggests that leek, placed in drink, confers blessing and protects from danger. The Skalds often used the term leek as a metaphor. 'Sea-leek' is the mast of a ship, for instance, and 'lauka loggr' are 'laws, as straight as a leek'. In general, we may assume that leek symbolises fresh, straight growth, prosperity and general well-being. LaukaR is also one of the earliest names of the L rune, the other being 'lina' (linen, linseed). We meet both of them on a small scraping knife from a female grave in Floksand:

'lina laukaR'.

The two concepts also occur in a legend of Olaf the Holy (*Flateyarbók*, II), given by Düwel. Here, a pagan farmer family had the custom of venerating a horse penis called Völsi before meals. The item was passed from hand to hand and everyone had to say a few words of praise. The farmer's wife started and declared: 'You have grown, Völsi, you have been received, you are clad in linen and conserved by leek.' Shocked by the performance, Olaf threw the penis to the dogs and converted the family.

Two L runes without text appear on the Alamannic fibula of Bülach. The bracteat of Ars shows a head and a horse, just like most bracteats do, and the inscription 'laukaR'. The bracteat of Skrydstrup, north Schleswig, shows a standing man with uplifted hands, a horse, a horned beast, a bird and a snake. The inscription reads:

'laukaR ula'.

The bracteat of Börringe, Schonen, shows head, horse and bird and reads:

'tanulu : al laukaR'.

Tanulu may derive from Anglo-Saxon: tennen, OHG: zennen: to excite, provoke. It may be a woman's name.

LaukaR was occasionally shortened, we find the word as 'lkaR' on a Danish bracteat that disappeared from a Berlin museum in 1945.

Then there is the word 'lathu' which means 'to invoke, to invite'. We find it on the bracteat of Schonen, showing a man with a bird-shape hairdress (or hat?), a bird, horse, swastika. He makes the thumb to mouth gesture so familiar from Celtic myth (Taliesin, Fionn) and Germanic lore (Sigurd). Thumb to mouth signifies the initiated adept who has tasted the elixir of enlightenment.

'Lathu laukaR gakaralu'.

Not that we could understand it. Some have attempted to identify the last word with 'cuckoo' (ON: gaukr, LHG: Gauch = cuckoo), and the end of the word may be the familiar alu. Should we read it as ' invocation of well-being, cuckoo, magical protection'? Just what does a cuckoo signify? Springtime? Illegitimate children?

Lathu appears on the bracteats of Hojstrup and Gutfiles. The bracteat of Damrum, North-Jutland shows a male head and the thumb to mouth gesture, the inscription reads: 'frohila lathu', Frohila being a personal name.

The bracteat of Skonager, north Jütland, reads: 'niuwila lthu' and shows a horse, bird and male head, the latter with a spear in his neck, and a triskel. The word 'niuwila' may be a misspelling of the name Niujila.

Some words of power remain mysterious. The bracteat of Lellinge, Seeland, reads: 'salusalu'. What happens when we combine alu with the letter s?

The bracteat of Olst, north Jutland, shows a male head with extended tongue, horse, swasticas, cross and triskel, and reads: 'hag alu'. May we take 'hag' as hail and sudden destruction? Does the bracteat signify protection from danger?

Better is the bracteat of Körlin, showing head and horse, and reading 'waiga'. It comes from ON: veig, meaning power or intoxicating drink.

Several elder rune inscriptions refer directly to the gods. They often appear on talismans. Here are some examples.

'Logathore
Wodan
Wigithonar
Awaleubwinix'

The inscription on a fibula from Nordendorf, near Augsburg, c.600. 'Logather' means 'craftsman of deceit', possibly a reference to Loki, who is otherwise not too well known in continental Europe. 'Awaleubwinix' may mean 'awa and leubwini shall give luck', we do not know whether these are people, forces or deities. 'Wodan' is clear, what a relief, and 'Thonar' is Thunder, i.e. Thor.

Here is an unusual talisman found at Ribe, Denmark. It consists of a well polished, round bone-disk (made from a human skull), to be worn as a pendant, and inscribed:

'Ulfur Odin Hydyr'

The central part is easiest to understand. The 'ulfur' might be a reference to Ullr, the god of hunting, shields, archery and snowshoes, patron of duellists, who was worshipped in groves of yew trees in southern Scandinavia. More likely the word is a form of 'ulfr', the wolf. What the wolf does in company of Odin is ambiguous, to say the least. 'Hydyr' is completely mysterious.

Two interesting spearheads, showing great similarity, were unearthed in Brandenburg and Kowel. The Brandenburg spear has an inscription reading 'Ranja' or 'Vanja', which might remind you of the dreaded goddess of the oceans, Ran, who gathers the souls of the drowned in her aquatic otherworld. Lewd Ran offers seat and bed to the drowned heroes (*Frithjofs Saga*). The word Ran is common in Indo-European languages, it designates running, flowing water, as in the words rain, Rhine and Rhone, and the concept of running. Krause (1966, 77) proposes that the idea is to make enemies run, or to make the blade run into the body. The spearhead shows a triskel, a swastika, a crescent and a mysterious abstract sign (which some Nazi historians immediately identified as a 'solar symbol'). What is the meaning of this arrangement?

The Kowel spearhead reads 'Tilarids' and shows several chevrons in a row, a swastika, various circles, a blend of the sowelu rune with the wolf-hook and a crescent. The age of the items is an open question, they were discovered long before any sort of proper dating was available, but the inscriptions make use of the elder futhorc. It is likely that these spears were not used for simple fighting and hunting but served a cultish purpose. The spear is Odin's weapon and Nordic myth is full of references to the use of spears in sacrifices. People who wished to go to Valhall had themselves marked by a spear if they could not find death in battle.

Frequently, a spear was hurled over the enemy army, accompanied by the shout 'I give you all to Odin!'. The flight of the spear was taken as an omen, predicting the way the battle would turn out. The dedication of the entire enemy host turned the fight into a blood sacrifice on a large scale. Prisoners were not taken, the defeated were all sacrificed and, as far as we know, the corpses were not plundered. We have evidence for several battles where all enemies were promised to a god and subsequently slaughtered. After the battle of Arausio (105BCE) the victorious Cimbri destroyed the entire spoils of war. Prisoners were hanged in trees, horses drowned in the river; armour, weapons, clothes were destroyed and gold, treasure and valuables cast into the water. The Cimbri had prayed for victory, not for material gain. They promised all goods and prisoners to their gods, and kept their word.

In a similar way, the Romans slaughtered in the battle of the Teutoburgian forest were left to decay in sacred groves. When Drusus 'Germanicus' found these gory remnants (15CE), he was upset to see horses, weapons and human bones rotting in the open. Nobody had looted the dead or attempted to gain material wealth from the victory. It is likely that the two spearheads were connected with sacrifices, but we have no way of knowing whether it was the annual sacrifices of peacetime or the emergency of war.

Fragments of magical rune inscriptions appear on the damaged stones of Noleby and Järsberg, both of them c.500.

'runo fahi raginakundo'
'runes do I colour that are known to the gods'

and

'ubar haite, hrabnar haite, ek erilaR runor writu'
'ub am I called, raven am I called, I, Eril, wrote these runes'.

Now the term 'erilaR' appears on several old rune inscriptions. Some have interpreted it as a title, and propose that it means 'rune-master'. Others, less romantic, claim that it is a tribal reference, and means 'the (H)erulian'. The Eruli were a north Germanic people among whom rune writing was fairly popular. The third possibility is a derivation of the word earl, (OE:eorl, GMC: *erlaz). This makes the writer a nobleman. Almost all inscriptions featuring the word erilaR date from the 6th century and a small geographic area. Another example, the Lindholm bone amulet (c. 500):

'I Erila, am called mighty in sorcery.
aaaaaaaaRRRnnnbmuttt: alu'

Stone of Nordhuglo, near Bergen:
'ek gudija ungandiR ih'
' I, priest (gudija), not exposed to sorcery in huglo…'
Stone of Vetteland, Norway,

(The stone is in fragments and parts are missing):

'/// flagdafaikinaRist ///
magoRminasstaina /// daRfaihido'
'(This place) is threatened by flagda (troll-women, monsters)
(I, n.n. set) the stone of my son
(I,) …d painted (the runes).'

As you can see, most of the interesting inscriptions are disappointingly short. Here is a magnificent exception. In a megalithic monument, a group of standing stones at Bjorketorp, south Sweden, we find a rune inscription dating c. 675:

'Forecast of doom.
I, master of the rune row
hid mighty runes in this place.
Restless through evil
shall die, whoever harms
this monument
of a hidden death.'

The stone of Eggjum, Norway, covered a grave. The inscription was on the underside of the stone, invisible to the casual observer but easy to read by the deceased. The outline of a horse was carved across the text, . The translation is still far from satisfactory.

'Not to be touched by the sun
Nor cut with iron is this stone.
Do not (lay?) it bare (expose it?)
When the waning moon travels across the heavens.

May no misguided men lay it to the side!
The man (the writer?) has cast the flood of corpses over this stone
And rubbed it into the oars of the (tired?) boat.
In what shape did the god of warriors (Odin? Tyr?) arrive
Here, in the land of riding warriors?
Fish, floating in the dark stream
Bird, screaming into the host of enemies!
Alu against the evildoer!'

The 'flood of corpses' is one of the many kenningar (poetic metaphors) meaning blood. The writer rubbed the blood into the inscription to make it magically potent. This custom was widely popular. When you scratch a rune inscription on a piece of wood or bone, the lines are barley visible. To make the words easier to read, a bit of colour comes in handy. For ordinary purposes, ashes or soot were rubbed across the inscription. In a magical context, it was often blood. Now blood could come from several sources. Some made use of a sacrificial animal, usually a sheep. This relates the practice to the 'blót' (to strengthen), the major sacrificial rites of the Germanic Scandinavians. As you read earlier, it was common to kill an animal and to seethe it ritually in a sacred cauldron. The blood of the beast was usually collected in a special cauldron. It was sprinkled over temple walls, sacral pillars, divine images and the entire congregation. This custom appears in several sagas, it is also alluded to in the *Hyndluliod*, 10, the *Song of the Hyndla* (the Wolfish or Bitchy One), in the *Poetic Edda*. Freya states of her devotee Ottar:

'He built me a house of stone
Like glass the walls are gleaming
Often he drenched them with oxen-blood
Devoted to the goddesses was Ottar always.'

Blood also appears when it comes to activate a rune spell. Here is an example from *Egil's Saga*. Egil was a historic person. He was a famed skald of Iceland and a dedicated follower of the pagan gods.

'Then Bard went to the queen and told her; here would be a man causing dishonour to her, for however much he drank, still would he claim to be thirsty. Then the queen and Bard mixed a drink with poison and carried it inside; Bard blessed it and gave it to a serving woman, who gave it to Egil and asked him to drink. Egil drew his knife and cut his hand, he took up the horn, carved runes into it and rubbed the blood over them. He spoke:

Runes I have carved into the horn
gave redness of blood to the signs
words did I chose for the beast's (the aurox)
the wild one's, root of the ear tree (the horn)
draught of merry maidens
we drink as we will.
Wisdom I seek, how wholesome
is the beer that Baröd blessed?

Then the horn shattered and the beer splattered over the straw.'

As could have been expected, Egil immediately went to take his revenge. The passage combines the three essentials of rune consecration: the union of signs (runes) with word (song) and deed (the blood letting). Put another way, the spell combines visual, acoustic and kinaesthetic elements and spells a powerful message to the deep mind. Suggestions are always stronger when you use several sensory channels at once.

Now blood, though popular, is not the only elixir that may be used to activate a rune spell. Crowley's *Liber Al vel Legis*, III, 24 proposes:

'The best blood is of the moon, monthly'

This recommendation echoes the secret rituals of Kaulas, Kulas, Vamas, Nathas and other devotees of Left-Hand-Path Tantra. Such blood appears at the rite time, flowing naturally, and is, when properly charged, a prime menstruum of magickal manifestation. The fluid is much superior to the quality one may get from killing an animal. But menstrual flowers are not the only possibility. Sperm does the job just as well, and better still are the combined secretions. Even spittle can be used. Just consider how the Aesir and Vanir made peace by spitting into a cauldron. Mead, as a sacred drink, was also used to consecrate runes, see *Sigrdrifumal*, 18. Egil improvised on the spot by cutting his hand, a good gesture as it showing initiative and dedication. If you bind a spell with your own blood it's much like signing a contract: you are directly connected, concerned and responsible. The

gods like that. Anyone who gives freely of her- or himself is much superior to one who lets others bleed. Crowley's alluding to the runes can also be seen in *Liber Liberi vel Lapidis Lazuli*, V, 47-48:

'He shall await the sword of the beloved
and bar his throat for the stroke.
Then shall his blood leap out and write me
runes in the sky;
yea, write me
runes in the sky.'

The link between blood and magick can also be found in the German word for 'sorcerer', which is 'Zauberer'. It goes back to OHG: Zaubar, MD Tover, OE: Teafor. All three words mean literally 'red colour, red ochre, to colour in red'. Need I remind you of Neanderthal and early Cro-Magnon funerals, where red ochre played a fundamental part? How old is this connection? But it did not remain in use for funerals. Ochre also appears prominently in cave painting. There are even rock formations resembling female genitalia that were coloured in red! Closely related may be *Voluspa* 18, referring to the creation of the first human beings out of an ash and an alder (or elm):

'They had no soul, nor sense, as yet
nor blood, nor motion
nor flowering colour.
Odin gave soul, Hönir gave sense
Blood gave Lodur and rich colour.'

What applies to the creation of humans

out of trees can also be applied to the consecration of rune spells and talismans.

Another fine example for practical rune magic comes from *Egil's Saga*. In chapter 72 of that violent epic we are told how Egil came to a house where a farmer's daughter lay sick and suffering in bed. When Egil inquired about her exhausted state, Thorfinn, his host, told him that healing runes had been carved for her, to no avail, as she had grown weaker. So Egil had the young lady lifted from her bed. Under the blankets he found a fishbone bearing some runes. Egil scowled at the inscription, carefully erased it and threw the fishbone into the fire. Then he had the people carry all blankets and pillows outside, to clean them by exposure to the sun and wind. He spoke:

'None shall carve runes
who does not know their use.
Many meanings have I found
inside the mad man's staff.
Ten of the magic runes
were badly suited to the bone
and folly did prolong
the sorrow of the maiden.'

Then Egil carved some runes and placed them under her pillow. His patient was immediately refreshed and told that she felt as if she had only just woken from sleep. This passage is worth considering. Note that Egil did not immediately throw the wrong inscription into the fire. Throwing things into fires does not always destroy them, indeed, some spells only become stronger when they burn. Egil erased the runes first and destroyed their carrier, the fishbone, afterwards. Good thinking. As to the poem, it gives a much needed warning that you have to know runes really well before you can use them in spells. Such knowledge cannot be derived from reading books and being well-informed. You have to explore the runes, live them and weave them into your own magickal universe before you can even start to be sure about spells. Odin's Rune Song (*Havamal*, 145-146) contains the injunction:

'You know how to carve? You know how to guess?
You know how to find? You know how to seek?
You know how to ask? You know how to offer?
You know how to send, and how to slay?
Better not to give, than to give too much:
the gift wants re-compensation.
Better not to send, than to slay too much;
so Thundr carved, as a guideline for people
then he departed to his place of origin.'

Runes were not only carved on bone and stone. A popular talisman is a rune staff, often a short piece of wood inscribed with a spell or a helpful suggestion. Here is the inscription of a rune staff of yew, Groningen, Westeremden, c.8th century:

'Hamlet confronted Opham.
Before his yews, the breakers calmed.
The surf slowed before his yews.'

Yews often appear in northern folklore as a material for talismans. The tree was considered strong against enchantment.

As we come to the subject of rune staffs we leave the inscriptions in Elder Futhark. The following items were written in the younger futhark of 16 runes that became popular in Scandinavia in the Viking age.

Several fascinating rune staffs were unearthed in Bergen, Norway, where a complete settlement was excavated. A good item dated around 1200 is:

'Be happy and of good cheer, Thor shall receive you, Odin will call you his own.'

This is remarkable, as paganism was supposed to be extinct at the time.

One of the longest inscriptions appears on a rune staff. Sadly, the wood is partly rotten and the text contains a lot of gaps:

'I carve healing runes
I carve safety runes
once against elves
twice against giants,
thrice against trolls (…)
Against her who gives evil.
The valkyrie of the giants (?)
so she may not
however much she wants to,
the doom-knowing woman,
hurt your life. (…)
I will send you, I will spell you
the evil and restlessness of the wolf.bitch.
May you be restless,
and full of giant's wrath,

never sit, never sleep (…)
You love me like yourself.
:thurist: rubus: rabus: eth: arantabus: laus: abus: rosa: gaua:'

This spell contains many riddles. It looks part protection, part curse. The last part seems to be a love spell and the final words sound like Latin. Is it an exorcism or a love spell? Perhaps you will be reminded of the Eddic *Skirnirsmal*, relating how fertility god Freyr falls in love with the frost giant's daughter Gerd (earth), whom he has espied from Odin's high seat. He sends his servant Skirnir to woo her, but Gerd refuses gifts, sweet words and promises. Skirnir, finding kindness futile, threatens to curse her by carving a TH rune (for Thurs, 'giant') and three staffs: impotence, ill-temper and impatience (Simrock), or perversion, madness and restlessness (Düwel), unless she consents. Under a shower of threats and curses, Gerd gives in. There is a hidden nature symbolism in this passage, as earth has to accept the wooing of fertility. The Nordic winter eventually ends, the sun becomes strong and the frozen earth unthaws. However, she has the right to chose her own place and time. She offers to meet Freyr in the forest of Barri, after nine nights. Nine nights appear frequently in Norse myth. The glad message almost breaks Freyr's heart, as nine nights are almost an eternity. I suggest you study the song, for though it is a nasty case of coercion, it is also a treasure trove of Nordic cursing. Could the staff of Bergen belong to a similar category of sorcery? And did the enchantment work? Personally I doubt it. If you enforce what should be given freely, you'll get something of little value for a high price. Such spells have a nasty tendency to backfire, interfering with the true will of others and violating the wholeness of your self.

How much more simple hearted is another rune staff fragment from Bergen, 12-14th century:

'ost: min: kis: mik:'
'Kiss me, Love'.

Bergen also offers an inscription reading 'Smid fucked Vigdis of the Sneldebeni'. Did it commemorate the event, was it a bit of slander or the expression of wishful thinking?

More eloquent is a staff from Bergen, early 13th century, reading: '…the old burden of the troll wife reversed itself early for me to the beautiful, dangerous woman…' whatever that may mean, and adds a quote from Vergil, in Latin: 'Love conquers all. Let us forgive for the sake of love' This quote was well known in the Viking age, parts of it were found, engraved in runes, on the leather of a shoe from Bergen. The missing part may have been on the other shoe, which we haven't' found. Spellcraft or simply someone making a fool of himself?

In the chapter on memorial stones, I mentioned that none of the Scandinavian rune stones gives the name of a pagan deity. I was wrong. The rune-stone of Karlevi, Öland, c1000CE, has the following enigmatic text.

'Buried lies, he who was followed, as most know, the greatest deeds,
Of Thrud, the tree in battle, in this hill.
There will not reign a viðrir of riding/ carriages,
Strong in battle, in Denmark, on the wide land of Endil,
Honourable over the land.'

Tough reading. In those days, any piece of poetry that could be understood at first glance was not artful enough. Most skalds prided themselves on perfect alliteration, metre and a vast store of abstruse metaphors, and the more incomprehensible a piece of poetry was, the better. Let's look at the details. The stone was obviously set for a hero and a war-leader ('who was followed'). He was a 'tree in battle', i.e. he stood as if he were rooted and did not move one inch. Thrud is the daughter of Thor, her name means (possibly) 'strength'. The 'Viðrir of carriages/riding' ('Við RR Rad A') is a reference to Odin. Viðrir is the 'weatherer' or the maker of hard weather, a title of Odin as a god of wind, storm and rain, and the buried was compared with him (Mondfeld 1986).

More enigmatic is the following inscription. It comes from the stone of Gorlev, Seeland. One side of the stone bears the text: 'Thjodvi raised this stone after Odinkar' This is followed by the younger futhark and a formula to keep the deceased safely in the grave: 'niut ual kum(l)s': 'enjoy the grave well'. The other side of the stone bears the following cypher:

'TH:M:K:III:SSS:TTT:III:LLL'

This text, obviously in code, was not supposed to be easy reading. We have a section made up of triple letters (I, S, T, I, L), while the beginning offers three runes: TH, M and K. When we read the text using the three initial runes, we may arrive at Thistil, Mistil, Kistil. The first could be a reference to the thistle, the second to the mistle(toe) and the third to the chest, cask or box, G: Kiste. Now mistletoe immediately brings Balder's death to mind. If this were true, it might imply that the chest is a coffin. What thistles have to do with it remains anyone's guess. Thus, the runes may or may not allude to Balder's assassination, not that we'll ever know for certain.

Let's have a few more examples. Here are some from the great Norman exhibition (Wikinger, 1992). The rune stone, Tingstad, Sweden, informs us:

'Afrid made this bridge for Hemkel and Sibbe, her sons'.

A fairly common dedication, you might think, but unusually, the text is carved on a simple double line curved like an upside-down 'U'. Could it be a reference to the rainbow bridge leading to Asgard? Is the rune stone a bridge to the gods or does it symbolise the ritual function of bridging the way of the deceased to the unknown?

A rune amulet, bronze with ring, c.1000CE, was discovered near Gorodisce, Russia. The inscription was written in cipher, which turned out to mean 'May you never lack potency'.

When we come to rune staffs, we encounter a few that carried messages and some that were meant as talismans. An example of the first sort is 'Thorkjell master of coins sends pepper to you' (Bergen, Norway, c.1200).

Much more enigmatic is a spruce staff from Staraja Ladoga, Russia, 9th century:

'The tail is covered with fluff, the gleaming (or sharp) attracts prey for all in the great host'.

Maybe this staff was part of an arrow-shooting trap used for hunting. Or consider the pine staff from Narsaq, Greenland, c.1000:

'On the sea, sea, sea, is the place where the Aesir are in ambush, Bibrau is the name of the maiden who is seated on the blue (sky?)'.

The reverse of the staff shows some runes in code and a version of the 16 rune futhark.

Bone occasionally served the same purpose. Much like the inscription from Bergen mentioned earlier, a bone from Oslo, Norway, late 11th century, reads 'kiss me'. Maybe it was a talisman, a daring message or a primitive love letter.

Runes were also used in a Christian context. A bone fragment from Sigtuna, Sweden, 12th century, is inscribed with the names of Mary and the evangelists, it probably worked as an amulet. Another inscription on bone, same place, same period, informs us:

'The king is very generous. He gave the most. He is popular.'

Well, generosity was the chief virtue of nobles and kings in most of northern Europe, but why record it on a piece of bone? Are we dealing with a positive suggestion (spell) carried by someone who wants the king to be generous?

Quite obscure is a piece of red-deer antler, Dublin, 11th century, which states: 'Horn of deer...' and nothing else. Or take the bone from Sigtuna, 11th century, which is inscribed with the 16 rune futhark (the runes Isa and Nauthiz are exchanged) and the cryptic text: 'BA BA'. Such texts look as if they were spells or sigils, but they don't enlighten us much.

Last, let me mention a fascinating rune staff, made of box-tree, from Lödöse, Sweden, 12th century. This item supplies a calendar. It shows 657 signs, some of them runic, while others are straight lines, crosses and dots. It has two broad sides with a total of 365 lines for the days, divided into a winter side (November - April) and a summer side (May - October). Isn't this remarkable? A Viking rune staff giving the same division of the year as you find among the Gaelic Celts! Is this a bit of cultural cross-over, maybe from a Viking who had been in Ireland or Scotland? Or were there Vikings in Sweden who ordered their year like the Gaels did? The sagas give no confirmation on this point. The two narrow sides of the staff show small signs. Some of them refer to festival days of saints, others were probably used to calculate movable festival days. Another sort of signs may have been something like a commentary to the year, showing lucky and unlucky days.

5 Memorial stones

The angular, straight shapes of the rune letters are especially suited for enduring inscriptions in wood or stone. The text was made legible by the application of blood, ashes or earth colours. Most rune texts on wood or bone have decomposed with the passage of centuries. What was carved on wood was written for the moment. Inscriptions in stone were for eternity. A considerable amount of rune texts have survived by being committed to stone. Most of these come from Scandinavia. In Sweden, some 3000 rune stones have been found. Most of these stones had nothing to do with magick or religion. They were carved as memorials, to give a measure of immortality to the persons and events mentioned in the text. A very early example of this custom comes from Tune, south east Norway. It is dated around 500 which makes it one of the earliest rune texts in existence:

I Wiw
after Wodurid the bread-keeper
worked the runes.
For Wodurid
the stone was prepared
by three daughters,
the funeral feast
by the most noble heirs.

Wiw, (the consecrated) was probably the pupil and replacement of Wodurid (wild rider) in the priesthood. The stone is remarkable in several respects. At the time of writing the memorial stones had not yet become a popular fashion and were probably reserved for members of the priesthood or royalty. It is typical that early rune inscriptions are very rare and usually mysterious, suggestive of magick and ritual. Late rune inscriptions are pretty common and contain few if any references to pagan belief. The custom of setting memorial stones peaked at a time when most aspects of rune magick had already been forgotten, i.e. around 800 with the beginning of the Viking period. By this time the church had almost extinguished the use of rune letters on the continent.

In Scandinavia the church had a weaker hold over the population, so that a measure of simple rune sorcery would still be used on occasion. Nevertheless Christianity was the dominant religious and political force, which may account for the lack of pagan symbols or deities on memorial stones. Most of these stones come from the period between 900 - 1200. For the people of the Viking times it was fashionable to commemorate their deceased or absent relations with rune inscriptions. The stones are often very beautiful, with complicated design and original ornament. The inscriptions, however, are often dull, repetitious and deal almost exclusively with mundane themes. As Thompson has shown in his detailed study of Swedish runography, the contents of these inscriptions fall under four headings:

1. Memorials. E.g. 'X set this stone for Y, his father.' The text is usually brief and lacks all details. In most cases fixed formula were used.

2. Prayer. Another standard phrase to call for divine blessing. eg; 'Guð hialpi X and ok guðs moðir!' (God help X and also God's mother) The name 'Guð' (ᚷ ᚢ ᚦ) could be used by Pagan and Christian alike. None of the old gods are mentioned on any of these stones.

3. Addition. This was added when the praying stone had become a memorial stone through the death of the person named.

4. Signature. Here the stonemason signed his work, often in a grand manner that required almost as much space as the rest of the text. eg. 'X risti staein' or 'X markaði runar'.

All contents of the inscription follow set formula. We can only guess how these stones were used. Quite possibly people prayed for an absent relation or for a dead ancestor. European folk legends are abound in stories of how the dead may return from the yonder-world to help their relations - that is provided their memory has been kept alive. There is a touch of Paganism in these stones that may go back to earlier periods. The text was usually carved between two lines, top and bottom, with the words in between. These lines formed serpent or dragon creatures, whose coils and convolutions made up for all the dullness of the text. The words were obviously of minor importance to the artist, and could be read from left to right or vice versa, at times in changing directions, as suited the stone and dragon shape. The dragon is a very old symbol so deeply rooted in Pagan traditions that to the Christians it was often synonymous with the devil himself. It was perhaps a concession to Christian belief that many of the dragons of the memorial stones appear to be bound i.e. limited and controlled.

The dragon symbol reminds us of the

Dragon shapes from rune stones in Uppland, Sweden, Viking period. **Above:** Dragons from the Tassilo Challice, Kremsmünster, 8th century AD.

earth dragon out of whose flesh all reality was created, like the warring red and white dragons of Arthurian romance, the Midgardworm who surrounds the known universe, Skadi's serpent in the skies (the Milky Way) whose dripping poisons make bound Loki convulse in agony and the death dragon Nidhoggr who strips the souls of the deceased of all waste material. This popularity of the dragon idea is remarkable, especially when we consider that much of Scandinavia is too cold for snakes and reptiles.

Another common motif is the cross. Whilst the dragon represents a presence that is all encompassing, the cross supplied a fixed point, a focus centering the stone. This cross is not the Christian cross. Usually the length of its arms are equal. In some cases they are composed out of a central circle with four triangles radiating from it.

Arguably the customary use of the dragon motif comes from the old religion, and was popularized in Viking times as it added to the mystery of the stones. The historical illustrations below give some examples of the dragon pattern (without the inscriptions).

The shape is highly useful for magick talismans, symbols, stelae etc.

6 Runes and fascism

This chapter intends to give some insight into the use and abuse of Celtic and German nature religion during the twentieth century. It is an important topic, as many occultists consider the runes to be tainted by their application by the Nazis. It is also a rather complicated topic, as most of the 'facts' about the esoteric aspects of the Third Reich cannot be proven. There are rumours, gossip and of course there are plenty of stories of people who supposedly talked too much and then disappeared.

As a non Nazi, I have no access to those circles which may or may not be informed on the occult side of National Socialism. Indeed, if you asked anybody on the street about it, you would notice that very few people in Germany are aware of the esoteric dogma of the Nazis. Those who remember the war would tell you that the school kids had to read about German/Icelandic mythology, that there were rune signs on certain uniforms and flags and that children had to celebrate some of the old pagan festivals. Probably you would also be told that there was nothing esoteric to the whole affair, just a few old customs resurrected by the state. If you asked about runes you would probably get a shrug for an answer, perhaps a bit of Wagnerian mythology, and an uneasy 'well, this is all Nazi stuff, isn't it?' To most of those who remember the war, these memories are pretty unpleasant and much rather forgotten.

It is no coincidence that most books which deal with esoteric Nazi gnosis, such as *Hitler's Secret Science* or the works of Pauwels and Bergier, were written outside of Germany.

How much magic was there in Nazi Germany?

A recent book by reverend Haack (employed by the Catholic Church to investigate any new religion or cult) gives some interesting insights. Haack lists some prominent members of the Thule Society. This group was a nationalistic order which financed the rise of the National Socialist Democratic Party and supported its leaders with cash, dogma and a certain amount of magical training. They educated the non-entity Hitler, supplied a secret doctrine and helped rig the elections in favour of the Nazis. Thule members were, among others; Adolf Hitler, Fuhrer and Chancellor of the Reich; Rudolf Hess, Deputy Fuhrer; Hermann Goring, Reich Marshall; Heinrich Himmler, head of the SS and Reich Marshall; Alfred Rosenberg Reich Minister; Hans Frank, National Socialist Reich Leader and Governor General of Poland; Julius Streicher, SA leader; Professor Karl Haushofer, Major General, ret.

Not all of these people were active occultists, as the Thule Society was not only an esoteric order but also a political club. The Thule Society's head was Freiherr Rudolf Von Sebottendorf, author of a book on Turkish Freemasonry which taught certain hand gestures plus concentration exercises. Two famous occultists, Guido Von List and Jorg Lanz Von Liebenfeld were its secret masters.

How much did these people practice Magic?

Some sources see the entire Nazi movement as a case of black magic, while others express the opinion that most Thule members were simply superstitious and power hungry. If we look at the historical development we find that the Thule Society was a somewhat nutty right wing organization prior to the Nazi's rise to power. These people were busy recreating a 'national identity' by blending Icelandic sagas with Wagner operas, trying to resurrect the 'original German' who would have been out of place anywhere except in Bayreuth. Such movements existed in most north European countries. At the same time France invented a pure Gallic race, while Britain indulged in a Celtic sentimentality, and of course everybody pretended that their own ancestors came from a pure and ideal race which had nothing to do with the rest of Europe. These 'Celtic', 'Gallic' and 'Germanic' movements were typified by blind romanticism, heroic ideals, naivete and the overwhelming need to be not just special but superior.

When the Nazi Party came to power in 1933, the Thule Society supplied the necessary dogma to create a state religion. This religion was developed gradually. As most of the older people were of Christian faith, the indoctrination was focused largely on children, with the long-term perspective of abolishing Christianity entirely. The substance of this new religion came from a curious mixture of Eddic legends, Grimm's fairy tales, Wagner's operas, old country customs, Arthurian myths plus a lot of material which the SS expedition under Karl Haushofer brought back from Tibet. Tibet, or rather *Schampulah*, was considered as the home country of the Aryan race. Consequently several SS expeditions were sent out to climb mountains, meet the Dalai Lama, search for the entrance to the centre of the earth and to bring back esoteric symbols, such as the Swastika. They also invited a number of Tibetan monks (rumours vary between 200 and 2000) who were found, dead by poison, when the American army entered Berlin.

Meanwhile the Thule Society worked hard on the acquisition of 'secret wisdom.' The SS raided all occult orders which would not cooperate with the Nazis. The head of the Fraternitas Saturni, Fr. Gregorius, was asked to undertake 'scientific' work to create a perfume to be used for the manipulation of large groups of people. Gregorius refused, and fled. Others, the unlucky ones, ended their days in concentration camps.

There were a number of highly bizarre projects, which are mentioned by Pauwels and Bergier, such as the search for the hollow earth, the 'world-ice' thesis and so on. Some claim that the SS also sent a couple of thousand soldiers to Brazil, where, according to rumours, they are to this day, living deep in the jungle in mystical ruined cities of elder races, killing all who are unlucky enough to stumble upon them. As with all stories on the Third Reich, mythology and superstition obscure the picture. Fanatics are not made with facts but fantasy, especially when the two cannot be kept apart.

What about the runes?

Though the Old English rune poem was known in Germany (one of the Grimm brothers wrote a little book on it) this material was for some reason ignored. Guido Von List, however, popularized a rune system of eighteen runes which he received, complete with new names, during a time when he was blind for reasons unspecified. Von List's rune system was apparently the basis on which so many other reactionary rune meddlers built their curious structures. Von List published his new and improved rune row and gave some 'meditation aphorisms' for each sign. Here are some samples. They say more about the Nazi way of thinking in terms of struggle, control and dominance, than the runes.

ᚻ the creative spirit must be victorious!

ᚴ respect the ancient fire!

ᛁ Through the unquestioning consciousness of your own mental might can the waves be controlled, made frozen and be hardened into ice. Not only waves (or will alone) but all life is obedient to the masterful will!

ᛦ embrace all in yourself and you will rule all!

ᚱ your blood is your greatest treasure!

ᛣ I am my rod (right), this right is inviolable, thus I am inviolable, as I am my right!

Interpretations of other rune experts of the period are by no means easier to digest:

ᚱ through pain, failure, need, temptation and suffering did I realize the true life! (Kummer)

ᛁ I will self-consciously experience all, self-consciously do all, self-consciously be my own! (Marby)

ᛉ I am my own right and knight! (Kummer)

One of my favourite aphorisms is given by Karl Spiessberger in his *Runenmagie* (where all of these quotation come from). Behold and tremble!

ᛉ the deluding insanity of matter shatters before the awakened one! Strength triumphs over the lust of the senses! O holy might of the runes! Redeem me from the root demon of women's nature! Woman, be human!

It seems hardly surprising that this sort of barely translatable garbage leads to highly eccentric systems of mystical insight. The attribution of runes, gods, god homes and old month names to the signs of the zodiac was created by the Guido Von List Society during the war. It is still used and circulated by the 'Armanenorder', who continue the Von List tradition to this day.

If this table proves anything at all it is the hopeless confusion of the Nazi gnosis. What the Nazis really believed is a riddle that cannot be unveiled. As in most old style orders, there were different instructions for different grades in the hierarchy.

Every one of those leading Nazis was busy with intrigue, trying to gather more power, influence, secrets, and when the war turned out against them (as the Tibetan state oracle and Hitler's personal astrologer are supposed to have predicted), a goodly dose of paranoia entered the picture. Himmler, so it is claimed, is said to have sent out an SS research team to find the Holy Grail, while others were keen to acquire the magical jewelry and weapons of escaped magicians, thinking the ownership of such tools would give them the power to work miracles.

The runes and the various popular symbols were meant to control the masses. The Nazis were quite aware that the release of emotional energy could be associated with specific symbols, and that these symbols could subsequently be used to trigger the desired emotional response at will. This sort of thing is used by most states, as any mage should know. However, I do not think that the emotional hysteria the Nazis evoked had any lasting effect on the runes. The runes, after all, have considerable power and consciousness that comes not only from cultural conditioning but also from their deep-rooted similarity to our mind structures. The Nazis, who ignored these eldritch connections, thought that they could inflict an entirely new and artificial meaning on these symbols, and expected the system to function as they had made it. As history shows, it did not work out. Had they invented new symbolism they might have conceivably 'charged it' the way they intended to. The way it was, they tried to re-name and control a phenomena they did not understand.

To an extent the association of rune symbols with emotional energy did function. If you ask the man or woman on the street what they remember about the runes, you will find these symbols associated mostly with shame and guilt.

Runes	Home	Gods	Old month names	ZODIAC
ᛉ ᛁ	Gladsheim	Ziu-Tyr, Ostara, Magni	Ostermond	ARIES
ᚡ	Alfheim	Freya,Gerda, Nerthe Freyr-Fro	Wonnemond,	TAURUS
ᚱ ᚺ	Ydalir	Bragi, Idun	Brachet	GEMINI
ᛉ ᛗ ᛃ	Sokkwabek	Saga, Urd, Nanna Wilbert, Loki, Hodur.	Heuert	CANCER
ᛗ ᛉ ᚺ ᚠ	Breidablick	Baldur, Sif,Werdandi	Ernting	LEO
ᚲ ᚾ	Vokwang	Frigga, Hertha, Honir, Skuld.	Scheiding	VIRGO
ᚱ ᛉ	Glitnir	Forsetti, Gefion.	Gilbhart	LIBRA
ᚴ ᛉ	Walhall	Holle, Odin-Wodan.	Neblung	SCORPIO
ᛜ ᚦ	Trudheim	Donar-Thor, Three Norns	Julmond	SAGITARIUS
ᛒ ᛉ	Thrymheim	Skadi, Widar, Uller...	Hartung	CAPRICORN
ᚦ ᛉ	Himminbjorg	Heimdall, 13 Valkyries	Hornung	AQUARIUS
ᛏ ᛉ	Noatun	Eir, Hel, Ran, Njord.	Lenzing	PISCES

The teachings of Nazi religion did not disappear at the end of the war. Some of the esoteric research materials were supposedly collected by special units of the American and Russian forces, and were never heard of again. What remained were dozens of small, fanatic groups. Such groups exist to this day. Haack mentions several of them in his work *Wotans Wiederkehr*. They share a mutual belief in the divine mission of Adolf Hitler, in racial purity and in a number of religious practices. Many of these groups consist almost entirely of idealistic young hot-heads, barely controlled by the older generation. Such groups are known to play war with genuine weapons, as they all eagerly await the day when the Russians, the Jews, The Third World Nations and all sorts of 'sub-human' races come to take their sacred fatherland away.

One of them is called the 'Gylfi-Youths', named after the legendary King Gylfi whom you may find in Snorri's prose *Edda*. Gylfi youths practice pagan nature festivals, rune divination (on the basis of the eighteen rune system) and have a mantra which they are supposed to repeat daily; 'Omi-Odin, Omi-Odin, Omi-Odin, Har, Here, Here, Har.' Gylfi dogma says:

> 'Pray to Gylfi for strength of faith, pray to Hermann for the purity of Germania, pray to Adolf for the unity of Deutschland.'

In a fantastic attempt to become completely isolated, the Gylfi movement has even developed its own language, composed of old High German, Old Icelandic and some completely artificial words. All this is done to cleanse the speech of the true Aryan from the *evil* influence of the Latin tongue.

More serious work is done by the Armanen order. From what one hears, the Armanen have recently reorganized and claim to be apolitical. The old Nazis, they say, have left the order. I have no idea whether this claim is true. The old Armanen order, as it existed uo to the mid 1980s, was definitely nationalistic. They used to celebrate nature rituals at old historic sites, which was a lengthy and complicated procedure involving many speeches, prayer to the Icelandic gods and to Adolf (who is supposed to feast at Odin's right in Valhalla), slow and pompous circle dances, rune divination, rune postures, ritual gestures plus sacrifices to the elements of earth, water and fire. Air is missing in their program. Perhaps they simply did not feel comfortable with it. In their old form the Armanen, who developed out of the Guido Von List Society, were keen on breeding a pure, Aryan super race, which was supposed to leave this planet in the next 2,000 years and good riddance! Their old self description ran as follows:

> 'The Armanen order fights for the true realization of the divine world order on the foundation of the old Aryan understanding of God as it is revealed in the hereditary forms of religion and cult in the ancient German myths of the gods.'

The bloated style of the original is even worse. Whether these lines are still acceptable to the new and reformed Armanen order I do not know.

Another interesting development can be observed in the various forms of Odinism. From what I hear some of them seem to lean strongly towards 'white superiority.' The 'Odinist Hof' for instance, has pointed out that 'Odinists also believe in caste. . . the Indian code of Manu was issued forbidding marriage between different castes. This is an Odinistic concept.' (English *Odinist Hof Review* number 9, 29, 2, 22, 34 re.) Recently a group of Odinists tried to boycott a performance of Wagner's *Ring* at an Oxford theatre because it dared to cast black singer as 'Wotan', an idea which the Odinists considered 'religious sacrilege.' In the old Pagan days, any person able to sing would have been thought blessed by Odin/Wodan, who is the god of speech and song, no matter the skin colour. It should be noted that a good many Odinist groups, even non-racist ones, habitually use an 'Eddic' vocabulary full of aggressive metaphors. Life, they consider, is battle and war and humans are free as long as they are willing to fight. Only heroes. who have died fighting, will go to Valhalla, so they believe - an item of Icelandic mythology out of touch with most of Europe, where people were not quite as extreme. It is moot point how many of these martial metaphors are still useful in modern society. Where Icelandic heroes relied on a stout sword and a supporting clan, modern people rely on manners, law and the state. Indeed it seems that the more magicians describe themselves as 'warriors' the more troublesome does their life become. Warriors imply war, enemies, aggression, life and death struggle - none of which is beneficial for a peaceful and productive existence. Moreover, people who play the warrior game are in real danger of taking themselves too seriously and mind you, when something become serious, you are probably doing it wrong.

I am glad there are other Odinists with less narrowminded dogma. In a time when we should, at long last, learn to consider the earth as a single living entity, there should be less emphasis on the supposed differences of colour, creed and nationality.

7 Titles and names

Now for a look at the people who practised magick and religion in old pre-Christian Europe. The works of Greek and Roman scholars supply a description of their functions and activities. But these authors should be taken with a large pinch of salt: many of them were more interested in a lively propaganda story than a realistic account. However biased these tales may be, they are pretty much all that there is known of those early Celtic and German forms of religion.

In pre-Christian northern Europe, the various tribes were pantheistic. As everybody knew, there were lots of gods, goddesses, spirits, clan totems, and whatnot, most of them with a distinct personality and a specialized function. Each of these spiritual entities had a specific job to do, be it to make thunder, help lovers, bless the harvest or to grant victory. Now these gods often had different names or images, which varied from tribe to tribe. Their functions, however, were universally understood. People prayed to the deities who were important to them; when they had a problem they turned to the deity in charge of that subject, and as there were lots of gods, one could be sure that all aspects of daily life were regulated by one specialist or other.

In these early and tolerant forms of religion, there were mystery and secret lore for each deity. People could participate in the worship of many deities, or be members of several cults, and as the gods of the time were neither elitist, exclusive, nor jealous, everything was fine. Consider the Celtic tribes of Julius Caesar's Gaul. From what we know today, it seems that there were hundreds of deities with distinct names and attributes, many of them completely unknown to us. Though some scholars have tried to work out the 'chief deities' of ancient Gaul, such projects have not been successful, as maybe the tribes were too independent to care much for the god-forms of their neighbours. Indeed it seems that the earlier Celtic and Germanic tribes were not interested in 'chief deities', as all gods were of importance one way or another.

These people were highly religious. Daily life included a lot of ritual customs, such as prayer and offerings, and these were practised by everyone. In Celtic Gaul, the more important ceremonies were conducted by the druids. Druids, as Caesar tells us, were members of a caste, and enjoyed a number of privileges. Some of the druids functioned as priests, healers or prophets. Others were judges, diplomats, historians, scholars, singers or simply officials. It seems likely that these druids, with their secret rites and their lengthy education, had some sort of monopoly on intellectual activities. Many Celtic tribes of the time were organized in a strictly theocratic fashion, meaning that the priests controlled the kings.

In such societies - think of ancient Egypt, Sumeria or Tibet - a criminal offence, such as theft, is not seen as an offence against the state, but as sin against the deities who made the laws. Now an organized priesthood, such as the druids, is only possible when people live close together, and there is enough wealth to support them. In Gaul, many people lived in walled towns, some of them with more than 20,000 inhabitants, which made it easy for the druids, and later the Romans, to control the population. Celtic southern Germany had similar cities. In eastern and northern Germany, however, religion was a less centralized affair. Many of the German tribes preferred to spread loosely all over the country, rather than cluster in fortified cities. These people enjoyed tiny villages, with lots of distance between neighbours.

Under such conditions, a professional caste of priests is highly impractical. Possibly there were some priests who lived near sacred sites, or organized the great ting-feasts on the mountaintops, which had people travelling for days to participate. In everyday rural life, people were often too far from any priest to 'go to church' regularly. As a result, the head of the family assumed a priest-function for the various minor rites of daily life. Of course these people had no regular religious education. Many of the wise women and cunning men of these days acquired their skills from like-minded practitioners living at the fringe of society, or received their knowledge directly and first hand from the gods and ghosts of the wild woods. It logically follows that such people developed inspired, and highly individual, systems of religion. Some of the north Germanic cults had regular priests who travelled across the country. These people often journeyed in big groups, with lots of wagons. Some of these carriages contained images of the gods, or holy objects, while the better part of them was reserved for the money and gifts collected from the population. Often these priests were accompanied by merchants and entertainers, people came to worship, to trade, to feast, and carouse, until the church put a stop to the fun. While in mainland Europe, most of the fun was over by 800, the old religion continued for a while in Scandinavia. The Vikings believed in many of the old gods of Germany, and developed a professional priesthood with strong political influence and lavish temples, wherever there was a wealthy king to support them. In the more rural parts, the priests had to work for a living, and were rich peasants, warriors or traders.

In Scandinavia of the Viking periods the original forms of pantheism were somewhat distorted. Such ideas as 'only those who die fighting go to Valhall' were fairly unknown on the continent, they are later developments, meant to motivate warriors into suicidal fighting rages. Similarly the mainland 'Wode' is an important deity, but not a patriarchal 'chief of the gods' as the Scandinavian Odin. That deity changed from a storm god (Wode) to a god of ecstasy and rage (Wodan) to a god of rulers and warriors (Odin), and will change again, attuning to the new aeon, to assume a mask that fits our time. Now you might ask whether these people who worshipped in old northern Europe were 'pagans', or whether they had a common term for themselves. If this was the case, this common name has been lost - though it seems more likely that there never was a common concept, in our modern sense. The idea of a single common German or Celtic religion is a modern one, as in the old days each district had its peculiar rites and attitudes. The Romans did much to control the organized priesthood of the countries they occupied, and the Christian church went beyond that. When Charlemagne, with God on his side, united the 'German-Catholic empire' his opponents, many of them believers in older faiths were termed 'pagans' or 'heathens' - city people's words for rustics living in the country. When the last Saxon tribes had been suppressed or massacred, the country became officially Christian.

Now for our terminology. I'll give a brief list of various magical and religious professions and activities, basically titles, functions, and insulting names, such as you may encounter in your research. The idea behind this list isn't so much to supply you with a lot of new and exciting labels to stick to yourself, but to give an idea of the many different practitioners mentioned in old literature. Those who like to call themselves by fancy names should perhaps consider that a title is a crutch to support the ego in times of doubt and worry. If you need a title to do your thing, this merely indicates that you can't do it naturally.

Helrunar, Haljarunae, Hellirunar, describes people who 'rune' (speak, sing, whisper) with Hel/Helja, the goddess and realm of the underworld. 'Hell', in its original meaning is the hidden realm, the dark and foggy place where the dead and unborn dwell. Often the term is used with a sinister meaning. The Gothic Bishop Wulfila mentions a group of 'Haljarunae' (feminine form) who were evicted by King Filimer because of their sorceries. Incidentally Filimer was not a Christian but a Pagan king. Others connect the Helrunar with the practice of 'utiseta' = 'to sit outside' (the whole night through) to evoke spirits, raise the dwellers from under the hill or to practise necromancy. In reading this book and exploring the runes, you are raising the dead spirits of a forgotten magick of the past. Joe Revill kindly informed me that 'Helrunar' is a plural, the singular in Old Norse being 'Helruna' (female) and 'Helruni' (male). In Anglo-Saxon it's 'Helrunë' (female) and 'Helruna' (male). It means someone who is familiar, possibly intimate with, the goddess Hel or her hidden realm.

Druid. A Druid was a member of the Gaulish or Island-Celtic priesthood. Julius Caesar gives an interesting account of the Druids in the sixth book of *Bellum Gallicum*. The word Druid has several interpretations. Some link it with *duir*, the oak (from *dorw-) and *derwydd* which, according to Robert Graves, is Welsh for 'oak-seer'. *Deru- is the Indo-European root of the word 'Tree' and the closely related ideas 'true' and 'trustworthy'. Others claim that Druid comes from the Celtic roots *dru*, strong, full and *wid*, wisdom, vision, wit. Nowadays Druids are often connected with runes, which is rather absurd as the original Druids are said to have used no writing, and the Irish Celts themselves wrote Ogham, if they wrote at all.

Erilar, is a name or title that is frequently found in rune inscriptions. Some witches claim that it means 'rune master' whilst scholars say it signifies 'the Herulian', which is a tribe

from northern Germany that used more rune writing than others.

Goði, Guðja, Guði, Gudija. A Goði is a priest of some cult or religion, who deals with ritual, ceremony, sacrifice and similar offices. The name connects with the word 'god' (< ᚢ ᚦ. = cuth) which was a title for several deities (Gautr = Odin) before the Christians monopolized it. 'God' can be traced to the Indo-European roots. *Gheue- = to call, invoke (OHG *gud-igaz* and OE *gydig* = possessed, insane, giddy) and *gheu* = to pour, to sacrifice.

Éwart, meaning the eternal law (êwa) guardian and *Eosago* or *Asega* meaning the 'law-speaker'. See also the Ehwaz (ᛗ) rune for further meaning of this word.

Wicce is the root of 'witch'. Gerald Gardner tried to connect it with 'wit' and 'wisdom', making his version of wicca 'the craft of the wise.' Linguistics, more prosaic, traces it back to 'wicked' which means 'crafty, cunning, twisted', and indicates that the 'title' was probably an insult.

Tunrida is found in most German languages. It means 'fence rider', i.e. a person who sits on a fence, one leg either side of reality.

Hagzissa, root of the modern German *Hexe* (witch) has a similar use. It means 'hedge sitter.' Hedges were used, from Neolithic times, to protect settlements (see *Thorn* rune). A person who sits in the hedge, or passes through it, interacts with known reality (the village) and the dangerous realms beyond, relating the world of mortals with the realm of the spirits, gods, ghosts and demons. In Robert De Boron's version of the Merlin mythos (c.1180) Merlin is spellbound under a flowering whitethorn bush in the forest of Brocceliande in Brittany. In later periods the 'Hagzissa' became the 'hag', which in the original version could be applied to both sexes and all ages.

Galdarmadr, Galarkuna, are men and women who practice 'galdr' 'galdar' or 'galstar', which signifies song and chant magick. The Indo-European root *Ghel-* means 'to call, shout, sing, scream.'

Vala, Wala. These are names for the priestesses in Germany.

Volor, Volva. This is the later Norse equivalent of Vala or Wala. It supposedly connects with *valr* 'the staff', making the volor 'staff-bearing women'. Famous walas were the women Weleda and Albruna, who upset Roman politics for years as they roused several tribes to revolt. Wala seem to be a regular part of the priesthood while the Nordic Volor tend to travel through the country on their own or in small groups, healing diseases, selling spells and foretelling the future. Some claim that the *Valkyrie* (val = the dead, kyrie = to choose, select, devour) are really a distorted vision of those priestesses. Several Eddic songs mention women who were Valkyries, and who had the skill to fly, astrally, to the battlefield to aid the hero of their choice.

Seiðkona, Seiðmadr. These words describe the people who practise Seid-magick, i.e. the art of seething. Seid-artists, as far as they are mentioned in literature, have a reputation for selling sorcery. Snorri tells us in *Ynglingasaga* 4-7, that Odin invented seidr, but that it was so dangerous and unclean that it was left to the women. Seid magick is used to make weather, work spells, heal, bind, divine or curse. The practice revolves around the use of chanting and the phenomena of obsession which causes the typical seething and trembling described below.

Zauberer. Is still a common word for 'sorcerer' in German. It comes from OHG *zauber*, OE *teafor*, meaning 'red colour, red ochre' and suggests the common practice of blood sacrifice. Runes were consecrated by a few drops (or more) of blood, while the red earth is probably the oldest religious colour ever used. The Neanderthal people used to bury their dead in red earth, or to place their skulls in a bed of that substance. While our direct ancestors enjoyed painting their cave walls with the red stuff. 'To redden' an object means to consecrate it.

Fortune Tellers. They had numerous names. A *Wizago* (wizard) is a 'wise speaker', the same thing as a *Spamadr/Spakuna* in Old Norse. A *Troumrater*, OHG, is an interpreter of dreams, a *Tan Hlyta*, OE, a person who throws lots, i.e. rune staffs. A *Zeichnaere*, OHG, is a person who works, causes or interprets signs (*zeihhan*), nowadays a '*Zeichner*' is a graphic artist. *Sortileg* is a Gothic word for people who divine with lots while a *Tôtrunar*, OHG is a necromancer who has his fun with the dead.

Berserker meaning literally 'in bear skins' describes a special warrior who can call on his fylgia (guardian animal) and transforms into a beast. Many berserkers used to fight naked, heavily in trance and rage, their beast-consciousness making them so mad that they didn't even notice when they were wounded. The *Ynglingasaga* claims that this practise was invented by Odin.

8 Ancient cosmology

The order of the world and the order of the mind are related. To observe how this order of consciousness evolved, let us cast our minds back to the beginning of time, when the world appeared young, vast and chaotic. Norse mythology begins, like the mythology of many countries, with a vast emptiness, with a void, a vacuum, predating all creation. The *Edda* calls this phase *Ginnungagap* (gaping void). Within this empty space, polarity develops. From the north, the frozen mists of *Niflheim* (fog home), came rolling to meet the fire sparks that came from southern *Muspelheim* (home of dried earth, home of destruction). As the heat and the dampness met, a secret alchemy took place, poison drops fell, which formed the ancient giant Ymir. In the beginning was the age when Ymir lived, and Ymir was all life at once.

This is the Edda's first aeon, a time of chaos and beginning when laws were unknown and the ancient ones dwelled on the earth.

Ymir, as the first life, is too vast to know itself. Some scholars suspect that the modern German 'immer' (always, ever), lies hidden in Ymir's name. This is a valuable (though unproven) idea as it describes giant-consciousness so well. 'Immer' suggests a certain timelessness, a consciousness that experiences 'as now', ignorant of past and future, ignorant of causal thought and wide-eyed in the wonder of the primal aeon. In terms of history, the legend of the giants can be understood in many ways. If you study the evolution of human beings, you will notice how swiftly each new species appears. Somehow in the distant past, a group of apes developed into human beings. It happened, as far as we know, in a series of rather sudden mutations. To each stage of this development, the previous stage appeared both wise and primitive - wise because the 'older type' had plenty of time to find a good way of life, and primitive, as each new mutation had an altered consciousness which somehow transcended the abilities of its ancestors. To each new type, the older types were 'giants'.

The development of the human being begins with the discovery of individual rather than group identity. This change can be deduced from burial customs. An ape group does not bury its members. Maybe the dead ape is covered with a few branches, or some of its close companions stay nearby for a while, but soon enough they realize the finality of death and move on. For the early humans, and this includes the Neanderthal people, burial was a much more complicated business. We may safely assume that the burial of definite individual has taken place when we encounter burial customs in which the dead, whole or part, were ritually eaten, or covered in red ochre; when graves are carefully built and designed to resist carrion eaters; when the dead are placed in customary positions and receive offerings; and when they are given weapons, tools, artifacts, ornaments or power links (such as mammoth ivory, ibex horns, fresh flowers etc). We may also infer that some notion of religion and a possible after-death state were common.

Now the discovery of identity begins with the 'I am', but speedily extends into the 'I am xyz.' For xyz, we may fill in one or more names, symbols, personal history, function in the group, skills, talents, problems, status in the hierarchy and all sorts of games which humans use to define themselves. Apparently it is not enough to be, we also insist on being this and that. It seems likely or so the spirits assure me that the 'group I', the value of the herd, lost meaning when each member began to acquire personality, uniqueness and creative expression.

As many mythologies suggest during these aeons of beginning, the ancient ones came to earth and formed our consciousness in their image. These primal entities obsessed and inspired our ancestors, taught them self-discovery and self-expression, and filled them with great lusts and drives, with passion and longing, until our ancestors became the living expressions, the human counterparts of the ancient and forgotten ones. This process by which out ancestors established their sense of identity may been wild and anti-social, they had great drives and few inhibitions. The ancient ones inspired them with the overwhelming intensity of their sentience, a sentience that has been considered evil and awful by most of the cultures that developed out of it.

Identity is a question of continuity. It requires a notion of time, definition of self and a couple of durable belief structures. As people began to discover the continuity of their personality not as a single state ('who am I right now?') but as a continuous process of development, they began to search for the cycles and regularities of nature. You will probably agree that a known, lawful and predictable world (or identity) is a much safer thing than the vast and wonderful chaos world of the beginning. Essentially we perceive the world as it suits our minds. Bandler and Grinder have pointed out (*Structure of Magic* Vol 1) that we cannot perceive the real world (whatever that may be): what we experience is a sensory representation of the world. We cannot perceive the real world directly: what we perceive is a model. Our sense experience is selected, ordered and represented by parts of our deep minds, which supply our conscious mind with a small, suitable and edited summary, which we, in our usual naivety, consider the entire universe. The deep mind does an excellent job shielding our conscious minds, our ego with its limited notions of 'I', from the overwhelming impact of whatever it is out there. Much of the order of nature is a reflection of our mind's order: the world is experienced according to our beliefs. Often enough, the restrictions that limit us do not exist in the real world but in our representation of it. During the nameless aeons, the ancient ones and their human incarnations had a wild and wonderful time. When the ice ages ended people began to settle and developed agriculture in ever increasing communities, organized and rational society developed requiring strict social, ethical and religious laws. The ancient ones found the new world too small for their liking. The chaotic forces of the dawn ages were banished, repressed and forgotten, and overwhelming ancient beings replaced by reliable gods with clear character and definite functions. In the *Book of the Forgotten Ones*, we are told:

'The bright gods did replace us on your altars,
the dark gods hid us in their temple veil.
The starred ones stirred within their awakening-time,
and cried our call of returning unto man.
We come, flesh-children,
through the midnight portal,
to the noon tide mountain,
to the waking mind.
Know us, and embrace us, and be whole.'

In the *Edda*, we read that Ymir is slain by Wodan, Willi, We, and that out of its body, the entire world is fashioned. We hear of the Hrimthursen, the frost giants, keepers of the primal knowledge of the Ice-Ages, who were slain or driven into exile when the gods established order. We learn that the Fenris wolf had to be bound, and that in the process of binding, the bisexual sky god Twisto (the twinned one) lost a hand and became the one handed god Tyr. We also hear that at the end of the season, the chain bursts and the wolf runs wild. After the chaos ages with their outbursts of wild talent and reckless self-expression, the worlds had to be ordered. For a stable society, moral codes were needed, laws and social customs, traditions of behaviour and belief, a structure of natural science and knowledge which made the world a more reliable and limited place. These restriction are the forces that keep the wolf locked.

In the *Voluspa* we learn that the gods went

to the chairs of law giving for names and paths to the stars, to order the times of the day, the quarters of the earth and the seasons of the year. We can examine this order when we observe the use of numbers in symbolism.

Zero: This corresponds to Ginnungagap, the gaping void before creation. This is the primal nothingness out of which all came and into which all returns. In a sense, this void is of ourselves and we share it with all that exists. What do we have in common with all that may possibly exist? Nothing. Nothing at all. I find that reassuring.

Unity: All is one. This is the basic state that knows neither separation nor difference nor change. In a sense, Ymir is one, and this one begets children with itself. We may see unity as a symbol for a 'here and now' consciousness that is typical for wild giants, aged mystics and small children.

Duality: This is the primal sexuality, in which we have an 'I' and a 'you', which communicate. The two are apart, and different, or at least they seem to think they are. In the *Edda*, duality can be found in the two extreme states of Niflheim, which is cold, pale, misty, veiled, and Muspelheim where the fire giants wallow in lava, fire and heat. Such polarities reflect the way our brains are built, which may explain why new-age prophets are often so anthropocentric to speak of 'cosmic laws of polarity' where they should more wisely speak of 'our typical human way of ordering the world.' The point is that people like to perceive polarities, and feel quite comfortable and reassured by it. However, the simple binary model is not the only one. The mind is quite capable of transcending the basic 'yes or no?' by adding 'maybe'. Do we have to choose? The world is a big place and many things are possible.

Trinity: Out of duality, a threefold mystery develops which transcends its primal elements. 'Thou art that which thou dost prefer' wrote Austin Spare in his *Focus of Life*, 'the seer, the instrument of seeing or the seen.' If unity can be seen as 'I everywhere' and duality as 'I and you', trinity goes beyond by adding 'I and you and the communication between us'. In pagan mythology, starting with the triskell spirals of the megalith period, the three-fold mystery is of major importance. If we look at the world Ash, we recognize its triple symbolism. The tree, which was originally a mountain ash or rowan, consists of three units: roots, stem and branches. These three items correspond to the three levels of consciousness, which are known from many mythologies, especially from the Chinese.

1. **Roots**. This level corresponds to the earth, to flesh and form, to nourishment and manifestation. The roots level includes all past experience, all past life times and, in the genetic coding of our cells, the entire scope of survival skills developed by our ancestors. This includes wild instincts, power drives, sexual lust and all sorts of obsessions which civilized people feel shame and unease about.

2. **Stem**. This part of the tree connects heaven and earth: in essence, its joy lies in standing between the realms of the absolute (heaven) and the particular (earth). In cosmology, it

can be considered the human level as we, just like the trees, live between the worlds. In human terms, this level corresponds with such ideas as reason, emotion, communication, change and social interaction.

3. **Branches**. The branches are the outfolding of the tree, its source of fresh energy, suppliers of breath and inspiration. In the branches we find seeds, and out of these seeds the next generation will be born. These seeds are potential trees in themselves. Thus, we may see the branch level as a symbol of potential for future development. In the heavenly plane we encounter the ideal forces, the ideal perceptions of ourselves, the gods and angels, the notions of what we may be like one day, leading to the idea of 'future selves'.

It should be obvious that the three levels of the tree function best when each of them can live according to its nature. We can apply the model to our own consciousness, to realize that a whole and holy being requires harmonious functioning in each of its parts.

Now the world tree is also a triple tree. Around its three branches and its three roots, three worlds may be found:

The world of ideals is the god-world **Asgard** (land of the Asir).

The world of instinct and obsession is the giant realm **Utgard** (out-land).

The world of reason and emotion is the human realm, **Midgard** (Middle land).

In **Asgard** the tree is called 'Yggdrassil'. This word means 'Yggr's horse', 'Yggr' being an aspect of Odin/Wotan; the name means 'the terrible one' and is the source of 'ogre'. In many shamanic traditions, the shaman had to climb a world tree (or a world mountain) to receive initiation between the worlds. Here the shaman is free to understand and bind heaven and earth, and is also 'outside', and open for the spirit union. The *Edda* tells us that Odin received the rune vision as he hung from the tree between the worlds. This ritual should be seen as a way of transcending the limits of ego, as a formula of exhaustion, of going out and beyond. It is not a rite of masochistic self-crucifixion, as some of the Christian scholars would have it. The career of Christ ends with the cross and its formula of suffering, that of Odin begins with the vision in the tree, and with the encounter of the spirit helpers. Had Odin died up there, the ravens and wolves would have devoured the carcass. Odin lived, but still the ravens and wolves devoured him, and became his friends for a lifetime and more. To understand this riddle I suggest you contact your own beasts. In the god world, there is a well at the root of the tree. Three Norns live there, Urda, Werdandi, Skulda, who weave destiny, purify all life in Urda's well, and create reality through divination.

In the world of the giants, the tree is called 'Mimameith', or Mimir's tree. In the common German tradition, Mimir used to be the ruler of the hidden waters that flow through the earth, of the sacred springs, swamps and water currents, sometimes even the high seas.

Mimir's well is the spring of all memory, and to drink from this source, Odin paid Mimir with one of his eyes. This eye became blind to the world, but opened up inside, into the brain, so that Odin sees outward and inward at the same time. We may learn from this episode where the sacred well of Mimir lies. In the *Fjölsvinsmal* we are told that Mimir's tree is so vast that no one can know its roots and branches at the same time, and that the tree is eternal. This corresponds nicely with giant-consciousness, which knows neither past nor future but the eternal now.

In the human world, the tree is called 'Lärad' which means 'giver of peace and silence'. This is the living tree, not the ideal tree of the gods or the numinous tree of the giants but the manifest tree which lives on earth. The *Voluspa* lists numerous animals which feed on this tree, live in its branches or creep beneath its roots. This tree is eaten and constantly regrows. It is the functioning eco-system, a community of life forms which interact and depend on each other. Lärad is destroyed and reborn at the same time, a changing tree in a changing world, and this suits us humans very well. There is also a well at the human root of the tree: The 'roaring cauldron' *Hwergelmir*. This is the well of Hel or Helja who is the Queen and/or personification of the underworld beneath.

In Nordic cosmology, we have already encountered the three primal states Ginnungagap, Niflheim and Muspelheim. When the worlds were established and cosmos ordered, these three realms were repressed, and acquired a curious in-between status.

Ginnungagap, the gaping void, surrounds the earth now, and protects us from the giants who live among the stars.

Niflheim became the classic underworld. When people die, they encounter after-life visions of paradise that suit their nature.

However, there comes a time when the illusions fade. No matter how glorious Valhalla may be, after a time the warriors, and even the gods, are done with glory, and find that the vision fades. Then the gates of hell open and Helja receives the dead. The prose *Edda* tells us she rules over nine worlds, over realms of fog and forgetfulness, over dim and twilight realms, over the places where people become shadows, walking endlessly through mist and fog, in an atmosphere that knows no time nor place, only the eternal veils of fog. You would do well to understand that this is not a punishment. From one point of view (Valhalla) all life is glory and battle and feasting. From another, Niflheim, life is an illusion peopled by shadows searching for meaning and purpose, and finding none. Helja is our lady of the veils, in that she may cloud our minds or reveal with clarity; in that she hides, and brings forgetfulness, or sings a song of memories revealing ancient mystery. From her point of view, human aims and strife and struggle are rather meaningless, coming to terms with this is something that people learn in Niflheim. However, it is not only our world which is seen as the roll of the mists, but also our notions of ourselves. In Niflheim there is an eagle, 'Hräswelgr' (to indulge in carrion) and a dark dragon, 'Nidhöggr' (to crouch underneath), who destroy the dead bodies of

belief and strip the soul of its name, purpose, past and future. Freed of this accumulated baggage, the soul spark is sucked up by the 'roaring cauldron' and comes to be reborn elsewhere. The idea of reincarnation is common to Germans and Celts alike. Sadly, we don't know how they thought reincarnation would work or by what laws it was governed. Now if you should chance to stumble into Niflheim, which is an experience I can highly recommend, you would do well to consider your ego and your identity as shadows, or mist illusions, which may be but do not need to be. There is no certainty in this realm, nor will you find reality, as all is illusion. If you understand this, you will realize the truth behind the veiling fog.

In **Muspelheim**, the 'home of dry earth', things are very different. This is the reals of Loki and the fire giants, the white hot heart of our planet. Here you will enjoy surges of passion, lust and overwhelming instincts. Muspelheim is hot and bright and so intense that the feeble human reason is a plaything to the great pulse of magma, fire, flame and gas. If we can leave our egos behind, we can learn to dance in the eruptions of this primal fire.

Now you may wonder what such models are good for. Remember that the mythological model supplies a topography of the soul, and that the order of the world (no matter how bizarre or fanciful) is also a map of the mind. You may have heard of the 'astral projection', of people who 'leave that body' (meaning body awareness is largely forgotten) and travel in the astral world, which is the world of dreams and imagination. Through this art,

which is explained in practical way in chapter 27, the trained mage may travel into parts of the mind which are usually unconscious. These 'parts of the mind' will represent themselves to consciousness as countries, lands and spaces, through which the mage may travel, and where s/he can encounter strange beings, who are the representatives of these countries (or parts of the mind). These magical journeys change the structure of consciousness from within. Should you meet Helja, for instance, you get a wonderful chance to come to terms with the parts of your deep mind which are symbolized by Niflheim, and perhaps you will even learn how to use the inbetweenness of Niflheim to contact other worlds. The fog is everywhere and nowhere, so that all worlds can be touched. Or you may meet Loki. You would learn some surprising things about yourself and you may even enjoy them (provided you enjoy Loki). Your personality may disintegrate, but then, worse things could happen. Identity and personality are plastic after all, and are meant to be taken apart from time to time. The ego is there to be changed, and if you ask humbly, Helja and Loki will no doubt be eager to help you in this job.

One of the ways to learn about runes is to travel to the tree, from there to any inbetween state, and to find a way into the rune worlds. Each rune can be used as a gate or doorway, and if you are in harmony with it, pass through, and come into an astral (imaginary) world that describes the rune much better than any book could. If you travel in such a rune world you will discover your own meaning for the rune, which will be the genuine, meaning in that it works for you, and is inspired by your deep mind. Some of these worlds will be beautiful, others may be incomplete, diseased or otherwise out of balance. If you travel into them you get a chance to heal them, to right the balance, and when you return to your body and the 'real' world, you will realize that the healing has changed your reality from within.

I should perhaps add that such encounters can be dangerous. True, the visions are 'imaginary', they are not 'objective' entities and places but dream-like representations. This does not change the fact that the deep mind, which is the reality that these visions represent, is very real, and indeed creates all the realities that you perceive. You act in a representation, but the reality behind the representation is as real as anything you encounter in this lifetime. If you meet Helja for instance, you will certainly learn about the horrors of death, forgetfulness, exhaustion and illusion. Your visions will involve corpses, bones, disease and will probably show your own death with lots of variations. Now you might say that all this is the imagination. True, it is experienced as imagination, but behind it lies a reality. If you say 'you are not real' to Helja, she may reply 'neither are you', and you would both be right. Or you might travel to Muspelheim. Instincts and obsessions will arise which you were never conscious of, and which, once evoked, you will have to accept and integrate. The *Edda* tells us that when the gods tried to repress Loki's chaotic fierceness they had to chain Loki. It also tells us that the chains broke, and that the resulting outburst

resulted in the end of the world. This is an important lesson. If you meet Loki, forget about the chains. Have a good laugh with him and become his blood brother if you can. Not an easy task, but a damned sight better than restriction.

The Norns and other Germanic trinities.

Nyrnir means 'weavers', the word refers to the spiders who build their realities by weaving, creating and devouring long strands of protein, creating a universe consisting of structure, connection and the spaces between them. The Norns weave fate, they cast lots which bind destiny and prophecy a future that creates itself through being divined. The *Edda* mentions three Norns by name:

Urda, who refers to the past, has the syllable 'ur' in her name, which denotes great age, originality, and the primeval (especially in German). (see Uruz rune).

Werdandi is the same word root in another time. 'Werden' in German means 'to become', and refers to the present time.

Skulda can be found in the English 'shall' and 'should', and refers to the future. The modern German *Schuld* contains her name, it means 'a debt' or, in a negative complex, 'guilt'. The original word had no negative implications. It simply pointed out that the bill is not paid yet, for good or evil.

The three together are 'wyrda', or the 'weird sisters'. Modern writers frequently pretend that these three Norns are the only ones, a centralized fate-producing unit for all worlds. Such centralized notions ('they bind the fate of all') are typical for our modern outlook. In the *Edda* we are told that there are many more Norns, some of them Aesir, some elves and some dwarves. Perhaps we should conceive destiny as a complex weaving that is done by many Norns in many places, each of whom processes space and time in her or his own way. Ultimately, this leads to a model in which every mage functions like a spider, building a mandala of realities and projecting it on the substance of the world. Indeed we are the Norns of our own lifetimes.

Another trinity evolved around Odin/ Wotan. In the prose *Edda* we meet him, for example, as Har (the High), Iafnhar (equally high) and Thridi (the third). These three hold a riddle game with king Gylfi, in which each aspect supplies a different point of view.

Then there is the trinity of the brothers (aspects).

1. Wotan.
2. Willi. 3. Weh.[1]

1. **Wotan** is unity. This refers to pure self, pure awareness and energy. Wotan, as you read in the history chapter, was originally a god of rage, of shamanism, of wild trances, song and ecstasy.

2. **Willi** connects with our word 'will', and the 'true will' being the individual expression of the universal and evolutionary will. This will includes change, evolution, transformation.

3. **Weh** or Ve. 'Sanctuary' or 'holy grove', i.e. the natural temple. Modern German *Weh* is something painful, like the English 'woe!' German *Wehen* are the pains of childbirth, while a *Weihe* is consecration and initiation. Sometimes the *Edda* gives us 'Honir' for Willi, Honir is a silent watcher figure, and 'Lodur' for Weh, who is 'flaming', an aspect of Loki. These three created human beings out of the 'ask' (ash tree) and the 'embla' (alder or elm). In the *Voluspa* we are told that Odin gave soul, Honir gave sense and Lodur supplied blood and rich colour. It is no surprise that the triskell, (the triple spiral), can be seen as a symbol for the Norns and Wodan alike.

These triads may be useful for divination. We might consult the Norns when we want to know how something will develop. We could select three runes, or throw three dice, so that the first rune refers to the beginning, the second to its present situation, and the third to what should develop out of it. The Wodan, Willi, Weh pattern can be used when we wish to understand three aspects of an idea. The first rune, Wodan, describes the essence, the second rune its motion, energy and meaning and the third its manifestation in body, earth and reality.

---

[1] This triplet may be familiar to Qabalists. Perhaps Binah is Weh, Chokmah is Willi and Kether is Wodan.

The number nine.

Where three is already the entire universe in north European nature religion, the nine, as 3 x 3, is beyond comprehension.

The ancient tree, for instance, connects three worlds, three planes, three wells and three guardians. It has three basic roots, but nine branches spreading over all worlds. When Odin spent nine days and nights on the tree, or Frey has to wait nine nights for his marriage with the frost-cold northern earth, or Grimnir waits for nine long nights, chained between the fires, it will appear obvious that the number nine meant something like 'forever'.

The four quarters

Another basic pattern is the fourfold symmetry. The four is really an extension of the two, a doubling of the double, a cross and the crossroads that connect the world. You are here, at the centre. In the *Edda*, we encounter the four dwarves who support the world; Nordri and Surdri, Austri and Westri. Often the quarters of the earth are connected with solar symbols. For the time being the sun rises in the east. This connects the east with the idea of birth, spring, beginning. In the south, it is strongest, which makes south the quarter of light, heat, summer and fire, unless you happen to live in Australia. West symbolizes age, and the going down of the sun. In many cultures, west is the direction of death. Then follows north, which is the direction of maximal darkness, and thus a fitting representative of winter, earth, cold and the sparkle of the stars. North is the direction of the night, its darkness is the sleep of the unborn. To the Celts and Germans, the night came before the day, just like pregnancy comes before birth. The Gaelic year began in November, after all stores were gathered in, with the celebration of the ancestors. Winter was seen as a preparation for the year to come. It is an interesting fact that most pagan traditions place the altar in the North, which is the direction of the Tir-star (north star), which was considered the 'need nail' around which the heavens revolve. The Christians, with their sun and light orientation, introduced the custom of placing the altar in the east, which is quite fitting for their solar 'birth, glory, crucifixion, resurrection' symbolism.

When we recognize the order of the seasons in the times of day, in the four elements, in the directions of the earth, this is a case of a basic model that gets deeply integrated in our notions of cyclic development and evolution. To our ancestors, each of the seasons meant a different outlook on life, and indeed, a different lifestyle. When modern witches celebrate the wheel of the year, they are continuing a tradition that is more important than ever. By celebrating the seasons, we keep ourselves in tune with the natural world. Many cultures believe that if they stop celebrating the seasonal festivals, all nature would get out of order. In our modern world of concrete, plastic and neon, our nature is

out of order. By celebrating the rhythms of change in nature, we keep our own nature in balance. The seasonal festivals are not only meant to harmonize humanity with nature. They should, in my opinion, also be opportunities to give our thanks to the natural world, and to send joy and blessing to all living beings. Nature itself needs healing in our days of pollution and waste. By going out into the wild we remember ourselves.

Systems of cosmology, such as those described in this chapter, are more than idle theory. Where they are not based on natural facts they rely on psychological ones. Cosmology is an attempt to order awareness in meaningful patterns. As in every functional Qabalistic system, the model you believe will soon reveal itself in all aspects of life. Once you begin to think in terms of trinity for instance, all life will appear threefold to you. Now the important thing is not whether you order your world in twos, threes, fours of six-hundred three score and six, as each and every model has its advantages. What matters is that you remember that no model is quite like the truth, and that truth includes the freedom to use all models, and to go beyond them. Any model which is believed with sufficient intensity will soon produce its own confirmation. A model is a bit like a mask, in that it covers reality and rearranges it. Truth wears many masks and models, and every single one of them is false. If you will freedom for your own thoughts, feel free to use any model that suits you.

9 Runes and nature

The Celtic and Germanic people, and the cultures which preceded them, considered themselves to be parts of nature. Tacitus tells us that the Germans would not tolerate cities or large settlements: 'they live alone and apart from others, wherever a spring, a field or a forest suits them' (*Germania*, 16). This accords with the needs of cultures that still possess the ability to identify with the ecological system that surround them. Apart from the ceremonies of the yearly cycle (during which whole tribes travelled for days to meet at some important site), they observed a number of religious practices closer to home. Sacrificial offerings would be laid out for the spirits of the house and the fields, and frequently memorial stones erected nearby.

The peasant of pre-history was more closely bound to the earth than we can imagine: the land was life, meaning survival and the continuation of the family or clan. Where a state-bound, centralized civilization (such as Sumer, Egypt, Rome) can afford to build monumental palaces and churches, a tribal system has neither the necessary labour force nor the use of temples or domes. To the pagan people of the north, the gods had not become as sophisticated as they were to, say, city-dwellers of the Near-East. To realize their existence, they had but to look at the wildness of the elements, the living forces of nature, the perfection of the system as a whole. They rarely built sacred houses for the gods, as the gods were everywhere, spoke in the roar of the oceans, the thunder of the storms, whispered in the foliage, danced in the flames or dreamed in the ageless silence of the earth. These gods were both terrible and beautiful; life-giving and death-dealing; overwhelming and unlimited. Other, invisible life forms were named 'elves' (called Alfen, Alben, Ilben, in the *Edda*). It hardly matters whether one considers the gods, elves, dwarves in an abstract or anthropomorphic way. The gods give power and idealism to humanity; humanity gave form and character to the gods.

To understand nature religion, one has to realize that everything, be it the elements, the seasons, the plants, beasts, minerals, the people, the depth of the earth and the width of the skies, is sentient and alive. Modern people have largely forgotten what it means to experience the elements. To understand nature we have to give ourselves into her care, and to experience first hand what heat, cold, day, night, hunger, nourishment, strength and exhaustion may mean. Who remembers the old days when possession of fire meant the difference between life and death? To learn about runes one should not only practice at home but go and dare the wilderness. The language of the runes is a language of nature. Many rune-forms are growth forms. 'Giving oneself' (gebo) means to open up to new experience. To walk in the woods, by day and by night, and in all kinds of weather. To feel the passage of the seasons. To be cold, to get wet with rain or snow, to lose one's way, to stumble around in the dark, to rest in the sun, to flow with the fog and to dance with the wind. To watch the stars, to collect herbs and leaves for healing and nourishment, to learn the ways of the beasts. To run madly cross-country, to scream, to laugh, to celebrate feasts on the mountaintops. We remember the meaning of nature insofar as we give ourselves; and each memory is a memory of ourselves. The wildness, beauty and passion we find in nature is an expression of our own being, and an expression of those states so clumsily called 'god,' 'self,' 'all-being' etc.

Loving nature means to love oneself. Nature religion is sterile without nature experience. This may sound self evident, but far too many witches and magicians nowadays never dare to leave their comfortable temple rooms. Catching pneumonia in a snow storm is far less dangerous than suffocating in an armchair. You may find that nature, in all her joyous and dangerous moods, can initiate you much better than any temple or cult can. We are nature and the discovery of the wilderness is the discovery of our primordial self-hood.

Of course it is possible to activate the rune powers in any place, be it on the mountain top, in a desert or in the middle of the city. Will is the essential factor. Many readers may have to do most of their practice indoors or at home. No harm will come from this (apart from complaining neighbours) provided you keep some nature contacts up. A 'nature contact' is a place or a situation that allows access to the elements and the primal levels of our being. A moderate nature contact would be a room immediately under the roof, a garden or maybe a river or park nearby. A walk in the fields can be useful, or a real fire at home. Once a week, however, one should go out into the wild, if possible alone. Remember Algernon Blackwood's haunting phrase 'the wind is roaring in the forest . . . further out.' We go into the wilderness to remember.

In ancient China, a system of nature study developed that sought to understand and control the forces of earth, water, fire and wind. According to the Chinese 'Feng Shui' tradition, the body of our planet is criss-crossed by energy channels or meridians that distribute life force across the land. These energy channels are also found in the human body (microcosmos), where they are balanced and stimulated by means of acupuncture, moxa and similar therapies. The energy channels transport the ch'i, the life-force, to harmonize the functions of the body and to connect it with other life forms. Human beings are said to relate to life and nature as the earth does to the stars. Where a *ch'i* line runs across the earth, the scenery is shaped by and shapes that power. Body and spirit influence each other. A similar tradition of energy flow once existed in Europe. We have no idea what this science was called; nowadays it is mostly referred to as 'geomancy'. Chinese and European geomancy use the term 'dragon lines' to designate the energy channels. Mountain ridges and cliffs frequently indicate the flow of these lines. According to Feng Shui teachings, the cosmic ch'i touches the earth of the mountain tops. From the height, the energy flows along the ridges and hills towards the valley. When the ch'i reaches the plains, it is brought to diffusion and transported to the oceans by rivers and streams. Given proper training, one can learn to feel the flow of the ch'i in the earth, and to follow the dragon lines through the wild.

To our ancestors, the energy currents of the earth were far more obvious than they are to us. Where they would have known 'places of power' modern people generally only feel 'funny' or 'spooky,' if they notice the difference at all. Geomancy is mainly a question of sensitivity, not of theoretical comprehension or abstract study.

Geomancy teaches that the earth and the quality of its energy influence one another. The energy does not simply flow downhill but seems to interact with the scenery. At some spots the ch'i bursts out, at others it collects, at some it is swept away by rivers and streams, and at some we find the ch'i stagnating, which makes such sites unhealthy for habitation. In Chinese Feng Shui we find a number of more or less useful practices to find out the proper sites for living. The three sorts of homes - temples (gods), houses (humans) and graves (ancestors) all have different energy requirements. Very little is known about European geomancy. It did not survive the 'Dark Ages'. That a system did once exist, however, can be deduced from folklore, rural customs, the locations of old shrines etc. If you practice rune magick in the open, you will soon learn that the energy flow differs from time to time, and place to place. The state of your inner world (set) and the state of the outer world (setting) influence each other. By generating rune energy, you will find yourself involved in a form of communication, that is, an exchange of energy/consciousness between micro and macrocosmos. This exchange is different in certain surroundings,

so that we may attribute certain states of consciousness to certain forms of scenery. More so, we find that all over the world specific landscapes and clime have produced very similar forms of nature worship. Here are a few notes on the meaning of scenery to the Germanic/Celtic way of life.

Mountains. In middle Europe, we frequently encounter 'ring-wall' systems on the mountain tops. Some of them, called *oppida* by the Romans, were fortified towns housing up to 30,000 inhabitants. Oppida are common in southern Germany, Czech, Austria, Switzerland and France. Smaller ringwalls were in use as forts, a place of refuge in times of war. A ring wall was usually a thick wall of boulders, earth and massive oak trunks. Most ring wall systems consist of several belts, or are worked in spiral fashion. Julius Caesar describes the construction of Oppida walls in the seventh book of *Bellum Gallicum*. Academics tend to believe that the Celts built the ring walls for military purposes. There are indications, however, that some ring walls are much older that the Celtic culture. Fortified ring wall systems had to be rebuilt repeatedly, as the wooden structures of the wall tended to fall apart every couple of decades. From their geographical location, we may deduce that not all ring walls were meant as fortifications. Some of them seem to have been religious sanctuaries or meeting places for the population. On top of the mountain, the forces of heaven and earth unite. The mountain top parallels the shamanic world-tree insofar as both are places between the worlds. There were few settlements on high mountain tops, usually the weather was too drastic and the water supply difficult. But there are many remnants of religious activity surviving to this day. Religion and law were closely connected in the old days. Thus we find 'ting-places' on the mountain tops, sanctuaries where the rituals of the seasons were celebrated, laws were made and the population met for judgment, festivity, decision making and 'symble' carousal. (see Tacitus *Germania*). Political activity was balanced by the symble-customs (the syllable 'sym' meant to 'to join' to 'be together') i.e. getting dead drunk with divine sanction. Mead is a very pleasant way of harmonizing the relations of gods and mortals. Such sites would be marked by holy trees, small shrines or blessed wells. Often, it was dangerous to approach such places. The religious sanctuary was usually secluded and difficult to reach, so that the exhaustion of the traveller constituted part of the initial purification. On arrival, the exhaustion and weariness would swiftly transform into clear-minded exhilaration. The element of danger is vital for this. If you have ever had the pleasure of stumbling across a ring wall with its thousands of huge stone boulders at night, you will come to appreciate the meaning of commitment. The importance of ring walls for military purposes increased in the late period, particularly during the Roman occupation. On occasion, whole tribes fled to these places of 'divine and human justice,' even if the supply of water and food was difficult. The Romans, after months of weary siege warfare, developed a process of drenching the wooden structures with oil. Then they laid fire and waited for the wall to collapse. At some ring walls the very earth is drenched with fury, blood and despair, so that a sensitive person encounters unpleasant surprises. Not only the gods were supposed to live on the mountain tops; we may also find stone giants or dwarves in such places. Fairy-tales commonly relate that there are 'forgotten gods' or 'kings from under the hill' resting inside mountains, dead but dreaming, and waiting for full resurrection in the time of wholeness.

On some mountains the earth power is so strong that the very rock seem to pulse with it. To understand the flow of the earth currents we should remember that the earth, like everything else, flows in waves. Observe how the earth once streamed and you can see the avenues of energy, some sweeping to the valley, some reaching across the mountain ridges to other peaks. Observe the growth of the trees. Along the 'dragon lines' we frequently encounter so called 'dragon trees,' i.e. trees with a coiled, wild and intense appearance which seem to vibrate with the power of the place. Where the power is diluted, trees look uniform, but where the energy is dense, trees are highly individual, and very much awake. Wind is also important. Exposure to storm wind does more than just blow away the heat, it can sweep much of the earth ch'i away. The same goes for water. Flowing water transports the ch'i, swifter than the earth does (the colder the water the more energy it can hold), so that a simple little stream may drain all the energy out of its

surroundings, and rush it downhill with great speed. To understand geomancy, you have to feel with your eyes. There are thousands of signatures everywhere which suggest the essence of each place. To see a mountain (or whatever) you could look into it, go beyond the surface and feel its substance. Seeing the form, penetrate to the interior and unfold from inside. Through identification, love and voidness you may realize the essence, which is also the essence of ourselves. Each mountain has its own distinct character and reacts to magick, rune practice, music etc., in its own way. We cannot touch the mountain with our reason. Only by being the mountain may we may touch the its sentience, the living meaning of its form. We are one with the earth; and this statement should not be the result of logical comprehension but of direct experience.

Hills. Here the earth force is already modified and calmed. Just as the mountains are home to gods and giants, we may encounter human heroes resting under the hills. Many of these are the ghosts of warriors, indicating that hilltops, like mountaintops, were widely used to build fortresses. Celtic burial customs often required the erection of a small hill over the grave chamber, a custom that may go back to megalith religion with its earth covered dolmen and barrow graves. Hill country is hunting territory. If we consider hunting as the highly religious affair it used to be, we find that it is not human power but divine grace that supplies food, hence survival. The gods gives life, the hunter kills to feed the community. By sacrifice of plants, beasts or occasionally humans, many tribes attempted to redress the balance and to give back in symbolic form, what the gods had supplied.

Sacred groves were places of sanctuary, where the seasonal fire festivals, sacred marriages or blood sacrifices were celebrated. (see *The Golden Bough* by Sir George Frazer). It is not true that the sacred groves consisted entirely of oaks. Roman superstition attributed a single species of tree to the sinister ceremonies of the Druids, with whom they were hardly on friendly terms. Modern study indicates religious activity for just about any sort of tree at one time or another. There were cults of the birch, beech, rowan, hazel, elm, willow and many other species. In Germany, and Scandinavia, many sanctuaries were dedicated to Ullr, lord of winter, hunting, killing and the Yule ceremony, whose sacred tree was the yew. See my book *Visual Magick* for further exploration of sacred trees and related folk customs.

The Plains. The earth energy is usually diffuse when it reaches the fields and settlements. The magick of the plains is agricultural and social. It is not the primal gods of forest and wilderness that trouble the peasants of the Neolithic ages, but the more human shades (ghosts, doppelgänger, ancestors) and the numerous spirits in charge of weather, fertility and growth. The fields are cultivated - humanized, so to speak. They are limited and protected with walls or thorn hedges and this relates to the Thurisaz rune(ᚦ). Also, they are property. Property, in the sense of ground owned and inherited, is probably an idea that began when people stopped travelling and began to work the earth. To the farmer the fields are an extension of the body: they are the future of the clan. Settlement means commitment, endurance and stubborn determination. The cults of the fields concern themselves with human problems. Typical examples are house spirits, ancestor worship, protective spirits, human ghosts and the beings of nature, elves, sylphs, fairies etc., who supply the blessings of growth, abundance and good weather. Together with such beliefs exist a number of customs to limit the forces of the wilderness, to keep the ancient ones away and to exorcise the repressed energy that will always accumulate in society. The gods themselves appear more distant and controlled - where each hunter of the nomadic aeons used to relate personally to the deities and demons of the wild, the peasant community employs a tribal shaman to speak with the unknown and to keep up the psychological health of the clan. The cults and life-forms of the plains are frequently fatalistic and emphasize security and limits.

Rivers and streams. They are conductors of energy. Cold water binds energy and distributes it through the land, concentrating the power in some river bends and draining it in others. Chinese Feng Shui teaches that each curve in a river has a side that accumulates power, and a side that is constantly emptied by the rushing waters. This may be important for your practice. Some sites may exhaust while others may overload the practitioner. When the aura is overcharged through misapplication of rune energy or through contact with unwholesome places or people, cold water (a shower for instance) us useful to clear the aura up again. Warm water is not as efficient, as it already contains some power of its own. Some rivers functioned as trade routes long before roads were known. Travellers on the water or settlers near the shore usually personified their river, attributing character, taste and habits to it and perceiving its consciousness in the form of water spirits, undines, kelpies etc. Many of these river spirits could on occasion be violent, so that the peace of the river had to be bought by regular sacrifice of beast or man. Some rivers have a rather gruesome reputation in this respect; if the sacrifice was omitted, the river took what it desired.

Springs and wells. These symbolize doors and gateways into the deep. Here is the spot where life (water) rises from the dark. The idea of birth, purification and passage is an obvious one. Some wells in central Germany were dedicated to Holla and popular place to pray for children. From the birth idea comes the use of springs for purification. This is the major use of Urda's well at the roots of the Yggdrasil tree. Missionaries fought it with all their might, exorcising and baptizing hundreds of sacred wells on their way across the land. A well may also allow passage to the underworld. Many fairy tales, such as the 'Frau Holle' (Hel, Helja) begin with some person falling into a well and through the water into another world. In Celtic Germany and France, wells were used for healing. Sick people undertook long journeys to live near a sacred well for a while. To 'take the water' and to consult the druids about their ailments. When the Romans occupied the country, they continued the custom. A holy well of the Gallic-Roman period was graced by a big stone stele showing three goddesses with baskets of fruit. These *Matrona* looked very much alike and of the same age, so we cannot inflict the popular wiccan trinity of virgin, mother and hag on them. Commonly these sacred wells were surrounded by hostels. Many of them became spas and are popular to this day. In some countries we find the sacred wells guarded by specially trained attendants. Where service was neglected or the well left open by mistake the waters of the bottomless deep were likely to rise and drown whole valleys. A number of lakes in Wales are said to have been born this way.

Swamp and marshland. These are among the oldest landscape types known to man. When the ice retreated, people began to journey across the new land, an open and barren country with few trees (mainly birch, rowan, willow) and sparse vegetation. Winter made the Tundra an icy desert with howling snowstorms. Summer turned the marsh into a muddy, mosquito infested bog. The first settlers in this country had to travel in order to survive. The tribes carried small hide tents and made their meagre living through hunting, fishing, collecting berries, mushrooms, herbs etc. In winter, people came close to starvation while in summer they lived off migrating reindeer and horses. In some swamps the

remnants of numerous reindeer sacrifices were found. As the climate grew milder, people began to settle. However the memory of the swamp as a place of danger and magick continued. The moors too remained a sacred (and haunted) place up to the Roman occupation. In its own way, the swamp is as inaccessible as the mountain top. The bog symbolizes the state between worlds, i.e. a reality between firm and fluid. Here we have a place of great danger where a transition between worlds may occur. A power-site where objects may be given to the earth/water/deep without necessitating the effort of digging a hole. In geomancy the earth energy is said to stagnate in swamp territory, giving a delicious touch of morbidity and putrefaction to the atmosphere. When you transcend prejudice and fear, the beauty of the swamp will reveal itself. To enter swampland sanctuaries creates a state between tension and commitment that is useful to the magician. The spirits of the moors are usually imagined as very beautiful, unrefined and untrustworthy. They have received sacrifices during all aeons of human evolution - food, clothes, jewellery, ornaments, beasts, small models of boats or ceremonial carts, weapons and frequently humans. In the war against the Romans, the swamps were considered a useful place to get rid of prisoners of war or selected criminals. Even the sophisticated cultures of the Celts and Germans continued the customary sacrifice to the swamp dwellers, however much their gods (ideals) were concerned with loftier realms. When 'sinners' were sacrificed, their hair was cropped very short (which gives the recovered swamp corpses an innocent, almost juvenile look) while the bodies were tied into a foetal position, much like the Pertho rune (K). In this state the sacrifice could be returned into the deep much like it had come from the womb. In the older Futhorc, the swamp was symbolized by the Eohl rune (Y). In the sixteen rune Futhorc, the swamp became mixed up with the sacred yew grove (both ideas imply sanctuaries closely connected with death and danger) and was symbolized by the Yr rune.

Caves and dolmens. They symbolize the unity of womb and tomb. Caves are the oldest religious sites known to us. The cave is inside and yet outside the known world, a transition phase in a journey leading both ways. Caves were rarely used for living, though there is plenty of evidence indicating settlement very close to them. Most of our dawn-age knowledge comes from caves. Indeed dawn-age art stood few chances of surviving in open places. The distribution of certain beasts and symbols in various cave rooms seems to indicate they were used for special purposes.

The big hall in Lascaux seems to have been a public power-site, whereas the small room with the en-tranced, bird-headed sorcerer (see illustration) above the chasm seems to be more concerned with the mysteries of death and rebirth. The sorcerer, the dying European buffalo (with spilling guts) and the woolly rhino that has just dropped its manure (note the characteristic position of the tail) above the opening to the deep, have successfully confused several generations of scientists. To simulate the psychological effect of the cave, the megalith people invented the dolmen (Bretonic: 'table-stone'). The dolmen consists of a low-lying entrance, a long passage with a low ceiling (either the megalith people were smaller than we are, or they wanted to make people stoop) and a slight curve (at the bend, we usually encounter a stone particularly rich in quartzite) leading to a large, round chamber. Sometimes there are one or two small rooms to the sides of the passage.

Several Bretonic dolmens have small windows that allow the sun's rays to enter the sanctuary and to illuminate special symbols in accordance to the time of the year. Bretonic dolmens contain many abstract symbols, most of which are too obscure for easy interpretation. These symbols were deeply cut into the rock (the eternal) and coloured on ritual occasions (the temporal). One of the more frequently found symbols is attributed to the earth-mother.

The largest of these is the symbol from Mané Ruthual (428cm x 321cm) where it is carved into the ceiling, pointing more or less to the north west. This 'gate-symbol' can be used for astral projection. The journey to the 'other world' is described by the following symbol from the dolmen of Petit Mont, where a way is leading to and from the gate. The symbol, like the dolmen itself, expresses three phases: entrance, passage, exit.

This may parallel the pattern of the journey; universe A, in-between-ness, universe B. Dolmens were built to last for eternity, so that the journey can still be made. The feminine idea (womb) was balanced by the Menhir (Bretonic; 'standing stone') with its phallic symbolism. Not all periods produced such sophisticated dolmen structures of Brittany. The dolmens of north Germany, Denmark and southern Scandinavia are younger than the Bretonic, and consist of a simple chamber with a short entrance. Few symbols can be found in them. The ceremonial dolmen-temple of the early megalith period (around 4000BC) was soon replaced with the conventional barrow grave. The ritual meaning of the structure was forgotten and the stone chambers were used to bury chieftains and

Symbols from Locmariaquer and the Gulf of Morbihan.

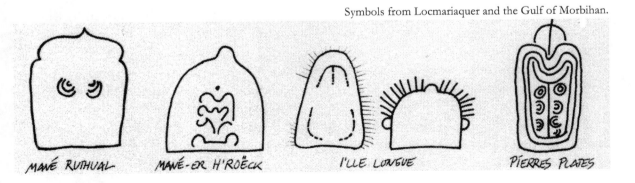

MANÉ RUTHUAL   MANÉ-ER H'ROËCK   I'LLE LONGUE   PIERRES PLATES

other individuals of questionable importance. Celtic and Germanic tribes attributed the dolmens to giants (big people to build with big stones) or the dwarves (the ceiling was rather low, after all) and imitated the form (a burial mound) to bury their own chiefs. Barrow graves were not only built for nobles, but also near the battlefields for fallen warriors. Many of these contained gifts for the dead. This attracted grave-robbers. Most barrow graves were plundered at some time. They remain. as half-collapsed mounds, containing disturbed bones and often a very angry protection spirit. A group of damaged mounds can produce a very gloomy atmosphere. If you want to practise nearby, try to come to terms with the spirits of the place first.

Sea and islands can be considered a realm of the fluid, uncertain and transcendental. In the old cultures, people believed that the earth floats in the sea like a child in the womb. Jormungandr, the Midgard serpent, divided the outer and inner realms of that vast ocean, not so much to keep the people inside but to exclude the forces of chaos and the numerous exiled giants living among the stars. To journey over the ocean meant to commit oneself to an alien realm. Etymologically, the word 'soul' ('Seele' in German) is related to the word sea ('See' in German), which may suggest a vague memory of womb consciousness. Tacitus tells us of an island in the north sea where the Nerthus-cult celebrated its rituals. Nerthus (feminine) may be an earlier form of the Vanish god Njord. There are indications that the 'Njord' figure came out of a matrifocal society. *Lokasenna* 33 has him speaking for the freedom of women to select their lovers, while Loki's reply suggests customs known from sexual magick. In other countries Njord was called Nodens, Nydd, Lydd or Llyr. In Holland and the Friesian islands, the deity of the oceans was called Nehallenia, and represented as a woman holding a fruit basket with a ship and a dog. The Romans sacrificed to her before sailing to Britain. Spanuth has attempted to show that the island of Nerthus was identical with the 'king's island' Abalus/Basileia mentioned in the Atlantis texts. Abalus shows some similarity to the Celtic 'sunken paradise' Avalon/Affalon (apple island), to the Cornish legend of the drowned land Lyonesse or the Bretonic tale of Ys, sunk for the crimes and blasphemies of her priests. Spanuth attempts to show that 'Abalus' was identical with the sacred isle of the Friesians, an island dedicated to Forsites, god of the oceans, who appears in the *Edda* as Forseti, son of Nanna and Balder (see *Gylfaginning* 32 and *Grimnismal* 15). Forseti, literally the 'one who sits before the assembly' i.e. chairperson, is a god of justice and lawgiving. There is a curious tale of twelve sailors adrift on the ocean. They appear to have lost their home country and were floating aimlessly when one appeared among them (the thirteenth) who could direct their course through the sea. He revealed to them and island, fertile and green, and gave them a couple of laws. As the ship reached the land he hurled an axe into the ground and disappeared. Consequently the island was named after him Forsitesland, and became a religious sanctuary. In a later version of the tale, the sailors were law-speakers expelled from germany as they had not acknowledged the reign of Charlemagne with proper enthusiasm. Another name of the island was 'Farra', which means 'cattle island' and may refer to the Fehu rune. Forsitesland appears in numerous chronicles. The isle lay close to the cliffs of Helgoland (the holy land), which still exists. The cliffs with their characteristic red, black and white stones, are mentioned by Plato as landmarks. 'Farra' was sunk around 1200BC. Parts of it reappeared in historical times and were described by the Greek geographer Marcellus who related them to Atlantis, and by a number of Christian missionaries who describe the island's appearance and the rituals held for Forsites. Between 1200-1300 the last remnants of Forsitesland vanished once more under the waves. That 'Farra' is fairly identical with the Platonic 'Atlantis' has been demonstrated by Spanuth's overwhelming researches. The tale of that north-sea civilization may have influenced Homer's account of the island of the Phaeacians in the *Odyssey*. There are plenty of similarities between the Platonic description and the Homerian version.

There is a tale speaking of an island of glass which can be found in nearly all countries around the north sea. 'Glass' is a word older than the material we associate with it. In the old days it used to mean 'amber'. Amber was highly treasured by the mediterranean civilizations who imported huge amounts of it from the north sea. Abalus was the source of this mineralized tree-resin. The glass temple is mentioned vaguely in the *Hyndluliod* and in the Celtic legends. A curious poem called 'The Spoils of Annwn' tells how Arthur raided the four-sided castle to obtain the cauldron of inspiration (a Pagan prototype of the holy grail). This castle, called 'Caer Sidi' (revolving castle), 'Caer Pedryvan' (castle of riches) and 'Caer Wydyr' (four cornered castle), 'Caer Vedwyd' (castle of revelry), 'Caer Golud' (glass castle) is considered to be identical with Annwn (the Celtic underworld) and is found on an island in the ocean. Apparently the journey to 'Caer Pedryvan, in the isle of the strong door, where twilight and pitchy darkness meet together and bright wine is the drink of the host' was not completely successful.

'The first word from the cauldron, when was it spoken?
By the breath of nine maidens it was gently warmed.
Is it not the cauldron of the chief of Annwn?
What is its fashion?
A rim of pearls is round its edge.
It will not cook the food of a coward or one forsworn.
A sword flashing bright will be raised to him,
and left in the hand of Lleminawg.
And before the door of the gate of the cold place
The lamp was burning when we went with Arthur - a splendid labour!
Except seven, none returned from Caer Vedwyd.'

Taliesin (Trans. Squire)

The tale of wondrous islands that are drowned by the ocean usually combines historic examples with the archetypal motif. We need not insist on any specific location for Atlantis, Avalon, Abalus, Anoeth and Oeth (note the similarity to the name of Njord's home 'Noatuan'), Ys, R'lyeh or R'lin K'ren A'a when the theme of the myth is such a common one. There may have been several such island civilizations. These legends usually have a common essence. The civilization they describe is considered rich, highly developed and in league with the worst demons of the dawn ages. We will never know these things for certain, and every magician is invited to dream, remember and imagine as s/he wills.

In some shamanic religions, we find the journey to the underworld paralleled by a journey across the ocean. In Scandinavia there are a number of megalith cult places in the form of a long ship. These ship-forms were obtained by placing a double row of big, flat stone slabs upright in the ground. Possibly these stone-ships were used much as certain north-American shamans, celebrate their group journeys in the 'spirit canoe'. This practice is related in M. Harner's *Way of the Shaman.* Another magical ship is mentioned in the prose *Edda* (gylf. 43), 'Skidbladnir,' big enough to carry all the gods and yet small enough to be folded up like cloth and be carried in a bag. Another use of the 'journey across the sea' is the fire burial. The union of fire and water is clearly described in the account of Balder's funeral. A combination of the fire and boat theme can be found in the Kenaz rune. On the island of Lundi in the Bristol channel is an ancient Christian cemetery, said to contain the graves of St Patrick and Vortigern, - it too is ship shaped.

It is vital for the rune magician to gain a genuine understanding of the faces and moods of nature. As the rune current flows through the body, height and depth, the three aspects of being are joined and the practitioner relates to the land in a subtle mode of communication. This understanding arises not through intellectual insight but through a feeling of unity, 'opening up' and embracing the world. Landscape is not the only variable in our experiments. Other factors are weather, time, season, lunar phases and so on. A diary is an important tool. It improves recall and observation, and allows us to cultivate a certain form of continuous awareness that far surpasses the meaning of the experiences we record. There are several methods of practical geomancy. Dowsing and pendulum application are fairly well known, and there is plenty of literature which will give you more data than you will ever need.

Another popular technique is 'ley hunting'. Ley (field) lines come in two varieties. One is the 'natural' ley line, which is more or less identical with the dragon lines that follow the shape of the land. The other is a more abstract phenomena that can be discovered by the use of a good map and a ruler. Using the map we mark all sites that can be of interest, old shrines, wells, sacred trees, ruins of old churches or castles, hill tops and the like. Note that both the Roman army and the Christian church occasionally occupied pagan cult places. The stones of several hundred ancient dolmens were incorporated in monasteries and castles in northern Germany, and no doubt the situation was not different in many other countries. Using a ruler, you may try to find straight lines that integrate several such power-places. Special consideration should be given to places on mountaintops, which may have been used for signal fires. When you find more than four power spots on a straight line, you may have discovered a ley line. Be sure to use a large scale map and a very fine pencil, then go and check.

Tree transformation

There are a couple of imagination exercises to develop sensitivity for geomantic phenomena. These practices are meant for people who have had a solid training in meditation. One of them consists of transforming oneself into a tree. If you have found a site you wish to learn about you should first calm yourself to reach a measure of inner peace and silence. Stand with your feet together, the arms hanging relaxed at your sides, eyes closing slowly. Allow your mind to grow silent and empty. Breath should flow easily with no effort or strain. As you embrace silence and simplicity, let go of your human identity. Feel how your feet and legs become a single pillar, and allow them to turn into roots. Let the roots reach downward into the deep, rich, silent earth. Feel the transparent water and nourishment, feel them embrace the soil, the stones and rocks that dream in darkness. As you drink of the dark and the deep, feel how the bark encloses you. Strong rugged tree bark, layer upon layer like silence wrapped around the central core. Winds flow around the surface skin, yet there is restful emptiness inside. Branches and twigs reach upwards, spreading into the height of heaven, adorned with foliage or naked according to the season. As breath moves slowly through the tree you feel the sap move under the bark, and as the wind sings in the leaves you feel your body swaying slowly in the breeze. With practice, the transformation will be easy and natural. You will come to understand how trees live in the yearly round. How they retreat deep down in winter time, how freshness and expectation rise in spring, how summer has them drowsing in the sunlight and how autumn is celebrated in a last outburst of flaming exhilarated joy giving way to the dreams of the dark season. Then there are the sensations of the moontides and the feeling of communication that flows among trees and joins the forest as a whole.

A similar practice is suitable for the warm season. Lie down on a blanket and descend into a half-sleep (alpha) state. Simply merge the body with the earth until your flesh has become an outgrowth of the soil, and the ground itself part of your being. This practice makes the self 'atmospheric,' expanding the limits of body to receive the full flow of being. By becoming one with the earth, surprising insights may arise, reflections of other ages and new modes of being.

More difficult are practices which allow you to merge into night and nothingness. Maat magick offers a similar method. Here we settle down, relax, go into trance, and then imagine how our skin stretches out, expands, and outfolds into the world until the entire scenery has become an extension of the body. 'Lust of Result' is is anathema to these experiments. Do as you will, not for any specific result but for the rightness of the doing. Analysis or evaluation should come after the practice. . . above all, do not struggle for conclusions and certainties. While in action, we should suspend judgment, belief and disbelief. It is useful to begin and end such meditations with a few ritual motions. If we begin them with a little ritual, we may find it easier to clear the mind from the usual everyday nonsense that occupies our weary thoughts. If we end them with a little ritual activity, we will find it easier to return to human consciousness and functionality. The ritual ending of each session should help us to remember that we willed to be human, and that our contribution to the all-consciousness of this planet is human awareness.

10 Runes and qabala

There have been a number of attempts to relate the various rune systems to the qabalistic system of the Hebrew/Egyptian/Sumerian tradition. In both systems, each letter, sound and symbols can be related to a certain type of consciousness. In the qabalistic systems each letter of the alphabet corresponds to a number, colour and path on the 'Tree of Life,' not to mention divine names, god-forms, beasts, plants, stones, symbol, magical weapons, classes of being, parts of the anatomy etc. The word 'qabala' (QBL) means 'a message or teaching from God,' i.e. a language by which God (all-self) may speak with us, and vice versa. (We are speaking of qabala in an unorthodox sense in this chapter. Where the term is used it is meant to imply the innovative qabalistic methods as taught by such authors as Crowley,

Grant, Regardie, Fortune etc., not the thoroughly abstract teachings of orthodox qabala with its notorious lack of practical applications.) The language of QBL uses certain words, signs, symbols and alignments to speak to levels of the mind which would not react to normal suggestions or prayers. The language of reason cannot even touch these levels, but a language of seemingly irrational symbols can do so very well. In a certain sense, the runes are a 'qabalistic' system. We may speak with the height or depth of ourselves by using runes, and, using the same language, receive meaningful answers. This phenomena is essential to magick and divination. Divination permits us to receive images from levels of consciousness inaccessible to our 'everyday self,' and magick uses the same images to influence and change this 'everyday self' and its reality; QBL, in short, is communication.

To the novice, of course, things do look a little different. Working one's way into a qabalistic system usually implies endless hours of study and meditation, getting acquainted with absurd theories, bizarre names and overwhelming lists of more or less obscure relationships between symbols of all varieties. After a time, however, the teaching does begin to make sense in its own crazy way and from that point unfolds meaning and creates and re-interprets the 'new world,' the magical universe. Once this process has begun, QBL can be used to produce valid psychological changes under will.

For example: A rune magician who realizes that s/he lacks, say, power, drive and determination may try to improve the situation by concentrating on the practice of such runes as Fehu, Sowelu, Thurisaz, Teiwaz.

ᚠᛋᚦᛏ

S/he might aid healing by creating an amulet which combines these glyphs, or by travelling through these and similar rune tunnels, so that the frustrations, inhibitions and restrictions are cleared up 'from within'. The qabalistic magician would solve the trouble in a very similar way, even if different symbols were used. S/he would invoke the spheres of Geburah, (power), attributed to the planet mars, and Tiphareth (beauty), which corresponds to the sun, and the heart centre of consciousness. For this purpose the temple might be decorated in red (mars) and gold

(sun), as might be the personal clothing. There could be six (sun) red (mars) candles on the altar, as well as a wand and a sword. The proper divine names would be intoned, sharp and hot food would be eaten, warm red wine be drunk, there could be wild and martial music and perhaps a spontaneous dance with the sword. In either case, consciousness is flooded with the highly concentrated essence of the energy/experience desired, until the practitioner feels easy and natural with it and has forgotten all his previous lack of energy. Similar tactics can be used to heal most psychological defects. Properly applied, QBL is not a philosophy but a system of practical consciousness-engineering. The interested reader will find plenty of useful data in Israel Regardie's *Tree of Life*, Dion Fortune's *Mystical Qabala* and in Aleister Crowley's *777* or *Magick*.

It should be obvious by now that each and every religion has developed its own 'qabala' language. Even in monotheistic religions this phenomena is found. Observe the myriads of highly specialized 'saints' with their specific symbols, attributes, totem beasts etc, in, say, Christianity or orthodox Buddhism. Similar systems exist all over the world, often with great similarities between them. Differences arise out of local conditions. Some religions have fairly simple systems of ordering the world, while others, such as the Chinese system, have developed into fantastic complexity in the millennia of their evolution. In all qabalistic systems we find the attribution of certain symbols to certain states of consciousness. Much of the original rune-qabala has been destroyed or forgotten during the persecution times. Consequently, attempts to relate the rune-order or the Germanic/ Celtic gods to existing systems of QBL (astrology, tarot, I-Ching, numerology or whatever) have failed for the sheer lack of reliable material. Such mixtures may be of personal value (individual insight) but cannot be verified with the existing historical data. This is especially the case when the cultural context of the joined systems differs. If we attempt to relate the rune signs to the tarot, for instance, we will soon come to the realization that both systems, though complete and balanced in themselves, describe different visions of reality. As the the habitat of the magician differs, so does the scope of possible experience and the psychological realities that relate to it. The near Eastern/North African systems include experiences of heat, desert, dryness and scorching sunlight which would seem rather strange to the rain-drenched, arthritic sorcerer from Northern Europe. Similarly as the Egyptian priesthood would have had little sympathy for the beauties of hail, fog or the howl of the snowstorm. Both traditions have similar aims (will) and similar tools (the human mind). Their difference comes from culture, climate, geographic conditions, mentality, way of life and the uniqueness of each individual consciousness.

For example; Most mythological traditions attribute certain beasts to the ideas of 'death'. Such beasts devour the corpse and carry the deceased into the 'otherworld'. In Egyptian religion this function is symbolized by such deities as Anubis, the jackal; Sebek Mako the crocodile, or the vulture of Maat, who leaves but bones, the 'naked truth,' behind. In Paleolithic periods, wild dogs and hyenas symbolized this idea. None of these beasts lived in the cold north, instead, we find Wodan accompanied by two ravens and two wolves, suitable representatives of death and transcendence, or the Morrigu flapping over the battlefield in the mask of a carrion crow. In Oceania death is symbolized by the divine shark. The symbols may differ, the basic idea remains the same.

We should not only study different qabalistic systems but develop our own 'personal qabala'. The study of symbols is useless unless it is inspired and streamlined by constant practical application. You will not understand the inner dynamics of any system unless you embrace it, feel it, live it and manifest it in living flesh. What is the use of an oracle that is so foreign to your daily life that you have to look up the answer in a book? The same goes for all attempts to influence the psyche through symbols which are only known from theory. Literature from all countries supplies us with thousands of symbols from all kinds of traditions - do not rely on others but seek the essence in yourself.

Where I attribute certain symbols to certain realities I consider these a suggestions not facts. True understanding of the runes comes from life, not merely from study but from life, and years of development have to go into it. Your idea of each rune will change repeatedly in this process, as the system is infinite and so are you. There are no shortcuts, no 'instant oracle practices', no methods to 'transform the world in ten easy lessons by

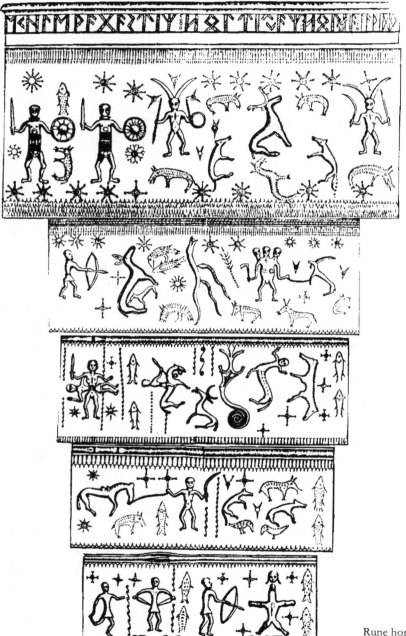

Rune horn from Gallehus.
Drawn by J R Paulli, 1734.

correspondence'. If you are successful in your practice, this will be the result of involvement, commitment and dedication. As you change, so will your vision of the world. One of the advantages of the runes is their capacity to stimulate the imagination. Even the most narrow-minded historian is apt to arrive at all kinds of bizarre interpretations without even realizing it.

Neither the Celtic nor the Germanic priesthood had much faith in the use of scripture and theory. The required knowledge was memorized, usually in a state of light trance and in rhymed form. Many of the songs in the *Edda* are catalogues of information, such as the *Grimnismal, Alvismal, Voluspa,* etc, and some of them have stored memories from the Ice ages and earlier periods. A form of 'natural succession' keeps such memories up to date, for as the study of mnemonic technique shows, the mind does not remember what it is not interested in.

One of the qabalistic techniques is called 'gematria', and is used to transform the letters of the alphabet into numbers. Words that produce the same number are supposed to be related to one another, or to contain a shared, if hidden essence. To find this essence, and to balance seemingly paradoxical ideas, is one of the tasks of qabalistic meditation. There are indications that a similar system of rune-gematria did once exist. Heinz Klingenberg has demonstrated this fact in his interpretation of the famous gold horns from Gallehus, Jutland. (See illustration). The two Gallehus horns were found buried in some Danish fields. Probably they were originally buried as sacrificial gifts or to hide them. Their age is highly disputed between 100BC and 500 as is the question of their cultural origin. The numerous bizarre figures shown on them cannot be satisfactorily explained by any known mythology, though there are dozens of scientific theories that attempt to do so. In 1802 the horns were stolen from Copenhagen museum and immediately melted-down by the thieves. A number of fairly exact drawings survived, one of the horns had a runic inscription:

E KHLEWAGASTIR HOLTIJAR HORNA TAWIDO

Compare with the illustration. Note that the last word is worked in a different style of writing. The inscription is usually translated as 'I Hlewagastir Holtijar made the horn'. ('Tawido' means 'to do', 'to make'). Klingenberg tried to interpret this inscription with gematria. Using a common 24-rune futhorc, he assigned a number to each rune.

(This is one of the common 24 rune rows. Of course there are variations, especially in the positions of the last runes.) The inscription contains four groups of rune signs.

A) E K H L E W A G A S T I R.
    19 6 9 21 19 8 4 7 4 16 17 11 15
13 runes, sum = 156.

B) H O L T I J A R
    9 24 21 17 11 12 4 15
8 runes, sum = 113.

C) H O R N A
   9 24 5 10 4
5 runes, sum = 52

D) T A W I D O
   17 4 8 11 23 24
6 runes, sum = 87

The inscription consists of 32 runes and 16 dots. The runes form 13 syllables. Of the 24 possible rune letters, 16 are used, plus the sign of the dot. Now there are some regularities in these numbers.

$$156 = 12 \times 13. \quad 52 = 4 \times 13$$

Add group
A + ... + B = 273 = 21 x 13 (.... = 4)
B + ... + C = 169 = 13 x 13.
C + ... + D = 143 = 11 x 13
D + ... + A = 247 = 19 x 13.

Note that
A + B = 21 runes.
B + C = 13 runes.
C + D = 11 runes.
D + A = 19 runes.

16 rune letters are used, plus the dot sign.

A	R	K	G	W	H
4	5	6	7	8	9

N	I	J	R	S	T
10	11	12	15	16	17

E	L	D	O
19	21	23	24

$$= 207 + . = 208 = 16 \times 13$$

These consist of six vowels

A	W	I	J	E	O	=	78
4	8	11	12	19	24	=	6 x 13

And of 10 consonants plus the dot.

R	K	G	H	N	'R'
5	6	7	9	10	15

S	T	L	D
16	17	21	23

$$= 129 + . = 130 = 13 \times 10$$

Whatever this may be it is not coincidence. What is the meaning of the 13? Thirteen has not always been an 'evil' or 'unlucky' number. The 13 appears prominently in some of the earliest nature religions and is closely connected to the lunar calendar. There are 13 full moons every other year, and if we consider the connection between the moon and menstruation, we come to understand the importance of the number to cultures who were possibly organized in a matricentristic way. Remember the importance of blood red colour to rune magick! On the magnificent stone stele from Laussel (see illustration) we observe a woman holding a horn. There are 13 notches in that horn. Note that the curve of the horn shape is already suggestive of the moon sickle. The Stele of Laussel is dated between 20,000 and 15,000BC. With the advent of patriarchal religion the phenomena of menstruation came to be considered 'dirty' and 'unclean', 'thirteen' was considered an 'unlucky' number and the use of body fluids (from either sex) was replaced with the use of sacrificial blood in ritual practice. The Gallehus horns indicate the existence of at least one gematric system in rune magick. Of course we do not know what individual meaning was attributed to each number, nor how widespread the system has been. As any occultist knows, there are as many systems of numerology as sand at the seaside. In the expectable scholarly fashion, Klingenberg wrote a whole book trying to organize each and every item on the Gallehus horns in groups of thirteen. Maybe there were really 65 stars (5 x 13) in 13 different types with a sum of 117 rays (9 x 13) involved in the design, yet how accurate are the drawings that we base our research on? Without the originals, such claims can hardly be verified. It remains to future generations of rune magicians to decode the surviving rune texts if possible, with the help of a computer.

11 Vision and crisis

I know how I hung
from the windswept tree
for nine long nights
pierced by the spear
given to Odin
myself to myself
from the branch of the tree
of which nobody knows
from which root it has grown.

They offered me neither
bread nor drink
then I bent over
took up the runes
took them up screaming
and fell to the ground.
(...)

Then I recovered
began to think
grew and felt well
word out of word
gave word to me
work out of work
gave work to me.

Runes shalt thou find
and staffs of advice
very strong staffs
very mighty staffs
coloured by Fimbuthulr (Odin)
given by the great gods
and carved by the highest of regents.

(from the *Havamal* 139, 140, 142, 143)

These lines from the 'Havamal' describe how Odin came to discover the magick of the runes. 'Initiation on the world-tree' reflects a shamanic custom that has been in use for millennia and is still practised in several traditions. The 'tree of life', be it as Yggdrasil, Laerad, Mimameithr, be it as the world pillar (north axis) Irminsul, be it as a model of the human spine with its energy centres, connects all worlds and all dimensions. The young shaman climbs this world-tree in order to receive his or her vision between the worlds of heaven and of earth. A magnificent example of this practice is given in Michael Oppitz' book and documentary movie *Shamans of the blind country* which deals with the shamanic tradition of Nepal. After days of exhaustive preparations, purifications, ceremonies and endless dances the young shaman is led to a 'tree of life' erected in the centre of the village. This 'tree' is especially prepared for the occasion; the bark has been stripped off and white cloth ('against witches') hangs from the few branches remaining at the top. A little platform has been built half way up the stem.

The candidate, in this case a young woman, has participated in so many dances to and from the village that she is by this time almost delirious. She wears a heavy 'armour' of headpiece, ornaments and special clothing adorned with cowrie shells, animal skins, feathers, bells of all varieties and a generous amount of ironware, some 14 kilos altogether. At the height of the ceremony her eyes are blindfolded and the pulsing heart of a sacrificial goat is shoved into her mouth. Then she is helped up the tree where she remains standing on the platform while all the shamans of the neighbouring villages dance around the pole. As the shamans circle the tree they repeatedly change direction. If the candidate above them moves in unity with them this is a good omen. Her 'human consciousness' has been thoroughly dissolved by then, her body quivers and convulses, obsessed by the spirits that will aid her healing work. Like all of her vocation, she has become the living representative of the mythical first shaman Rama Puran Tsan.

The same formula - initiation through crisis and ecstasies - can be observed in Odin's experience on the tree. We should not mistake Odin's rune initiation with the usual instances of suffering and martyrdom. Odin and Christ may both experience important similar events up on the tree or cross; this does not change the fact that the reasons and results of their transformation differ considerably. To Christ, death on the cross implies the culmination of a holy lifetime in a gesture of sacrifice and suffering. To Odin, the nine nights on the tree are but the beginning of the magick to be. The suffering of Odin is undergone for a purpose, voluntarily, and this purpose transcends the meaning of pain. To the pagan mind, the exhaustion and pain undergone during initiation are but technical aids to achieve a certain state of consciousness. Christianity, on the other hand, starts out with the absurd idea that the flesh is sinful, and finds fulfillment in its punishment, the act of suffering being the height of holiness itself.

We should realize that exhaustion and suffering are keys to dissolution, which may lead to transcendence provided that conditions are right. Without this element of will, suffering becomes an exercise in masochism. There is no special grace in giving one's life for others, or enduring torture for some noble idea. Where pain is experienced, the purpose of this pain lies in shattering the normal human limits of consciousness, releasing what has hitherto been dormant and repressed. 'Pain' is just one tool for this purpose, and not even the most efficient one. Exhaustion is far better, be it through dance, hunger, isolation, physical strain, art, music or sex. As Austin Spare had it 'there is no need for crucifixion.'

The purpose of exhaustion lies in dissolving identity and opening the mind for the glory to be. If pain occurs, and is experienced as such, the whole operation fails through the negative conditioning it creates. In the state of absolute exhaustion time seems to stop and the 'eternal now' reveals itself to us. Out of the in-between-ness (life/death) the new gestalt may flower and a new way of life arise out of the vacuum. In this fashion the novice dies and the shaman is born. In magical literature the transformative process of 'life, death, rebirth' is referred to as the 'formula of IAO'. 'I' stands for Isis, and symbolizes growth and fresh development. 'A' for Apophis/Set, symbolizing crisis, obstruction, frustration. 'O' for Osiris resurrected from the dead. This formula, which should be studied in the works of Aleister Crowley, describes the flow of evolution, learning, and development. The pattern repeats itself time and time again, a spiral flow that has to be lived in order to be understood. The crucial point is our behaviour during

crisis. To the magician, crisis offers freedom from habit and a chance to change. There is no final stage to this process, as life and change are continuous. 'IAO' is a formula that reflects solar 'life-death-rebirth' symbolism. We find the formula suggested in the shape of the Sigel ᚼ rune: Isa ᛁ growth, ᚱ obstruction, ᚼ fresh growth. We all die and are reborn continuously. The babe had to die to permit the child to live, the child died to attain youth, the youth was slain in order to become adult and so on. As we live and die, our values, desires and needs transform. The more one struggles to avoid change and dissolution, the harder will the crisis be. All has to change, and if it doesn't change voluntarily it will be changed by force.

The magician changes much faster than most people do, and soon learns to embrace crisis and dissolution with a laugh. His or her problems come from the question of 'right measure'/balance in motion. How much crisis/dissolution are needed? If you believe that 'more pain equals more enlightenment' you will suffer for that delusion. It's not our conscious mind's decision how much crisis is needed. If we are sufficiently honest with ourselves we will get exactly what we need - usually a little bit more than we dreamed necessary, and a little bit less than we dreamed possible. To avoid crisis or to indulge in it are typical beginners' problems. We need not imagine that a single crisis will solve our problems once and for all. The 'abyss' will be encountered again and again. People who believe that they have come 'through the abyss' show all too clearly that they have simply lost their way in it. A touch of crisis is often useful to break the dominance of identity and to open the gates to the deep. This is the reason why Austin Spare emphasized the use of vacuity and the 'death posture' as vital conditions for the consecration of sigils.

How much crisis is needed to open the gates? It depends on how much ego and self-importance you have. A magician who habitually re-forms mask and identity can easily open up, while an ego-centered pompous ritualist of the medieval tradition needs endless periods of abstinence, prayer, fasting etc., to achieve the same results. The more ego you have the more effort will be needed to break its control. Such cases need fantastic amounts of ritual equipment, drastic and melodramatic gestures, months of preparation, all of which look very impressive to the novice who believes that 'more effort equals more results'. To a magician who cultivates a degree of humility, honesty and humour, things look somewhat different. If you live at the edge of reality, in the full awareness of your hungers, frustrations, shortcomings and hang-ups you will make the transition with less effort than the numerous magicians who concentrate on ego-building practices, positive suggestions, pride and certainty.

It is vital to understand that crisis and exhaustion open the gates, they do not effect the congress that takes place after that. Indeed, if you indulge in crisis for its own sake you will only produce constriction. The energy force for union is not crisis but joy. Magicians who try to energize sigils (or spells or whatever) by massive exhaustion only cause the mind to associate the sigil with strain and tension. Exhaustion should be used to open, to purify yourself from waste materials before you start to do magick. Once the vacuum has been created, exhaustion is not needed any more, indeed it will only obstruct the passage of the proper energy (self, god) which arises on its own accord, without your effort, control or involvement. First exhaustion, then vacuity, then channeling through oneself.

How were the runes received?

Some authors seem to believe that Odin received one of the many futhorc alphabets in his state of enlightened dissolution, preferably the 'original' futhorc, whatever that may be. Now the mind shaken by initiation through crisis and exhaustion is in no state to receive anything as abstract, complicated and absurd as an alphabet. The exhausted mind is void and simple, and easily overwhelmed by sensation. Normal objects reveal a fantastic scope of beautiful or terrible implications, vision is vast, wide-eyed and wonderful. Had Odin seen the futhorc alphabet as we know it he would have died laughing.

What, then, was received in the timeless instant? One possibility is suggested in the chapter 21 on divination. Perhaps a method of seeing was received, vision that revealed a myriad of symbols and signs out of the growth of branches and twigs. With experience, these symbols would then be refined to a scope of basic runes. Structures which later developed into the various futhorc-alphabets. Another possibility would be a sign or a symbol that contains all possible rune shapes. Such symbols are called 'Binderunen', German for 'bound runes'. I will offer some examples and ask you to develop your own. Binderunen can be used for many sorts of magick. They can be used as a concentration focus, as parts of the altar design, as tools for divination. They can be carved on wood or bone and be used as 'magical mirrors', as described by Franz Bardon (Initiation into Hermetics). They are also useful for meditation practice, particularly for the cultivation of an empty mind. Practise looking into them while keeping the mind void and silent, this may teach you how to 'open up'. Strain and effort should be avoided. Simply allow your awareness to fix itself on the symbol while the mind grows silent and peaceful. Do not expect results. Simply practise dealing with the awareness flow. Learning to produce vacuity and silence 'under will' is important for the transmission of energy/consciousness between the worlds. As the ego usually struggles against silence and voidness, exhaustion is often the first act. By 'letting go' into silence, we give our suppressed selves a chance to emerge. Beyond identity, in between the worlds, in the 'void place of belief' we are free to see anew and to accept change where it is willful. In between realities, we can choose to change the world and ourselves as we will.

'Thrill with the joy of life and death!'

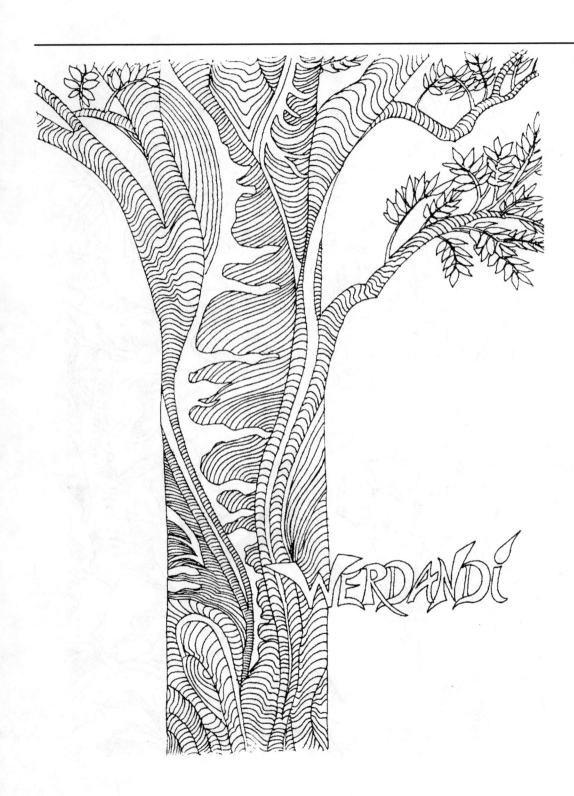

12 Introduction to Werdandi

As has been mentioned repeatedly, rune practice involves a number of physical exercises that permit the mage to experience the form and flow of each rune in the body. These exercises have beneficial effects on body, mind and soul, they give reality to the abstractions of the symbolism, they evoke and earth the current. The postures can be used for ritual, ceremony, dance, meditation, energy work, gymnastics, to balance and heal the flow of vitality, to clear up blocked energy and to bring the idea into living flesh. Above all, they are an interesting field for practical experiment in body, energy and consciousness.

It is a sad fact that many aspiring students of the oh-so-occult arts forget the physical, the exoteric side of reality, concentrate on the refinement of the exalted spirit and the subtle forces, all the time repressing body and flesh as 'crude illusions' meant to be 'transcended'. Often the body is ignored or even damaged, be it by bookishness, to much fasting, asceticism, sexual abstinence or the blind use of will-power, and when disease, weakness, overpressure or some other 'weakness of the flesh' reveals itself, this is usually 'healed' by more concentration, more spirituality, more esoteric effort, 'acceptance of karma' and the attempt to 'think positive'. We all know occultists who look positively uneasy in their flesh, feel no delight in the senses, lack the basic lust and joy of life and live out a tepid existence of serious and dull intellectual mind-games.

Where we divide body and consciousness we are violating both. We incarnate in flesh because we willed it so. Flesh is our medium of interaction with the world. The ego or persona is the vehicle of communication between humans and need not be a prison or a trap. The very simple state of physical well-being is the basis of 'advancement' of consciousness. It is remarkable how a few simple and natural practices, so obvious and basic that few occultists ever bother to think about them, increase the sense of living within body and the universe. A healthy and happy body is capable of lust, full emotion, pleasure, delight and honesty in all experience, it feels good, radiates self and confidence to embrace the world. Without this basis of joy and energy, spiritual progress needs much more effort and discipline, provides less pleasure and more trouble. We try to work with body, not against it, and this means much more than just a measure of dutiful tolerance for a 'biological machine'. Unless we can come to see body as something positive to care for and delight in, our spiritual ambitions lack roots in reality. Not duty but pleasure should make us do our exercises. As long as you have to force yourself to move, dance, breathe, love etc., you are at war with yourself. So much for today's sermon to the unbelievers.

Have you ever wondered how body and mind influence each other? If you study the works of Wilhelm Reich you will encounter the concept of 'character armour'. Reich discovered that areas of chronic tension in the body often parallel chronic repression/ neurosis in the mind, and that healing one without the other is usually impossible. According to Reich, neurosis grows where vital desires cannot be lived out, because of fear, social conditioning or lack of opportunity. Vital desires that find no fulfilment are 'stored' in chronic tension. Sexual hunger, for instance, causes a feeling of frustration in the genitals. Then the conscious mind tries to repress/ ignore the troublesome awareness and tries to reduce sensitivity in the area. Muscular tension does this job, and when the trouble becomes chronic, so does the tension which is now considered an 'armour'. Israel Regardie wrote about it:

> Basically this comprises at least two elements, the psychic armour which for convenience sake may be compared with the Freudian super-ego, and muscular armour which is the sum total of all the bodily tensions of the organism. The function of the armour - whether on the psychic level or the muscular level - is to repress impulses and feelings that are not morally acceptable in terms of cultural environmental attitudes and early family training . . . One represses with one's body as much as with one's mind.' (Introduction to Crowley's *World's Tragedy*)

Plainly, a complete therapy must equally dissolve the armour of body *and* mind. The healing of the mind requires honesty, self-knowledge, reflection, deconditioning of negative thinking, meditation and the transformation of repressed memories, desires, dreams (opening Pandora's box). While healing of body involves the rediscovery of relaxation, joy, sheer lust, organic pulsation, energy flow, full breathing and dynamic motion. All of these are basically sexual, as is all perception and interaction of form. 'All things fornicate all of the time' wrote Austin Spare, to the disgust of the esoteric scene of his day. The discovery of body and mind in union is equally the unfolding of the repressed all-sexuality.

Sexuality is one the the key problems for civilized people. Here follows a simplyfied synopsis of Reich's analysis of the development of bodily armour out of a repressed sexuality. In early infancy, the child learns that the genitals/anus are taboo areas. Puberty increases these troubles. Attempting to decrease sexual feeling, the hips are tensed and become 'frozen'. This effectively clogs the body's natural resource of life-energy. Belly breathing, which used to be natural becomes restricted; now the chest is burdened with the task of breathing, which it does with less efficiency and more haste. Consequently the general tone of vitality drops, which generally weakens health and gives a gloomier outlook on life. As the chest moves out, one's centre of gravity rises. The socially acceptable good posture derives from a military ideal. (Chest out, belly in, legs straight, eyes forward etc.) This effectively prevents emotion through an exo-skeleton of sheer cramp.

This is intentional and a vital part of the brainwashing that turns uncertain adolescent youths into obedient, soul-hardened killers. With the freezing of the hips the legs usually become tense, which in turn increases the armour of the pelvis. By now the energy flow is severely restricted by muscular tension. Soon enough the shoulders follow, cramping the neck area and cutting off the head. It is hardly surprising when such an agglomeration of chronic armour becomes insensitive, that the energy channels get blocked and the very joy of life disappears into a nightmare of duty, obligation, rules, routines, achievement orientation and the like. Sexuality itself becomes a partial release of local tension that has little to do with the rest of the body, let alone the soul. If we are honest we have to admit that we are considerably more diseased and constricted than we would care to realize.

Healing is not acquiring something new but to becoming conscious of the restriction and then deconditioning ourselves. This is why such simple activities as deep breathing, love play, dancing, rune practice or Kung fu (Chinese: Wu Shu) require so much work. We cannot expect to get rid of character armour, cramped posture, low vitality and morbid attitudes in a few short months. How surprised you will be when, in a few months, you think back to the time when you read this book and consider all the changes that the practise worked for you?

Life-energy, be it called 'rune power', 'chi', 'od',[1] 'orgone', 'prana', 'pneuma', 'vril' or whatever, can only be perceived and channelled when the major cramps have been dissolved. Many beginners complain that they do not feel anything, and try to improve the situation by forcing results. Others feel that 'something happens' and get terribly upset...

---

[1] The name coined by F von Reichenbach for the life energy he discovered - he name it after Odin.

people often cling to their armour, as they sense that its dissolution will certainly confront them with the feelings and desires they have evaded for years. Armour equals security to those who have found shelter and protection in it. Doing without armour means, first of all, confrontation of the repressed, accumulated pain and admission of one's vulnerability. It is remarkable how we all try to rationalize our armour, to explain it away and to endure it willingly. The armour seems to offer protection. That your armour is dispensible may be acceptable in theory, in practice it is damned hard work, constant vigilance and repeated deconditioning of self-imposed limitations.

Rune stance practice can help us in this great work. It helps us to become aware of ourselves, to breathe, stand, sing naturally, clears blocked energy channels, increase vitality and gradually erodes the armour acquired by habit. Where resistance is reduced, the universal life-energy is free to flow and pulse through our being like water through a living sponge. In spite of the opinion of several occultists, the rune energy flow is nothing new, special or alien. The energy flows at all times of our lives; without it, we would not live at all. Rune stance practice merely improves the clarity of perception, the ability to open-up, to accept the flow of the current and to channel the energy as accords with will. We are not acquiring a new faculty but remembering an old one; what we discover is ourselves.

13 How to proceed

The proper assumption of a rune stance (or any other posture in magick, yoga or Wu Shu) depends on a number of variables. No doubt you will have a measure of talent already, but that in itself does not suffice. Things begin to work when all the variables (stance, breathing, sound vibration, energy flow, imagination etc.), have been mastered sufficiently to function in cooperation. People who expect instant results will certainly be disappointed. If you persist in practice, however, the many problems will gradually dissolve and the many separate skills fuse into a simple and natural activity. There will come a time when the whole thing seems so easy that you will wonder what the fuss was all about. To the beginner, everything seems difficult, as all the required talents have to be developed at the same time. Sorry, but that is the way it is. As you are learning through the indirect communication of a book you will have to very watchful and open minded. You will have to check, re-check and experiment a great deal, as there will not be a teacher who drives, controls and guides you. This burdens you with a lot of responsibility, you are in care for your own development, and if you want to know whether you are doing right you will have to observe yourself for an answer. Of course it is easier to learn by imitation, but then I expect that you are the sort of person who enjoys independent research.

The principles of rune stance are quite simple. You assume the form of a rune with your body. You imagine the shape of the rune into yourself, breathing deeply, you sing out its name/sound until you feel the corresponding flow of vibration, energy, sentience. This basically, is how it is done. It is not quite as easy as it sounds, but you will find that out soon enough. Our major problem, as was mentioned before, it the sorry state we are in. The average person has bad posture, chronic character armour, shallow breathing, low vitality, repressed sexuality and does not dare to sing, chant or scream loud. Apart from these minor troubles there is the vital question; 'what if it works too well?' One can easily get an overdose of energy, it is a common problem among the more determined mages. Before you begin to practise you should acquaint yourself with the chapter dealing with troubles and strange symptoms. (Chapter 17)

Here are some points for consideration.

- The energy flow depends on clear channels. To an extent, the energy will clear those channels up. If the channels are overly blocked through tension and armour, an increase in energy may cause problems. Whatever you do, do it gently. Do not force results.

- Health. A healthy, rested body that gets enough sleep, food, sex and activity is the best foundation. Though the advanced practitioner can work with rune posture in times of disease, weakness or crisis, this may not be easy for beginners. If you decide to learn these exercises, do it when you feel moderately well. Also, avoid practice with a full belly.

- Relaxation. All tension restricts energy, breath and flow. This goes for the chronic character armour just as for the tensions that come from lack of motion, stress or one-sided activity. Now we may dissolve such tensions through depth-meditation, self-hypnosis, or some similar tactic. This means that we use mind to relax body. We can also use body to relax body, which is often a very useful method to deal with unconscious tensions. It means, sorry, that you get up and do something.

- Physical exercise. Oh I can imagine how you sigh and curse at this, which goes to show just how deeply you need the dreaded activity. Lethargy and melancholy are often symptoms of vitality hunger, and the longer one lazes about the worse things get. Edginess, nervousness or a heated temper may come from the other extreme - excessive energy accumulation that requires activity to find release.

Here the learned witch-doctor prescribes long walks in the country and the generous use of a punch-bag. Rune stance (or most forms of meditation, for that matter) is much easier when we move around before the practice, jumping, stretching, twisting, warming up, that sort of thing.

I often start by jumping around for a few minutes, forward, backward, sideways, on one leg, running on the spot, jumping high etc. This warms the body up, increases oxygen circulation and releases a lot of tension. Then I work on the joints. Rolling the knees gently is the beginning, then follows a good session of hip rotation. The pelvis is rotated in small and wide circles, sideways, forwards and back, in irregular curves and so on. It is also moved by pushing the genitals up and down (back); this motion should come from the pelvis, without any other motion of torso or thighs. The discovery of free hip motion is absolutely essential. Most civilized people have frozen hips, even in coitus they have to move most of the torso and the upper legs as the hips cannot move independently. It is a useful practice to involve more pelvic motion into your dancing. Do not try to move the hips by letting torso and legs shift them, but instill the pelvic area with awareness and let it move on its own accord, the rest of the body following. Try it in front of a mirror. Do such motions look vulgar and obscene? Welcome! You've just met a neurotic belief that lies hidden in the armour. Loki advises that you persist in your effort, and try to look as obscene as possible. When you can do it with complete indifference or even pleasure in public, much of the armour will be gone.

Next, the shoulders are exercised. Stretch out the arms and swing them in wide circles, going very slowly. Breathe in as the arms move up, breathe out when they move down. If you go fully into the sensation you will feel freshness and joy radiate all over.

Then the neck is eased by *gentle* rotation of the head. Imagine that you have a piece of chalk perched on the tip of your nose and that with it you are trying to draw a circle on a blackboard. Sometimes this is easier when one gets down on the floor on hands and knees, in this position the hips, shoulder and neck can be exercised very fully. Try to imagine you are a cat. Stretch out the claws, move the back up and down, allow the pelvis to move in circles . . . experiment. These, and similar practices make the torso warm, fresh and flexible. Perhaps they do not look very spiritual or refined, but then, they work, and that is the vital issue.

14 Rune stance practice in history

I'd dearly love to tell you that the rune stance practice is a continuous and old tradition, cherished and honoured from that primal day when our arch-ancestor did the impossible and dared to stand erect. . . Alas, I cannot, no matter how deeply popular paganism yearns for the protection and support of a true tradition (with pedigree) that goes back to the famed 'wisdom of the elders', whatever that may be. I've tried to think of some examples for that wisdom, but all that came through had to do with head hunting, tribal feuds, human sacrifice and a million incomprehensible taboos. . . But I am violating the sacred beliefs of a good many witches, and I should not do that, at least not all of the time.

Broadly speaking, some of the postures or stances used in rune practice have been known and used in ritual, dance and ceremony for several thousand years. Pictures of simplified humans in such stances can be found in stone-age art, in the carvings of the Neolithic periods, the rock art of the Alps, the figures engraved on Scandinavian stones and so on. They also appear outside of the Indo-European realm, in places like North Africa, Meso-America or Australia, which would indicate that such signs and gestures as Isa |, Algiz ᛉ, Teiwaz ↑, Gebo ✕, . . . etc. are not acquired by learning but are rooted in the deeper levels of the collective unconscious. We have a tendency to express certain feelings and states of consciousness in very definite gestures, and the ones that express religion, belief, passion are very similar. Such magical gestures work in two ways; on one hand they suggest a state of energy/awareness, thereby producing it, and on the other they reflect the inner awareness and express what is felt, when ordinary postures will not suffice.

In a general way, the rune stances are as old as human beings, but in the particular way that assigns specific names and sounds to postures and song the tradition becomes sketchy. There is no historical evidence indicating that Germanic priests practised rune stance the way we know it today. Memorial stones etc., show that some postures were used by the priests. How they used them and to what end, remains an open questions.

The specific practice appears in esoteric literature around the turn of the century in the wake of the pagan-nationalistic revival. Where it came from is not known. During the Nazi dictatorship the practice became popular, both in the Fascist orders and in the opposition. Then all non-Nazis orders were suppressed and Nazi gnosis confined the practice of rune stance to their peculiar 18-rune system. As the Nazis destroyed all esoteric literature they didn't agree with and the Allied forces destroyed or stole most of the Nazi material, the origin of the rune staff practice cannot be traced.

Practices involving posture and song can be found in several countries. In Yoga people sit and drone their mantra till their ears fall off, the same happens in Chinese Taoism, though in a livelier fashion. Mantak Chia, who wrote a few excellent books on Ch'i flow and the like, shows examples of posture, breath and vibration in *Taoist ways to Transform Stress and Vitality* (Healing Tao Press 1986). Certain sounds are chanted to stimulate various organs and the whole thing looks much like rune stance practice, or would if his programme did not require the practitioner to sit on a chair. This seems to be a modern adaptation, in the old days people did their thing in a solid horse-stance, and rightly so. Keith Dowman gives a fine example of Tibetan rune practice in his translation of Drugpa Kuenleg's biography *The Divine Madman* (1980). Kuenleg was all a saint should be. In one scene he demonstrates the entire set of letters of the Tibetan alphabet by imitating their shape with his body. Perhaps this is inspired improvisation and perhaps it is a genuine tradition. Kuenleg was mad enough to do it, and saint enough to leave us guessing.

15 Breathing

Breathing. Aaah.... Breathing.
So simple and so difficult.
Let us take a deep breath and proceed.

Basically, breathing is one of the factors that determines the efficiency of the energy-household. It is a sad fact that very few people breathe properly, which seems rather strange when we observe that children usually do. Unlike adults, children have little character armour, and this lack of repressed crisis and chronic tension makes them open to feel fully, be it pleasure or pain, and to adapt swiftly to fresh experience. In the process of growing up our breathing capacity is reduced and we acquire a shell of armour ('this cannot hurt me!') which limits our ability to respond with full emotional freedom. Soon follows the classical freezing of the hips to reduce sexual urges (puberty) and this reduction of self-experience leads to the usual grown-up-

gloom that goes with lack of joy, need to achieve and reduced expectations. Most adults in the civilized world have a chronic tension in the belly and pelvis which plays hell with sexual pleasure and the ability to live and love. Consequently the rib cage has to be used for breathing which raises the point of balance and makes the body top-heavy.

Of course there are exceptions to this phenomena. Those who have to feel and breathe fully - children, barbarians, yogis, taoists, martial artists, opera singers, dancers, actors and other savages. All these must breathe with the belly, and much of their training is devoted to the re-discovery of this art. Belly breathing has several advantages. It utilizes more lung volume, for instance, which provides more oxygen with less effort. This energy flow gets directly focused on the centre of the body, the 'tan-tien' which lies a little below the navel. This improves balance and energy distribution.

We have all grown up with the cliche of the huge chested, muscular, self-conscious athlete. Seen from the energetic point of view, the professional body-builder is a functional cripple - the body is top-heavy, the hips are stiff, the knees are tensed and locked - the muscular overdevelopment does not accord with functionality but with an 'aesthetic ideal'. The mind is often dull and empty and the whole magnificent strength-apparatus works in separate muscle groups, not in unity. Compare this with the natural athlete. Some 'uncivilized' jungle dweller, for instance - and you will observe that body looks less impressive but can act with more grace, endurance and strength. This is so because it acts from the centre and applies the power of the whole being.

Now perhaps you would like to breathe more fully. How do you do this? The usual western approach would be to take deeper breaths, to increase the expansion of the lung volume, to draw more oxygen in. This is rather typical of consumerist thinking. Instead of utilizing the capacity that exists we try to get more of it. Let's go the other way. Instead of saying 'breathe air in' we may try to 'breathe more air out'. When we breathe out fully we require no effort in breathing in. Most of the lung volume is occupied by stale air no matter how one breathes, so 'let it out' is an easier way of increasing the quality than 'force-more-in'. This is one of the essential secrets of breathing; it is of especial importance at times of stress, when singing or during bouts of asthma - simply let it out. The other essential is the ability to utilize the belly. This is very hard for adults. Some psychologists such as Reich, Lowen and Laing claim that the armour of the hips and belly is an attempt to reduce sensitivity, feeling and flow. It is no surprise that many people become paranoid when they feel some part of their armour come apart. They struggle to control, try to behave and limit themselves with rules and routines rather than confront the suppressed beast or god.

Opening the armour is a way of surrendering ego to the self: that which is suppressed rises into consciousness, which can be rather unnerving. Healing requires that you make peace with those suppressed urges and drives. You can learn to dissolve armour, on a regular basis, but you will also learn to be watchful as armour - useful as a means of repression - tends to reappear in times of stress and crisis. The important thing about breathing is not the exotic exercises but the flow of breath in daily life.

People with strong character armour frequently point out that those without armour are easily upset, shaken, over-emotional or get carried away. Like children they cannot control their emotions. They live and love too deeply for proper adult behaviour. On the other hand this dangerous vulnerability allows them to recover and adapt. Like children they can grow. The armour cannot grow. It only becomes more tense. It says much about our society if we value ideals of self-controlled, independent, unemotional coolness. Living has been replaced by owning, making by consuming, expression by functional efficiency; the virtues of the mercantile machinery.

'These are dead, these fellows; they feel not.' *Liber Al*, II 18.

It is not the intention of this book to supply a course in proper breathing. Easy breathing may take years of work, occasionally even the help of a therapist. I do not believe in burdening people with complicated breathing techniques when the basic essentials, how to breathe naturally, have not been developed. Here are some hints which may be of use:

Belly breathing is easier to learn when one lies flat on the ground. A bed is not as good, it might be too soft or invite you to doze. Try to leave the chest immobile and to move the belly gently. As you breathe in the belly moves outwards (do not force it), as you exhale the belly falls in. Sometimes it is easier to feel when one places a hand or light weight on the belly. Try to feel the sensation. Do not insist on any particular rhythm. At times it may be good to take deep breaths by conscious effort (when tight or constricted) but on the whole body will know its own rhythm, you needn't involve your mind in the process. Some systems of meditation advise beginners to count the breath. This may be good to sink awareness into a comfortable half-dream state, but it has nothing to do with the ability to breathe naturally. If you have to do something with your mind as you explore breathing, how about enjoying the event as fully as you can?

When you have learned belly breathing in a lying position you can try it kneeling or sitting. Keep your knees apart and your belt open, the belly must be mobile and free. When doing the practice standing (waiting for a bus or whatever) keep the legs flexible. Walking is another good occasion for practice. Experiment by pushing the belly out in a horizontal way for a while. Then try to push it down, it feels as if you are trying to breathe into your feet - and moves the hips. Next try to move the genitals forward and up (the pelvis moves) as you exhale. These are just experiments, they may give you more experience. The hip motion may be remembered by the position of the △— rune. The illustration will show you how this looks. Wilhelm Reich used this posture to teach the 'orgasm reflex', which is a pulsing energy rush moving the entire body as a whole. Wunjo, wyn, means joy and pleasure (*Wonne* in German), and deep, free breathing is a blissful experience. The pulsing motion observed by Reich takes place when the armour dissolves and breath/energy move in accords with nature. He linked it to the motion of an amoeba that attempts to fold itself around its food with the entire body.

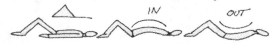

During the exhalation the hips lightly leave the ground, the belly moves in and the shoulders move up a little bit - this may sound difficult in theory, in practice it happens on its own accord. The matter is described in *The Function of The Orgasm*, which is highly recommended. It is not enough to simulate the motion; the goal is to transcend technique so that the natural pulsation can arise.

16 Vowel song

Here are some practices that are useful to get acquainted with sound, breath and vibration. Several magical systems use these, or similar exercises - in the most complete form they are treated by Gregor A Gregorius of the Fraternitas ∴Saturni∴ in the *Die Magische Erweckung Der Chakra im Aetherkorper des*

Menschen, (Berlin, no year). I'll spare you the convolutions of the theory, it is the practice that counts. Like many other traditions, the system attributes certain vowels to different regions of the body. The head is connected with the element of spirit and the sound of the 'I'. Neck and throat correspond with breath, which is air, and the sound of the 'E'. The solar plexus, controlling the body's 'central heating' with heart, liver and stomach, is connected with fire and the warm sound of 'A'. In the lower belly is the region of water - corresponding with the intestines, kidneys and bladder and the sound-vibration 'O'. Last there is the bottom of the spine, with genitals, perineum and anus plus the legs - this is the realm of earth and the depths below, and the deep-sounding 'U'.

Now try this: Stand or sit down in a posture that feels easy and comfortable. The spine should be more or less erect and the belt, trousers, or skirt open so that the belly can move without restriction. Try to avoid stiff legs or hips when you stand. Take a deep breath and sing: 'I' - The sound should be high pitched and extended. Take care that you exhale fully (this is much more important than full inhalation) but do not force the breath. Tension distorts the sensation. Concentrate on the clarity of the sound, not on breaking the world record for extended howling. When you hit the right pitch you will feel a vivid sensation touching the head and moving along the spine as if you were a pillar of energy. You will have to experiment. There is no single 'right sound' so try variations - raise and lower the pitch, make the sound waver or flow straight, try different degrees of loudness and so on. A couple of strange sensations may occur (see chapter 17).

'E' - This vibration touches neck, throat, the lower head and the upper chest. Sometimes it feels as if it would rush along the arms and makes the palms thrill. Some use this vibration to energize the hands before doing massage. The German 'E' sounds a little different from the English ... do not use the 'E' of English, 'excess' etc. but as in 'head', 'very', 'energy'.

'A' - touches the heart. It connects with an emotion of warmth, sympathy, love, you will easily feel whether you heart is open or armoured at the time. The sound should arise with a feeling of 'opening-up'. Focus on a sound like 'half','far', not on 'admit', 'action', 'aeon'.

'O' - vibrates in the centre of the belly a little below the navel. This region is the power house of the body, its vibration increases the sense of balance, heightens vitality and energizes the etheric body. The sound should arise with a feeling of wonder and expansion. Sometimes the vibration seems to expand and surround the aura like an egg. This phenomenon is used by certain magicians who habitually charge their aura every morning before going about their business. The sound is more like 'not', 'want', than like 'onion', 'only', 'other', but as there exist no real approximations you will have to experiment. The mouth should be open wide and the lips rounded.

'U' - is a deep, dark sound. U vibrates in the sexual realms and the levels below. There is something full and dramatic about this sound, it vibrates in passion, sometimes in beastliness. Some Fraternitas∴ Saturni∴ texts claim that U 'evokes the archetypes'. It is sometimes used for earthing. The U sound is much like 'do', 'foot', 'utopia', 'usual', not like 'urn' or 'up'.

I hope that you enjoyed this. Once you have learned to sing/vibrate/feel each of these vowels, you might proceed by combinations. Using a single breath you could sing 'iiiiaaaauuuuu' which yields a vivid sensation of downward motions, or 'uuuaaaiii', rising up. You could try to sing each vowel at its highest pitch and then drop down the sound as deep as you can manage. Some use this to earth rune energy: they sing out a given rune name starting high and then allow the sound to sink. The feeling evoked by this downward vibration helps to pour the power into the ground.

Of course it is not enough to do this exercise once or twice. The practice prepares you for the more complicated vibration of the rune sounds, it establishes a few clear and vital sounds around which the sensitivity for the rune sounds can evolve. If you really want to learn you should do the exercise daily, for at least a month. Each vowel should be sung out three or five times, that should be enough for most people. Rune chanters have to find a workable balance between doing too little and doing too much, and you alone can know just how much you need. If you start gently you give the system time to become integrated, and your body time to accept the vibration. Irregular practice, done with determination and strain, can seriously damage your health.

Though many people will have the problem of getting minimal effect (at first), there will be some who will get too much. The techniques of release, discharge and the like are treated in chapter 17. It is a good sign if the practice changes your consciousness. Now this does not necessarily mean something wild or overwhelming, but it can happen that your mood changes or your awareness becomes more intense. Full vibration can provide a 'reality leap' into a state of lucidity and freshness. It could also make you uneasy. This may happen because:

- Ego/sanity feel threatened.

- The armour dissolves, which gives rise to repressed fears, horrors, needs etc.
- You have just had an excess of energy and cannot let it out.

The first two reasons signify that you are doing very well, so well, indeed, that your ego feels afraid - it would prefer its habitual limitation, neurosis or armour - and tries to make you stop. The last reason would indicate that you should ease up, not that you give up but that you give more consideration to your body's needs.

Then there are some typical beginners' problems arising from the oh-so-protective limits of ego. Most of us have seen beginners who boast about magick and then cannot get their mouths open in the circle. Why else do so many magicians rely on set ritual formulae, on reading aloud invocations written by others? Why do they have to insist on fabulous words of power and precise rituals sanctified by their 'genuine sources' and their supposed 'antiquity?' Free screaming in chaos language (any sound is acceptable) is much more efficient than the standard 'words of power', and freely spoken invocations have the advantage of coming from the heart. As the magick should transform you, there is little use in applying the speeches of other people to the work. The magick that makes an invocation efficient is not the grandiose style or the poetic vocabulary but that you mean what you say.

One of the first problems with rune practice is the shyness of the beginner. The exercise may appear dreadfully loud, extroverted and possibly crazy. Here we encounter ego. Ego says I want to be normal, I want to do sensible and meaningful things, preferably the same ones I've always done! And just what will the neighbours say? What would my friends think? I can understand this problem. I've had it repeatedly, and so have my neighbours. Such minor problems should not keep you from doing the great work. It is a sign of success when you forget your shyness, second thoughts and feeling of acting strange and when the sensation becomes so clear that you simply 'take off' and go with the flow.

At a more advanced stage you may do the exercises silently, working the sound only in the imagination. This, however, does not mean that the imagination is better than the real thing. The adept should be free to decide on any given volume, enjoying the richness of the experience. The beginner always wishes to be less conspicuous, and as long as this tendency exists, you do well if you are very loud.

Other practices are suggested by *AL*, II 22. Such methods change the ability to perceive the vibration. They are not 'more' or 'less' efficient than normal practice, they simply teach to sense it differently.

Then there is the question of group work. A group that practises rune stance or vowel song together creates a shared field of energy and experience which unifies group will, brings the participants into close touch and balances power in the group structure. Group practice effects a mutual reality leap, this is particularly useful when some people feel weak or depressive. It also helps to get rid of shyness - if all in the group produce some bizarre behaviour, it is much easier to the join the fun. The group energy can be easily perceived, even by beginners, which swiftly convinces them of the validity of the action. Vowel singing is something which can be done almost like a party game. All participants could hold hands and sing in unity; creating a sound that flows continuously. Singing vowels while holding hands with one's beloved is a very intimate experience.

The advantage of magical group work lies in its reinforcement of individual belief- this is usually increased when all participants dress alike, wear the same talismans, repeat the same invocation and so on. The pattern is familiar enough, it is used by most cults, religions, schools or armies. In a sense it is useful, in another it is a trap. Groups that depend on such toys can rapidly descend into separatism, minority feelings and persecution mania. A flexible (living) group can accept non-conformism, doubt, criticism and spontaneous change: the group that stagnates does so with strong insistence on rules, laws, regulations, dogma, tradition, obedience, hierarchy-behaviour and the usual secretiveness. All symptoms for a character armour on the large scale. The human mind is a funny old thing. This, basically, is the problem in group work. Primates tend to organize in hierarchies, meaning that the strongest, loudest and oldest ape tells the others what reality is like. When we sing runes or sounds together we ought to try to find a mutual level, both in sound and in the mode of singing. The problem is that some will believe that they are more competent than the others, and insist on 'being right'. This often happens unconsciously. Those who believe in their own inability will try to imitate those who do not feel that way, and those who keep believing that they are always right will find it quite natural and good if they are imitated. Often enough the advanced cases (primates who feel more at home in the territory than others) will automatically insist on their own sound-level, possibly show-off with their prolonged exhalation and believe that the others should 'do it right', meaning 'just like me'. In such cases of habitual control/submission it works wonders when the authorities behave like fools and the functions of control/leadership are rotated, no matter whether people believe that they are competent or not. Loki advises that leadership in ritual should be diced for.... No doubt this will produce any amount of errors at first, but on the long run it might create a group of equals with more efficiency and self-assured independence than any of the hierarchical organizations could ever dream of. Of course it rarely happens this way. Quite a few people who join groups do so as they lack the discipline to work and experiment on their own, and most leaders enjoy their position out of a deep-rooted belief in the inability of their fellows. They usually have strict codes of behaviour to explain their standards, instead of helping beginners to develop their own unique will they try to tell them what that will would be. Surrounding themselves with copies of themselves, they feel proud of their followers and just a little disappointed that none of them is quite as good as they are. Magick is learned by imitation, true, but it is also learned by opposition. Behind these two, imitation and opposition, should be the essence; discovery and expression of self... This subtle art requires no rules or regulations.

17 Problems, troubles and how to deal with them

Twitching, energy jolts, sudden spasms are a sign that body is regaining the ability to pulse freely (Reich links these phenomena with the 'orgasm reflex') and that the energy, as it begins to flow, is passing through channels that were hitherto locked. Such reflexes are a sign that tension is dissolving, and they should be welcomed.

- Swaying happens when body attunes to some energy and begins to pulse in sympathy. Swaying can also happen in trance states of silence and vacuity. The phenomena of hospitalism is connected with this. Swaying has a calming effect on consciousness. Hospitalistic swaying is basically an attempt to soothe oneself. We may observe it in zoo animals who feel bored, it also happens in the wilderness. Waiting elephants often sway or dance on the spot, and polar bears waiting at ice-holes for the emergence of a seal also sway. Swaying can give access to a variety of gentle trance states. A feeling of absent-minded seeing may easily make people sway, on the other hand the feeling may be produced through voluntary swaying. It sometimes happens when I stand void-minded on the ringwall, with the icy blast of the wind tearing at me and the vortex whirling over the stone circle. Swaying that occurs during rune practice may involve a strong urge to rotate on the heels. Some authors, such as Frater Amenophis of the Fraternitas∴ Saturni∴ consider this a sign of success and advise that one should go with the motion, allow the rotation and do the runes in several directions.

- Warm sweat is usually a sign that body is heating up and cleansing itself. It often happens in ch'i practice that sweating is used to wash toxins out of the body.

- Cold sweat however is a danger sign. Probably your circulation is shaky and you had better stop.

- Shivering and trembling are possibly signs of the beginning of a *Seidr* trance. This theme is treated in another chapter.

- Yawning and belching are ways of getting rid of stagnant ch'i. The urges may seem irresistible, you practise a little and find all your song disturbed by one yawn after another, and maybe you will wonder, 'am I that tired already?' Yawning releases stagnant air. It also has an energetic function; 'pockets' of blocked ch'i are released (particularly at the trouble spots - back of the neck, throat, etc.) which can leave you a little exhausted, as the energy excess is gone. Other symptoms of clean-up operations are the unexpected churning of the bowels or the need to fart. It is also possible that the increase in ch'i flow brings out old pains and afflictions that have lain dormant for years. Usually this is part of the healing process, but this does not imply that one should not watch them very carefully. If they do not go away, see a doctor.

- Energy hunger, as Wilhelm Reich demonstrated, is a source of biopathical diseases in the average population. Most people suffer from chronic energy hunger, but when they get more energy they often cannot deal with it as the armour itself prevents balanced distribution. Rune practice, deep breathing, gentle lovemaking, dancing, etc., all help to supply more energy, as do journeys in the wilderness (nature contacts), sunbathing, fresh food and the like.

Typical symptoms of energy hunger are a chronic tendency to resign, to shut up, withdraw, feel unhappy, small, tense and depressed, aptly symbolized by Reich's metaphor of the amoeba that tries to shrink, to make itself small and harder in times of stress. In such cases the vital problem lies in opening the shell and letting the pressure out. Stored desires, unacknowledged conflict and repressed needs all become poison unless they are released, confronted and dealt with. Art is a useful channel to let the pressure out, but then, we all know how hard it can be to get up and do something. Singing and screaming very loud can also be helpful, or the practice of martial arts. Sometimes we have to trick ourselves into a better mood.

- Energy excess is a rather common problem among artists and magicians. We all tend to call up more than we can deal with, especially during those early years when true Will is unknown, power a constant temptation and all development takes place by trial and error. Beginners often 'try-out' sigils, rituals and all manner of sorcery, then drop them when they believe that nothing (or too much) is happening. No release of energy is ever lost, the lack of immediate results does not mean that there will not be results at all.

Then there are those who believe in grandiose invocations and forget the license to depart, what happens to the energy? We need not pretend that only amateurs have this sort of problem. We all make mistakes and accidents do happen - woe to the mage who pretends to be beyond errors and crisis. All magick, conscious or not, is half known and half concealed. We may be moderately sure about what we are doing (at the best of times) but we will never be certain.

Now it is fairly easy to evoke energy/consciousness, the trouble often arises out of the 'what shall I do with it?' i.e. the question of earthing. Earthing means that the power has to go beyond the limits of our being. It has to take on some sort of body to leave our system in balance. If the power comes into us and finds no way of release we get magical constipation. If it is only a little bit of power, this results in making the mage tense, cramped and edgy. If it is a lot it may well tear the ego apart, possibly even kill. It is no damn good having fabulous visions and miraculous insights unless these experiences are allowed to come out, causing communication and change. Going to heaven may be fun, but unless we come back to earth it is just another form of escapism. This is what commitment means, we care for the earth, it is of us and we of it. Magick is no pleasant hobby for the select few, it is a way of life.

Reich pointed out that the inability to release sexual energy and emotions is one of the roots of cancer and other biopathies. The energies encountered by the artist/magician are frequently very strong. We ought to bear that in mind when we play round and pretend mastery.

Earthing has many forms, depending on the nature of the mage. What we need, first of all, is a form of expressing our vision, of giving flesh to the dream. This starts with a well-kept diary, it is useful to put down experience in a definite form, if only to release pressure and to free the mind to think of other matters. It does not matter whether you draw, write, sing, cook, act, carve, build, make music, love or enact absurd events (group rituals, for instance), the vital issue is that something happens, that the current does not stop but flows through you, clearing the way for fresh impulse. This sort of earthing cannot be overemphasized. There are too many part-time magicians who believe in doing a little bit of magick (to feel special and successful) while keeping up their comfortable everyday routines and limitations. In the long run, this sort of division between 'occult' and 'profane' activities causes a peculiar sort of schizophrenia that spoils either of them. The honest magician offers the fullness of life to the current and goes with the flow, embracing joy and crises as they come to be. Genuine magick transforms the entire universe.

Earthing is one of the issues that marks a difference between old aeon and 'Nu' Aeon practices. The old Aeon mage thinks in terms of property, 'my' tradition, 'my' rank, 'my' task, 'my' achievements, 'my' initiations . . . illumination is 'gained', secrets are 'kept' (if not hoarded), the tradition is 'guarded' and so on. Old aeon mages are what they own and usually they sit on it until it starts to putrefy.

The nu Aeon mage is more concerned with being and becoming. Here we encounter the virtues of 'let it out', 'share it', the love that gives meaning to communication

Art and communication can help us to release, to express what is moving within. Honesty requires that the joyous vision is expressed just like the vision of pain, fear, crisis, guilt and whatever else lies repressed. The old Aeon mage may believe that such revelations would damage his authority; the Nu Aeon mage knows that holding back kills. So much for earthing on the large scale.

On the small scale we may still get an overdose of energy (be it through rune practice, yoga, *ch'i-kung*, ritual, beast forms, contact with the gods etc.) on occasion, and such an overdose should not be underestimated. The physical symptoms differ according to disposition. For me it is usually accompanied by headaches or circulation trouble. Yours will probably be different . . . look out and learn.

Sometimes serious problems arise from energy overcharge. Once, after doing depth massage I was too lazy and careless to release the energy excess that had accumulated in my hands. Within a few hours they got swollen beyond recognition and throbbed with a dull, regular pain. It took several hours of discharging, bathing the hands in a forest stream, before the pain left and several days before the size was right again. Another time, in youthful enthusiasm, I created dozens of sigils and elementals in a desperate attempt to force change. One night, during a group ritual on the ringwall, something snapped and I

went physically blind. That was something of a shock. I had a few extreme visions, lost a great deal of vitality, collapsed on the ground and only regained my eyesight by accepting the situation and coming to terms with it. It was Austin Spare's cryptic aphorism 'Does not matter - need not be,' which open the knots in my mind. A friend got partial face paralysis for quite some time because, as he put it, he had refrained from releasing the excess energy of his rune experiments.

Ways to release energy

- Small amounts can be earthed easily. As you stand, imagine that a line runs through your body from the height of heaven to the centre of the earth. The power is not confined, it passes through your being. As you exhale deeply you allow your body to relax. Your head sags, the shoulders slump, knees bend as if you would fall within yourself. Do this little trick a few times. Each time as you let go (partial collapse) you feel the excess of power rushing down through your feet and into the ground. Imagine that the charge goes deep, you do not want to dump it on your neighbours in the flat below.

- Larger amounts require more commitment. Imagine that the earth's surface opens, revealing a deep tunnel. Get down on hands and feet, so that the palms and foot soles rest on the ground. Arms and legs should be slightly flexed. This will feel rather awkward, but that is the way it is. Combine your exhalation with the vivid imagination of energy release, the power washes through your body and rushes down. As it passes through you it takes along all your burdens and restrictions: the knots of tension, fear, worries, seeds of disease and pain. This practice should be done with vivid emotion, let it out, let it all out. Keep voiding until you feel clear, light and well. Then close the tunnel again.

- More intense scenes, such as obsessive shaking (Seidr), can occasionally reach a stage where one fit follows another, time stops and one cannot get over it. This may be alright under suitable conditions but when it happens in a snow storm on the mountain top there may come a point where the fit must stop or the body will suffer. At times the only way to stop the trance is to fall down and to pour all the power into the ground. 'Earth drinks, is never drunken' tells us the *Havamal*... The earthing must suit the energy with a appropriate degree of intensity, technique and imagination. If nothing else let go with all the being.

- Energy imbalance is not the same as energy excess, it moves through body erratically and upsets your mood and health. In such cases we have to balance the power. The Gebo X rune is often used for this purpose, but more important is another practice. Focus the energy in the lower belly. This area, called *tan tien* by Taoists and *hara* by the Japanese, is a little below the navel. It is the centre of the body and the cauldron of etheric energy (ch'i, orgone, vitality). The Taoists teach that the centre point can store excess energy and distribute it through the organism. The 'dragon's castle' in the centre distills and refines power. To the front of the body it functions as the accumulator of energy (belly breathing) and to the back, at the spine, as the distributor of it. Focussing awareness to this realm causes the ch'i to flow. After your energy practice you simply concentrate your attention on the centre point. Place your hands on it and rub it in spiral motions, feeling the energy circle inwards to the deep. Taoist tradition claims that deosil circles are yang and widdershins circles are yin. From this they advise that men should do more deosil circles and women more in the counter-clockwise direction. This does not mean that one only uses one direction, merely that one does a little bit more in the direction corresponding to one's sex; we are after all male and female in our souls. If you do this well you will feel that the belly gets warm and that the energy, as it is gathered in the centre, gives off a warm and happy glow that radiates all through the body with a feeling of laughter and joy. For more on such Taoist practices see *The Secret of the Golden Flower*, published by Richard Wilhelm and C G Jung, Mantak Chia's excellent *Awaken Healing Energy Through The Tao: the Taoist secret of circulating internal power*, and Michael Saso's *The Teachings of Taoist Master Chuang*.

Some rune stances make contact with the deep. They can be used to raise power, they are equally useful to release it. The crucial point lies in your will and active imagination. To release, try Othila ⧼, Gebo X, Uruz ⋂, Teiwaz ↑, Laguz ⌐, Berkana ⌐, Wujo ⌐.

- In some states, earthing is easier when one uses physical help. Wind, for instance, can carry excess energy out of the aura. Water is even more efficient in attracting and storing energy. Some assume the stance of Laguz ᛚ, placing the hands on the central heating or in a wash basin and using the flowing water to take the energy excess away. Taking a hot shower is not efficient - warm water does not accumulate energy so easily - but if you end the hot shower with a minute or two of ice cold water you will release the excess and give your circulation a good kick to make you clear, active and positive. Tub baths are not too good, they gather some energy, but then you still soak in it.

- When you charge talismans, sigils, power tools or give a depth massage to some part of the body (yours or another's) that is tense or armoured, you hands may easily get overcharged. One way to get rid of the excess is to make a motion the looks as if you would fling water from the fingers. You exhale deeply and imagine that the energy flies off. This is done until the hands feel free again and the excess is released into the atmosphere. An easier method is to wash the hands thoroughly in cold water, imagining that the power is swept away. Now it may look tactless if you end a gentle massage by rushing to the tap but it can be downright stupid to avoid it.

- Other forms of energy excess can be channelled into activity, long walks in the wilderness, hard physical training, dancing for a few hours, anything that releases through exhaustion. In spiritual matters it can be good to pray and rant and rave and scream to release poison, it is the same method, in another realm. After a while you'll come to a point where you can laugh about yourself.

18 Learning to tune in

Here is a simple exercise introducing the rune stances of:

Isa $|$,
Uruz $\cap$,
Algiz Υ,
Teiwaz $\uparrow$,
Laguz Γ,
Gera ς.

0. Prepare yourself. Give yourself a moment of silence to calm your mind. Then do some gentle physical exercise to loosen the body and release tension. Jump around, shake your arms and legs, rotate the hips. Then stand in silence facing north. The feet should touch at the heels, the knees are slightly bent, the arms hang at the sides, the shoulders are relaxed. Feel the breath flowing to and from the belly.

It may be also useful to do a brief invocation of Odin/Wodan or the Norns.

1. Assume the stance of the Isa rune $|$. The feet solidly on the ground so the body feels very erect. Now the arms are lifted to form a single, vertical line. The palms face forward or each other (a matter of taste). The posture is not very comfortable - still, tension should be kept at a minimum. Breathe deeply and exhale well. Imagine that the Isa pillar connects the height of heaven with the depths of the earth, a single line of focused energy. Now take a good lungful of air and sing out the word 'IS', the 'I' should be high pitched like the clear sound of a bell and the 'S' like a prolonged serpent's hiss that fades into silence. Do not try to force the sound. Tension only

distorts the sensation. Sing/vibrate the 'IS' three times.

2. Now bend over almost touching the ground. This is not a stretching exercise, the knees are not locked. It is recommended that the position is comfortable. Let the head hang down between the arms, the fingers pointing to the earth. This is the stance of the Uruz rune ᚢ. Here use the imagination to let go and reach for the primal depths, the roots of being. The rune connects with Urda's well which washes all pain and tension away, it also signifies the wild ox who symbolizes the power and wildness of the beasts.

Whether energy flows down or rises up depends on will and imagination. Vibrate/sing the word 'ur'. The 'u' sound should be deep and sonorous, and the 'r' may be rolled or done in a coarse, guttural fashion. Try also the variations 'uruz' or 'ururur..' Repeat three times.

3. Now reach upwards till you stand erect as in the Isa posture. Then let your arms relax a little so that they drop sideways into the stance of the Algiz rune ᛉ. The palms should face upwards, the posture feels top heavy but not as tight as Isa. Be careful that your shoulders are not hunched up or tense and that belly moves properly in breathing. This posture is known as 'Algiz' in some systems and as 'Man' in the Scandinavian futhorcs. I suggest you try it with both titles. The important issue is the vibration of the 'aaa'. The word to vibrate is 'man' which starts with a closed mouth, then opens wide with the 'a'

(a feeling of release) and closes with a droning 'n'. 'Man' should not sound as the English word 'man', the 'A' should be rendered as in 'harbour' i.e. 'mmaaaahnn'. If you have practised vowel singing you will know which sound to produce. The rune does not refer to the male of our species but to humanity and the idea of reaching for the skies and embracing heaven.

4. Now let your arms sink down at the sides until your stance looks like the Teiwaz rune ᛏ. As Algiz connects with heaven, Teiwaz releases downward and the current is poured into the ground. This is often a very vivid feeling. Teiwaz has to do with blood letting, evolution and the flight of the arrow to the stars. Where the current flows into the soil, life begins to grow. Sing the word 'tir' or 'tiu'. If you allow the sound to drop this makes earthing easier.

5. Move your arms inwards until the hands, palms up, meet. Your stance now looks like Laguz ᛚ, from the side. Laguz is a rune that has to do with the ocean and also waterfalls and the act of washing oneself. It also refers to 'the law', which is, as all Thelemites know, 'Love Under Will'. Sing out the word 'lagu', 'lauga' or, as is common in Germany nowadays, 'laf/love'. The 'F' can be done to resemble the foaming of the waves on the beach. If you do this well, your body will sway with the water.

6. Pull your hands inward to the belly, so that the palms cover the centre point and the

elbows stand out sideways. Some do this stance with the hands at the hips, but if we use this rune to round things off it is more appropriate to touch the belly itself. Your stance should look like a variation of the Jera rune ♦ (see illustration). The word pattern to vibrate is 'gera', 'gara', 'gea', 'jara'. This is an agricultural rune sign which symbolizes the garden, the seed and the living grain that grows out of it. After vibrating you can rub the belly and spiral the energy inwards to store it, or release the excess into the ground, as was described elsewhere.

Do these six runes daily, with three or five repetitions of each. This sort of practice should be done for several months until each sign immediately tunes in to some state of energy/consciousness. It is useful to make notes in the diary in regard to climate, weather, time of day, place of working, state of health and your mood before and after. *Remember to earth properly.* When you have mastered the whole series begin to vary the conditions. Try to vibrate with less noise, or in a whisper, finally learn to sing in the imagination alone, or alternate loud and silent play. Then try these exercises out of doors, or integrated in ritual. When you are well used to them you can discover the feeling and flow of the other runes. By then you should be able to experiment on you own, replacing my boring 'dos and don'ts' with a livelier spirit of enthusiastic experiment.

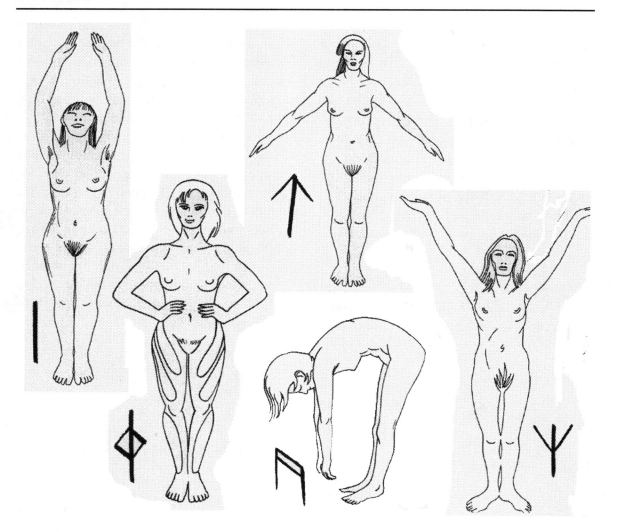

19 Runes for health?

Literature on rune magick abounds with hints concerning the healing of various diseases. One encounters lengthy accounts of anonymous enthusiasts who cured this or that exotic illness through rune practice, and some lodges go so far as publishing neat lists attributing rune symbols to dozens of diseases. Such tables of correspondence are very popular among the result hungry. For the serious magician they are a waste of time.

Rune stance practice may have indirect healing qualities where the disease is a biopathy, i.e. a disease of the autonomous life system. According to Wilhelm Reich, who coined the term, biopathies are afflictions that are rooted in a lack of vitality. Rune stance practice tends to ease that condition, as does any sort of activity that makes people breathe deeply, exhale fully, assume good posture, regulate the energy circulation and release tension in song, sound or screaming. Such practices can be found in most systems of magick. They stabilize the bio-energy network, which gives body a better chance to cope with its problems and to enjoy life.

Nevertheless, the runes are no cure. We should not attempt to replace a competent doctor or natural healer with some rune pattern that is supposed to cure anything. Rune practice is of little value in such cases as arise from vitamin or mineral hunger, not to mention various infectious diseases, sprains, broken bones or broken hearts, regardless of holistic positive thought and the like. Nor should runes replace the use of healing herbs or natural medicines. Most biopathies - energy hunger or excess - are closely related to the Reichian character armour, i.e. vitality ceases

to flow freely when aspects of self are repressed and 'stored' in muscular cramp. The same energy hunger, without the neurotic repression, can happen if we spend too much time sitting in a cramped posture or doing work that utilizes only parts of the anatomy.

Some of the more extreme biopathies arise from sexual hunger and the inability to function and feel freely. The sexual function requires a relaxed body and a peaceful state of mind, a sense of sharing, loving, caring for the other as for oneself. While making love a lot of energy gets raised which works its way through the system, provided the couple function in energetic unity and body-mind is not cramped by armour. Where the channels are blocked, the experience is partial, unsatisfactory and leads to separation. The sensations of exhaustion, weakness, feeling drained or vampirized or abused arise from an inability to feel, flow and love freely. Where people feel apart in coitus there will always be a sense of 'losing energy' for the male (causing unconscious frustration) and a sense of 'being abused as a container' for the female, who frequently has little use for the charge deposited in her. One solution to this problem is the well known practice of holding back ejaculation (as taught in certain forms of Tantra and Taoism). It has the distinct disadvantage of requiring conscious effort and control, meaning armour and separation. Also, the practitioners have to be very capable in distributing and storing the unreleased excess of energy. Another method, which is more a way of life, requires that the couple share love, trust and honesty and go beyond

the notions of I/you, achievement, aims, effort, technique, before/after etc. It means that making love is free from lust of result and that one gives oneself to the event without holding back. This is obviously quite another matter than to use each other to release frustration and tension.

When the couple functions in unity, their energies merge. The shared radiation eases any imbalance. This implies that one allows plenty of time for the event and spends even more in close embrace after orgasm, breathing in unity, so that the energy can circulate through both as one, restore balance and heal the whole. The shared breath balances power, breath in discord just wastes life away.

This sort of thing is more than copulation, it is mating, and the best cure for character armour that exists. I will not go as far as Wilhelm Reich who claimed in his *Cancer Biopathy*, that cancer, angina pectoris, asthma, cardio-vascular hypertonia, epilepsy, catatonia, paranoid schizophrenia, fear neuroses, multiple sclerosis, chorea and chronic alcoholism arise exclusively from sexual hunger. Among artists and magicians the problem of energy excess is quite as common and causes similar troubles. Reich claimed that 'all biopathies have in common a malfunction in the natural pulsation of the whole organism.' Rune practice (or vegetotherapy, yoga, ch'i kung etc) may gradually erode the armour of tension, restore the ability to feel and recharge the organism with fresh energy. This will not change the original problem that caused the armour and the biopathy. Reich was surprised to discover that it wasn't enough to merely to dissolve the armour and restore the natural pulsation of his clients; these people must actually changed the life-style, which had produced all the cramp and frustration in the first place.

Often the disease is nothing but a symptom/solution for some deep-rooted need. Healing such a disease will only make body/mind produce another one that serves the same function as the original disease, and this sort of vicious cycle can go on for quite some time. An excellent method of dealing with such 'secondary gain' is given by Bandler and Grinder in their writings on 'reframing'.

There is just one disease that can be directly influenced by rune practice, and that is a very humble affair compared to all the wonder recipes... behold the miracle:

How to clear a clogged nose.

A) Do some rune stances, vibrating rather loud. My own favourites for this problem are Algiz, Teiwaz, Ansuz, Gebo, divination will reveal others.

B) Sit down. Keep some tissues ready. Vibrate some deep droning sounds, such as 'om', 'ong', 'oaoaoamng' which shake up the nose and the facial bones. It does not have to be very loud, just enough to make you sneeze. Do not force things, go gently.

C) Now for the particular channels. Close on nostril with a thumb. Vibrate gently through the other one. Switch sides repeatedly. Now close both nostrils. Vibrate/drone as before, then let your thumbs slip off a little bit then close the nostrils again. Close one nostril and tap against the free channel as you vibrate. One can produce and impressive number of absurd sounds this way. Concentrate on the feeling. Good vibration makes the entire nose area, from the roof of the mouth to the eyebrows vibrate and thrill. When it feels like a nasty itch or an urge to sneeze you are doing well. Be very gentle in this stage. You want to release pressure, not increase it.

D) Rub your hands together until they feel warm. Now massage your face, head and neck until they feel warm and relaxed.

This exercise often causes strong flow from the nostrils. Soon you may hear a high pitched sound from your nose cavities and the pressure is gone. This does not mean that you have to keep droning till release occurs or your head turns purple. Sometimes it takes some time before the pressure is released. You do well if you practice this technique gently in small doses but repeat it every half hour or so till the pressure is gone. Of course, this is no therapy but a specific help for a minor problem, commonly found among sorcerers who have been out in the rain and cold for too long. If your nose troubles are chronic you should see a doctor.

20 Divination

'She went to her handbag, picked it up, squatted on the floor of the computing room. She was breathing heavily. Jerry watched her as she took something from her bag and threw it on the ground. It was a handful of chicken bones. Miss Brunner was casting the runes.' Michael Moorcock, *The Lives and Times of Jerry Cornelius* (1976).

Technically, rune divination is a simple matter. There are three stages to its performance, namely:

1. Tune in and ask your question.
2. Select your answer.
3. Interpret the information.

All of this would be simple and easy, were it not for a number of very human problems and shortcomings. Divination is not developed from one day to another. If you expect assurances, guarantees and firm predictions you will be disappointed. The runes require experience to work well, and experience can only arise from practice. You will have to become familiar with each rune sign. Some people consider divination as a party game. They get themselves some more or less adequate book on this or that system, do the ritual required and look up the answer. If the answer fits the question in a more than general way, this may be coincidence, synchronicity or latent skills in prophecy. It is not a phenomenon that can be relied upon.

In the earlier phases of study you may have to look up a lot of items. The real answers, however, cannot be given by a book. They arise from intuition, and this is a faculty that requires cultivation. Imagine that you ask a question and receive, say, Nauthiz as your answer. There are at least three interpretations, so what can we make out of it?

The book will not be able to tell whether the rune is meant as (1) need, trouble, lack, hunger, necessity; (2) knots, the binding of two streams, karma, union as mutual change, unseen connections; or (3) the Norns as the weavers of fate and reality, compulsion, drive, impulse, desire. Only intuition could tell you which one is appropriate, a book cannot.

If you lack training and familiarity with the signs, you will easily deceive yourself. It is so absurdly easy to select the convenient answer, and to congratulate yourself on your superior insight and far reaching intuition. The rest is done by selective memory. If you wish to work divination properly, you will have to *live* with your system. The rune posture, chant, dance, handgrip, astral projection etc., are the very tools that will make the futhorc come to life for you. Without these practices, the runes will remain an abstract thing that has few, if any, connections to reality. Now I cannot tell you just how intuition should appear if the answer is right. You, for yourself, will have to learn which sensations you may trust, just as you will have to discover which questions invite misinterpretation and self deception. You will make plenty of mistakes, and rightly so. The mistakes are a vital aspect of your magick, they provide a good opportunity to learn something new and with hindsight often provide a source of amusing anecdotes. Beginners should carefully note their questions, rune answers plus their personal interpretations in a special diary. Consider what you expect from divination. If you desire 'true answers' with 'definite meanings' you will often be disappointed. Would you foretell the future? What is this future to you? A fixed destiny, like pearls on a string, or an outfolding of various possibilities along streams of probability? Would you live in a limited universe? The past does not exist, inasfar as memory tends to reinterpret experience time and time again. The future is just as impossible. Divination can indicate possible developments, can give 'educated guesses', can reveal trends and tendencies. It cannot supply guarantees: the future, after all, is shaped by each single instant (and this includes the very act of divination). Only the weak-willed like to believe in fixed destiny. Fatalism is self restrictive; a magician requires an open universe.

The greatest value of divination may perhaps be discovered in the present. It works best at describing the status quo, at giving a new vision of the present situation, at changing your point of view. Through divination, we may discover new insights, which may lead to different attitudes and new possibilities. Most of our problems are self inflicted. Divination may allow us to see beyond these limits, and to shape the world anew. Nor is divination but a simple matter of re-definition. Here is an ancient riddle: do the runes reveal or do they write, and make the prophecy come true?

We should embrace divination with as few pre-conceptions as possible. One of the greatest obstacles is the value attributed to the technique. Some 'serious' magicians consider the runes so thoroughly sacred that they only use them for matters of greatest importance. Quite a pity, as they will never become very familiar with them this way. True enough, the runes are sacred. However, they are no more sacred than you are, so there is no need to pretend pompous sincerity or to approach them like a servile imbecile meeting god almighty. Sacred does not mean serious. The more dread, awe and importance you involve in the act of divination the less natural and easy will it be to you. Serene ritual may be helpful, it is never obligatory. A person who requires pomp and grand gestures is probably incapable of getting results without strenuous effort, or needs the outer props to reassure himself that the answer cannot be wrong. The more seriously you take your divination, the easier will you deceive yourself. Good style requires a lot of experiment. Try divination in a variety of moods, ranging from serious/ceremonial to playful/spontaneous. Wodan (priest) and Loki (clown) are blood brothers. The part of your mind which does the divination for you (i.e. selects the answer you can understand) is equally serious and full of jokes, and unless both aspects are balanced, will certainly fool you. It is you who makes the divination valid. The signs themselves are just signs, a good blend for a specific purpose, but really no better or worse than any other signs. If you accept divination as an act of 'controlled folly', both serious and in jest, you will find that the answers come to life. Loki is a trickster!

There are occasions when unclear or misleading answers may be vital for your development. I remember receiving thoroughly 'wrong' answers which led to right (willful) action where 'right' answers would have given the game away at a far too early stage. In other cases one may find that one's question is ignored (as trivial) and that one gets commentaries on far more important themes (conveniently ignored previously). We are not consulting a machine but dealing with intelligence. Divination is not just a skill, it is an adventure.

Let us begin with the question. What do you want to know? Get a clear idea of your problem - this may involve some contemplation - and phrase the crucial point in a simple question. This is a delicate issue. There are so many things to avoid! In our asking, we frequently reveal our errors and misconceptions. So many questions revolve around egoistic desires, mine/thine, I versus you, how to control others, how to achieve results, how to rationalize problems, how to avoid responsibility and decision, the eternal 'why me?' etc. Neither your subconscious mind nor the gods or fylgjar give a damn for such matters. They cannot understand egoistic troubles properly - such things are alien to their consciousness. It is even worse when you expect them to decide for you. Asking a god 'should I do x?' is an infantile way of making another agency responsible. Maybe the gods of the last Aeon were keen on obedient servants - not so the deities of the

Nu Aeon. Chances are that their reply will be as invalid as your question. Then there are badly worded questions. If you ask: 'what course of actions is required to achieve a satisfactory resolution of problems ABC in relation to D without involving E' you will get the confusion you deserve. Remember that you have to operate with a rather limited vocabulary. Twenty-four runes are not much when the problem is this complicated. Nor is it so helpful to ask 'will it be good if I do ABC?' It may be good for you - as seen by the gods - but that does not ensure that you will enjoy it. *Maybe* it is good for the magician to invoke the chaos giants... but *certainly* it will be terrible.

Practice will teach you how to word the question. Keep your words simple, honest and short. Indifference is another vital issue. If you urgently desire any specific outcome, and you may not even be conscious of your desire, if you feel pressure, need, drive, lust, hope, loathing, hunger or any similar sensation, your question may be flawed by wishful thinking, and your answer be interpreted by a mind cluttered with preconceptions. Such answers only support what you believed anyway - they are worse than no answer at all. What we need is an attitude of open-minded friendly indifference. Our troubles do concern us, true, but during the act of divination we want to learn. This means that we should keep our minds open to the new, and that we should not take ourselves too seriously.

Practice will teach how to let go of fear and misery, how to open a gap, a pause, a silent interval. This vacuum phase of consciousness allows us to work the divination without fear or desire concerning the results. It hardly matters whether we achieve this state of suspended belief/disbelief through the cataclysmic convulsions of the Seidr-trance, through refined silent meditation, sexual exhaustion or the absurd hilarity of a laughing cramp. In all of these cases our human troubles are dislocated and we are ready to send out our question and receive the reply in full honesty.

Well, we have constructed a suitable question and are eager for the working. Many practitioners begin by invoking the gods, the Fylgjar or their inner genius/subconscious mind. This is an excellent practice. Explain your problems, voice your troubles, give them a definite form. Beginners tend to be tongue-tied in such situations. They prefer 'mental invocations', and overlook that stating things honestly and loud is a vital aspect of the healing. 'Mental invocations', of course, are only efficient when you can do them just as well aloud (and louder). These are your gods and friends. Say what you feel and you will find that the problem gets clearer, and the pressure decreases. You will not need any special names of power or complicated formula. Speak from the heart and allow the words to rush out, meaningful or not, cascading floods that flush out the poisons. If need be, scream. Then, when you said what had to be said, calm down and go into voidness consciousness, into the freedom of the undefined.

Focus the mind on the question. There should be no anxiety in you, just a friendly and detached interest. Say the question aloud, once, twice, again and again. A good and simple question is much like a mantra; it sounds like music, and rotates with a rhythm. Allow the voice to fade out and continue to circle the question in your mind. By now the words should have become almost meaningless. Continue. Allow the question plenty of time to 'sink in'. Your body may begin to sway to the pulse of the inner rhythm. This makes the trance more profound. Go into it deeply. Still repeating the question-call you should pick up your tools. Dice, rune staffs, rosaries, bags containing pebbles or wooden chips can be held in the hands during the asking. They can be breathed upon, to make the link to you stronger, or anointed with various fluids. They can also be clapped, clicked or rattled in rhythm to the inner call - this, again, amplifies the trance. We get the same effect when shuffling tarot cards or casting Yi King coins. The monotonous sound focuses the mind on the rhythm, and the rhythm allows the question to touch deeply. Sometime during this process you will spontaneously perform the proper selection. Your hands may clutch the proper rune signs, scatter the dice, hurl the staffs to the ground or grab the proper symbols on the rosary. This may happen suddenly or with intent, effortlessly or with the wildness of heavy obsession.

Well then. You have received your data. What does it reveal? No, do not grab for the book. First, you should simply look at the rune sign, and feel the sensation/emotion that comes through. Spontaneous first impressions are useful; they arise without consideration or second thoughts. Use your own brain before looking at traditional interpretations. Ask as many questions as you can cope with. (complicated issues often require several operations.)

After the working a brief thanksgiving to the gods and Fylgjar is required, and a period of silent contemplation. Give your thanks freely, but also say if you are still confused. Do not use set formula, speak from the heart - it is worth much more than all classical 'licenses to depart'.

21 Rune alignments

When Gaius Julius, the future Caesar, was busy expanding the frontiers of his domain across Gaul, a Suebic king got in his way. His name was Ariovist and he had been invited into Gaul some years earlier to support one Celtic tribe against another. He had gathered some like-minded friends and crossed the Rhine to make himself at home in the centre of Gaul. According to Julius Ceasar's account, when he arrived nearby weeping Celtic nobles invited the Roman army to get rid of the Suebian troops for them. Caesar was always ready to help the downtrodden Celts on the road to civilization. In the ensuing war, the outnumbered Roman army was surprised to find the Suebians ready for small fights, but reluctant to join full battle. From questioning prisoners he learned:

'It is custom among the Germans that the family mothers, using runes and divination, decide when the battle is to be fought. They had declared the gods were against a German victory should they battle before new moon.' I Book 50

The delay was much to the advantage of the Romans, which may say something for the efficacy of religious divination for warfare. After Ariovist was beaten and his troops put to mad flight, the Romans freed some captives who had been held in chains by the Suebians. Among them was C Valerius Procillus, a friend of Caesar's, who told this tale:

During his captivity, three times had lots been thrown in his presence, to decide whether or not he should be burned. Each time the oracle had kept him unharmed. If his account is true, it raises some interesting questions on the Suebic relationship with their gods. Did those people believe that it is important to ask the gods whether they wanted a sacrifice? Quite a few cultures would have sacrificed Procillus without asking, on the time honoured assumption that war gods are always hungry.

Tacitus, in his *Germania*, gives a well known account of divination by lots among some unspecified Germanic tribes.

'no one cares so much for signs and divination by lots as they do. They cut a branch of a fruit bearing tree and divide it into small pieces. These they mark with a sign and cast them randomly, as chance would have it on a white cloth.'

Next follows prayer to the gods, which is performed by a priest, if the divination was public, but by the father of the house, if the divination is private. While looking skywards, three signs are picked up and interpreted.

'If the result is unfortunate, no more questions will be asked on that topic for the day, but should it be auspicious, it still has to be confirmed by other signs.'
Germania 10

This is what we know of the traditional methods. If you like to try it, the equipment for this form of divination consists of the following items:

a) One bag to contain the runes.

b) A complete set of rune signs. Use whatever variety of Futhorc you feel easy with. Carve the signs on wood, bone or pebbles. Don't buy them ready made: making them is an important stage in getting used to the system. Consider; the tools of divination are parts of your body and extensions of your mind. The closer they connect with you, the better.

c) A bit of cloth to mark the divination space on the ground. A simple cord can be used to the same purpose.

Esoteric literature abounds with complicated rules as to what invocation to use, what garments to wear, where and when to work the divination and so on. As very few of these rules make any sense save in giving beginners a complicated ritual to believe in, I will not bother to burden you with them. (A shrug, a smile - do what thou wilt!).

Let's experiment. You may shake the rune signs within the bag (use a big one), gripping and mixing them in a steady rhythm that accompanies the question's repetition. You may also scatter them on the cloth and mix them there - it depends on your preferences. The eyes are kept shut, out of focus or averted. The hands select the appropriate signs by feeling.

One rune layout

- Simple answers are received by selecting a single rune. This method may be a bit primitive, nevertheless it is very suitable for beginners who want to avoid confusions and wish to learn about the Futhorc step by step. Look well at you answer. Does it make sense to you?

What could it mean? If the sense of 'certainly! It means...' is lacking or if the answer seems meaningless, you may use the following practice. Imagine a curtain. It should be of a soft, heavy and dark material, and should be pictured (with closed eyes) until it looks real. If you need advice on visualization see my book *Visual Magick*. When the image of the curtain is clear and well developed, imagine that you pick up your wand and draw the rune sign in lines of vivid light on the cloth. Do not hurry! Get your image clear in your mind. You will sense when the fire of the lines has 'made contact', has called forth the 'real thing'. Then you may imagine that you slowly draw the curtain open. Some will immediately find images arising, others will encounter emptiness or trivial thoughts. In the latter cases you may repeat the process, and open another curtain. You could work a little banishing to get rid of the useless garbage that tends to clutter the upper levels of the mind. Also, you could assume the appropriate rune stance and vibrate its sound to tune into the image.

Some practitioners like to imagine some sort of mirror behind the curtain, be it a real mirror, a black mirror or a natural one, such as a small pond, a well or a spring. Note that all of these visions require practice. When you wish to work with a spring image, for instance, you will get used to the scenery around it, to vegetation, fauna and atmosphere. These things give life to the vision, they make the imagination solid and congruent. If you have imagined them often enough, your answer will come through easily. Take care that you close your curtain and or mirror properly,

even if it seems that nothing has happened. Such 'windows' are gateways to the deep; they should not be left open unattended.

Another related method uses the rune sign itself as a window; you press it against your brow and try to 'see' through it with your imagination. Such practices require training. Give yourself time to get used to them.

Two rune layouts

Two signs can be selected to describe the dual aspects of a problem. The right hand selects a rune for the 'day-side' of consciousness, the world of reason and law, a known world connecting to the knowledge of ourselves. The left hand selects a rune for the 'night-side' of our being, for the dark and deep realms of chaos and potential where unknown beings move unseen. Thus, the right describes the outer, visible appearance, the surface of the subject, while the left suggests what is going on underneath. Meditation on the day and 'night-side' of your being should make this model easy and natural. See the works of Kenneth Grant for ideas on the night-side.

Three rune layouts

Three signs have many applications.

1) Use a layout in triangle pattern. The runes are related to

(i) Wodan.
(iii) Weh. (ii) Willi.

To put it simply, Wodan is being and self, Willi is will and development (motion) while Weh describes body, colour, substance. If we ask for the description of a person, (i) will tell us of the essence, the inner substance, spirit. (ii) of the changes and transformations that occur; and (iii) reveals the material aspects, the nature of the life led, the earthing of the ideals and manifestation of the whole.

2) To observe the flow of development, we may select three runes for Urda, Werdandi, Skulda. Urda tells us the roots of the matter, its beginning and birth, Werdandi reveals the becoming, the present instant and Skulda suggests how things shall be, or should, or might, be in the/a future.

3) Norse and Chinese cosmology agree in that they speak of three levels of consciousness in each person. These levels are symbolized by (i) beasts, (ii) men, (iii) gods. If we lay out three rune signs in a vertical row, the bottom sign tells us of the beasts. This is the level of instinct, of survival lusts, of body needs, territorial behaviour etc. It is the realm of our 'past selves' insofar as it contains, in living flesh, the genetic memories of several million years of struggle for survival. The middle sign reveals our conscious, human state of mind. It deals with human interaction, with communication, reason, work, society. This is the realm of 'identity', and of the many masks we dance each day. On top is the realm of the gods. Here we find our 'future selves', images of what we would like to become, ideals, possible solutions to old problems, and visions of ourselves enthusiastic, inspired, immortal and forever young.

Thus, the three levels describe three aspects of single person. We can draw three runes to find out what our personal status quo is. If we want to observe relations between persons, we may select three runes for each of them, and then compare the needs and urges for each plane. This practice is excellent for couples. But be sure to use the full set of runes for each person, not one set for both.

Four rune layouts

Four signs can be interpreted in relation to the solar formula. Lay them out to quarters of the circle and judge them in reference to the direction. East = birth, south = life, west = age, north = death.

Five rune layouts

Five runes can be laid out like a pentagram. As some claim the five pointed star is a symbol of humanity. ('Every man and every woman is a star.') Each of the points relates to an element. Thus, if you wish to find out about vitality, you look at the rune sign in the fire position, and if you care to observe the state of mind you are in, look at the rune in 'air'. This layout, once more, gives a complete description of any person. Should there be confusion, ask for a simple sign to describe the whole and put it in the centre. A multiply-rune layout can also be useful when you want to contemplate choices and their outcomes. Draw one rune for each choice and them compare them. In more delicate issues you can draw three runes for each choice and observe how each tends to work out.

Now we could continue like this for quite some time, producing ever more complicated layouts. In practice, they are rarely needed. We ought to focus on communication, not on complexity. If you have asked well, the deep ones (call them gods, beasts, demons, guarding spirits, inner self or whatever) *want* to communicate with you. This means that they will do their best to send you the appropriate idea or inspiration. If you are ready to receive, this will usually require very few rune symbols. More symbols equal more confusion. Why employ a dozen signs when a single one does just as well? Remember that the runes themselves are not the answer. Then answer is *suggested* by the runes.

Modern tools

- Dice. Get yourself three or four wooden dice. Three dice are useful for the 16 rune futhorc, each Aettir gets one dice, and two spaces remain open. These may be filled with additional runes, remain empty or carry some personal symbols (such as '?', '!'). Four dice are ideally suited for the 24 rune futhorc, though of course the Aettir pattern is broken. You might lay them out in a 'cross-roads' pattern and invoke one god for each quarter. (Finding out who lives where in your cosmos is a vital aspect of your development). Dice have the advantage that they are easy to handle, which makes them useful for the sort of trance state that has you scatter bits and pieces around.

- Rosary. Carve the rune signs into wooden beads (a small file does wonders) and string them up. Use beads with big holes, so they glide easily. This is a useful tool for meditation, it is also excellent as a pocket computer.

The disk. Here is a tool for Arachnophiles. Cut out two solid disks of cardboard. The diameter should be at least 30cm. Glue the two disks together. You may want to include a few personal items in between - symbols, glyphs, hair, binderunen, feathers, fluids or whatever. The rune symbols should be written on the outer rim of one side. Give each sign a field of equal size. Paint a black circle into the centre of the disk. Using a pencil, mark the boundaries of the rune fields on the other side of the disk. Draw lines to the centre and design a spider web. Now each web pocket at the rim equals a rune field on the other side of the disk. Lay the web on your knees. After the invocation, begin to circle your finger on the net, around and around, the rhythm should parallel your breath and the inner rotation of the question. Sometime your finger will be drawn to the outer rim, and will stick to one of the web-pockets. Now turn the disk around and find out which rune sign belongs to the field. The black centre may be used as a mirror for the imagination - project the rune into it, and see what comes out.

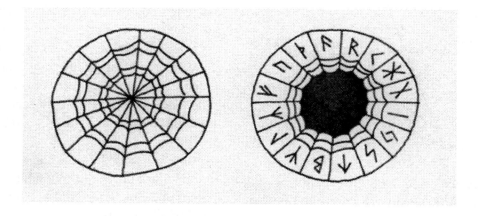

22 Unusual methods of divination

Apart from the customary oracular practices using rune symbols or dice, a number of advanced techniques have been developed that function with little or no equipment. The basic idea behind these methods is simply that you and the world reflect each other in countless subtle ways, so that by seeing with an open mind, the signatures and meanings of all ideas can reveal themselves to the magician. These methods require a certain amount of experience in 'seeing' techniques.

Leonardo Da Vinci introduced a basic technique for 'Eidetic vision' into the history of art that is of great importance to our studies. You will perhaps be familiar with this technique from childhood games or Rorschach tests. It works on the basis that the mind tries to understand the unknown by means of the known. Leonardo Da Vinci advised his students to select some unusual shape, such as one rarely ever observes consciously or with full attention to detail. A friend of his is said to have come upon this technique when he passed a wall against which local persons, especially the sick, used to spit for some superstitious Catholic reason. Leonardo's friend, no doubt an artist of surprising vision and genius, was amazed to find a myriad of fantastic forms arising from the spittle and the stone, and spent hours studying them in sheer ecstasy. Now you will not need something as drastic as this (though it can be valuable to go so deeply into a disgusting sight that nausea disappears and a sense of aesthetic pleasure arises), an ordinary aged brick wall (without slime) will do fine.

Mind you, slime (without bricks) can also be used.

Open your eyes, still your mind, see what reveals itself to you! In the 'meaningless' forms of rot and decay, in the mosses, lichens, cracks, dirt, dust and changes of texture or colour all kinds of bizarre visions can be found. Try to see without naming them.

Do not bother to tell yourself that this is a bit of loose stone, and that an aged cobweb. Simply go into the shape without explaining it; see it in an attitude of wide-eyed, empty minded awe, so that the form itself, without conceptualization, can work its magick on your mind. Soon you will find all kinds of strange creatures, faces, symbols, beasts, cities, flowers, bizarre scenes and strange events.

This practice is vital to the artist as it teaches to see in a holistic way without analyzing, questioning or naming. In 'drawing from nature', be it landscapes, portraits or nudes, the act of seeing should take place with as little interference of reason as possible. You do not portray this or that person (who relates to you in such a way) but try to see simply the form of the face, with no concern for the person or yourself. Analytical seeing takes place during pauses or afterwards, not while in the act of doing it. The practice is vital to the magician as it teaches to 'open your mind and let the pictures come' in a playful, easy fashion. As the mind tends to feel uncomfortable without the support of reasonable thought and familiar patterns, it does its best to create meaningful shapes out of the basically meaningless arrangement communicated through the senses. This goes for brick walls and the rest of reality. In doing so, the mind reveals materials that have hitherto been 'unconscious' to your waking mind.

With practice, it will become easier for you to stop the inner dialogue, see what is and evoke vision from it. You should train in this art until you can make such pictures appear out of all kinds of objects, be they weather worn stones, decaying vegetation, cracked earth, folds of cloth, growth of mosses, twisted roots, splitting ice, towering mountains or whatever.

Man-made objects can also supply surprising insights at times; even that famous can of tomato soup can be interesting, when viewed with sufficient intensity. Advanced practices aim at seeing whole ranges of scenery in this fashion, though this is difficult, as it is hard to forget that 'these are trees and here is a stream and over there the naked earth comes out...' We are learning to see form without explaining it to ourselves. Small objects are easier to start with, or unusual ones that are not familiar to the mind. It is typical for us humans that we like to see random sense impressions in ordered, meaningful structures. This habit is a safety mechanism. The amount of sense impression we receive each instant is so overwhelming that our mind reduces them to priorities, fits them into comfortable patterns, ignores most of them, (repression) and fits new interpretations to some of them (projection). Through techniques such as these we can break our observation habits and open up to see reality in new ways.

Among the earliest cult objects of humanity were flat slabs of stone into which the shapes of several beasts were carved. These beasts were scratched on top of each other, so that the lines overlay and mingled. On first sight, such Paleolithic stelae look like a meaningless jumble of crude lines with the odd head or hoof sticking out here and there. To the stone age shaman, such a stone could contain a whole series of power beasts. If you look at the twisting lines with the necessary open mind and inner silence, you will find the beasts arising out of the confusion; one after another the lines coalesce and show meaning to the seer. Possibly the 'random shapes' (networks of criss-crossed abstract lines) found in some Neanderthal caves (Île De France and elsewhere) had a similar use. In many cult caves (some of them barely big enough to hold a single human) the walls were decorated with scores of scratches - horizontal, vertical, diagonal, curved, star shaped etc - which show no recognizable pattern, no meaning or purpose.

In a state of deep silence, however, aided by the flicker of the flames and the dance of the shadows, such scratch-networks soon became an homogeneous 'field' out of which certain simple shapes emerge on their own accord. These 'simple shapes' are selected and emphasized by some part of the mind we are 'unconscious' of. Many of them show great similarities to rune signs. We may use this technique for rune divination. Here is one method. Go into the wild. Walk around for a time to dissociate your everyday consciousness and attune to the living world.

A little sweat and exhaustion can be useful. First you will need some item that can supply the data you want. Aged rocks are useful for this purpose, or great trees, thorny hedges, sedge grass in the swamps, twisting weeds or simply a few blades of grass reaching for the skies. We may use any living, organic object that shows sufficient complexity in its form to reveal a scope of rune shapes. Note that some objects tend to produce some runes more frequently than others, depending on the direction of growth. Practice will teach what particular item supplies the information you need, and what consciousness you will be most relaxed with.

First you will have to build up a connection. Walk around your object, touch it, observe the nuances of its structure and the environment around. Send your vision into the core of its being and try to feel what it is like to be that particular rock or tree. The form expresses meaning: Feel the sensation, identify with it, embrace the very heart of its being. With a tree, you would allow your sight to glide through the branches, to touch each little twig, to feel the density of the wood, the pulse of the juices, until you realize the 'rightness' of the growth, and the fullness of the personality. Again this art requires practice.

The secret of contact is not intellectual apprehension but a flow of love and sharing. Understanding comes out of union, and union requires the ability to receive. As the Zen saying goes: 'first, empty your cup.' We cannot touch trees with the intellect, as trees do not think, but we can touch them through the sensations we share with them. When you sense contact, focus on your question or problem. Try to keep your inquiry clear, short and simple. Allow your question to sink deep into your mind - which is also the tree's - repeat it silently as you let your gaze glide slowly through the branches. Well phrased, the question sounds rhythmic and musical (like a mantra), this rhythm makes concentration clearer. Gradually, a state of calm should come over you. The eyes go out of focus or close entirely and the question fades away. When you feel the impulse, open your eyes wide and allow your sight to be caught by the first structure that attracts attention. Spontaneous reaction is required; do not think but do. Often, your answer may be there already. If not, use the seeing technique (outlined above) and allow your answer, a rune shape, to emerge out of the structure. Some practitioners find it easier to look with one eye for this purpose, as vision can then become two-dimensional.

Here we have an indication how Odin 'received' the runes on the tree. When you have received your answer restore the balance. This means that you give your thanks and gently disengage from the object of your vision. It is particularly easy to learn this technique in the cold season, when the branches stand clear and dark against the frozen skies. Given sufficient practice, you will find 'signatures and signs' appearing in this fashion as you walk the woods, and appearing effortlessly, *en passant*. As your sensitivity increases, you will become adept at picking up omens from a fantastic range of items.

Indoors, you may adapt this technique by using a number of staffs. Collect a bundle of at least nine staffs, each should be as long as the length from fingertips to elbow. These can be clacked rhythmically as you focus on your question, and are scattered on the ground to supply your answer. This divination technique is fairly advanced, as the resulting layout often creates several rune shapes in several layers. Some rune shapes will leap out at you whilst others require more effort. See whether they lie on their own, or pointing in some direction. You might also scratch a web of random lines into damp earth, or do the same using a thick pen and paper. To the seer, everything is revealed everywhere. Again, I'd emphasize the need for practice. Divination is a matter of communication. You have to learn a language before you can speak it.

23 Sigil sorcery

Here is a branch of the magical tree which I love very much. Sigil sorcery is a way of effecting change. It is based on the realization that it is not the conscious mind but the deep mind which works the greater changes. In essence, we may call sigil magick a technique to ask the deep mind to produce a specific change. It is our job to specify just what we want changed, and the deep mind will find surprising ways of making the change come true, provided it wills to do so. In this respect, the practice is based on trust. In magick, we frequently encounter aspects of the inner and outer world which we would like to change. Some of these changes may be easy to effect. Such changes may take place - with the help of the deep mind - if we pray for a while, speaking to the deep mind, the gods, the spirits, and tell them what troubles us, and ask for help or insight. Such direct requests can be very efficient. They let out some of our worry and tension and use this energy as a contact to the deep realm, which usually tends to know much better what is good for us than the conscious mind.

Sometimes the direct approach may be too simple. As we all know, there may be problems which require change, but try as we might, the conscious mind will not come up with worthwhile solutions. This is often the case, and not very surprising, if we consider that the conscious mind is usually the most limited aspect of our being. The ego likes to do things as it always has, and if this does not work, it can get desperate and stubborn. In many psychological troubles, the ego is quite helpless. It may try to work changes, using the old methods and thought patterns and this change probably will not happen. We observe the same thing in psychotherapy. The ego of the client may spend years describing its conflicts and the ego of the psychologist may spend years trying to get useful insights from this, but all in all this practice will effect few changes, except in the therapist's bank account. If the ego could have understood the problem, or if the ego could have made a worthwhile change, it would have done so long ago.

Now the client comes to therapy, and the mage to the gods, or the shaman to the spirits, for the very simple reason that the ego did not produce a solution. Indeed, in such cases it is often the conscious identity, the ego, itself which prevents the desired change. If we want this change to happen, we will have to ask our deep minds to work this, and often enough we will have to hide this request, so that the deep mind can do its job without the interference of our conscious personality. Quite possibly, the ego will have to be changed so that the desired change may take place, and quite probably it will try to meddle, try to control this process. This is precisely what we wish to avoid. So we veil our request with a sigil.

What is a sigil? A sigil is usually a visual glyph. This sign contains our request and is transmitted to the deep. The deeper self-aspects receive this message, and when they consider it a willful request, they will make it come true, sometime, somewhere, and with more grace, understanding and wisdom than the conscious mind. Using sigils for magick is a very old art. The medieval grimoires, for example, supply us with the names and sigils of hundreds of spirits, who may be contacted by these means. These sigils are traditional, in that they were received once and handed on by the tradition.

Modern sigil sorceries, such as those developed by Austin Spare and Kenneth Grant, work on the idea that the Nu-aeon mage should develop her or his own sigils for the work. Spare's method of sigil crafting is quite well known nowadays. First you ought to meditate on your problem for a while, to find out what restricts, and what sort of change you desire. You do not have to be quite precise, the important thing is to 'think into the the right direction'.

Now you would formulate your desire in a simple phrase. e.g. 'I desire good health', 'I will power', 'all is healed', 'we love', 'life is joy', 'initiation now!' 'I desire money', 'fresh inspiration', 'astral vision is easy', 'the spirits appear', 'conflicts are solved' 'love and laughter' etc.

To make a sigil out of 'love and laughter', you would first kick out all double letters. Love and laughter = love and ~~laughter~~. Now take these letters and construct and glyph out of them. Some examples:

So far, the practice seems quite easy doesn't it? Here are some points to remember in the sigil's construction.

- Keep it positive. If you say 'I want no disease', your deep mind represents the ideas 'I' 'want' 'disease' and then tries to cancel the disease it has just imagined. This may cause some confusion.

Exercise: imagine clearly what these phrase mean.

1. 'I want no disease', 'I want health'.

2. 'My emotional troubles disappear', 'my emotions are healed'.

3. 'I am feeling not bad', 'I feel well'.

4. 'Do not do this wrong', 'Do it right'.

5. 'Do not be loud', 'Do be silent'.

When your deep mind tries to make sense out of such suggestions, the negations can be difficult. The mother who tells a child 'don't fall down', communicates 'do - negation - fall down.' To make sense of this, the deep mind has to imagine 'do fall down' and then has to cancel the whole thing. This is a complicated procedure, as the undesired effect has to be conceived before it can be denied, and often enough our little brat will get a strong impulse to fall in the process. 'Be in balance' would be a much better suggestion, as it is a simple and positive concept which can be imagined easily. Some pioneers of hypnotherapy, such as Schultz, believed that 'the subconscious mind cannot understand negations.' Modern research indicated that it can, but not as easily. Apparently it needs more time to make sense of negations and more effort. When in a hurry or under pressure, negations can easily be overlooked. Also, it is an interesting aspect that our deep minds do not enjoy imagining negative events. To imagine 'fall down' is not pleasant and your deep mind will not like to imagine it. Even if we cancel the imagination with a 'don't', the end result will still be unpleasant, while the idea 'be in balance' feels quite attractive from the start.

- Keep the phrase short. This keeps the letters few and the sigil can remain simple and uncomplicated.

- Avoid specification of details. If you say 'I will love' this will make very good sense to your deep mind. If you say 'I will love with X under conditions ABC, but not if DEF are involved', your deep mind will hurl the sigil into the rubbish heap where it rightly belongs. Please consider:

Can your ego know whether person X wills to love you?

Can your ego know which conditions are required?

Can your ego know how this love should take place?

Can you Ego know which changes you'll need to adapt to each other - of course it cannot. If we use sigils, we do so precisely because the ego has not found solutions, and is probably not competent for it either. We use sigils as we can trust the deep mind to solve our problems, and like any other specialist, the deep mind will know quite well how to work the willful change. Would you tell your doctor how to take out your appendix? The deep mind is much more competent in working changes and effecting a healing than you are. It will know what to do, and how and when and with whom, much better than your ego can. This means that a general suggestion will give the deep mind a lot of freedom, while a specific suggestion may well be aimed at what the ego believes important, and which may be completely beside the point. Keep your phrases open and diffuse, you want to stimulate change, not to specify and control it. Certain speech patterns have been found useful for this task, see the work of Milton Erickson and *Trance-Formations* by Grinder and Bandler.

The sigil is an abstract glyph; its shape should not remind us of what its actual meaning is. This abstract glyph contains its meaning, but does not reveal it. We can transmit the sigil to the deep mind, using various trance states, without attracting the interference, control, doubt, hope, judgement, fear, desire or evaluation of the ego.

We have formed a sigil for a desire. What do we do with it? First of all, we dissociate the original desire. This means that we *forget, or pretend to forget*, what the sigil is good for.

We may lay it aside for a while and busy ourselves with other matters. When we come back to it, we should pretend that we do not know what it means, that is is simply a neutral and abstract shape which we wish to communicate to the deep mind. It is not our job to worry about its meaning and fulfillment; we are simply there to pass the message to more capable hands. This task of forgetting may seem difficult at first, especially if the sigil was meant for something vital. Austin Spare advised to construct several sigils at one time, and to communicate / transmit these days later, so you would not be quite sure which desire you are working with. This forgetfulness, whether real or pretended, assures that the ego will not involve itself in the process.

Transmission.

This is the last, and crucial stage. First, you require a time when you are receptive. You will need a clear mind for this. Drugs might complicate the process as they may cause confusion. For instance, you could ask your deep mind; 'Hey! You spirits and friends! I want to communicate this seed-shape to you, and I would like to ask whether you want to receive it?' This way, the deep mind may tell you when the channel is open.

Another way is to use a 'magical time'. This might be a time during ritual, or when you are out in nature, a time of joy and openness, of exhilaration and ecstasy, when you are especially in tune with yourself.

Some mages use crisis to get the contact open. Crisis and exhaustion, as was described before, can be very useful to break the control of the ego, to shatter habitual belief and to open our armour so that the sigil may slip through. The problem with crisis is, that it tends to associate the sigil with a lot of unpleasant emotions. Crisis can cause cramp in more ways than one, and if we connect the sigil shape with the cramp sensation, our deep minds will not accept it. Thus, if you wish to work a sigil in a crisis state, be careful to use the crisis only to open you up. During the act of transmission, the ideas of pain, crisis, cramp, need or desire should all be avoided; what we want is an open-minded friendly attitude.

Right then. The time and space are fine and you feel open and energetic and wish to transmit the sigil shape. There are plenty of ways. I like to work in a dual fashion, alternating intro- and extroverted methods.

For instance, I would start in silence. I would look at the sigil shape and allow my eyes to move with the lines, to feel the lines, to feed on them, and as my mind becomes quiet I sense that more and more awareness sinks into the sigil, and that the shape begins to pulse, and I centre myself on the shape, and sense it, and somehow the deep mind makes contact, so that I can feel how the sigil flows through my senses and through my open and silent mind into the deep regions. 'Wide-eyed vacuity' is a good description for the process. After a while I would grab my rattles or drum and begin to make music while concentrating on the sigil shape. If this music gets loud, wild and abandoned, things are working fine. After some of this I get so carried away that I begin to dance around the sigil. Then, sometime I collapse on the ground and begin to stare at the sigil in silence. This alternation of silence and music is repeated several times, until the sigil feels very much alive. This technique involves both transmission under great clarity (the silence) and the channelling of energy and power. As the two phases alternate, the problem of cramp can be avoided. Maybe you will twitch and shudder a bit, but that is quite alright.

Whether the sigil manifests or not is something the deep mind decides on the basis of the true will. If the desire for the sigil is willful, it will manifest when the conditions are ripe, just like a seed in the earth that feels that spring has come, and begins to grow. If the sigil is meant to satisfy a mere egoistic craving, it will not be connected with the force-field of the true will, and will not manifest. Maybe you will get a chance to live the experience in an instructive and refining nightmare, but all in all such sigils are expelled out of the system.

If you are not ready for the sigil's manifestation, your deep mind will see to it that you change, and that your world changes, until the conditions are right. Each sigil may be transmitted several times, then its material body (the paper you wrote it on, or the wood, bone, metal, leather or cakes you used) is destroyed and the entire working forgotten. It is no use to be on the lookout for results. The deep mind will manifest the willful changes, in its own good time. Experience teaches that some sigils manifest very swiftly, others require some time and some will not manifest at all. All of this is outside of your control, so give it a shrug, a smile, stick to your work and allow the world to surprise you. And as Milton Erickson put it 'everyone like a nice surprise.' If the sigil is willful and conditions are right, the desired change will happen so naturally that maybe you will not even notice.

Austin Spare's method of sigil working was something new to the magical world, in that it allowed the magician to create original and unique sigils for any change conceivable. Spare's method of binding letters connects with the art of rune sigils, or 'Binderunen' (German: bound runes). The rune masters of the old days used runes to write words, and as they could read these quite fluently, they had to veil the nature of their desire by combining the runes in an abstract glyph. Let us work out some examples.

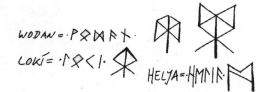

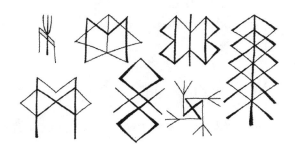

Sigils of this sort can be useful tools if we want to make contact with the gods. If we want to contact a new god-form, or spirit, we may sigilize the name and focus on it. If this is combined with prayer/invocation, dance and a bit of wild chanting, the chances are good that contact is made. Maybe you will not be so conscious of it during the first attempt, but then, the energy which you release will not be lost but lie dormant, and will accumulate to make the desired communication possible. Of course you can also sigilize desires using binderunen, by using the methods described previously.

Another interesting use is talisman work. You might select a few runes for a specific force field, and combine them in a single glyph. This sign may be carved into wood or bone, might be drawn on paper, leather, your skin or the front door (if you feel like this). Meditation and charging the sign with its rune energies will soon make the glyph come to life, it can then be used to attract sympathetic energy or to banish hostile influences, and may be carried around with good effects. Such talismans should be treated like living entities, i.e. they should receive a proper name and be told quite clearly what they are meant to do. A rite of baptism may work well.

Here is another age old system of rune code, which is based on the three 'aettir', which means 'eight' or 'families', into which the futhorc alphabets are usually divided. Most rune alphabets are divided into three groups. One of the old German rune alphabets appears in the following order:

The position of each rune determines its code.

Fehu = 1. aettir, 1. rune. Kenaz = 1. aettir, 6. rune. Pertho = 2. aettir, 6. rune. Ehwaz = 3. aettir, 3. rune. Laguz = 3. aettir, 5. rune, and so on.

(It should be noted that there are local variations to this order, and that in Scandinavia the aettir are shorter, and appear occasionally in reverse order, i.e. Teiwaz = 1 aettir, Hagall = 2 aettir, Fehu = 3 aettir.)

Here are some examples for rune codes, given by RI Page in his *An Introduction to English Runes.*

Isruna and other rune cyphers

The code is based on the Isa rune

ı||| = ᚦ (1/3)   ıı|||| = ᛋ (2/5)   ııı| = ↑ (3/4)

'MIMIR', IN ISRUNA, WOULD LOOK LIKE · ııı|||| ıı|||ıı ııı||| ıı ||ı |||| ·

LAGORUNA. ᚾ = ᚠ (1/1)   ᚾᚾᚾᚾ = ᚱ (1/4)   ᚾᚾᚾᛉ = B (3/2)

'FREYA' = · ᚾᚾᚾᚾᚾᚾ ᚾᚾᚾᚾᚾ ᚾᚾᚾ ᚾᚾᚾᚾ ·

HAHALRUNA = ᛉ = ᚦ (1/3)   ᛉ = | (2/3)   ᛉ = ᛗ (3/4)

'FREKI' = · ↑ ᛉ ᛉ ᛉ ↑ ·

MORE EXTRAVAGANT CODES ARE THE FOLLOWING

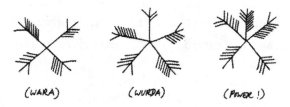

= ⊰ (2/4)   ᚦ (1/8)   ᚦ (1/3)   ᚲ (2/6)   ᚴ = H   ᛉ = 8

ᛒ = ᚱ   ᛒ = ᛐ   = ᚲ   = < (ALL EXAMPLES CA. 9th CENTURY A.D.)

In another system we encounter wheels, coded in a tree pattern.

(WARA)   (WURDA)   (POWER!)

The use of such codes lies not in keeping secrets from others - after all the cipher is rather primitive - but to code the message so that one is not constantly reminded of its original meaning.

If you are not fluent in rune writing yet, such codes will not be needed. You will get good enough results from writing a letter to your gods or Fylgjar, using futhorc letters. The resulting message will look like a homogeneous collection of strange signs, and can be transmitted easily enough. Once you become fluent in reading runes you may apply any code that strikes your fancy, or develop your own.

So far, the technique works for all sorts of sigils. Here is a variation for rune magick. If you wish to give a name (personality) to some weapon or tool, to create an artificial elemental, a talisman, or to work some similar spell, proceed as follows:

Make a sigil out of the name of the object. The rune letters of the name should suggest the character. The sigil is engraved into the object, then coloured with red earth, ashes, blood or other fluids. Speak the name aloud in repetition. Lay the object on the ground, between or under your feet. Now invoke the runes of the name by use of posture and vibration. As the current runs through you the object is charged. Objects (weapons, jewellery, talismans, masks, figures etc) given such a 'taufe' (baptism) should be treated as living entities. Unlike normal sigils (which are frequently buried, sunk, burned or hidden after transmission) the 'object consecrated' stays in use, it is not forgotten.

Last, there is an advanced variety of sigil working that takes place in Seidr, i.e. in states of direct obsession when the mage is 'seething' with the energy surging through body. In normal sigil magick we try to calm and void the conscious mind to get the sigil to the deep without distortion. In Seidr, the conscious mind has been occupied; the deep has risen and taken control. The Seidmagician is obsessed by the current, by the gods, the Fylgjar or the beasts, by rapture, joy and energy. Seidmagick accepts that self is much more than we are aware of. The deep ones rise and work the rite; they may take up the sigil and work with it directly.

In such episodes there is no need to attempt 'tranquil transmission'; there is no choice but to cooperate with the power or to suffer a blackout. They, your 'guests', are also you, and will make their own laws and conditions. In their own wild way they may work and earth the sigil directly. Note that in Seidr the 'conscious I' (identity/ego) is merely a witness. You are free to call, to watch, to accept. If you interfere or resist you may simply be overwhelmed, black out, or suffer loss of memory. If you cooperate, however, and enjoy the fun there will be some surprises in store for you.

24 Seiðr and Seething

The people of the old north were well versed in several dark arts of sorcery. Most dreaded was the art of seiðr. We are fortunate to have a few, if fragmentary accounts of seiðr. The term is a little enigmatic. Seiðr can be loosely translated as sorcery, but this description suffers from being so uninformative. There is lots of sorcery in the Viking age, including rune-spells, necromancy, trance journeys in the imagination and people going mad in berserk-consciousness, but such activities were not classed as seiðr. When Karl Simrock made his classic German translation of the *Eddas,* he chose to translate the term seiðr with Sudkunst, German for the 'Art of Seething'. Now seething is worth considering in depth. In German, the 'Sud' is the broth, and you would use a Sud, a broth, in order to make beer. Here we have the first link to

magick: the production of a consciousness changing beverage. Beer may be only a drink for you, but for the people of elder times, beer was sacred. Just consider that the word ale is connected with the strongest 'word of power' of the rune inscriptions: alu. A Sud or broth is also the stuff you would need to cook up other things. Here a lot of potions come to mind. The sagas have quite a few references to poisons and elixirs, and even include potions that induce sleep or forgetfulness.

Another interesting reference to the term seething comes from sacrificial custom. The Vikings never sacrificed raw or grilled meat to their gods. The proper preparation consisted of seething the meat gently in a cauldron hanging from the roof of the temple. This was not simply custom, it was a sacred act. We find this idea in the Gothic word *sauths*: an offering or sacrifice. It means literally 'what has been seethed'. Old Norse sauðr is the ram, the most popular meat for sacrifices. In Old Icelandic, the term sauðr means a sheep, literally 'something seethed for sacrifice'. The suðnautar were the 'seething companions', i.e. the worshippers who partook of the sacrifice. In other words, there was a sacred quality to seething.

However, things were more complicated than this. In Nordic lore, there is just one attempt to define the art of seiðr. You can find it in the *Ynglingasaga*, 6, in a lengthy text describing the sorceries and skills of Odin, who appears as a semi-divine but human magician. I have quoted the passage in full in *Seidways*, where you can find a thorough study of seiðr in the old north. Here it should suffice to quote the short passage.

> 'Odin understood the art that has most power and used it himself, which is called seiðr. And so he knew the fates of people and events yet to happen, could give death, ill-chance and disease to people; also he could steal wit and power from some people and give them to others. And this sorcery, when it is practices, had such an 'argr' nature that the men thought it not without shame to deal with it, and so the art was taught to the goddesses.'

The term 'argr' is of interest, it can be loosely translated as something that transgresses social gender norms. When Odin transformed into a wise woman and deluded the people of Samsö, Loki accuses him of having an 'argr' nature (*Ägirs*/*Lokas.* 24). Odin, in turn, accuses Loki of having been under the earth for eight winters as a milk-giving cow and mother, another act of 'argr' nature. Sex changing is one of the things that seemed 'argr' to the Vikings, in spite of the fact that several of their major gods enjoyed such activities. According to the Duden, the term 'argr' had a composite meaning . It could mean 'fearful, cowardly', 'horny, lustful' and '(ethically) wrong', its root being the Indo-European term '*ergh-' meaning 'to move heavily, to tremble, to quiver, to be excited'. Related is the old Greek orcheisthai: quivering, leaping, jumping, dancing. It's the source of our word orchestra. This is a fascinating thought that should be considered deeply. Just what is the nature of Odin's seiðr? We know what he did, but just how did he do it? What is the trance practice behind seiðr?

Let us consider the Tungusian word 'shaman'. It comes from various words designating the ascetic, the healer and the priest, but deep down at the root we encounter the Sanskrit 'shram', which in a religious context means austerity or bodily toil carried to the point of exhaustion. Shamanic activity, as the term is loosely used in ethnology, is based on a few typical practices which differ from the stricter profession of the ceremonial priest. A shaman is one who works with one or more helping spirits, be they beasts, plants, fungi, crystals, gods, angels, ancestors, archetypes or whatever; who has fits of inspired possession, enjoys ecstatic visions, travels into the otherworlds by ritual and astral projection (in the imagination) and has a range of magical techniques that involve ritual, dancing, song, music and visual symbolism. The same goes for the people who practice seiðr sorcery.

Sadly, the sagas give few details. We frequently encounter brief references to seiðr, but as the Vikings were given to compose long sagas using as few words as possible, such references are often enigmatic. One of the best documented cases of what might be seiðr is given in the *Saga of Erik the Red* (see *Seidways*). Here we have a wise woman who appears on a farm in Greenland, where she performs a rite of prophecy. To simplify things, the seeress was seated on a seiðrhjallr, a seiðr-chair. Pagan sorcery songs (vardlokkur) were chanted, then the spirits appeared to her and she began to prophecy. This tale is well known and cited as an example of seiðr, in spite of the fact that the seeress is called a spakona, a foreseeing woman. The term seiðkona, seiðr-woman, appears only once in the account. The rite itself is an oracular trance, well and good for prophecy, but a far cry from the sinister seiðr-sorceries ascribed to Odin in the *Ynglingasaga*. This raises the question whether the most popular account of seiðr in Nordic literature is really an account of seiðr at all. Maybe the seeress was a seiðkona, but functioned as a spakona for the occasion.

Other tales reveal a more dangerous form of seiðr, see the examples given in *Seidways*. These rites occasionally involved a seiðhjallr, possibly within a black tent, but they are not public nor are they concerned with prophecy or visions. In fact many of the seiðr sorceries were highly secret events. To the Vikings, seiðr was not a popular art. Seiðrfolk had a reputation of performing destructive magic for payment. They were dreaded for their skill in stealing wits, bringing bad luck and making accidents happen.

Here is another tale. In *Frithjof's Saga*, the three evildoers Helgi, Halfdan and King Hring engage two seiðwomen to destroy the protagonist, Frithjof. The latter is at the moment on the high sea . As the seiðr begins, a terrible storm erupts around him, churning the waves and tossing the ship about. Frithjof and his companions fight the waves and do their best to reach land, but the cold, foaming sea rages against them. Frithjof gazes into the waves and sees that a huge whale is circling the ship. There are two witches (also called werewolves) sitting on the back of the whale, and whenever the ship comes close to the shore, the whale's might forces it back into the open sea. In his despair, Frithjof steers the ship straight at the whale. The sorcerous monster disappears and the ship's prow crushes the two witches. This ends the episode from Frithjof's point of view.

A little later, we read that at the same time the two seiðladies fell from their seiðrhjallr. So the spell had two sides. Physically, the seiðladies were ashore and trancing on a seiðrchair. Astrally, in the realm of inspired vision and imagination, they were out on the open ocean, directing the storm and fighting Frithjof by means of the whale, who seems to be their ally, vehicle and power beast. As the spell breaks, the sorceresses catch the full recoil of their efforts. This story is pretty shamanic, and also sinister enough to fit the seiðr-account of the *Ynglingasaga*. However, seiðr was more than just astral projection with wicked intent. The *Ynglingasaga* mentions astral projection (i.e. journeys in the inspired imagination) a little before it deals with seiðr. The passage is quoted in the chapter 'Vision of the Runes', further on. It is good evidence that such journeys, and even beast transformations, were part of Odin's sorceries. However, such skills are explicitly not described as seiðr. Nor is the seiðrhjallr a must. There are several tales that deal with seiðr and most do not mention a special chair.

Now for the speculative side.

As you recall, Simrock connected the ideas of seiðr and seething, and seething is a brilliant metaphor for a shamanic practice well worth developing.

The seething cauldron is more than a metal tub for cooking. In another sense, it is your body, and 'by the same mouth' it is the universe you live in, the world that surrounds you and cooks you to ripeness. 'Seething' is a marvellous expression for what happens when the mage lets go and becomes inspired/excited by the appearance of a spirit, by obsession, ecstasy or the rush of an energy current. The body begins to shake and tremble like water in a cauldron.

Now the interesting thing is that the body seethes, that is, it trembles at a light and easy frequency. Seething is not the same as boiling (which is too strong) or simmering (which is too weak). When you allow your body to seethe, you are striking a perfect balance between activity and passivity. There are wide differences between awareness during light, medium and strong seething, you find them explored at length in *Seidways*.

Each seething trance is very much unique. The fire of the seething comes from excitement, and excitement leads to the tremors that make body shake and shudder. On the other hand, shaking can produce excitement. It's a feedback mechanism. Excitement of mind can produce shaking of body, shaking of body can produce excitement of mind.

The result is a trance state that looks wild and crazy to the outside observer. Things are very different when you experience it yourself. What looks active and energetic can contain a calm and smooth state of mind. It is easy to forget your body when it is shaking at a regular rhythm, and as you will know, a dissociation of body consciousness can be the very thing that makes your mind clear and your visions lucid.

Shaking is cultivated by many shamans the world over. In *Seidways*, I have devoted several chapters to a comparison of cultures that use shaking for trance activity. My examples range form the healing dances of the San people ('bushmen') of the Kalahari to Haitian Voodoo, Japanese mediums, Nepalese and Siberian shamans, the Egyptian Zar cult and the mad seers of medieval Wales. I also included a few examples from European history, such as the Shaking Quakers and the Mesmerian movement with its 'healing crisis'. These examples, I hope, are sufficient to demonstrate that shaking is a natural and efficient form of trance magick that has been used by numerous cultures all over the world. It is an art, and like all arts it may need a bit of training and refinement. Now the curious thing about seething is that it is not learned by effort but by release. You have to relax into your excitement to get a good shake going. The tremors are best when you enjoy them. If you attempt to force shaking, you may get a very inferior sort of 'trembling-by-effort' that doesn't take you very far. If you ride the tide of excitement and let go into the joy and passion of the art, you can enjoy the tremors for hours.

This can take a bit of deconditioning. As a child, I used to get such 'fits' of trembling when I became excited, especially when I was drawing pictures. My parents were worried about my harmless little habit and dragged me to a few doctors, who could not find anything wrong. The shaking was certainly not epilepsy. It could be reduced by being less excited, and increased by being more excited. Of course nobody was really happy about it, and so I gradually (and unconsciously) learned to repress the impulse. It was only when I was well into magick that I rediscovered the shaking. This took several years. At first, the shaking happened sporadically when I was getting carried away, when praying wildly, for example, or when transforming into a beast. But I still had a latent bad feeling about it and a vague fear I might be going insane. Then I encountered the phenomena in literature and saw Nepalese shamans shaking quite happily in Michael Oppitz's documentary *Shamans of the Blind Country*. It certainly released me from a lot of uncertainty. Shaking was not something negative, nor was it a side effect of trance practice but one of the methods that make ecstatic shamanism possible. The next surprise came when I learned that I could start and end the 'fits' as I wanted. Before, I had thought that 'shaking happens', soon I learned that it can be controlled. The term control has to be used cautiously in this context. If you think that you can control shaking with your everyday mind you are fooling yourself. A good seething trance can empty that everyday mind and open your self to a lot of unusual experiences.

One of the first is sexual. Good seething generally moves from the hips. This is not always the case, as body can tremble in numerous ways, but in general, relaxed and loose hips are just the thing to make it easier. When teaching the technique to others, the usual experience is that the more tight, cramped and armoured a person, the more difficult it is. Good seething requires a 'living pelvis', an ability to breathe freely and a sense of joy and lust. People who repress their sexuality, who are cramped by fears and shame or who prefer to look dignified, find shaking a difficult thing. Some begin to tremble and then all their repressed frustrations come up. In this sense, learning to shake is more than a trance technique, it also includes a measure of therapy. The best training you can give yourself to make shaking easy and natural is to enjoy a lot of dancing (emphasising hip movements), deep belly breathing and a good love-life. Seething is very close to Wilhelm Reich's 'orgasm reflex', a natural pulsation that happens as you let go of control. In shaking, first I come apart, then I come together and finally I come home to myself.

Now sexuality and lustful feelings connect beautifully with the term *ergh-. Such trances are both lustful and dangerous, or at least they seem dangerous to control-freaks and people with serious attitudes and a stiff upper lip. They also may not have been popular among the Vikings in general. Norse literature is often very prudish and tends to avoid such topics as sex. Perhaps you need an *argr* nature to enjoy a relaxed pelvis that can pulsate freely. Just ask yourself: what was so shamefully *argr* about seething that a practice invented by Odin was used primarily by goddesses? What were the Viking men afraid of? How come 'real men' tend to have a cramped pelvis? Why do women tend to learn shaking faster than men do? We have references to quite a few male practitioners in the sagas (they are called seiðmaðr and seiðberandi) but the colourful majority are female (a seiðrlady is called a seiðkona).

When you look at magick worldwide you'll find more shakers than you ever expected. East Asia has a lot of shaking in mediumism, in obsession trances and similar events. You find shaking in the more obscure traditions of Taoist beast-form Wu Shu (the trembling starts just before the martial artist transforms into a beast) and in Indian folk worship. The eldest reference I have found to shaking trances comes from earliest Indo-European literature: the *Rig Veda* (c.1200-900BCE) describes people who are called vipras. The Sanskrit vip-, source of our word vibration, means to tremble, shake, quiver, shiver or to be stirred. A vipra is a sage, seer, prophet, poet or simply inspired. The vipras were an early class of ecstatics, and though they seem to have existed separately from the common Vedic priesthood, they were certainly respected and honoured. Humans used shaking to have visions, to heal, to exorcise and weave spells in Vedic times, but the same goes for several gods. Thunder-god Indra, the storm-gods Maruts, the horse-deities Ashvins and of course Agni, the restless god of fire, are praised and celebrated as vipras.

Shamanic trembling has been called 'pseudo epilepsy' by academics, who observed that the phenomena, though not really controlled in its full form (obsession) can be induced and ended at will. Unlike the classical epileptic fit, shaking can go on for long periods and is often enjoyable. The shaker is not in danger of suffocation, nor is there a loss of bladder control. In fact it turns out that in numerous cultures, wild shaking is the very thing that makes a trance impressive. Healers who don't shake do not amount to much, this goes for mediums in Japan as for sorcerers in central Africa. There are many cultures where shaking is required as a sign of inspiration, much like diplomas in a doctor's waiting room. We may safely consider it, like much of the shaman's trade, as a mixture of genuine trance activity and excellent showmanship. And while it captivates the audience, it also allows the shaker to leave ordinary reality and to function in unusual realms of perception. One avoids the common problem of dropping out of the magical reality into limited everyday thinking, as happens so easily during pauses, gaps and interruptions of ritual.

And shaking is certainly a must in most forms of obsession. Now obsession is a term that has been misunderstood by a lot of experts. It certainly seems pathological if you grow up in a materialistic culture, or in one that violently denies the existence of spirits. In cultures where humans and spirits interact all of the time, obsession simply means that your ego takes a step seidways and the obsessive spirit starts to run the show. If this spirit is very different from your everyday personality, it may well appear violent, fierce or terrifying to the audience. If it is similar to your personality, the transformation can be so smooth and natural that few will notice the shift.

In Voodoo, for example, the novice has little experience of what it is like to be obsessed by her/his personal deity. When they deity enters the novice's body, that body tends to be tossed about, and shaking and trembling often seem rough and violent. In Voodoo obsession, the presence of a god within your body is generally supposed to mean that your conscious identity blacks out. This is what people report, and for many it seems to be the case. When the god leaves body, the devotee may simply collapse. S/he often has little if any memory of what it was like to be a god. With growing experience, however, the devotee and the god get used to each other. They adapt and transform, and the rite of obsession becomes a union that works by voluntary co-operation. When you become much like your personal deity, the shift to

divine consciousness is not such a shock any more and amnesia is not necessarily the case. Voodoo adepts can do the transition very smoothly and elegantly, and when the god begins to play its part, they do not have to suffer a blackout.

This is also the case in shamanism and in magical obsession. Where the religiously obsessed serves the community, the mage often wants to learn and transform through the union. Shaking trances are perfect for this. When you learn to give up your personal illusion of 'control' and trust in your personal deity, you may find that you can abide as a witness. You may co-operate with your deity, and your deity co-operates with you. It hardly matters whether you view your guest as a god, a spirit, your inner genius or as an archetypal expression of your deep mind. Don't worry about words and definitions. All magick is communication of self with self, if we remember that we are everything.

And shaking is changeable. Changes of awareness happen frequently, as do changes in shaking speed and power. Sometimes light tremors or swaying are the thing to take you into a gently and focused trance, sometimes it becomes wild and fitful, especially when you transform into some deity or spirit or project energies or thought-forms. All in all, a good shaking trance is something that needs variation. Body is exhausted when you try to keep up the same rhythm, pulsation and awareness all of the time. Changes are natural and should be encouraged. When I want to shake for long periods, I change the speed of the trembling, the location of the pulsation and my awareness ever so often. Shaking can have a lot of uses and applications. Forgive me for not going into details here. If you want to learn how to shake and trance, read *Seidways*, do the exercises and find out what seething can do for you.

Let me end this chapter by emphasising that my identification of seiðr with seething and with shaking trances cannot be proven by reference to Viking literature. While I find it likely that this was the case, there are a good many others who insist that shaking was never practised in the cold north. As I have learned since *Helrunar* and *Seidways* appeared, there are pagans who imitate the episode of the *Erikssaga*. They have a priestess on a high seat, who trances and weaves prophecy (without trembling), and a congregation of people who supply power to the ritual by means of chanting, drumming and a bit of suggestion to brighten up the visions. This is a good and innovative ritual format. It involves a lot of syncretistic elements, but then, we can't help being syncretistic. Little is known about seiðr, and less is reliable, so we have to fill the gaps by incorporating elements from other cultures and trance techniques. This is hardly unusual. Most religions borrowed stuff from other faiths. The better ones were honest enough to admit it.

In this sense I would like to add a few new ideas on the seiðhjallr, the seiðr chair. A high seat was one of the most important status symbols in the Germanic cultures. In the long halls, the warriors sat on benches. The kings, the highest nobles and a few guests of honour were permitted elevated (high) seats in a special section of the hall. Thus, a special seat could be a sign to set a person apart. The *Eddas* echo this custom. We have Odin sitting on his high seat in three different personalities (*Gylf.* 2) and we have references to the chairs of law-giving. Several mountain sanctuaries had a 'king's seat' from where the regents could gaze to the limits of their domain. The same pattern appears in medieval Celtic lore, just think of the dangerous seat in the Grail castle, at King Arthur's round table and on selected mounds. Now the Eddas mention something obscure that may or may not have something to do with the seiðhjallr. *Sigrdrifumal* 17 mentions runes carved into the 'seat of the seeress', without giving details. Then there is the Norn's seat. We do not know much about it. However, there is a fascinating item hidden in the late *Solarliod*. This poem is not always included in modern editions of the *Eddas*, as it is a late addition full of Christian material. The *Solarliod* is an account of the soul's fate after death, including many descriptions of hell and suffering that do not accord with Nordic paganism. The text emphasises a catalogue of sins and their due punishment. However, the poem is a compilation. It includes a few verses (51 - 57) that are definitely not Christian and well worth contemplating. We find the relevant passage within a lengthy account of the horrors of hell.

Nine days I sat on the seat of the Norns,
Then I was lifted on the stallion's back.
Severely shone the sun of the giantess
descending through night and fog.
Within and without I deemed to wander
through all seven underworlds:
up and down I sought the way fearfully
that was painful to travel.
Let it be said what I saw first
when I came to the places of pain:
Scorched birds, who were souls
were flying like flies everywhere.
From the west came the dragons of
madness
and covered the glowing alleys.
They beat their wings as if heaven
should burst, and likewise earth.
I saw the sun-deer coming from south
lead by two holding his halter;
on the field its feet were standing,
he lifted his antlers to heaven.
From the north came riding the sons of
sobriety;
Seven of them I saw.
They filled their horns with glorious
mead
from the well of the good god.
The winds grew silent, the waters
stopped:
 I heard a saddening sound.
With all their might, eager women
were grinding garbage for food.

And so it goes. The text continues with an account of hell and the fate of various sinners. Moral issues, ethical admonitions, the usual threats so familiar from medieval Christianity. But what do you think of the Norn's seat? What of the cosmology surrounding it? This may be a glimpse of an otherworldly initiation ritual. With a bit of practice you can turn it into a meditation and use it to explore the Nordic underworlds in your inspired imagination. Is this a key to the seiðr-chair? Helja be with you and good luck!

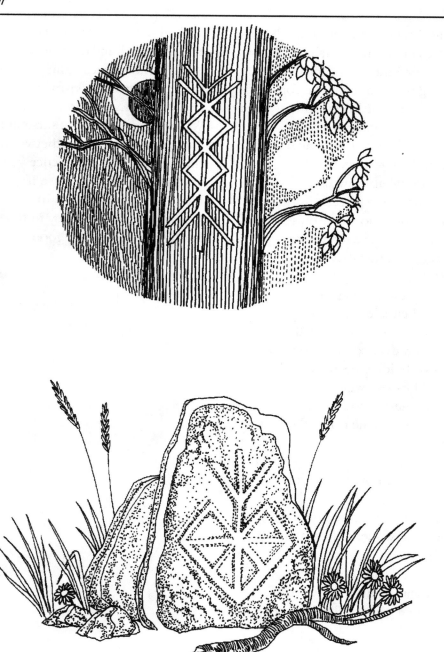

25 The magical use of energy

In this chapter I shall write from the shamanic point of view. I shall speak of spirits, which may upset some readers, but as was outlined earlier, the model that says that 'spirits are actual entities' makes quite as much sense as the model which claims that 'the spirits are actually projections of parts of our deep minds'. If this idea annoys you, well, here is a good opportunity to practice the lofty art of suspending judgement.

Let us try to look at ritual in a new way. When we examine a ritual, we can do so by concentrating on its meaning and contents (i.e. what is evoked? What is the intention? Which symbols are used? What exactly is said? etc.) which is the usual way people consider and evaluate such activities. Another way is to ignore 'who' and 'what' and to concentrate on the 'how' and 'when'. The

'why' is something you might work out for yourself, if you have a couple of decades with nothing better to do. Let us look at functions and syntax. Most rituals, no matter the creed, cult or tradition, have certain common elements and a similar syntax to effect specific changes. Usually they start with dissociation, which means that the mage detaches consciousness from everyday activities, work problems, overdue bills, loud neighbours and the daily newspaper. This is called banishing. We get rid of unwanted influences at this stage, and there are dozens of ways of doing so. Some do it quite simply by screaming 'all negative influences go away now!' Others wield a dagger, sword or a sharp stone, some 'empty their minds' while others draw complicated symbols in the air while vibrating names in Hebrew. This part is ended when the unwanted influences and thoughts are expelled. Then comes a brief pause, during which the end of the banishing is signalled with a bell, clapping hands or some such activity.

Next follows association, which means that we attach our awareness to whatever reality we intend to work with. Robes, clothes, temple equipment, symbols, altar layout, pictures, colours, scents, sounds, chants, gestures, ritual tools etc are all part of the vocabulary of association; they connect us effectively with the state of consciousness with which we want to get in touch. This stage is called invocation. Invocation usually makes use of speech, prayer, gesture, dance, symbolism and creative imagination, to direct our awareness the way we will. We call forth the desired consciousness, and we call it into ourselves. As is customary in most systems of magick and religion, the consciousness which we invoke is perceived in the various shapes of gods, angels, demons, nature spirits, beasts, spirit helpers, archetypes and so on. These beings appear masked in symbolic form. We clothe them in our imagination until the image is real enough to permit interaction and communication. Note that such a spirit is more than imagination. It appears in the form of imagination (i.e. in astral matter, or dream stuff) and reveals its nature in a shape suited to the magician's understanding.

The difference between a real spirit and a spirit which we imagine at an idle moment or while reading horror stories is that the former connects with realms of energy and consciousness and the power of the deep mind, while the latter is more or less constructed by the ego and connects with very little. Its shape is like an empty shell. The real spirit will have a mind of its own and enough power to upset the ego if needed, while the constructed spirit will simply reflect our wishful thinking, and this is a vast difference, no matter that their bodies are equally imaginary.

Now we come to a point which is frequently ignored. To manifest themselves, the spirits require a certain amount of energy. In the old days of sorcery at the cross-roads, the daring mage used to supply energy in several ways. The mage was supposed to be chaste, and to fast and pray for days before the act of evocation. This means that a lot of emotional energy - if not hysterical determination - was released when the actual time of the ritual came. Fear of the spirit added more energy to the event, not to mention the fear of being discovered at work. More so, it was often obligatory to slay a small beast, such as a dove, a black hen or a young goat, so that the spirits might feed on it.

What is the purpose of such slaughter? The soul of the beast had nothing to do with the rite. What was released through the blood-spilling was simple, physical life energy, the same living vitality which we have called ch'i, orgone, prana, bio-energy etc., in other parts of this book. As the sacrifice was slain, all of its energy was released at once. Now Aleister Crowley tells us (*Magick* p 219) that, '...it was the theory of the ancient magicians that any living being is a storehouse of energy varying in quantity according to the size and health of the animal, and in quality according to its mental and moral character.' You find the same sort of thinking among Nepalese shamans who frequently sacrifice sheep to feed the spirits and to keep them happy. Evil spirits, who are supposed to steal souls and bring disease, can be bought off with a sufficient amount of blood. The same idea can be found among Celtic Druids (who believed that to save a man you have to kill another), among Germanic priests (who preferred to kill oxen, but occasionally promised their prisoners of war to the gods of strife and slaughter) and among dozens of other cultures.

It may be interesting to note that in many cases it was permissible to eat a sacrificial animal after the gods and spirits had devoured its essential life-force. It was part of the old tradition that the spirits feed on the energy released. Personally, I do not believe that this is quite true. The spirits assure me that they require the energy not as food but as a medium of manifestation. They do not need the energy to live, as they exist independently of such rituals, but use the power to take on a form sufficiently solid to communicate with us and to effect change on the material plane.

Of course I would not expect you to believe this straight away. As a mature and sensible person you will undoubtably prefer to ask the spirits yourself, which is the scientific way of doing esoteric research. Let us concentrate on the essence of this operation. As I hope you will understand, it is not exactly blood which we need but its energy. We do not require blood sacrifices to get good effects;

the simple, biological life energy we need can be generated in many ways.

Michael Bertiaux gives one of the most wonderfully simple methods of raising such power. Let me quote from lesson 2 of his course in Voudoo energies:

'... then you will offer power to the spirits by rubbing your hands together for a couple of minutes and then holding your hands towards the altar with the palms open and extending the fingers upwards, so that the altar will receive the power as it flows out of the palms of your hands and to the spirit world. This is your gift to the spirits, the power of life or vitality which will be used by them in healing or in some other work.'

(*Voudon Gnostic Workbook.*)

Did you imagine it might be so simple? Well, let's look at other methods. There are many budding shamans, especially in modern countries, who fail to get contact with their power beasts for the simple reason that they try to work this 'mentally' or 'in the astral' and forget to involve the body. If you wish to contact a power beast you will have to supply a dose of power first, to get the communication going. Sitting down and thinking about it will not raise much power in the physical sense, the same goes for reading books and smoking dope. Try it the wild way, as wild spirits love wild people. A good initial invocation of a power beast requires that you call loud, chant, scream, howl and yell, that you play a swift rhythm on a rattle or drum, and that you keep dancing and chanting, if need be for hours, till sweat runs over your face and body shakes and shudders with passion and exhaustion. Such action will release plenty of high quality energy, and it is this energy which will attract the beast and allow it to appear to you (through the imagination). You may then allow it into your body, to live and enjoy in living flesh.

At later stages, when you have come to know your beast for some time, less effort will be needed. Both of you will have learned the mutual identity. There is a strange thing about this release of power. You send out a lot of your physical and emotional energy, which is seized and shaped by the spirit's manifestation. Then, however, comes a return flow, and union with the spirit fills you with power and joy far surpassing what you have initially sent out.

So far we have outlined that physical activity, dancing, chanting, emotional outbursts and wild music can be used to generate power for ritual. Voudoo people may say 'the *loa* (gods) like to see us dancing for them', but it is not the specific dance steps that attract the loa, it is the act of dancing in a wild and abandoned way that calls the gods and makes them want to indwell their human servitors. There are magicians who go to the disco to have fun with the spirits, and others who love to run, leap and climb in the forests.

Another potent source can be emotion. Prolonged prayer with plenty of passion is a good example, especially if you pray out of some crisis situation. If you spend eleven months praying for your Holy Guardian Angel to appear, it may easily burn its way straight through your mind in the hour of recognition. Some spirits create energy by the act of appearance. The ancient ones, and the forgotten ones, are excellent examples. The first contact with these primal yonder-entities confronts the conscious mind with the full impact of chaos and madness. The shape of their appearance is specifically designed to throw the ego into a fit of sheer horror which cannot be adequately described. These beings feed on your sheer and overwhelming horror, which releases the energy required for their manifestation. Of course with growing familiarity, the mage will come to understand their true nature and the fear energy will be replaced by sympathy, love and ecstasy.

This change in attitude, however, will require a little practice in the art of dissolving both reality and identity. No doubt it will make your ego squeak itself to death, but then, this is what the fuss is all about, isn't it? Just as the spirits can be manifested through fear energy (Castaneda gives some lovely examples) they can also manifest through the brighter emotions of joy, laughter, lust and love. The joyous rites of eucharist and thanksgiving, of drinking, feasting and laughing with the gods and spirits have their origin in this force field.

Artistic activity is another wonderful method. In a sense we can claim that we nourish our contact with the spirits if we express the wholeness of ourselves. People who live in close contact with the spirits by being busy manifesting and earthing will not require much effort to generate energy, as there will always be plenty of energy in all they do and delight in.

As you should have guessed by now, the energy released by rune practice or vowel song, especially when done in a group working, is another good power source. This energy field will pulse around the group until it is released in a willed direction. Ask the gods and spirits to make use of it.

One of the strongest sources of bio-energy is love making. So called sexual magick can produce an impressive force-field for the spirits to manifest in; the sexual fluids and the energy jolts of orgasm release much more power than the slaughter of some beast. Sexual energy, coupled with lust, love and joy of union is one of the strongest forces we may experience. Unlike the life-force of a sacrificial beast, it is created, focused and freely offered by ourselves. Many magical traditions claim that every act of love making tends to attract all sorts of vampires, spirits and quasi-entities to the field of energy. To use this force for magick can be a difficult matter, for, as Kenneth Grant notes:

'The mental exaltation generated by a magically controlled orgasm forms a lucid lense-like window past which stream the vivid astral imagery of the subconscious mind. Specific images are evoked and "fixed", they become instantly and vitally alive.' (*The Magical Revival*)

This is a force born out of the will to unite and the will to reproduce that generates children in every union. Its application requires training, which is why many magical orders make such a fuss of secrecy about it.

It need hardly be emphasized that if we offer the energy of our lovemaking, it should come from both partners. To use the energy of another to feed one's own spirits, as is quite normal practice in certain occult groups, is, in my opinion, an exotic variety of vampiristic abuse. If you cannot cooperate with an equal, a loving partner, you would be much better off energizing your magick with masturbation. Maybe it is less fun, but it is certainly more honest.

Seething trances or Seidr, which make the body shudder and shake, are another way of generating a force field. This phenomenon is quite common in shamanism, it attracts the gods and spirits to indwell and obsess the body of the shaman. Did you know that the old Indo-European word for 'spirit', *Gheis*, the source of the modern word 'ghost', used to mean 'to shudder, to be excited, to agitate, to stir up'? These ideas have to do with passion and energy, it is only in the last couple of centuries that the spirits (*Geister*, in German) were associated with the ideas of fear, dread and dead people.

Another possible energy supply can be found in the power currents that run through the earth. The earth ch'i may create places where the flow is so concentrated that the spirits may appear more easily. Such sites were often selected for sanctuaries, temple grounds or sacred groves, and sometimes several different magical traditions used the same places in the passage of the aeons. Their rituals gave sentience and meaning to the earth energies, and if we encounter such places today we may find unusual forces arising. Such places, provided the magician is in harmony with their force and intelligence, may provide an excellent power focus to amplify the contact with the unknown realms. Ancient sites, which may have seen several changes in their information over the aeons, will require the mage to bring them up to date, to attune them to our present aeons. Work in the Maatian way will permit a contact to other times, and other cultures working at the same site, both in the past and future. A key to communication across time is congruence. What do you have in common with the people who lived and loved at a given place and time?

Some spirits, such as the guardian angel, the totem beasts, the fylgia, our favourite deities or the patron demons seem to dwell in no specific place. These spirits can be considered part of us, just as our conscious identity is part of them. The energy we require to get in touch with them will create a communication channel within our system. Once this channel is created, we require fairly little energy to keep it open, provided we live in harmony and frequent contact with the spirit in question. The more the spirits are integrated into your life, and allowed to express and manifest their nature through you, the easier will communication become.

The spirit of Loki suggests that I end this chapter by emphasizing that all spirits are illusions, and that they are almost as illusionary as our everyday personalities. I agree with this - one illusion agreeing with another - and stumble to the fridge for a drop of champagne. Cheers!

26 The vision of the runes

The last section of this book deals with the tools of the working: the rune signs and the interpretations attributed to them. They are the fruits of the tree and the seeds of the work to be. They are your tools, and you will imbue them with meaning, purpose and experience as you evolve with the system. In this sense the last section is dedicated to Skulda, the norn of the future(s), and the magick of what should be, will be, and is manifest in living flesh.

What is the meaning of each rune?

There are plenty of books which try to tell you. Most of them give a garbled summary of the various rune poems, phrases, in simple words so the result-hungry won't get indigestion. Such explanations (A = B) are not worth much. While it may be true that A can be B on occasion, B need not be all there is to A. For one thing, the rune poems occasionally contradict each other. All of them were composed in periods when rune writing was approaching oblivion and the church was down on all pagan traditions. There are also ethnic differences between them. We may say; 'this is what runes meant in Iceland at the time when this poem was composed,' but this hardly suits conditions on the continent several centuries earlier, when runes were more of a sacred mystery, and less of a system of writing things down.

For instance in the Old English poem the Uruz rune refers to the aurox, a beast which had become extinct some centuries earlier, but still featured greatly in mythology and legend. The Old Norse rune poem, a few centuries later ignores the aurox and replaces it with the more common totem of the reindeer. Still later the Old Icelandic rune poem appeared, ignoring both beasts and resurrecting another old theme; the connection of Uruz with Urda's well of purification, in the glyph of 'rainshower' and 'drizzle'. Still more confusing and fascinating is the mixup of the yew tree and the sedge grass in the rune signs, Eihwaz, Algiz, or the way the Ansuz rune appears in three variations in the Old English poem. Clearly, a simple 'A = B' is impossible.

You might begin by forgetting *the* meaning of the runes. Over the centuries, each rune has had several meanings, many of which we probably do not know about today. Much more important than the traditional interpretation is the meaning the runes have for you. If you have done some of the exercises, you may have come to some sort of practical understanding of posture, chant, flow and the like. Now I would ask you to connect the rune practice with the rune wisdom which rests in your deep mind, so that the outer forms are clearly connected to the inner force fields of power, joy, understanding and self-realization. To do so, here are some simple practices which allow your deep mind to tell you what each rune is good for.

1. Passive meditation.

To make you more receptive to the messages of the deep mind, a light trance state is required. This trance level is often called 'alpha' as the brain shows the characteristic 'alpha-waves' when in it. You know this state from experience, whether you are aware of it or not. The alpha level is a comfortable state of half sleep and half wakefulness. There are dozens of ways of going into alpha. Most of them make use of relaxation and repetition. If you have never done this before, I suggest you find a competent meditation teacher or experiment as follows:

a) Go to a quiet place where you will not be disturbed.

b) Jump around for a few minutes, do some mild physical exercises, stretch the sinews, rotate the hips etc. This loosens body up and makes the energy flow, and relaxation easier.

c) Lie down on the ground. A bed is not recommended as you should not drift into sleep but retain a measure of wakefulness. You may use a blanket and a pillow for comfort, and if you like, you could place a thin cloth over your eyes.

d) Move around a little until your posture feels comfortable.

e) Now it may help to ask your deep mind for help in inducing a pleasant and tranquil trance state.

f) Calm down. Allow your body to relax. Awareness may move through body, and will tell you which sections are tense. When you notice such tension, increase it (tense it more!) and then relax. Tense it again and relax it. If you do this a few times you will know how to let go.

g) Allow body awareness in the four elemental realms.

Earth - first comes . . . the realm of earth . . . of living earth . . . solid and firm . . . and as you think . . . of the earth . . . as it supports you . . . you can feel . . . how heavy your body is . . . and how it rests . . . calm and relaxed . . . and how your weight . . . is on the ground . . . and your body . . . is like the earth . . . the flesh is like earth . . . and the bones are like stone . . . and you feel yourself . . . resting in peace . . . one with the earth . . . living and peaceful earth . . . the earth you love . . . and live with . . . and as you feel . . . how comfortable . . . and heavy . . . your body can be . . . you realize . . . how good it is . . . to rest . . . and relax . . . and enjoy . . . and you sense . . . that you are floating . . . into a deep trance . . .

Water And as you you flow . . . and float . . . you remember . . . the fluids . . . in your body . . . and in the world . . . the waters . . . that flow . . . and circulate . . . you might remember . . . the flowing . . . and fluid element . . . the water . . . that flows . . . in rivers . . . and in streams . . . giving moisture . . . and nourishment . . . and there is water . . . in body . . . which circulates . . . and refreshes . . . and as you float . . . deeper into trance . . . you feel your blood . . . as it streams . . . and flows . . . and circulates . . . and you realize . . . that the fluid . . . washes through you . . . that the blood pulse . . . is steady . . . and even . . . and that you feel comfortable . . . in this trance state.

Fire So you arrive . . . in the realm of fire . . . there is fire . . . in the sun . . . and there is fire . . . in the centre . . . of the earth . . . and there is warmth . . . body is warm . . . warm and comfortable . . . as it rests . . . the warmth . . . spreads through you . . . living warmth . . . gentle energy . . . and perhaps . . . you perceive . . . how the warmth . . . the inner glow . . . spreads from the solar plexus . . . from heart . . . and liver . . . radiant . . . a bright and shining . . . glowing sensation . . . or energy . . . and joy . . . keeping you warm . . . and comfortable . . . all body . . . warm and aglow . . . you feel well . . . and the energy . . . keeps the system . . . whole and healthy . . . as you go deeper . . . and deeper . . . into trance . .

.

Air And to . . . the realm of air . . . wind flows . . . as breath flows . . . under a wide sky . . . and as you feel . . . the lungs moving . . . and breath flows . . . out and in . . . out and in . . . the trance gets deeper . . . you feel . . . the gentle motion . . . of the lungs . . . and hear . . . how your breath . . . whispers . . . and flows . . . like the wind . . . free wind . . . clear air . . . an open sky . . . your breath flows . . . in gentle rhythm . . . and with each breath . . . the ch'i flows . . . and body . . . feels so good . . . and with each . . . outflow and inflow . . . the trance gets deeper . . . much deeper . . . and you are . . . comfortable and calm . . . and ready . . . to leave body . . . your body . . . gets along well . . . the system . . . works in unity . . . so your mind . . . is now free . . . to perceive . . . and sense . . . the deep mind . . . the unconscious realm . . . the world . . . of the spirits . . . and you know . . . and remember . . . that trance states . . . are pleasant . . . and that you may come . . . into your trance state . . . anytime you will . . . as trance is easy . . . and natural . . . and your deep mind . . . likes to be . . . in touch with you . . . that trance . . . can be . . . like coming home . . . and that . . . you can learn . . . what you have really . . . always known . . . you are . . . at home . . . within yourself . . . and with the spirits . . . you are whole.*

This sort of text is an example of the metaphors and manners of speech that can be useful to ease the body and induce trance. Try to read this text aloud to get acquainted with it. Each ' . . . ' signifies a pause, so that the words, which you speak, in a calm and slow and gentle voice, are very few, and that you get a chance to calm down. Ideally, you will learn how to speak freely in this system. When you learn this method of trance induction, give yourself plenty of time. Repeat the words in you inner voice as you rest on the ground, and try to see what you say, hear what you say, feel what you say. Going in and out of trance, ought to be practised daily for at least a month before you proceed. You will soon find out how to improve the process, and trance will come easy and naturally to you. You will progress faster if you are wise enough to proceed slowly.

---

* Consider what difference the address 'you' or 'I' makes to this practice

h) How to come out of trance.

Try something like this, allowing the words to come more quickly as you approach the end of the trance:

. . . and now . . . after this meditation . . . I want . . . to return . . . to waking consciousness . . . to wake up . . . to the world . . . and so . . . I give my thanks . . . for this valuable . . . and vitalizing experience . . . and return . . . awareness into body . . . I feel my flesh . . . and the breath flow . . . is getting stronger . . . the breath flow . . . going out and in . . . is increasing . . . and as breath . . . supplies more air . . . I feel . . . that I am waking . . . that the blood . . . flows . . . swifter now . . . and I begin . . . to move body . . . stretch my arms . . . and stretch my legs . . . feel . . . that I am waking . . . deeper breaths. Aaah! Now I arrive . . . and wake up . . . eyes open . . . hello! Awake now!

It is recommended that you move your body as you wake, take deep breaths, stretch arms and legs and open your eyes only when you are awake again. Sit up but stay seated for a moment or two. This is important for two reasons:

For one thing, it is sound practice to give a clear and definite beginning and end to your trances. This may help your mind to know just when each consciousness is wanted. Ringing a bell or clapping hands are excellent signals for this. For the other, it may happen that you relax so deeply that your body goes to sleep. In this case your breath-rate and your circulation will be slow, and it is not good to jump up too quickly. Perhaps you may think that this is an overly complicated way of going into trance. True, there are simpler ways. In some systems of meditation, you are simply given a key word, usually in Sanskrit. Then you sit or lie down and repeat your key word once with each breath. As you do so, you imagine that with each repetition, you are sinking deeper into trance.

Another way is to count breath. You start with 100 and count slowly backwards till you arrive at zero, and a good trance state. Each breath is one number down, as if you were in a lift. These methods are wonderfully simple and work so well that they have been exploited commercial by some organizations. However, they tend to dull the mind. Once you get used to them you may find that they are too easy, and that your attention goes elsewhere. The more complicated method given above is a mixture of four-element cosmology plus hypnotic speech patterns. It is very flexible, can be adapted to any system and belief, and induces (with a measure of practice) much deeper trance states than the more mechanical methods. For an excellent introduction to speech patterning see the works of Milton Erickson, Richard Bandler and John Grinder.

Your should spend some time making your body relaxed, warm, comfortable, with unrestricted breathing in order to move your attention elsewhere. When the body is comfortable, it will rest easily and free us to deal with the mind. If we ignore our bodies by concentrating on mind alone (which happens in the simple methods) it can easily happen that the body may intrude and trouble us. Others try to get past this obstacle by forcing the body to stay completely motionless. Some spend several months in the frustrating act of trying to be as motionless as a stone. Of course the body would fight it, and produce cramps, twitches, itches, and whatnot, all of which can be unpleasant. What is really needed is a comfortable trance state in which the body rests easily and does not disturb our magick. In a good trance, this happens naturally. Your deep mind can do this for you, and easily. It does so every night when you fall asleep. Now we don't have to be as stiff and tranquil as a corpse for this purpose. When we dream and sleep, the body is also in motion from time to time, and requires these motions to stay comfortable. People who do not move in their sleep, such as comatose alcoholics, tend to suffer numbness and paralysis of the limbs they slept on.

Sometimes muscles will tense or twitch a little, and this is quite right. Thus, if your body needs some movement while you are in trance, it's all right and much better to allow this than to spend energy and effort trying to prevent it. It's better to scratch and be done with it, than to waste minutes trying to ignore or fight an itch. These words are written - with a friendly laugh - for all the devotees of obscure yoga systems who have been taught that the 'real' trances only take place when the yogi is seated in some bizarre posture without any motion, stiff like a corpse for hours. Now this sort of thing may be an impressive performance in itself, or maybe it can happen as a side effect when mind is busy elsewhere - It is not obligatory. When body is comfortable and at rest - and this is easier in a natural posture on the ground than seated in some cramped asana - it won't bother us. The advanced trance-magician should be able to go into a deep and pleasant trance in any comfortable posture, as well as dancing, walking or seething.

2. Rune meditation

This is quite simple. When you are deep and comfortable in your trance, imagine one of the runes. You might imagine it glowing in lines of light. If you find this difficult, try to augment the vision with the sense of touch - how does that sign feel? Or sound - can you hear the rune name? Some find it easier to imagine the rune as a solid object (carved out of wood, for example), while others imagine that they sing its name to get the vision going. When you imagine sight, sound and feeling at once, you will get a strong representation. As you focus on the rune, observe any ideas that arise. For those who find it difficult, here are a few hints on how to use hypnotic suggestion to induce interesting visions:

'And as I float . . . in this trance . . . I perceive . . . clear and vivid . . . the shape of the rune . . . and I see . . . its form . . . in lines of light . . . and as I see . . . the image of —— . . . I can hear myself . . . vibrating its name . . . the call rings out . . . and I can feel . . . that the vision . . . is strong . . . and the power . . . flows through the sign . . . and makes contact . . . so that the deep mind . . . knows what I ask . . . and reveals . . . to me . . . the nature . . . of the rune . . . and shows . . . what I know . . . deep within . . . visions arise . . . dreams arise . . . and as I focus . . . on the rune____ . . . its meaning unfolds . . . so I may see . . . and hear . . . and feel . . . that I may recognize . . . and remember . . . that

there are messages . . . in each rune . . . and important insights . . . which I ask . . . the deep mind . . . to reveal now...'

Let the words fade into silence, open your mind and dream. Others use a curtain. They go into trance several times to establish (imagine) a curtain. They see it, feel it, hear the cloth and make the vision real. Once the curtain is well established and easy to imagine, they draw the rune shape on it, vibrate the name and feel the energy. When the rune is clear, they pull open the curtain and observe what is shown behind it. When the vision is over, they close it again. Erase the rune, give thanks and return to the waking world. Perhaps you don't like the idea of a curtain. In this case try it with a door. Others spend a week to imagine a mirror or pool. When the imagination is real, they project the rune into its depths and watch what comes out.

Maybe the visions were directly inspired by the rune, so you may congratulate yourself. Maybe they contained interruptions by Helja knows what ideas and memories. This method is passive, and you are open to receive all sorts of stuff. If the things that come up seem unrelated to the rune, concentrate on the rune shape, sound, and energy. If you do this well, the power of the rune will banish unwanted ideas. Please note that it is not for your conscious mind to decide what is adequate and what ought to be banished. The rune power will decide that, and will produce a field that throws out all alien elements. Some of the visions may be shocking. If Teiwaz gives you visions of crisis and bloodletting, for instance, it may not be pleasant, but it will certainly be appropriate. You are in trance *to learn something new from your deep mind,* and what your ego says to it is of no importance whatsoever. If you doubt the validity of your vision, concentrate on the rune. When you have worked with the runes in this state for a while you may learn how to see rune messages in waking consciousness also. This is a matter of practice. Don't count on instant results: the inner senses have to be developed. You can use this method if you want to trance with a partner.

Lie down, relax, and slow down until you into a good trance. Maybe your partner could talk you into trance, or tell you long stories of ancient forests and primal rune alignments which reveal themselves everywhere. When you are comfortable and deep in trance, you partner asks your deep mind which runes it wants to reveal. You wait until you receive an answer. Then tell your partner which rune you have selected - making sure you both know which one you're talking about. If necessary describe its shape and name. Next your partner assumes the posture and chants, vibrates or whispers the rune name a couple of times. Tune in to the sound and sensation. What ideas are raised? Now your partner earths the energy, and sits down to wait. Experience confirms that it is uncomfortable to continue with a given rune stance for as long as the other person needs to learn. Simply continue to learn from that rune until you feel satisfied. When you are ready signal it to your partner, who may then ask your deep mind to select another rune. This method has the advantage that it is the deep mind, not the conscious mind that selects the rune and provides the vision. We get very little conflict this way, indeed it may happen that your deep mind is so eager to cooperate, that your problem is choosing one of many to explore first.

3. Astral projection

Now we come to the real goodies. The last method was largely passive. True, you actively induced a trance state and true, you actively invoked a rune in sight, sound and feeling, but everything that came out of it was a matter of receiving. An active alternative is the time honoured method of astral projection. Start with an open mind. Maybe you have read about astral projection before. Most of what you have read will certainly be dubious rubbish describing in fine esoteric prose things that the authors have no direct experience of. If you expect astral projection to be like that, based only on gossip and hearsay, you may be in for some disappointments. This is what happened to me. Some of those authors say that in astral projection the 'soul' is 'completely outside of the body', possibly connected with it by a 'silver cord'. In my youthful enthusiasm, I tried more than 250 times to get 'completely out of my body', in various trances, which simply did not work. Nowadays I know that the 'out of the body experience' is a metaphor.

We do not need to be 'outside' of the body. It is quite sufficient to be unaware of the body, or to forget it in the practice, as our attention moves to other realms. The 'astral plane' is a term for the land of dreams and imagination. This is not really a land, it is not even a place, but a state of awareness. This state of awareness, like everything else, is a function of the mind. We don't have to go 'out of the body' to contact it as it is not a physical place to go to. As we grow more aware of the astral world, we will equally tend to forget or ignore our bodies. Maybe our awareness will function in both realms, or maybe you will notice that your body moves or requires adaptation of posture from time to time.

Traditional occultists would demand an 'either body or mind' division of sentience. This stupid idea caused the 250-odd failures, as I was so intent on being fully 'outside' that my struggle served to increase body consciousness which in turn disturbed astral, i.e. imagination awareness. Had I ignored the demand for a full split, the journey would have taken place much more easily, and before long I would have been so interested in the astral world that body would have been forgotten anyway. This is what happens when we try to learn something and expect our experience to accord with dusty old dogma. Other authorities state that during astral projection, the body gets stiff and cold, like a plank of wood, and that this is the proof that we are 'really outside'. If this happens I would consider it a side effect. Any introverted trance tends to product such effects, if you spend an hour at it.

However there are people who are very active during astral projection. Many shamans, especially those of Nepal, 'travel to the underworld' in the quest for a spirit, a lost soul of a client, or for self-discovery. Unlike the popular image, these sorcerers fly through the astral while their bodies remain seated. Many keep up a fast drum-beat while they are travelling. And some manage to sing and account of the journey simultaneously. When things happen, their body may sway, or shudder, or jerk about, then they may collapse and lie motionless, and suddenly leap up again to continue with the working. This, if anything, if firm proof that astral projection does not necessarily require a full dissociation of body and mind, and can be worked in numerous states between.

The important issue in astral projection is that your attention moves largely into the dream-land. If you retain some of your body awareness this is alright, and sometimes it can be useful, if you wish to drum or speak during the event. The 'silver cord' so popular in Theosophical literature is another metaphor. Some people like to imagine that they are in connection with their physical body, and so they imagine a silver safety line. Some say that the astral body, i.e. your body of imagination, has to be like the physical body. This is also nonsense. The astral is a representation of the deep mind in terms of imagination. The worlds you encounter are imaginary, and the body you inhabit in the journey is equally imaginary. In some worlds (or 'parts of your deep mind'), a human form can be a serious limitation. In the *Ynglingasaga* we are told:

'Odin could change his shape;
His body would rest as in sleep or death
But he became bird or beast, fish or worm,
To travel instantly to far countries,

In his own or other people's interest.'

In some of the darker realms of the astral, it may be useful to change into beast spirits or into some formless state of non-being. A common Maatian metaphor is to change into a 'black flame of voidness', which works wonders should you consider yourself not as a thing, but an absence. In other realms of chaos, the mode of integration is to become the entity which you encounter.

Another misconception says that astral projection is difficult. While it may be true that certain parts of the astral world (or the deep mind) are difficult to reach, this certainly does not go for all of them. Let me give a very un-occult example. In modern psychotherapy, there is a school of astral projection which is called *Katathymes Bilderleben* and was developed by H. Leuner as a form of active imagination or daydreaming. First, the client is allowed to sit or lie comfortably. The therapist may give some help so that the client relaxes well. When this is achieved - and it does not have to be a deep trance - the therapist asks the client to imagine a meadow. What sort of a meadow? When you think of a meadow it won't be the same meadow I am thinking of. It may be a large or a small meadow, one with flowers or tall grasses perhaps. There may or may not be animals in it, it may be healthy or poor growth, it may be on the slopes of a mountain or just a tiny lawn in the front garden. All of this is left to the client.

Now the client is asked to describe the meadow, to say what is seen, felt, or heard, and in the process of description the meadow usually gets more solid and real. The same thing happens when a shaman describes the 'under or overworld' in the process of travelling. Now the therapist asks the client to move around on the meadow, to discover more of it, and soon enough the client is busy walking through the imagination as if it were the material world. As Katathymes Bilderleben is a therapeutic process, we won't be surprised to find that many clients encountered trouble. Some find their meadow polluted, or fenced in, or diseased. And when they encounter such troubles, it's part of the therapy to find solutions to them, to open the fence for example. The therapist, by the way, should not offer directions. The client has to find solutions, and as health is restored within, the same will happen in the outer world. Now this methods offers a series of journeys into several environments. The meadow is just the initial experience. Other therapeutic journeys involve: 'follow a stream to the sea', 'climb a high mountain', 'come down from your high mountain', find a house and go exploring in it', 'go to the edge of a forest'. When the patient explores these psycho-active environments, s/he actively experiences parts of the mind which are usually unconscious. When the stream, for example, is blocked, the client gets a chance to clear up the obstruction, which gives a powerful message to the deep mind. Mountain-climbing is wonderful to find out about ambition and self-estimation. In the house, forgotten treasures may be found, and at the edge of the forest, dwellers of the twilight may appear.

More advanced journeys involve encounters with wild beasts, archetypal figures, caves and swamp-holes. Please bear in mind that the above is therapy, not analysis. The therapist is there to produce a state of consciousness in which the client may directly encounter and communicate with the deep mind, using the medium of active imagination. The less the therapist interferes the better. It is a curious fact that people who practise Katathymes Bilderleben over a time may run into guiding, guarding or helping persons or beings in their journeys. Such figures are often speakers or messengers for various parts of the deep mind. The same thing happens in shamanism, when the shamans fly to the otherworld to meet their gods and spirits in that environment.

What do we learn from KB? That it is possible, and sometimes more efficient to function in the astral and the physical at once; to journey in the imagination and to speak of it simultaneously. That astral projection can be easier and more natural than many 'occult authorities' would have it. That the astral environment accords with consciousness. In astral projection, we are communicating with our deep minds, and effect changes through this interaction. Here is a basic structure for astral projection.

A) Go into trance. Use some method that feels comfortable to you. As you lie down and relax deeply the awareness of the outside world is dissociated (i.e. you ignore and forget it) while you associate (connect yourself) with body awareness. Release any tension, regulate your posture, breathe slowly and so on, until a pleasant and deep trance is reached.

B) When the trance is deep enough, body is free to care for itself and your awareness is free to go elsewhere. This means that you dissociated body awareness and associate with astral awareness, i.e. imagination. Some do this by imagining that they are outside of their body and see it (however diffuse) on the ground.

C) Now you imagine a door, gate, curtain, tunnel, hole, or opening, which will be your passage into the astral world. When your image of it is clear and vivid, you imagine that you pass through, close the opening or gate from the other side. This dissociates most of your body awareness and associates you with the astral.

D) Now you follow the passage, which may change as you move along, until you arrive at another gate or doorway, preferably of the astral world you wish to visit. The 'passage experience' is important, as it gives you opportunity to adapt more fully to the astral awareness of realms which are usually unconscious to you. If need be, the passage gives you excellent opportunities to change your body.

E) You open the new door and pass through into a magical world. As you turn around and close the door behind you, the passage-reality is dissociated. As you tune into the new world, you associate with it. Now, you may go on exploring.

F) Going back to body consciousness is usually done by returning along the same route. With experience, you may find or develop short-cuts, or change into some beast which flies very fast. Be careful that you close all doors behind you.

Now I hope that you are eager to try this out here and now. Of course I cannot tell you exactly what and how you should do it, as you are a person with unique talents and hangups. I don't know which symbols get you going, or how you can best make the transition from body awareness to imagination. You will have to experiment to find out.

However, if it helps, I may describe how I usually travel to the rune worlds. Don't expect your experience to be quite like mine. Usually (not always) I begin by drawing a magick circle on the ground (using a length of rope), which helps to dissociate a great deal of everyday awareness and the world outside. Inside of the circle I do a little ritual, involving prayer, gesture and free chanting in chaos language. Then I vibrate the rune I desire to explore in the journey and assume its posture. Next I lie down on the ground, relax my body and go into a a a trance, much as it was described in the first exercise of this chapter.

I don't use the same method at all times, as this would make the practice dull, but introduce variations. When my body is quite comfortable, heavy, warm, relaxed and the breath flows easy and slow, I imagine that I am outside of it. Sometimes I imagine that I drift out of it like a cloud, or that I roll out of it sideways, or that I simply get up and stand in the air. The body I see on the ground is an imagined vision of myself in the circle. At this stage it is not a clear vision, as the imagination isn't quite solid enough yet, nor needs it to be. Sometimes I find my awareness moving from body (ground) to body (imagination) and vice versa very fast. It's important to stay tranquil at this stage, to go gently and slow. Don't expect that you will be entirely 'outside', or that body awareness is fully dissociated. Instead, focus on the doorway. I work with several doors, which lead to various magical realities, such as temple rooms, cult caves of the ancient ones, halls that open into the night-sky, etc. These magical spaces were discovered and developed through years of magical practice. If imagined repeatedly, the astral environment can become surprisingly stable. For a rune journey, I go to a gate with a black curtain. Then I draw a symbol on the curtain in lines of light, and say a word. When the symbol is clear and well-defined, I imagine that I open the curtain. Welcome to Niflhel (fog-hell)!

Behind the door, the mists are rolling. I walk through, then turn around, close the curtain and draw the symbol. Now I turn *slowly* and begin to take in the scenery. The ground feels moist, as is the cold air around. Veils of fog are writhing over a desolate and half-hidden landscape full of twisting roots, coiling tubes, ancient rocks, and walking shadows in the twilight gloom. To get used to it, I sit down on some root or rock and see, hear and feel the scenery. This will make the vision clearer. My increased awareness ('what do I see? What do I feel? What do I hear?')

associates more fully. After a while I go for a walk, have a chat with Helja or Nidhögr, perhaps do some magick and then proceed to my rune gate. This is a huge stone cliff rising out of the swirling fog. What will the rune gate be for you? A door, a tunnel, a gate, a spring or just a foxhole in the ground? It's part of the fun to find the right connections. Now I draw the rune sign on the stone, in lines of light, assume the proper posture, chant the name and focus on this calling until I sense that the idea has made contact, and that the proper world lies behind the stone. Then I leap into the rune sign, get spun around, and find myself elsewhere. This is another crucial moment. First I look at the gate through which I have come. It may look a little different from the other side. I draw the rune on it and sing its name.

Then I expand the vision. I look at the ground beneath, and at the frame of the gate, or rock, it is set in. Then I turn slowly, and sit down once again. I give myself time to get in tune with the new world. Perhaps the vision is a little unclear at first. It will get more solid the more awareness I give to it. If it doesn't, I assume the proper posture, vibrate the rune name, and use this energy to amplify the vision. Then I begin to walk around, to explore the new world. In a sense all aspects of my experience will reveal the nature of the rune sentience, the environment and atmosphere will describe the inner meaning of the rune, and so will all life forms which I encounter.

Often enough, rune journeys are lively experiences. We are not there as observers but have to act, to change, to do and communicate, so that the journey of discovery equals an initiation. Some of the entities of the realm may teach us sorceries, or special applications for each rune sign. You shouldn't expect these entities to be well-behaved. There are many curious creatures in the astral. Some of them may be friendly but some of them certainly won't. It can happen that you are cheated or attacked if you are not careful. Some of those beings will test you, challenge you, try to control you. In turn, you should test all beings that you meet. Blind trust is deadly in the astral, as it is far too easy to deceive oneself, to indulge in wishful thinking or to 'bloat' the ego with the dangerous 'oh how well I am doing!'

Let's say that you meet an angry giant, who begins communication by raising a huge axe. Now you might waste time saying 'Hello! I know that you are just imagination!' However, the same goes for you, which means that the giant is real enough, and that you had better act, preferably fast. This is the time for shape changing. You might grow, for instance, or turn yourself into a wild beast, or draw a dividing line with your magick sword. Or perhaps you draw the rune in the air, and intone its name. I don't know what will work: dare to experiment. Some mages do this by drawing a holy symbol in the air, and by saying a sacred word. You would do well to use a sign and word which really means a lot to you. In many cases hostile entities are banished through this act, or at least constrained to behave in a more friendly manner. Drawing the rune sign will tell you about the being's nature. If the being is a genuine dweller of that realm, the rune will make the vision clearer. If it is not, the sign will banish it. You can realize the nature of each astral entity by confronting it with a sign, word, gesture, that is vital to your magick. If it accepts the energy, it is probably in harmony with it. If it flinches, or tries to get away, it is of no use to you.

Now there are people who believe that we should trust anything we meet in the astral. Some say that testing is not polite, and only makes the spirits angry. I disagree with this. People who blindly trust any bit of imagination that comes their way have no way of distinguishing just what is a genuine expression of the deep mind and what is a creature constructed by the ego's need to feel self-important. If a given entity flatters you, be careful. Nema expresses this point very well:

'Again, caution is urged. The fluidity of the astral planes renders proper verification of experience more difficult. One has to be able to recognize the nature of entities encountered on the astral planes during the encounter. Our allies are not offended by the presence of a diamond shield about the aura; like all surviving sentient beings, they have armour of their own.

There is a simply method of 'field analysis' to determine the nature of an astral entity. Since Yesod reflects Tiphereth, the procedure is to radiate the essence of the sun of the hawk and the negative radiance of the black flame. The allies will match the radiance in tonal or harmonic frequencies; alien entities will flee or be rendered immobile. The radiance may be engendered by visualizing a sun-sphere bearing the Eye of Horus, and a black flame speckled with stars. Vibrate the mantram 'Lutis Nitra' and your astral body will emit the envisioned radiance.' (CJCM, Vol 1)

This particular technique makes use of the Maatian magical system. Replace the words and symbols by some from your own tradition, if they mean more to you.

Coming back from the rune world to the body usually goes by the same route. I take care to give my thanks for the experience, close the doors well behind me, and return to the flesh. Often it takes some time to wake my body, to get the circulation going, and to get up. Then I usually sing a little, before ending the working, opening the circle, and writing the journey down. Keeping a diary will help you to keep the memory vivid and clear. Using this, or a similar method, you can learn to explore any symbol, sign, glyph, or sigil that suits you. You don't have to know what it is good for: the deep mind will tell you by making an entire magical world out of it. Indeed it is a test for neophytes to travel into some unknown symbol. This book should supply hundreds of them.

For rune magick, I recommend that you visit each rune world at least three times and make careful notes of the event. You will notice that the journey gets much easier with each try. In my usual way to the rune worlds I tend to use Niflheim as a 'passage' or 'in-between' state. Perhaps this will also suit you (once you get used to the joys and horrors of the place) but probably it won't. I suggest you ask your deep mind to select some symbols, and then try them out, for who knows to which range of awareness they may lead? Maybe you will find that some runes can easily be visited, and others are more difficult. This would indicated you are in tune with the former runes. It would also tell you to give more attention to the others. Perhaps some of these worlds require more effort, or maybe you will have to come to terms with them (and the parts of the mind which they represent). Some worlds may even require healing, or transformation, and so maybe will you. It's part of the joy in such 'journeys in the spirit vision' that they can change the structures of your mind.

27 Rune companion

How To Use The Dictionary

Each rune is introduced by a commentary, followed by the rune poems, names and sign variations. The interpretation is loosely based on various word-roots, assorted ethnology plus a measure of my own visions. Some of these are highly subjective. I ask the reader not to believe them blindly but to do independent research. I am no linguist so there will probably be a number of misinterpretations in the etymology. If you know better, please write and correct me.

The ethnology is less speculative. I've had the pleasure of studying ethnology for a time, nevertheless you should bear in mind that such human sciences as history and ethnology are subject to human error, not to mention fashions and trends.

My principle authorities for etymology is *Der Grosse Duden vol. 7 Etymologie,* (Mannheim 1963); R Schützeichel: *Althochdeutsches Wörterbuch* (Tübingen 1974); Heyne-Schückings: *Beowulf* III, Glossar/dictionary, (Paderborn 1961); Kock and Meissner: *Skaldisches Lesebuch* (Halle Saale 1931); *The American Heritage Dictionary of the English Language* (Boston 1981) (appendix: Indo-European roots); K Simrock, *Translation of the Eddas* (1981, Wien, Heidelberg); Plus various bits and pieces gathered in the usual eclectic fashion. The rune texts come from three sources.

1. The Old English Rune Poem.

The manuscript (Cottonian MS Otho BX) is dated around 1000, though the poem is probably two centuries earlier. The original manuscript was lost in the fire of 1731. A copy, published by Hicks in his *Linguarum Veterum Septentrionalum Thesaurus*, London 1705, survived. The rune signs themselves were not included, but have been preserved by a collector who carefully drew them at the side of the text. The rune poem describes 29 runes in verse.

also the signs are given, but without text.

2. The Old Norse Rune Poem.

Published by Olaus Wormius in *Danica Literatura Antiquissima* (Amsterdam 1636) based on a manuscript from the Kopenhagen University library. The original was lost in the fire of 1728, several transcripts survived. The text is dated around 1200 and describes the basic 16 runes of the Scandinavian system.

3. The Old Icelandic Rune Poem.

Based on four manuscripts in the Arnamagnean library in Kopenhagen. The texts were written down around 1400, though they are probably older. The poem describes the usual 16 runes of the Viking period, ignoring the newly developed versions of ⨎ = EH etc. The order varies in the manuscripts, Man ᛉ and Laguz ᛚ are often exchanged. Each

of the verses ends with a keyword in Latin and an old title for 'king' beginning with the rune letter.

The three rune poems can be found in B. Dickins: *Runes and Heroic Poems* (Cambridge University Press 1915) and M. Halsall, *The Old English Rune Poem* (Toronto 1981).

The St Gallen rune texts, given in another chapter, come from *Aelteste Deutsche Dichtungen* (Insel Verlag 1964). The names and shapes of various runes can be found in R.W.V. Elliott *Runes* (Manchester 1959) and C.W. Thompson *Studies in Upplandic Runography* (University of Texas Press 1975) and C.A. Pushong *Rune Magic* (London 1978). Other relevant titles can be found in the bibliography.

The various symbols come from several volumes dealing with Paleolithic art and similar matters. These books are listed in the bibliography. **These symbols were selected because of their similarity. It is in no way suggested that any given cave art symbol is a direct ancestor of a similar rune shape, or that our stone-age ancestors thought the same about their symbol as did later generations.**

Abbreviations:

P = Paleolithic period. Cave art between 35,000 - 10,000BC. Nomadic way of life, hunting-gathering, following the beasts.

N = Neolithic period. Agriculture, settlements, stationary society. The Neolithic is not a specific time but a phase of development. Agriculture was probably discovered in the Near East and spread slowly from South East Europe when the glaciers retreated.

NS = Neolithic Spain from c.7000BC.

NG = Neolithic Germany from c.5600BC.

NSC = Neolithic Scandinavia from c.2500BC.

MB = Megalith period, Brittany from c.4500BC.

NA = Neolithic Alps from c.5000BC. Close connection with Etruscan, see next entry.

ET = Etruscan, proto-Etruscan. Letters from the alphabet, by sound value.

PH = Phoenician. Source of Greek and Roman alphabets.

IE = Indo-European. This is a reconstructed language and is therefore always prefixed by the symbol *.

OHG = Old High German 700 - 1100.

MHG = Middle High German 1200 - 1500

G = New High German from 1600

OE = Old English

ON = Old Norse

OICE = Old Icelandic

GR = Greek

GOT = Gothic

'Cattle' is the traditional interpretation of the **Fehu** rune.

The Indo-European root *Peku-* is the basis for the OE *feoh, feo*, (cattle, property, treasure (related to 'fee')), the OHG *fehu, fihu, fieu* (= cattle, beasts) and the OICE *fe* (property, wealth). The shape of the rune may suggest the head of a horned beast, which connects it with the fertility gods, Frey and Freya, who may still be found in the German words *Freude* (joy) *Freiheit* (freedom) *freien* (to woo) *Friede* (peace) and *Freund* (friend).

To the Northern Indo-European tribes cattle was an essential aspect of life. The cow or ox is a source of food, a worker on the fields and also the beast that pulls the heavy wagon on which the families lived during the migration years. The IE root *per-*, meaning 'forward', 'through' is the source of such words as 'forth', 'further', 'first', 'from'. Another word stream from the same root 'leading, to pass over', which can be found in OG *faro*, OE *faru* (to travel), OHG *faran* (to travel, to go), OHG *fuoren* (to lead). The cattle driven wagons of the Celtic and German migrations contained all the movable property.

Bulls were often slaughtered as sacrifice to the gods, as on the island *Farra* (bull island) dedicated to Forsites. The cow Audhumla licked the first human from out of the ice.

Another idea links Fehu with the primal fire. The primal fire (G *Urfeuer*) is the flame of self (OE *feorh* = life, soul, spirit), the white flame of unity and the black flame of truth. The flame of many colours appears in OHG: *fagar* (brilliant, radiant) *fehen* (to colour, to dye), OE: *fah, fag* (colourful, radiant, bright) and OICE: *fa, faa* (to paint, colour), and *fagr*, (bright, beautiful).

A third idea-stream connects with fighting, which is the logical outcome of all the great migration movements. *Pei-* (to hurt), *peik-* (to cut, mark) and a few similar IE roots attest to this, OE *feohte*, OHG *fehta* (to fight). Modern words such as fiend or foe come from this.

The frequent interpretation of ᚠ as 'cattle' is insufficient unless we understand the common source for these idea streams: it is the self-fire that expresses itself in the fight for survival, be it in stationary form (house, property, cattle, breeding, agriculture), in motion (migration, journeys) and in the usual warfare that enables invaders to win territory and to keep it.

The Old English Rune Poem

Feoh byth frofur
fira gehwylcum;
sceal ðeah manna gehwylc
miclun hyt daelan
gif he wile for drihtne
domes hleotan.

Feoh is a comfort to all men;
yet must every man bestow it freely,
if he wish to gain honour
in the sight of the lord.

The Old Norse Rune Poem

Fé vaeldr fraenda róge;
føðesk ulfr i skóge

Fé is a source of discord among kinsmen;
the wolf lives in the forest.

The Old Icelandic Rune Poem

Fé er fraenda róg
ok flaeðar viti
ok grafseiðs gata
aurum fylkir

Fé = source of discord among kinsmen
and fire of the sea
and path of the serpent
aurum = gold.

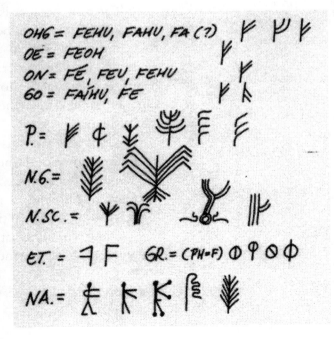

The Uruz rune has many interpretations. As the *ur* or *aurox* it describes a species of wild oxen that is extinct nowadays. The Ur is not related to the cattle we know. It was a much larger animal, with a shoulder height of up to six feet and could not be domesticated. The aurox was famed for its courage and primeval wildness. Caesar gives an account of its chase; the beast was driven into traps and killed by young men who wished to prove their valour. This ceremonial hunt was probably a 'rite of passage' marking the beginning of manhood; the trophies, ie. the horns, were important for ceremonial drinking (symble). The shape of ᚢ may easily suggest the outline of the beast with its massive shoulders. It is interesting that the aurox, still known to the author of the Old English Rune Poem, was unknown in Scandinavia and Iceland by 1200. In the former the reindeer replaces the Ur, in the latter both beasts are unknown and the meaning changes to 'drizzle, rain'.

Some consider Ur as a reference to Urda's well. The prefix *ur* is used in German to denote things of great age, such as *urzeit* (first time) *urtümlich* (original) *ursprung* (source), *urteil* (verdict), *urknall* (big bang) or the OHG *urtiefel*, the arch-devil. The three Norns, described in chapter nine, all go back to the IE roots **werad-*, branch, root, and **werdh-*, to grow, become. *Wyrd* describes both fate and disposition, which comes from **uer-* to turn, wind, bend, weave, become. The same as ON *orlog*, OHG *urlag* = ancient law. Urda's well, as is told by the *Edda*, restores to health, life and simplicity, washing away the troubles and pains and revealing the essential self. The same purification is reflected in the reference to dross which is the waste that comes out of iron in the process of smelting.

Drizzle and rain are both cleansing showers that fall from the heavens. If we turn the rune around we find a simplified horn from which the waters of life may be drunk, reflected perhaps in the OHG words *urlosa* (redemption) *urristi* (resurrection) *urruns* (rising) *urrunst* (beginning) *urspring* (source, well) *ursach* (first thing, ie. the root or reason for everything else). The rune posture is used to let go (of trouble, pain, sorrow) to bend to the deep and to resurrect the primal power of life and wildness. Two of my friends placed their hands on each other's shoulders to form this rune, and we able to seethe quite energetically whilst doing so.

The cleansing aspect is indirectly touched by the association of the horn with the moon: the Venus of Laussel (see illustration) carries a horn with 13 notches, which may refer to 13 lunar periods and 13 times of monthly bloodletting. The horn that appears aggressive in the aurox is receptive and good for drinking once it has been won. The symbolism is complex, I suggest you get yourself a drinking

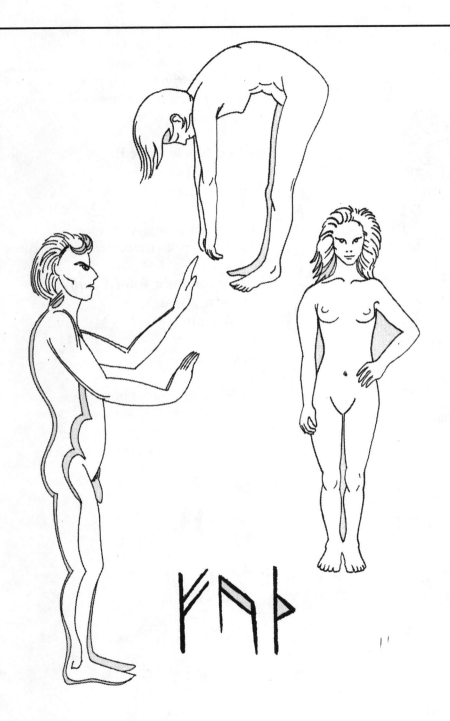

horn and settle down for a drink and meditation. This is what 'symble' ceremonies are all about.

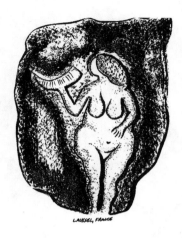

LAUSSEL, FRANCE

The Old English Rune Poem

Ur byth anmod
ond oferhyrned,
felafrecne deor,
feohteth mid hornum
maere morstapa;
thaet is modig wuht.

Ur is proud and has great horns;
it is a very savage beast
and fights with its horns;
a great ranger of the moors,
it is a creature of mettle.

The Old Norse Rune Poem

Úr er af illu jarne
opt løypr raeinn á hjarne

Dross comes from bad iron
the reindeer often races over frozen snow.

The Old Icelandic Rune Poem

Úr er skýja grátr
ok skára thverrir
ok hirðis hatr
umbre visi.

Ur is lamentation of the clouds
and ruin of the hay harvest
and abomination of the shepherd
umbre comes from imbre = shower.

The Thorn is one of nature's ways of protecting her fruits. Thornwalls have been used as barriers as long as human beings worked the fields and lived in villages. A girdle of thorn bushes used to protect every village and settlement, a hedge that divided the known universe from the dangerous and unknown realm beyond. The German 'dorf' and the English 'thorpe' both mean 'small village' and go back to the image of the thorn. Hedges were used to divide fields, sometimes even frontiers were fortified with thorn walls, such as the German/Danish border when it ran across the island Sylt.

Thorns offer division, restriction, protection, separation. They are sharp against intruders and offer berries and fruit to settlers. The word 'thorn' goes back to the roots *(s)ter*, stiff, hard, *ter*, to get over, break through, overcome (which is found in 'through' and 'drill'), possibly also *ter-*, *(s)tene*, (to thunder).

The ↑ variation of the rune, found in the St Gallen manuscript could resemble the image of Donar/Thor's hammer. Donar/Thor was an agricultural deity who fertilized the fields and drove giants away, establishing order and law. The wall of thorns, mentioned in some fairy tales, becomes a threat to the community if it is too open or too closed. In the enclosed thorn wall the people 'fell asleep' while the centuries flew by.

Now the rune is also called *Thurs*, which is an old name for the giants. The giants are a symbol for the primitive and obsessive drives that threaten the order of the world, possibly *thursa* connects with the OHG *thurfan*, which means 'oppressive need, necessity, desire, drive.' The ᚦ is called 'Hrugnirs heart' in the *Edda*, it is invoked to bind, restrict and control. Whether the thorn wall binds or protects depends on the situation and one's ability to pass through the barrier at will.

Merlin, who was spellbound into a hawthorn hedge by his beloved Nimue could nevermore leave his prison... but then he also became immortal, as being 'out of time', conscious through all the ages.

The *hagzissa* or witch, is a 'hedgesitter' who has learned to pass through the barrier and to connect the needs of the village (conscious mind) with the unknown world beyond (the collective sub-consciousness). That the passage can be dangerous and painful needs hardly be mentioned.

The Old English Rune Poem

Thorn byth ðearle scearp;
ðegna gehwylcum
anfeng ys yfyl
ungemetum rethe
manna gehwylcum

ðe him mid resteð.

Thorn is exceedingly sharp;
an evil thing for any knight to touch
uncommonly severe on all
who sit among them.

The Old Norse Rune Poem

Thurs vaeldr kvinna kvillu;
kátr vaerðr fár af illu.

Thurs causes anguish to women
misfortune makes few men cheerful.

The Old Icelandic Rune Poem

Thurs er kvenna kvöl
ok kletta búi
ok varðrúnar verr
saturnus Thengill

Thurs = torture of women
and cliff dweller
and husband of a giantess.
Saturnus = Saturn

OHG = THURISAZ, THORN
OE = THORN
ON = THURIS, THURISAR, THURS
GO = THAURIS, THYTH

P. =

N.SC =

ET. =   PH. =   GR. =

NA. =

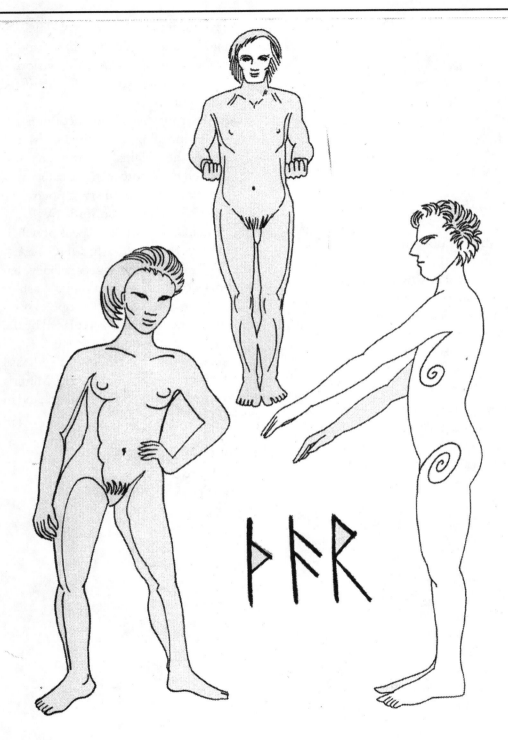

The Os rune has to do with the gods. The word *Aesir*, name of the ruling tribe of gods, is connected with it. The OICE *Oss* has three meanings, the Aesir, the height of a mountain and the '1' on a dice. The modern word 'ace' comes from this. According to some authors, the words 'ass' (singular) and Aesir (plural) go back to the ash tree, which is *os-* in Indo-European, OHG *ask*, OE *aesc*, ON *askr*. The word 'ass', they say, used to mean 'supporting pillar', which was a tent pole in the early days and the central pillar in the great hall in the days of agriculture. The meaning of the world-ash, connecting heaven and earth, is a central theme in the *Edda*.

Another meaning of the rune has to do with speech. Wodan/Odin has his essential initiation hanging from the world-ash, sacrificed to himself, and finding freedom in a scream, then in the speech of the runes. Wodan's name is rooted in OHG *wuot* (crazy, in rage), GOT *wods* (obsessed), OE *wod* (sound, voice, song) and OICE *odr* (poetry). The IE root: *os-* means 'a mouth', and the rune refers to speech, communication, breath, words and silence, to the wind that flows through the branches of the tree, (the original 'Woide' was a storm god, leader of the wild hunt) and to 'the same mouth' by which the vision is shared, the nectar joined and life exhausted into the beyond.

In the IE root *ansu-* we encounter the rather vague meaning 'god, demon, spirit', and perhaps the original phenomena was savage enough to fall into all three categories, but in the refined form of the rune poems the reference is definitely to Odin, lord of Valhalla. Odin's principal weapon, the spear of will, is also related to the world-ash; OHG *asck* = spear, OHG *asca* = ashes. It seems likely that the original world ash was a mountain ash or rowan. This tree spread over Europe as soon as the glaciers melted and was replaced by the modern ash tree at a much later age.

The three aspects of the tree, Yggdrassil 'horse of the terrible one' Mimameith 'Mimir's tree' and Laerad 'giver of peace' are treated in chapter eight.

The Old English Rune Poem

Os byth ordfruma
aelere spraece
wisdomes wrathu
ond witena frofur
and eorla gehwam
eadnys ond tohiht.

Os is the source of all language,
a pillar of wisdom
and a comfort to wise men,
a blessing and a joy
to every knight.

The Old Norse Rune Poem

Óss er flaestra faerða
for; en skalpr er svaerða

Óss is the way of most journeys,
but a scabbard is of swords.

The Old Icelandic Rune Poem

Óss er aldingautr
ok ásgarðs jofurr,
ok valhallar visi.
Jupiter oddviti.

Oss = aged gautr (god)
and prince of Asgard
and lord of Valhalla.
Jupiter

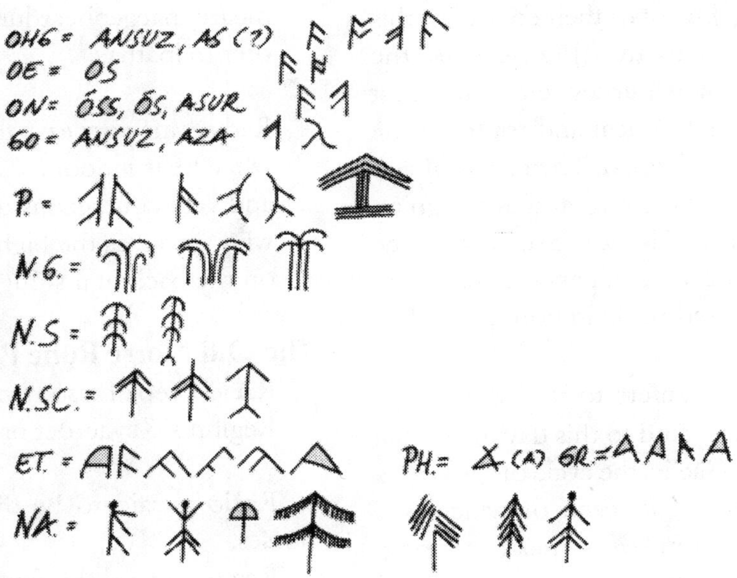

OHG = ANSUZ, AS (?)

OE = OS

ON = ÓSS, ÓS, ASUR

GO = ANSUZ, AZA

P. =

N.G. =

N.S =

N.SC. =

ET. =   PH. =   GR. =

NA. =

Rad is a very complex rune. Basically it refers to riding, to journeys and quests. We find this in such words as OE *rad* (street, path, road) OE *ridan* (to ride) OHG *rado* (swift) *girado* (suddenly), OICE *reið* (wagon) *reidatyr* (god of the wagons) *reida* (equipment, motion), all of which go back to **ret(h)*, roll, run. Rad is not just a journey - people rarely travelled for fun - but a quest, a knight (German = *Ritter*) errand. The quest is an old tradition, both for knights (who got most of their education this way) and for shamans (journeys to the underworld, healing journeys etc.) The quest involves challenge, ordeal and triumph: the rider returns transformed. The task is of less importance than the going, and in the going each step on the road is the sum of all the way. Such journeys are 'rites of passage' that allow transformation and re-definition in an alien environment.

In a sense, ᚱ refers to the wheel - the journey is a circle - and to this day the G *Rad* = wheel. In the Gaelic, the cycle of the year is divided into four *radh*, each of which is a season (*earrach* from *ear* = head - spring, *samhradh* from *samh* = sun - summer, *fogharadh*

from *fogh* = fullness - fall and *geamradh* from *geimheal* = chain - winter). As a parallel of the great yearly cycle, the council-circle assembles; the experience gained on the road is the quality that allows participation. The council-circle is the ᚱ rune as OICE *rað* (council, plan, advise, intent) *rada* (to give advise) OHG *rat*, *raht* (council, decision), OE *raed* (help, advise) *raedan* (to govern, rule). German *raten* = to guess, a *Rätsel* is a riddle.

The concept of the ruling *rath* goes back to the IE root **ar, *are* and **re-*, which equals 'to put together'. We find this root in the Ger rune, in the ᚱ context it led to such terms as 'harmony', 'art', 'order' and 'rite'.

The Old English Rune Poem

Rad byth on recyde
rinca gehwylcum
sefte ond swithhwaet,
ðemðe sitteth on ufan
meare maegenheardum
ofer milpathas.

Rad seems very easy to every warrior
while he is indoors
and very courageous to him
who traverses the highroads
on the back of a stout horse.

The Old Norse Rune Poem

Raeið kveða rossom vaesta;
Reginn sló svaerðet baezta.

Raeið is said to be the worst thing for horses,
Reginn forged the finest sword.

The Old Icelandic Rune Poem

Reið er sitjandi saela
ok snúðig ferð
ok jórs erfiði
iter raesir.

Reið = joy of the horseman
and speedy journey
and toil of the steed
iter = journey.

OHG = RAÍDO   R R R
OE = RAD   R R
ON = RAT, RAÍÞU, RÆÍÐ, REÍÐ R
GO = REÍDA, REDA   R K

ET. = ◁ ▷ ▷   PH. = ᖀ   GR. = P R Þ

NA. =

Ken is a very enigmatic rune. Its symbolism has much to do with fire, not the ancient fire (ᚡ) nor the solar flame (ᚺ) but the human expression of it. OHG *chien* and OE *cen* both mean a bit of wood which was cut from a tree and used as a torch. To this day a *kienspan* is a bit of pinewood used to light fires, and *kienäpfel* are the 'apples' of the pine. *Kynda*, OICE, is 'to kindle' a flame.

The torch is made by splitting (OE cinan) wood, the ken Itself shows a split/cleft (OE *cinu*). In the St Gallen rune manuscript we are told that < is equally 'split off' and 'glued to', the text is ambiguous and the symbol could be understood in both ways. Ken could be a wall with a torch, <. is clearly a cleft. It is interesting to note that the ulcer referred to in the poems burns just like a torch. The IE root **kenk-* (to burn) is the source of the modern 'hunger': the flame has to devour.

The poems also refer to disease and death. In some futhorc rows, such as the St Gallen versions, the ᚲ stands at the end of the first row and outside of the regular order. Indirectly we are reminded of the G *Kahn* (small boat), ON *kan* (boat, cup) and OICE *gin, kin*, (prow of a ship, open jaws, as in *ginnungagap* = gaping jaws, the gap of voidness that surrounds the world.) The boat or ship was often used for funerals. Sometimes a hill was erected over the ship and sometimes the boat was set on fire on the water, see for example the account of Balder's funeral in the *Edda*.

Some authors emphasize the presence of the *aethlingas* (nobility) in the poem, and connect < with the idea of kinship, from OE *cyn* = people, tribe, species. The heads of the clan are OICE *konung* (king, noble) and the queen, *kona*. Obviously such people are prime candidates for the development of stomach ulcers. Others claim that Ken comes from ON *kuna*, which is a 'young maiden'. If we view < as a cleft, this symbolism might work out, but if we consider the equally valid ᚡ the phallic symbolism cannot be denied. Both of them are fiery.

The Old English Rune Poem

Cen byth ewicera gehwam,
cuth on fyre
blac ond beorhtlic.
byrneth oftust
ðaer hi aethelingas
inne restath.

Cen is known to every living man
by its pale, bright flame,
it always burns
where princes sit within.

The Old Norse Rune Poem

Kaun er barna bolvan
bol gorver nán folvan.

Kaun is fatal to children
death makes a corpse pale.

The Old Icelandic Rune Poem

Kaun er barna böl
ok bardaga (för)
ok holdfúa hús
flagella konungr

Kaun = fatal to children
and painful spot
and abode of mortification
Flagella = ulcer.

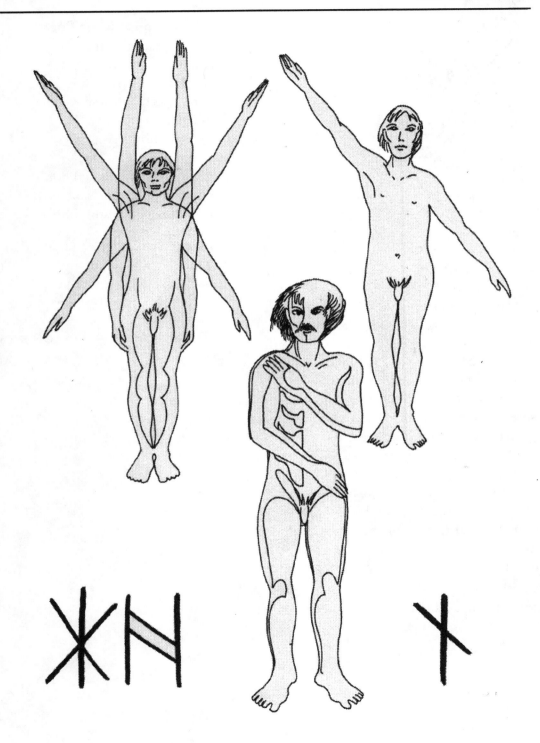

Gyfu is the seventh rune of the Old English poem, it does not occur in the Scandinavian systems. *Gyfu* means giving, (OHG *geban*, GOT *giban*, OE *giefau*, ON *gifa*) which evolved out of the IE **ghab-* to grab, take, carry, give and **gheb-* to give, to take. Curiously both aspects - giving and taking - occur simultaneously in the Indo-European. The word 'gift' (G. *Gabe*) comes from this. The gift is a sacrifice, a giving to all and a receiving in kind. The rune posture often used to release excess power, symbolizes a person who spreads and opens up. The original act of giving is the giving of oneself, it is the only thing one can be free to give. Possibly the OHG *gebed, gibet*, OE *gebed*, prayer, has to do with X. The X is also a gable, from **ghabholo*, fork, branch of a tree. The Old Germanic type of houses had a gable, with beast heads finials, usually dragons or horses. A variation is ᛤ which seems to be a simplified swastika, fire wheel. The sign ᛤ also resembles the popular peasant sign called the 'wolf-hook', the crossbar being the item that breaks the wolf's power.

The Old English Rune Poem

Gyfu gumena byth
gleng and herenys
wrathu and wyrthscype
and wraecna gehwam
ar and aetwist
ðe byth othra leas.

Gyfu brings credit and honour
which support one's dignity;
it furnishes help and subsistence
to all broken men
who are devoid of aught else.

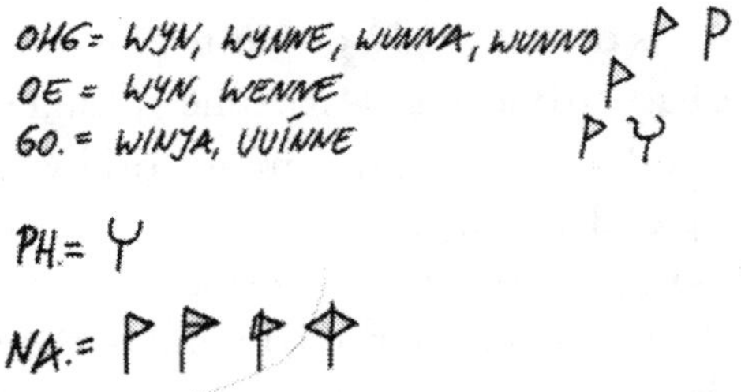

Wyn rune number eight in the OE poem, unknown in the Scandinavian texts. Wyn is a rune of joy and bliss. The IE **wen-* (to desire, strive for) can be found in OHG *wunno* joy, luck, bliss, lust, *wini* beloved, *weniz* hope, OICE *vingjof* joy, gift, OE *wine* = friend, protector. The German *Wonne* (bliss), the English 'to win' 'winsome' and the Latin 'Venus' come from this root, probably also the tribal name *Vanir* and the *vanadis*, Freya, goddess of love.

The sign ᚹ is something of a riddle. If we lay it down it suggests a posture that was frequently used by Wilhelm Reich and his followers to release the 'orgasm reflex' (see chapter 15). The bent posture of the legs frees the hip/belly region to move, tremble, vibrate, which in turn dissolves the sexual armour.

In another sense we can see Wyn as a pair making love, he as earth — and she bending over him ^, our lady Babalon and the Beast on which she rides. For some obscure reason this lucid symbolism has escaped the awareness of historical scholars, who tend to find their bliss among books and not in bed.

Old Norse Rune Poem

Wenne bruceth
ðe can weana lyt
sares and sorge
and him sylfa haefth
blaed and blysse
and eac byrga geniht.

Wenne he enjoys who knows
no suffering, sorrow nor anxiety,
and has prosperity and happiness
and a good enough house.

OHG = WYN, WYNNE, WUNNA, WUNNO ᚹ ᚹ
OE = WYN, WENNE ᚹ
GO. = WINJA, UUÍNNE ᚹ ᛉ

PH = ᛉ

NA. = ᚹ ᚹ ᚹ ᚹ

Hagal is the beginning of the second Aettir. Some attribute the rune to Wodan in his aspects of Har (high) or Höttr (the one with the hat). In one sense ᚺ is a rune of wintertime when the human and natural world went to sleep under a carpet of snow. Winter was the season of sleep, darkness, restoration, patience and rebirth. Outdoor activity and warfare had to be abandoned, the family stayed together at home, the 'whiteness from heaven' making travel and work largely impossible. *Hagal* is sometimes interpreted as 'hag-all', hag, root of the word 'hedge', from IE *kagh-* to catch, seize, wickerwork, fence. 'Ich hege das All' (I am custodian of all') is a common and modern German interpretation of the rune. It is the protective blanket of snow that refreshes earth, healing the natural world. ᚺ is often called a healing rune, but the healing suggested by winter is not a gentle affair. The cold cleans. The seed sleeps in suspension. The weak beings find death, the strong ones fresh strength. People retire indoors, where they have a long and dark season to come to terms with themselves. Such isolation could strengthen the family ties or break them entirely. Whether the enforced inactivity is a blessing or a curse depends on how we get along with ourselves. Wintertime was seen as preparation for the year to come. The old people would recount legends and tales - while the younger generation spun flax, worked on the loom or carved household goods. Nordic sagas mention up to three great winter feasts, each of which could last for days or weeks, depending on the wealth of the host.

The snow crystal is suggested by the ✳ shape, and to my imagination ᚺ is a snow drift between two trees. Another relevant interpretation relates Hagal with hail. This would connect the rune with spring and summer, when thundestroms are common and showers of hail threaten to devastate the countryside. Hagal is also rooted in the IE *kaghlo-* pebble, hail. ✳ is called a *Binderune*, as the rune posture can only be done in stages (such as ᛏ and ᛚ) or by a pair standing close together. When on your own, try (1) ᛏ posture, vibrate 'hag', (2) let the arms down into ᛚ, vibrate 'al'. There is a brief pause as the arms move, nevertheless the full word is done in one breath. The same procedure is used for ᛉ 'hag', ᛦ 'al'. The essential idea is to establish a six-rayed star. When working with your love, stand close together and imagine you two are a single shape. One partner does ᛏ while the other is in ᛚ Then both vibrate 'hag', switch postures, and complete with 'al'. The rune contains motion and is good for dancing also..

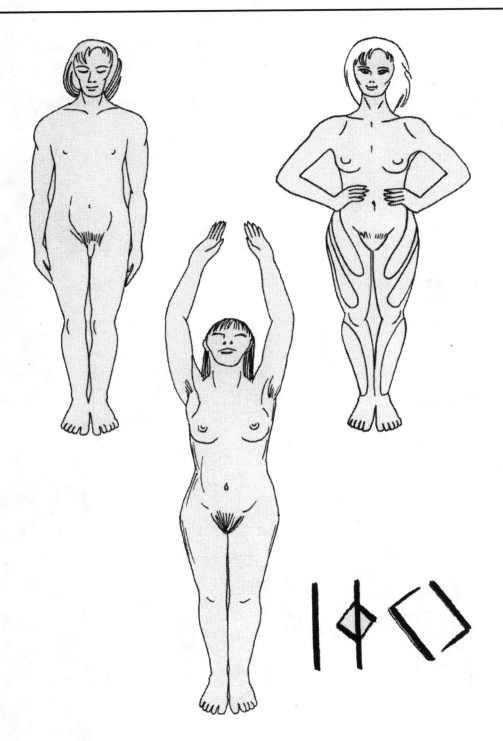

The Old English Rune Poem

Haegl byth hwitust corna
hwyrft hit of heofones lyfte
wealcath hit windes scura
weortheth hit to waetere
syððan.

Haegl is the whitest of grain
it is whirled from the vault of heaven
and is tossed about by gusts of wind
and then it melts into water.

The Old Norse Rune Poem

Hagall er kaldastr korna
kristr skóp haeimenn forna.

Hagall is the coldest of grain;
Christ created the world of old.

The Old Icelandic Rune Poem

Hagall er kaldakorn
ok krapadrifa
ok snáka sótt
grando hildingr

Hagall is cold grain
and shower of sleet
and sickness of serpents.
Grando = hail.

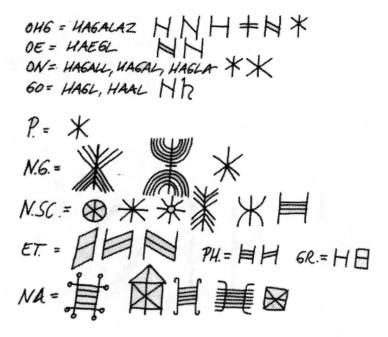

Nyd is a rune that has suffered too much negative publicity. OHG *niot, not*, GOT *nauths*, OE *nyd*, OICE *nauðr* all mean 'need, necessity, pressure, compulsion' and similar ideas. This 'need' is not quite as simple as it seems. The OICE *nauðsyn* is 'need-sin' while *njotta* = 'to enjoy'. OHG *niot, niet, nit* are 'desire, longing, to lust for', while *nietegi* is the dreaded 'lust of the flesh' OE *neod* is 'desire, craving' and *nyt* is 'urge, duty' and could even refer to an office. In all of these cases there is necessity, but not in the 'hunger and lack' ideology favoured by some scholars. Without the least historical verification, the eighteen rune system goes so far to introduce the modern 'eh' rune, which looks like ᛇ to oppose the doom and darkness atmosphere of ᚾ. with the positive concepts of marriage (*Ehe* in German). Now the ᛇ rune in its original sense could suggest imbalance, a posture in a dance of disturbed equilibrium. Another interpretation of the sign leads to the knot, the knitting and the net, from IE *kn- to press, contract, push, knead, bind. ᚾ is a rune of binding and dissolving, coming together and coming apart. The knot is a place/event. Here is the net worked by the Norns (Nyrnir = weavers), the spider web of all reality. All events are seen as the interaction of lines of force, combining to create the web of destiny. Where two persons, events, ideas meet, their lifelines show mutual change; they 'share a gesture' (Castaneda) and proceed to develop from the shared knot of their interaction. All rituals or moments of intense event/experience are knots in the fabric of the net. ᚾ refers to ties, known and unknown, the ties of hunger and fulfillment, the spells we work in need and the ties we form in joy and laughter with our beloved ones. Knot magick has its place here. When we seize the instant and tie or open our knot in fullness of consciousness, the lines of interaction change the pattern of the whole. The knot is imbued with its vision and communicated into the web of all life.

It should be noted that Nauthiz is sometimes drawn ᚾ and sometimes ᛇ There is no need to introduce that modern version of 'eh' when the 'not' idea itself includes the idea of bond-fasting, be it out of necessity or out of free will. Another interesting interpretation suggests that ᚾ is a fire drill (a drill plus a bow) which was used for the 'need fires', which are described in Frazer's *Golden Bough*.

The Old English Rune Poem

Nyd byth nearu on breostan
weortheth hi theah oft
nitha bearnum
to helpe and to haele gehwaethre
gif hi his hlystath aeror.

The Old Icelandic Rune Poem

Naud er thýjar thrá
ok thungr kostr
ok vassamlig verk.
Opera niflungr

Nauð is grief of the bond-maid
and state of oppression
and toilsome work
opera = work.

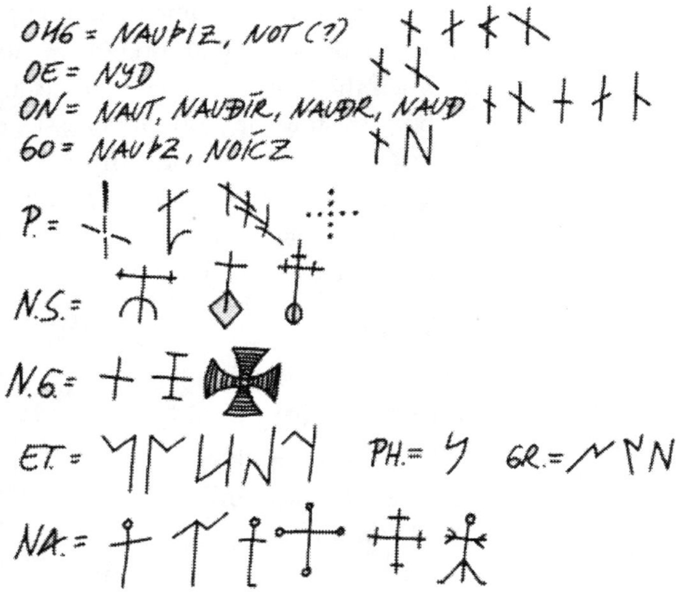

Nyd is oppressive to the heart;
yet often it proves a source of help
and salvation to the children of men,
to everyone who heeds it betimes.

The Old Norse Rune Poem

Nauðr gerer naeppa koste;
noktan kaelr i froste,

Nauðr gives scant choice
a naked man is chilled by the frost.

OH6 = NAUÞIZ, NOT (?)
OE = NYD
ON = NAUT, NAUÐIR, NAUÐR, NAUÐ
6O = NAUÞZ, NOÍCZ

P. =

N.S. =

N.6. =

ET. =   PH. =   6R. =

NA. =

Isa is the only rune that was never varied, no matter which futhorc version was used. The sign remained as it is, and this 'freezing of development' is one of its essential meanings. OE *is*, OHG *is*, OICE *iss*, all go back to the IE root *eis*- which is 'ice, frost'. In the *Edda* we find some very clear references to the ice-ages, to the creation of life out of fire and ice and to the giants of the ice, the Hrimthursir. Ice is frozen water, signifying that the fluid becomes solid (for a time), thereby suspending development and change.

Ice is cold, beautiful and dangerous. The crust of ice covers lakes and steams, even the shores of the ocean, and life has to continue in the darkness underneath, unseen. The ice-bridge may connect the shores but we have to walk with great caution and very slowly. Some sorts of ice are criss-crossed with myriad angular lines, which provide an excellent field for rune divination. Then there is the image of the mountain goddess Skadi who bound the sickles of the moon to her feet and invented skating.

The I posture has a strangely sobering effect. It 'freezes' the rolling astral tides and reduces the mage to the simplest possible form. A single line to bind heaven and earth. Tradition frequently links the I rune with the 'I-phenomena', and certainly all notions of identity are just frozen images that suspend what is otherwise fluid and in motion.

I is also connected with OHG *isarn* = holy metal = iron. The first iron, the 'holy metal', fell from the skies. Several Icelandic kenningar* use ice as a symbol for iron, such as the 'Valkyrie's ice' (the sword) or the 'arm-ice' (bracelets of iron or silver). OICE *isarn* and OHG *isin, isenin, isinin* = iron, often a symbol for any sort of weapon. Weapons also have to do with the 'I-phenomena', but there is little need to emphasize that point.

The Old English Rune Poem

Is byth oferceald
ungemetum slidor
glisnath glaeshluttur
gimmum gelicust
flor forste geworuht
faeger ansyne.

Is is very cold and immeasurably slippery
it glistens as clear as glass
and most like to gems;
it is a floor wrought by the frost,
fair to look upon.

---

* Poetic metaphors, very popular amongst the Nordic Skalds.

The Old Norse Rune Poem

Is kollum brú braeiða
blindan tharf at laeiða.

Is we call the broad bridge;
the blind man must be led.

The Old Icelandic Rune Poem

Iss er árbökr
ok unnar thak
ok feigra manna fár
glacies jöfurr

Iss is bark of river
and roof of the wave
and destruction of the doomed
glacies = ice.

OHG = IS, ISA

OE = IS, ISAR

ON = ISS, IS, ISAR

GO = IIZ, EIS

P. =

N.S. =

N.6., N.S6. =

ET. =   PH. =   GR. =

NA. =

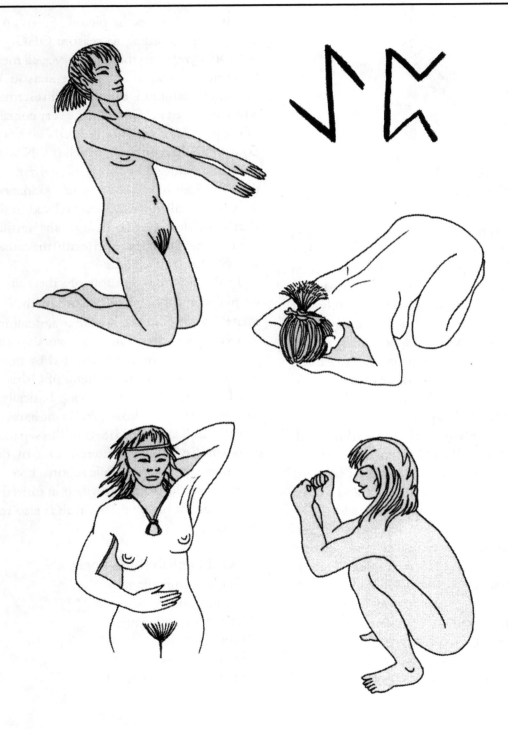

Ger is a rune that deals with agriculture. Consider the 'Neolithic revolution', the change in lifestyle and philosophy that came when new technologies were introduced and nomads decided to settle, possibly for generations. The age of the hunter/gatherer gave way to the age of the peasant.

The Indo-European roots *ger-* to gather, *gher-* to grasp, enclose, and *ar*, to fit together, produced a wide field of new words. OICE *jarda* (buried) *jarðriki* (realm of earth) *gardr* (settlement, garden). OHG *gard, gardo* (garden, circle, choir). OE *geard* (enclosed space, country, garden.) We are reminded of Asgard (Aesir land) Midgard (middle land) and Utgard (outland). Perhaps ◇ shows the enclosure of a field. To the peasant, land itself was survival. The hunter-gatherer relies on luck, skill and mobility, to the peasant endurance, law and long-term planning are vital. The soil is divided, worked, defended and passed on to heirs, which requires a new definition of law, order and property. Earth produces fruit. The ✦ or ◇ can be seen as an image of the seed or of the grain that grows out of it.

Time now enters the picture. Seeds grow into plants according to season: OHG *garo* and OE *gearn*, from the IE **garwa-z*, all mean 'complete, ripe, ready'. The season of fulfillment, autumn, is called *Herbst* in German, which is related to 'harvest'. The very concept of the year (OHG *jar*, OE *gear*, ON *ar*) has to do with the harvest time, which is ON *arnot*. *Airem* is a Celtic name for the ploughman. In the Old English land blessing the goddess of the earth is called *Erce*, closely related to the Earth-Goddess Gerda, wife of the fertility god Freyr, and Jörd/Fjörgyn (earth) the earliest wife of Odin in the *Edda*.

In the Scandinavian folklore the rune is simplified into ✦ or which balances with Nyd. That the Indo-Europeans were an agricultural society already deep into solar worship and patriarchal government is attested by many scholars. This is called the 'aeon of Osiris' is occult circles, Osiris/Asar being basically a corn and grain god who is killed in the harvest, then the fields are burned (Set) and his separate parts (the seeds) are scattered. Out of the barren earth the fresh life is reborn. Like all solar heroes, death and resurrection form the central part of his myth, the fruit is also the sacrifice.

The Old English Rune Poem

Ger byth gumena hiht
ðonne god laeteth
halig heofones cyning
hrusan syllan
beorhte bleda
beornum ond ðearfum.

Ger is a joy to men, when God, the
holy king of heaven,
suffers the earth to bring forth
shining fruits for rich and poor alike.

The Old Norse Rune Poem

Ár er gumna góðe
get ek at orr var Fróðe

Ár is a boon to men
I say that Frothi was generous.

The Old Icelandic Rune Poem

Ár er gumna goði
ok gott sumar
ok algróinn akr
annus allvaldr

Ár is a boon to men
and good summer
and thriving crops
annus = year.

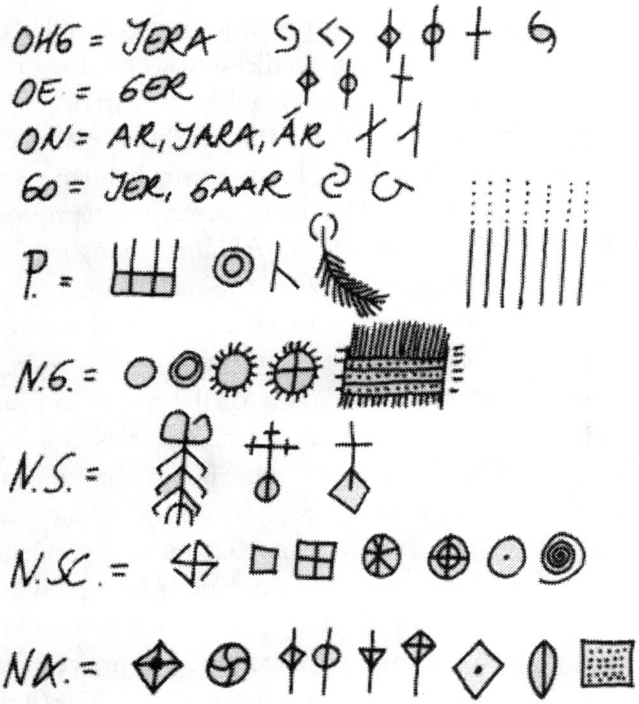

Ehwaz, Eoh; & **Yr** runes belong to a group. There has been a mix-up of meanings, leading to a degree of confusion. The OE ᛇ, meaning the sedge grass, appears in the ON rune systems in reverse (also in the St. Gallen version) ᛉ and refers to the yew tree. Simultaneously the ᛦ is explained as the 'man' rune (originally ᛘ) in the Scandinavian systems. To increase complications, the OE rune poem introduces another rune for the yew tree, it is the common ᛇ the 'e' of the common Germanic futhorc. The sound was probably like the 'I' in modern English, pronouced 'Aye'. The Old English Rune ᛦ may have been pronounced like an X, Z, Dg or Sh.

Thus we get: OE ᛦ = sedge, ᛇ = yew, ᛘ = man. ON ᛉ = yew, ᛦ = man (this version can also be found in the St Gallen texts, which predate the Scandinavian systems.) The sedge is missing in Old Norse. I think that it is rather futile to speculate about the 'true' meaning of these runes. For working purposes it is enough to travel into the rune tunnels: here you will find out which sign is a yew and which belongs to the swamp.

The yew is one of the trees that lives for centuries. Its hard, compact wood made it excellent for the purpose of hunting from Neanderthal times to the middle ages; bows and crossbows were made out of yew wood until the tree had almost died out. In the elder days a special arrow poison was distilled out of yew berries, needles and wood, the bright pink berry flesh being the only part of the tree that contains comparatively little poison. Our word for poison, toxin, comes from the yew's name *taxus*. The yew is a death tree. It produces its bright berries in fall and retains its fresh green needle coat all the year through.

Few yews can be found in the forests nowadays, the tree grows too slowly to be of economic use. Many of them can be found growing happily in cemeteries all over Northern Europe, there being a proverb that the cemetery yew has a root within each coffin. Scholars claim that once a yew cult had its sacred groves in northern Europe where the (Scandinavian) god Ullr was invoked. There is a curious connection between the ON ᛉ and the concept of madness. The OHG *irri, irre, irr* = confused, lost, free of, heretic,

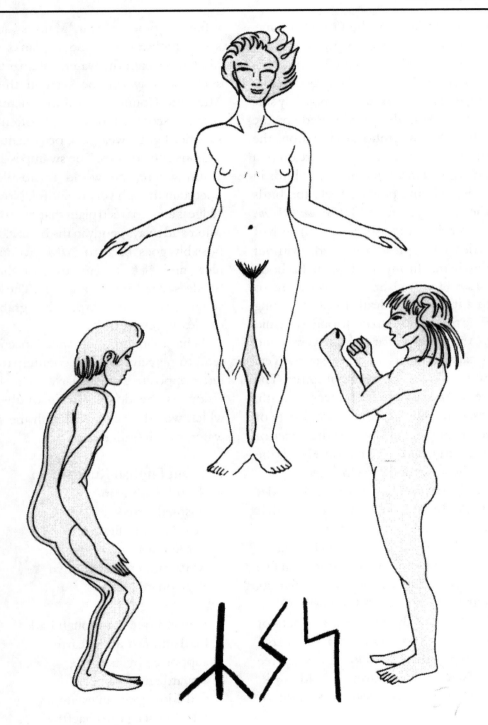

unsteady, crazy (root of the G *irr* = insane, mad, crazy) and the OE *ierre, yrre* = excited, angry, confused, wild, from the IE root: **ers-* to be in motion. These words aptly describe madness, rage and intoxication - possibly side results of handling the poison. Perhaps the change from ᛉ to ᛦ symbolizes the roots, the reversal of reality, the impossible dream of a tree that is green in winter and feeds birds in spite of its extreme poison. Well, the birds enjoy the bright (yew from OHG: *iwa*, OE:*iw*, OICE:*yr*= bright, reddish, colourful) flesh of the berries and spread the seeds without digesting them. Hironymus Bock in his book *Herbal Lore* (1577) claims that yews are so toxic that it is certain death to sleep among them. The toxin is said to be strongest in mid winter. Another popular use for yew wood was to carve amulets or rune staffs. Yew wood was said to drive away evil spirits. The mysteries of the yew are the trances of death, madness, confusion and that exalted state of inspired craziness that reverses the order of the world and goes beyond reason. Here is the realm of the jester and the clown.

The sedge-symbol also reverses the order of the world. In the swampland, solid earth is untrustworthy, the ground is treacherous, there is nothing solid or certain. The swamp breeds curious amphibious creatures that live in both realms. The elk or moose gave its name to the rune sign (elk = OHG *elho*, OE = *eohl*, ON = *alg*), as the moose is a variety of giant deer that thrives in swamp and marsh country. Its broad hooves allow the beast free passage where a person would sink. Swampland was often used as a place of refuge in times of war. Many swamps had secret pathways - wooden planks on stilts hidden beneath the water. Remnants of one such pathway can be seen in the British Museum. Countless swamp sanctuaries are being discovered nowadays, often rich in sacrificial gifts, weapons, ornaments, model wagons and corpses. The swamp is a magical realm where the world is hostile, fluid, uncertain though very beautiful. Now the elk sedge is a sort of reed plant that rises out of the water and sways gently in the breeze. Its name possibly goes back to **elkos-* wound, sore, ulcer and **sek-* to cut, root of the words 'sickle, sedge, saw, sax (sword)'. The leaves of sedge grass are sharp, who grabs them carelessly gets cut.

What follows now is sheer speculation. I tend to perceive ᛇ as a counterpart of ᛊ, a lunar opposite to the solar ᛊ. The ᛇ, in my vision, is the double sickle of the moon, which would nicely blend with the swamp/ water/marsh/sedge character.

The Old English Rune Poem

ᛇ Eoh byth utan
unsmethe treow,
heard hrusan faest,
hyrde fyres
wyrtrumun underwrethyd
Wyn on ethle.

Eoh is a tree with rough bark,
hard and fast in the earth,
supported by its roots,
a guardian of flame
and a joy upon an estate.
ᛉ Eohl - secg eard haefth

oftust on fenne
wexeð on wature,
wundath grimme
blode breneð
beorna gehwylcne
ðe him aenigne
onfeng gedeth
Eohl - sedge is mostly to be found
in a marsh, it grows in the water
and makes a ghastly wound
covering with blood
every warrior who touches it.

The Old Norse Rune Poem

ᛦ Ýr er vetrgronstr viða;
vaent er, er brennr, at sviða.

Ýr is the greenest of trees in winter,
it is wont to crackle when it burns.

The Old Icelandic Rune Poem

ᛦ Ýr er bendr bogi
ok brotgjarnt járn
ok fifu fárbauti
arcus ynglingr

Ýr is bent bow
and brittle iron
and giant of the arrow.[*]
arcus = bow.

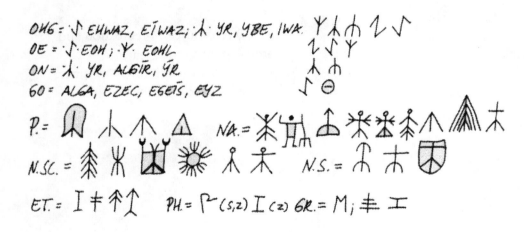

---

[*] Dickins translates *Faubauti* as 'giant of the arrow', who appears in the Edda as the father of Loki. The name seems to be ambigious and several scholars have translated it as 'fast to escape'.

Peorð is rune no 14 in the OE rune poem, placed between ᛇ and ᛉ. The text is obscure and defies clear interpretation. Accordinly, scholars have surmised that the sign refers to a game, a game-board, playing figures, drinking cups, the cauldron of food and whatever else might be enjoyed indoors. If the rune name is of Celtic origin it might relate to the Old Welsh Peir, a cauldron. This, however is very speculative. ᛈ seems to suggest an entrance into a room/space, possibly a cave. OHG *P(h)orta, borta* = gate, door, *p(h)orzih* = hall, hallway. Another possible root refers to the hill fortress, OHG *bergaz*, OE *beorg* (burg, borough), from IE **bergh-* to hide, protect, **bherg-*, high, hill fortress. German *Berg* = mountain. The earliest Bergs are ring-wall sanctuaries that were fortified in wartime.

The ᛈ is a squatting posture. It can be found in some swamp corpses; the sacrifice was bound into a ᛈ shape, like an embryo, before being strangled and sunk. This might link the ᛈ idea with the hall (uterus) and warrior (foetus). The posture could be of use in giving birth.

The Old English Rune Poem

Peorð byth symble
plega and hlehter
wlancum (on middum),
ðar wigan sittath
on beorsele
blithe aetsomne.

Peorð is a source of recreation and
amusement to the great,
where warriors sit blithely together
in the banqueting hall.

OHG= PEORD ᛈ ᛞ ET.= ᒣᒣ PH.= ? GR.= ΓΓΠΤΤ
OE= PEORD, PEORÐ ᛈ h
GO= PAÍRÞA, PETRA ᛈ Π

Sigel is a solar rune. In its name the IE roots *sawel-, *swen-, *sun-,* can be found, all of which refer to the sun. The sun, sunna, was a goddess in Old North Germanic culture. The solar formula, known in the western occult tradition as the 'formula of IAO' describes the usual pattern of life, death and rebirth. The same idea can be found in the ᚼ shape. Sometimes flowers or branches grow in the ᚼ shape. This happens when the original motion encounters obstruction bypasses the trouble and proceeds to grow in the original direction. It is the cyclic pattern of growth, crisis and more growth that makes the phenomena predictable, and if we inquire honestly, we find that this sort of evolution takes place in all forms of learning. We may also consider the ᚼ as part of the solar wheel, the swastika, which goes back to the ages when our ancestors celebrated the solar festivals by rolling huge fire-wheels down a hill. In another sense the ᚼ symbolizes the lightning flash, which was the first source of fire to our ancestors, divine fire that fell from the skies.

In the 18 rune system, ᚼ called the *Siegrune*. *Sieg* is German for victory, the word goes back to IE **segh-* to hold. The OE *sigel* (sun) is possibly related to such words as *sige-folc* (people of victory), *sige-leas* (without victory), *sige-rof* (rich in victory), the word 'siege' and such terms as *sigan* (to sink, fall descend) and *sigle* (jewellery, treasures). The ON *sigr* (victory) can be found in numerous names, such as Sigurd, Siegfried, Sieglinde, Sigmund or Sigrdrifa (the victory giver). Sigrdrifa is the name of the valkyrie in the *Sigrdrifumal*. After waking, she sings out a few lines which are considered genuine old invocation chants, greeting the day, the Aesir and asking that victory be given to the seated. Translated into body and posture the Sigel rune suggests somebody seated or squatting. Another aspect of Sigel is ON *sel, sael*, OHG *salig*, all of which signify 'blessed, holy, joyous, happy'. *Selig* in modern German is 'blissful'. The word *sal* can occasionally be found in religious blessings (or in symble toasts). Legend claims that once there was a branch of the priesthood called the *Seligen* who were known for their healing women and for a deity called 'Fru (lady) Saelda'. It is a curious thing that in German language the sun is feminine. Sigel got a rather bad reputation during the Nazi reign when members of the *Schutzstaffel* (security squad), the ᚼᚼ, adopted it as their symbol.

The Old English Rune Poem

Sigel semannum
symble bith on hihte,
ðonne hi hine feriath
ofer fisces beth

oth hi brimhengest
bringeth to lande.

Sigel is ever a joy to seafarers
when they journey away
over the fishes' bath,
until the courser of the deep
bears them to land.

The Old Norse Rune Poem

Sól er landa ljóme
lúti ek helgum dóme.
Sól is the light of the world
I bow to the divine decree.

The Old Icelandic Rune Poem

Sól er skýja skjöldr
ok skinandi röðull
ok isa aldrtregi
rota siklingr.

Sól is the shield of the clouds
and shining ray
and destroyer of ice.
Rota = wheel.

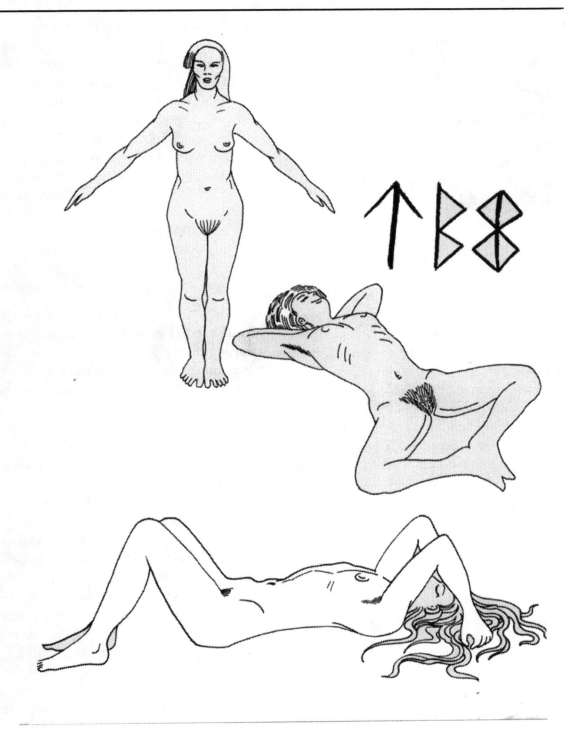

Tir has a rather complex range of interpretations. First of all the rune shows a spear (like that which wounded Odin) or an arrow (such as killed Balder 'by accident'); tools of blood letting. The arrow/spear points in a direction, suggesting motion, development, evolution. Evolution involves two basic forces; the aim is survival, joy, life, procreation and the prize is blood. We all kill to eat, or have others kill our food for us. It is the species that endures and the individual who lives it out. The symbol of bloodletting equals excretion. Two spread legs and something pouring out. Where ↑ reaches for heaven, ⋏ lets flow to the earth. Why was Odin wounded? Why did Tir loose his hand? 'Tiu, Tiwaz, Tir' is one of the oldest Indo-European deities. In the *Germania* s/he appears as 'Twisto' (G *Zwitter* = ambisexual), the androgynous ancestor of mankind. This stage is symbolized by two hands. When in the course of development the Fenris wolf (symbol of the gods of chaos) had to be chained (so that ordered society could develop) Tir gave a hand as a hostage. The wolf trusted Tir as Tir was both (I/you, man/woman) and as such the only honest judge. Now the wolf had to be chained, and in the process Tir lost his hand, and his duality. The god of bloodletting had become one-sexual, and as a male deity, menstruation was replaced by warfare. In the Germanic myths, Twisto transformed into Donar-Thor, god of thunder and into Tyr-Zis, the god of war. There is a similar division between the Celtic deities Taranis and Teutates, who come from the same Indo-European stock, as do the Greek Zeus, the Latin Deus, or the Devas of Indian mythology. The Indo-European root *deiw-* refers equally to the sky god and to heaven.

The ↑ or ⍍ were occasionally carved into sword or spear blades. Possible origin for the name is *ter-* to pass over, cross, go through, *ter-* to turn, *deu-* to lack, be waiting, *deu-* to burn, hurt. OHG *tiuno*, OE *teona* = injury, OICE *tjon* = loss, penalty. Another stream of meanings comes from *deuk-* to lead. OHG *tiuhan*, OE *teon*, to pull, draw, lead. OICE *tirr* = honour, fame. OHG *tiuri* = costly, valuable, dear, holy,. *Tiuren* = to praise; OE *tir* = fame, honour. The OICE *teinlautartyr* is a sacrificial vessel to receive blood. The figure of the twinned one, Twisto, continued in folklore as the twilight traveller, the double one or devil (OHG *tiuval*). OHG *tiufi* is the depth, the abyss. The spear/arrow points at the *tir-star*, the pole star, which is 'ever on its course over the mists of night and never fails'. In this sense the earth axis itself is the ↑ pointing to the north. The Tir-star was sometimes called the 'need-nail', the nail that holds the worlds in place and around which the heavens revolve.

The Old English Rune Poem

Tir bith tacna sum
healdeð trywa wel
with aethelingas
a bith on faerylde
ofer nihta genipu
naefre swiceth.

Tir is a (guiding) star;
well does it keep faith with princes;
it is ever on its course
over the mists of night
and never fails.

The Old Icelandic Rune Poem

Týr er einhendr áss
ok ulfs leifar
ok hofa hilmir
mars tiggi.

Týr is a one-handed god
and leavings of the wolf
and prince of temples.
Mars

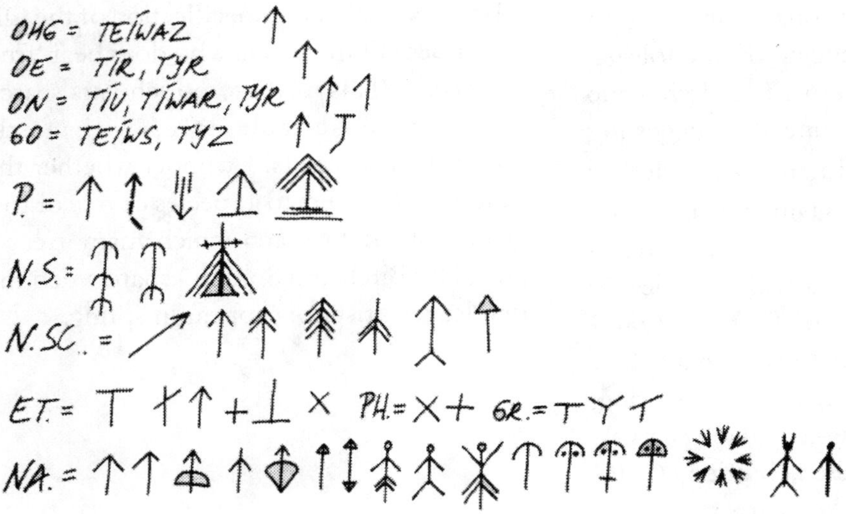

The Old Norse Rune Poem

Týr er aeinendr ása;
opt vaerðr smiðr blása.

Tyr is a one-handed god;
often has the smith to blow.

OHG = TEIWAZ
OE = TÍR, TYR
ON = TÍU, TÍWAR, TYR
GO = TEIWS, TYZ

P =

N.S. =

N.SC. =

ET =   PH =   GR =

NA =

Beorc is one of the tree runes. Though some scholars connect it with the poplar and the OICE poem mentions 'abies', the fir, the basic symbolism points at the birch tree, OHG *birka*, OE *berc*, ON *björka*, which comes from **bher-eg-* to shine, bright, white. The birch was one of the first North European trees to grow after the retreat of the glaciers, a tree of beginning that was involved in numerous spring festivals to sweep out evil influences (broom), to clothe the 'green man', the 'April fool', and to bring the blessings of fresh life, in the shape of consecrated twigs to each home. Sunlight dancing on the foliage; the first day of a new lifetime. The birch is one of the fertility trees, its rune sign suggesting breasts ᛒ, the breasts and a pregnant belly ᛒ, or a woman on the ground giving birth. The IE root **bher(a)-* to bear, to carry, to endure, to bring is closely connected with the idea of birth. Traces of this can be found in OHG *barnam*, OICE *barn*, Scots *bairn* = a child, ON *burthiz* = birth, OHG *brengan* = to bring, Celtic *endo-ber*, a carrying-in, OHG *bur*, OE *burlic* = borne up, exalted, burden, OHG *barwon*, OE *bearwe* = basket, barrow.

Then there are OE *beorgan*, OICE *bjarga, barg*. OHG *bergen* = to protect, to hide, shelter, which is the source for *Berg* (G = a mountain fortress), or *Burg* (G = a castle). The Edda mentions *bjargrunar*, runes that protect and hide. Allied is the concept of innocence and simplicity. OHG *bar*, OICE *berr* = bare, nude, open vulnerable, sometimes even 'without' or 'free'.

In a sense the Berg(mountain) concept (OE = *beorh, beorge*) refers to hills and dolmen. The dolmen structure is the feminine aspect of megalith religion, the womb of stones where rebirth was experienced, deep below the hill. Modern tradition claims that ᛒ is the rune of the mother goddess. The ᛒ shape can be seen as mountains, yet it can also signify the waves of the sea. OHG *ber*, ON *bara* = a wave. Last, there is the nebulous figure of the lady Berchte, who ends the 'wild hunt' time with her namesday the 6th of January. Her Irish counterpart, the goddess Brigid or Bride (meaning 'bright' and 'exalted') may also be related. Not all of the specification of the OE rune poem fit the Birch, who does bear 'fruit and seeds.' This made some scholars search for a more suitable tree, with fairly unconvincing results. I wonder whether the rune actually refers to a species of tree or to a quality of bright green which many trees - including Birch and Spruce - share when the first leaves or shoots appear in spring.

The Old English Rune Poem

Beorc byth bleda leas
bereth efne swa ðeah
tanas butan tudder
bith on telgum wlitig,
heah on helme
hrysted faegere
geloden leafum
lyfte getenge.

Beorc bears no fruit, yet without
seed it brings forth suckers
for it is generated from its leaves.
Splendid are its branches
and gloriously adorned
its lofty crown
which reaches to the skies.

The Old Norse Rune Poem

Bjarkan er laufgrónstr lima
Loki bar flaerða tima.

Bjarkan has the greenest
leaves of any shrub;
Loki was fortunate in his deceit.

The Old Icelandic Rune Poem

Bjarkan er laufgat lim
ok litit tré
ok ungsamligr viðr
abies buðlungr.

Bjarkan is a leafy twig
and little tree
and fresh young shrub
Abies = fir or spruce.

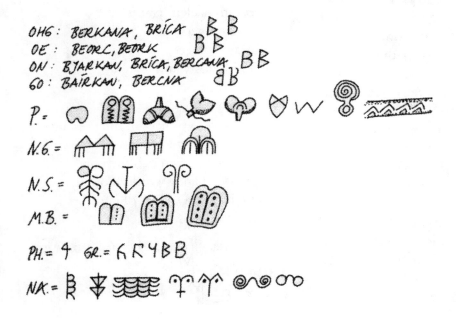

Eh is rune no 19 in the OE poem. The rune is called 'eh' which means *Ehe* = marriage in modern German. (This idea is suggested by the posture of two people in ᛗ touching hands.) *Eh* goes back to OHG *ehin* = one, *ea, ehwa* = eternity, right, law, forever, *e(o)haft* = just, holy, *ehwart* = high priest, *eban, ebin* = equal, just, in unity, even and OE *ewa* = marriage contract. OICE *ae* = always, ever, *aevi* = lifetime. All of these go back to IE *aiw*- meaning originally 'life force' or 'life span', which later developed into words such as 'aeon' or 'eternity'. The text of the poem is somewhat obscure. Eh is one of the runes which may be influenced by the Celts. We are reminded of horses (see Tacitus on horse cults), the horse being an animal of Epona with a hoof print like a moon sickle. Among the Venetian people, who lived at the German/Polish coast of the Baltic, it was a popular custom to keep white horses in the temple of Swantewit, the many faced god. These horses were oracles. For divination a number of lances were erected in a field. The god was invoked, the question asked, and then a sacred horse was released to run through the lances.

If it came through without touching or knocking any of them over, the signs were auspicious. But if it did touch any, the signs were bad indeed. Another version was to draw lines on the ground which the sacred horse had to cross without touching. This method was used every year to determine where the Venetians should go raiding. It was successful and Vineta, the island city, became the richest port in the Baltic before a mighty storm drowned it 'to punish these sinful people for their welath and greed' as the Christians later put it. Long after the ᛗ rune went out of fashion another 'eh' ᛉ was introduced in Scandinavia. It can be seen in certain monkish manuscripts.

The Old English Rune Poem

Eh byth for eorlum
aethelinga wyn
hors hofum wlanc
ðaer him haeleth ymb[e]
welege on wicgum
wrixlath spraece
and bith unstyllum
aefre frofur.

Eh is a joy to princes in the presence
of warriors, a steed in the pride
of its hoofs, when rich men on
horseback bandy words about it;
and it is ever a source of comfort
to the restless:

OHG= EH, EIHWAZ ᛗ ET.= ᚾᚾ PH.= ᚾ GL.= ᛉEₗH
OE= EH, EOH ᛗ
GO = ēgeū, eyz ᛗ E

Man is a rune that describes mankind. Some Nazi ideologists have tried to make it the rune of man (while attributing ᛉ to woman) but this sort of division has nothing to do with the original meaning. ᛘ comes from IE **man-, *manu-, *manw-, *manna-, *monu-,* = humans. The roots have much to do with mental activity, **men-* being the source for 'mind'. OE *gemynd* = memory, mind. OICE = *muna, man* = to remember. OICE *munda*1 = to remember, *munda*2 = to divide, make a difference. OICE *munr* is 1st sense, desire, sensation, feeling and 2 to judge, to divide.

OE *myne* = sense, thought, intent, *maenan* = to remember, dedicate, mention. In OHG we encounter the *minne* concept. *Minna* was originally 'memory', and acquired the additional meaning 'love, sympathy'. A *Minne sänger* was a travelling musician who played love songs at the courts, praising the ladies and barely escaping the wrath of their husbands. The term dropped out of fashion when *minne* had become a dirty word. In the ON we find the custom of *drekka minni*, 'to drink minne' out of the *mindebaeger* the 'minne cup', i.e. to drink in honour of someone. The minne cup was often adorned by a frieze of rune signs. Here are two interesting examples.

The latter includes both symbols; ᛘ and ᛗ in a form that suggests a chain of people, perhaps a circle of worshippers that link to join the force. Both rune postures, ᛘ and ᛗ have been in use as ritual gestures in almost any culture, no matter when and where ᛘ expresses 'reaching for the height' while ᛗ, folding the arms across the breast, brings the force down and in. ᛗ is also two people in the ᛚ position who embrace. The rune poems indicate that man is the 'augmentation of dust', which implies that we are 'lifted up'. They also point out that we are doomed to fail, and to return to the earth that was our origin. Both the Anglo-Saxons and the early Christians were fond of this sort of doleful attitude.

Another, though unproven interpretation suggests that ᛘ is a tree shape, or that of any other plant reaching for the light. We are reminded of the *Myrkwald*, the primal murky forest that covered the entire earth. In the *Edda*, the first two humans are called *Ask* and *Embla* (Gylf. 9) Ask is the ash tree and embla is the alder or elm, depending on which translation you favour.

The Old English Rune Poem

Man byth on myrgthe
his magan leof:
sceal theah anra gehwylc
oðrum swican,
forðam drihten wyle
dome sine
thaet earme flaesc
eorthan betaecan.

The joyous (man) is dear to his
kinsmen; yet every man is doomed
to fail his fellow
since the lord by his decree
will commit the vile carrion
to the earth.

The Old Norse Rune Poem

Maðr er moldar auki,
mikil er graeip á hauki

Maðr is the augmentation of the dust
great is the claw of the hawk.

The Old Icelandic Rune Poem

Maðr er manns gaman
ok moldar auki
ok skipa skreytir
homo mildingr.

Maðr is the delight of man
and augmentation of the earth
and adorner of ships
Homo = man.

OHG: MANNAZ, MAN
OE: MAN
ON: MAN, MAÐR, MANNAR
GO: MANNA

P. =

N.S. =

N.SC. =

N.G. =

ET. =   PH. =   GR. =

NA. =

Lagu is a rune of water. The IE *laku-, *loku-, a body of water, a lake, a sea, is one of its sources, as are *leg-, to dribble, trickle, leading to OE *leccan* = to moisten and ON *leki* = a leak. *Lou- to wash, to bathe, has to do with it and the words OHG *louga*, ON *laug* = lye OICE *laudr* = foam, soap, *laugardag* = bath-day, *laugask* = to clean oneself, *leygja* = to wash, rinse, *loekr* = stream, *logr* = ocean, OE *lagu* = ocean, lake, river, *lagustream* = ocean current, or the scotch *loch*. We are reminded of what psychology calls 'oceanic feelings' (Reich liked them and Freud did not), the sensation of drifting, flowing, expanding that goes with free sexual experience. In the 18 rune system the rune is called *laf* which is supposed to come from 'love'. Now 'love' comes from *leubh-, *loubh- = to care, desire, love, believe (→ leave, → libido). The connection cannot be proven, but this does not change the psychological relationship, the emotional truth. In another sense the rune has to do with law, which comes from *leg- = to speak, and developed into Latin *lex* = law (→ legal, → loyal, → privilege). ON *lag* = law,

laid down. Greek *logos*, logic etc, OHG *lekjaz* = enchanter. OE *laece* = physician, leech.

Thelemites know that 'Love is the Law, Love under Will'. A good law was called 'log laukjofn' or 'laukar löggr', i.e. law as straight as the leek plant (*allium porrum*). Leek is the first plant that appears after the flood (*Edda*, Voluspa), it was often used as a symbol of potency and purification. Before refrigeration it was the first green vegetable to appear after winter. It was sacred to the Celts and is still the national vegetable of Wales. The etheric oils of leek have disinfecting powers. The plant was frequently added to beer, ON *blódlaukar* = bloodleek, the herbs and spices that were thrown into the sacrificial beer. The German word *Lauch* (leek) often occurs in words that signify nobility.

In the St Gallen manuscript the ᛚ rune is called 'lagu the leohto', i.e. the glowing (light) ocean. 'Light' comes from a very similar family of roots. *Leuk-, *leug- = to bend, wind, to glow, to shine, being the source for OHG *laug, lauc, lauga*, OE *leig*, OICE *log, loga, leygr*, = fire, flame. This is the source of Latin *lux* and ON Loki... whether this phenomena has to do with the ᛚ rune is an open question.

The Old English Rune Poem

Lagu byth leodum
langsum gethuht,
gif hi sculun nethan
on nacan tealtum
and hi saeytha
swythe bregath
and se brimhengest
bridles ne gym(eð)

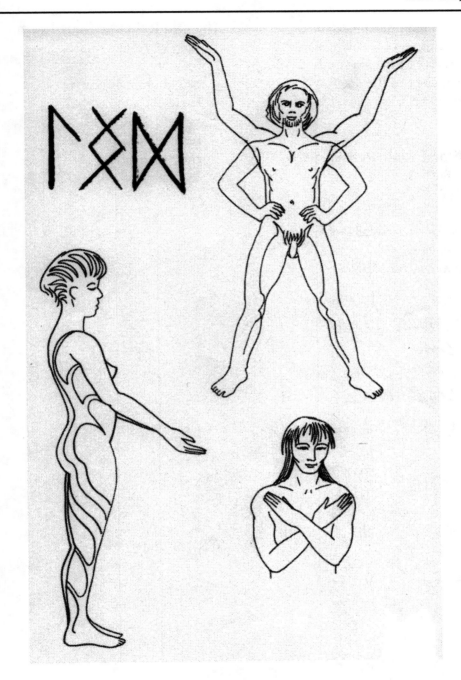

Lagu seems interminable to men,
if they venture on the rolling bark
and the waves of the sea terrify them
and the courser of the deep
heed not its bridle.

The Old Norse Rune Poem

Logr er, faellr ór fjalle
foss;en gull ero nosser.

Logr is a river which falls from
a mountain side;
But ornaments are of gold.

The Old Icelandic Rune Poem

Lögr er vellanda vatn
ok viðr ketill
ok glömmungr grund.
Lacus lofðungr.

Lögr is eddying stream
and broad geyser
and land of the fish
Lacus = lake.

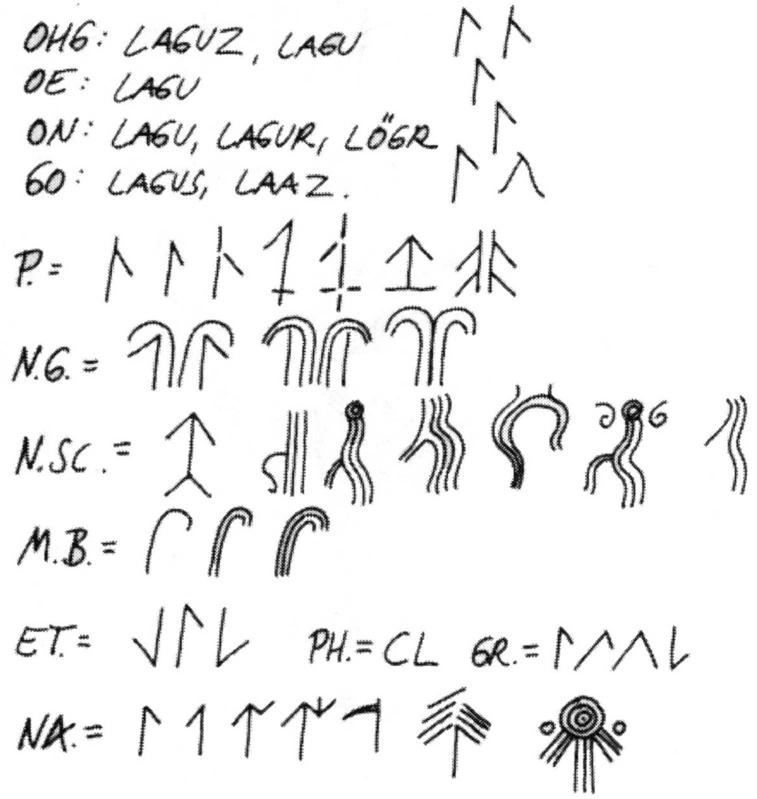

OHG: LAGUZ, LAGU
OE: LAGU
ON: LAGU, LAGUR, LÖGR
GO: LAGUS, LAAZ.

P. =

N.G. =

N.SC. =

M.B. =

ET. =   PH. = CL   GR. =

NA. =

Ing is a rune associated with the fertility gods Ingwi-Freyr and Freya. It is rune no 22 of the OE poem and the common futhorc. Some scholars cite a mother of Frey and Freya, called 'Inguna', but on the whole the name Ingwi describes Freyr himself. It might be a symbol reflecting the time-honoured custom of making love in the fields, the simplified ◇ being a field shape like ⬧ That the hero Ingwi travels eastward might suggest his re-entry of the source of his origin (east) but this is just guesswork. Some scholars got east and west muddled up and wrote that Ingwi was a Nordic king who travelled across the Atlantic to found the Inca kingdom, there are several of bizarre books on the theme.

The Old English Rune Poem

Ing waes aerest
mid East Denum
gesewen secgun
oth he siððan est
ofer waeg gewat;

waen aefter ran;
ðus Heardingas
ðone haele nemdun.

Ing was first seen by men
among the East-Danes, till,
followed by his car,
he departed eastwards
over the waves.
so the Heardingas named the hero.

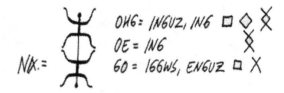

Dæg is rune no 24 of the OE poem. In some versions of the common Germanic futhorc it is the last rune, in others it is the one before ᛟ. IE *agh-* = a day, a span of time. *Dheg-*, to burn, heat, are the sources of OICE *dagr*, OE *deag*, OHG *tag*: day. The old idea of 'day' used to include 'night', indeed we are told (Tacitus) that time was calculated in nights and night was thought to precede day. Consequently the Germanic 'day' used to begin after sunset, with feasting and celebration. The two halves of ᛗ mightsymbolize this polarity, and the cerebral hemispheres which find the order of polarity obvious and natural (as it reflects them). The ᛗ symbolizes the double axe, which was a sacred weapon both for the megalith cultures and the Indo-Europeans. The double axe, in its earliest form, was made of stone and buried in sacred places. Stone double axes have been found under Menhirs in Brittany. They were also popular sacrifices in a number of megalithic and stone age cultures. Up until the last century, popular peasant belief called such axes 'thunderbolts'. They were frequently buried under farmhouses to protect them against lightning. The symbol was probably a sign of duality/polarity, much like the Chinese yin/yang symbol, like summer/winter, day/night and woman/man it reflects union, communication, equilibrium.

The Old English Rune Poem

Daeg byth drihtnes sond,
deore mannum
maere metodes leoht,
myrgth and tohiht
eadgum and earmum,
eallum brice.

Daeg, the glorious light of the creator,
is sent by the lord, it is beloved of men,
a source of hope and happiness
to rich and poor,
and of service to all.

OHG: ᴅAG, ᴅAGAᴢ ᛗ ᛘ   PH.: ᛈ GR.: ᴅ ᴧ ᴅ
OE: ᴅAEG   ᛗ ᛘ
GO: ᴅAGS, ᴅAAᴢ ᛗ ᶔ   NR.: ᛞ ᛏ ᛏᛏ ᛢ ⬡

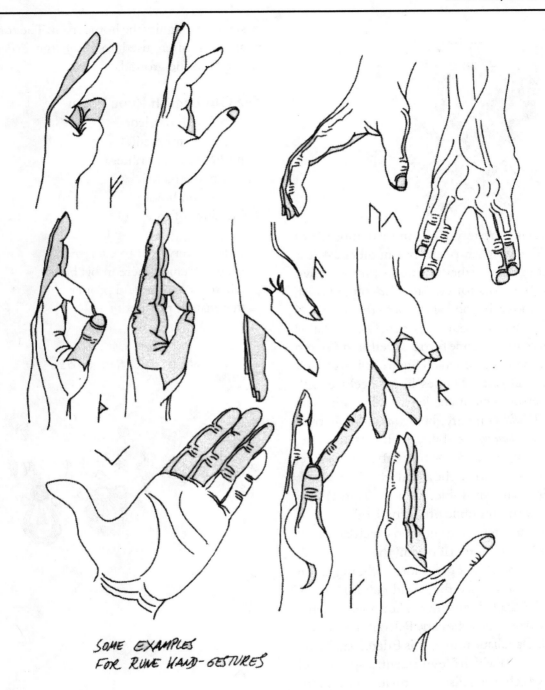

SOME EXAMPLES
FOR RUNE HAND-GESTURES

Ethel is a mystery. The rune is number 23 of the Old English poem but number 24 (the end) in some other common futhorc rows. Possible roots for *othil* are: **ud-* out, utmost, **eti-*, above, beyond and **udero-* the womb. ⊗ is the 'ancestral country', Eden, Daath, Dathyl or perhaps the bone fortress Oeth and Anoeth (→ Noatuan), of which Squire tells us that it was built out of bones like a beehive with numerous chambers like a labyrinth. The OICE *edli* = nature, being, *odal* = inherited country, *odlingr* = nobility, OHG *ot* = treasure, property, *uodil, odhil* = property, inheritance, homeland. It might be asked why the Futhorc begins with movable property (cattle) and ends with immobile property (land).

It is an interesting question which 'ancestral home' or 'country of origin' the ⊗ rune will reveal to you. Some get visions of the migration moves, others see the island culture loosely called 'Atlantis' and others, like myself, emerge in the dawn ages, the early Paleolithic periods.

In Qabalistic terms, ⊗ is Eden, Daath, the abyss out of which life and identity sprang and into which being dissolves on its journey into self (present and absent). The Nazis used the ⊗ symbol to signify the home front. The rune posture is often used to discharge excess energy into the ground.

The Old English Rune Poem

Ethel byth oferleof
aeghwylcum men,
gif he mot ðaer rihtes
and gerysena on
brucan on bolde
bleadum oftast.

Ethel is very dear to everyman,
if he can enjoy there in his house
whatever is right and proper
in constant prosperity.

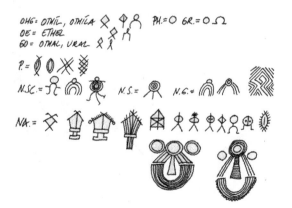

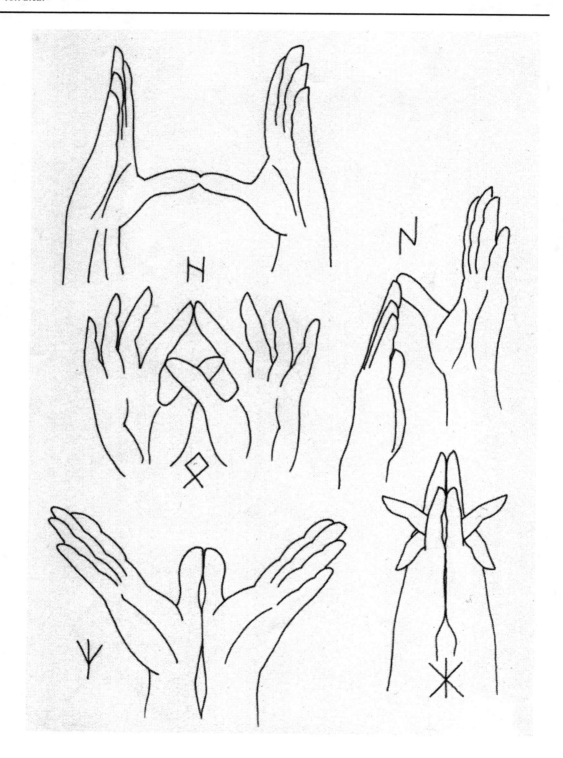

The 24 runes treated above are the commmon Germanic futhorc. In England several runes were developed out of the basic continental range. Some of them are described in the *Old English Rune Poem*. These runes are enigmatic. Few scholars have offered sensible interpretations, and I am no exception to the rule. I offer them for the sake of completeness. Do your own research!

Ac is a variation of ᚠ, its sound is an 'a'. The rune describes the oak tree (MHG *eich*, OHG *eih*, ON *eik*, OE *ak, ac*, from IE **ayg-*). Oak and beech trees were the food sources for pigs which were driven into the woods for fattening every Autumn. The word 'acorn' is related, from the IE **og-* growth, wild fruit. There is so much folklore connected with the Donar-oak that I can only suggest that you read it up in the usual source books. The oak tree is connected with the lightning flash, which may have to do with the fact that oaks love to grow on subterranean water streams. To the population, the 'thunder oak' was the place where justice was given. The oak is often a symbol for endurance and loyalty, this has to do with its ability to live long and the way it develops its foliage late in spring but retains it longer than any other leaf-bearing tree. The acorn, with its shape like glans penis, is an ancient symbol of fertility. Acorns were not just a welcome food for pigs. In times of famine, the acorns were watered for days (to get the bitter taste out) and used as meal powder for soups or bread. The bitter astringents of the oak supply a useful medicine that resolves wounds and sores, cleans the skin, eases swollen glands and helps - in the form of a rather ghastly tea - cure diarrhoea.

The Old English Rune Poem

Ac byth on eaorthan
elda bearnum
flaesces fodor,
fereth gelome
ofer ganotes baeth;
garsecg fandath
hwaether ac haebbe
aethele treowe.

Ac fattens the flesh (of swine)
for the children of men.
Often it traverses the gannets bath,
and the ocean proves whether Ac
keeps faith in honourable fashion.

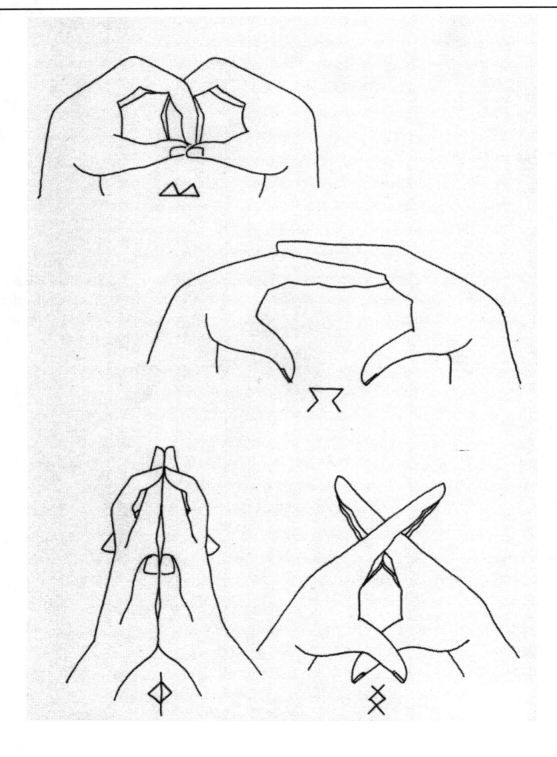

Aesk is the ash tree. The rune was developed out of the common Germanic ᚹ which looks like ᚨ in the OE poem (rune number 4). The symbolism of the ash has been treated in that chapter. The leaves and seeds of the ash are a good diuretic (increasing urine) medicine that is often used to clean the body of accumulated waste. External application is good for rheumatism, muscle-ache and arthritis. The mountain ash or rowan (not related to the ash tree) is also good for healing - the leaves and blossoms produce a tasty tea that stimulates the bladder and kidneys, eases stomachache and diarrhoea, the flowers being a good help against bronchitis and coughing. In the old days, it seems there were few trees which weren't used for healing one way or another.

The Old English Rune Poem

Aesk bith oferheah,
eldum dyre
stith on stathule,
stede rihte hylt,
ðea him feohtan on
firas monige.

Aesk is exceedingly high and precious to men.
With its sturdy trunk it offers a stubborn resistance, though attacked by many a man.

Yr is number 27, another version of ᛣ, it seems. As a commentary Dickins offers a well-deserved 'questionmark', and so far few scholars have found better explanations. The sign could refer to a saddle, a tent or a blanket, plus several dozen other items which make just as much sense. I leave the guesswork to you.

The Old English Rune Poem

Yr byth aethelinga
and eorla gehwaes
wyn and wyrthmynd,
byth on wicge faeger
faestlic on faerelde,
fyrdgeatewa sum.

Yr is a source of joy and honour
to every prince and knight,
it looks well on a horse
and is a reliable equipment
for a journey.

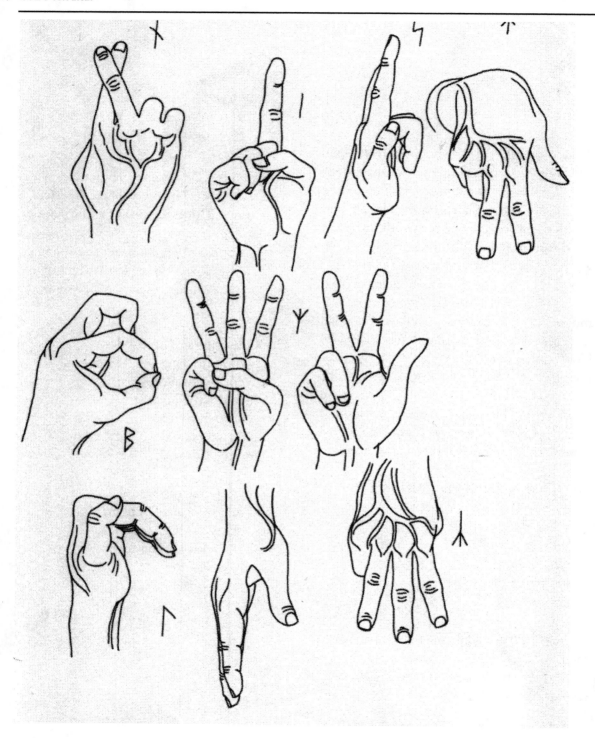

Iar, number 28, is a mysterious amphibious creature which cannot be easily defined . Attempts to explain it as a frog or eel have been made. My own guess is that ✳ is a picture of a beaver. Now you might complain that a beaver is no fish. This is true from the modern point of view. Up to the late medieval time the beaver (and the fish otter) were considered 'fish', which made them welcome food for the rich on fridays and during the fasting seasons.

The Old English Rune Poem

> Iar byth eafix
> and ðeah a bruceth
> fodres on foldan,
> hafath faegerne eard
> waetre beworpen
> ðaer he wynnum leofath.

> Iar is a river fish and yet it always feeds on land; it has a fair abode encompassed by water, where it lives in happiness.

Ear, number 29, is the sound *ea, eo*, and means 'water' in Old English. *Ea* in OHG = eternity. (see Ehwaz). It has been claimed that *Ea* is found both in 'sea' and 'earth' (from IE *er- earth, ground). Then there is a curious deity called Eor, Ear, Er, Iar who gave his name to the 'Irminsul', from OHG *irmino- large, whole, and *sul*, pillar. The Irminsul is the pillar that holds heaven and earth in place, the world axis, in a sense, and the human spine. OHG *ermin* = whole, universal. Several huge wooden Irminsul pillars were worshopped by the Saxons. Charlemagne had them cut down and confiscated the treasures (sacrifices) that had been placed around them. Below are three Irminsul symbols, 1 from a Philistine cup (1100 BC), 2 fibula of Vegstorp (Bronze age) and 3 the Old Saxon Irminsul sign. You may notice that the word and sign seem to have very little to do with the poem. Dickins proposes that Ear means 'The Grave'. Can you see a connection between these concepts?

The Old English Rune Poem

> Ear byth egle
> eorla gehwylcun,
> ðonne faestlice
> flaesc onginneth,
> hraw colian,
> hrusan ceosan
> blac to gebeddan;

bleda gedreosath,
wynna gewitath,
wera geswicath.

Ear is horrible to every knight,
when the corpse quickly begins to cool,
and is laid in the bosom of the dark earth.
Prosperity declines, happiness passes away
and covenants are broken.

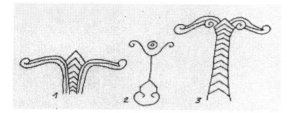

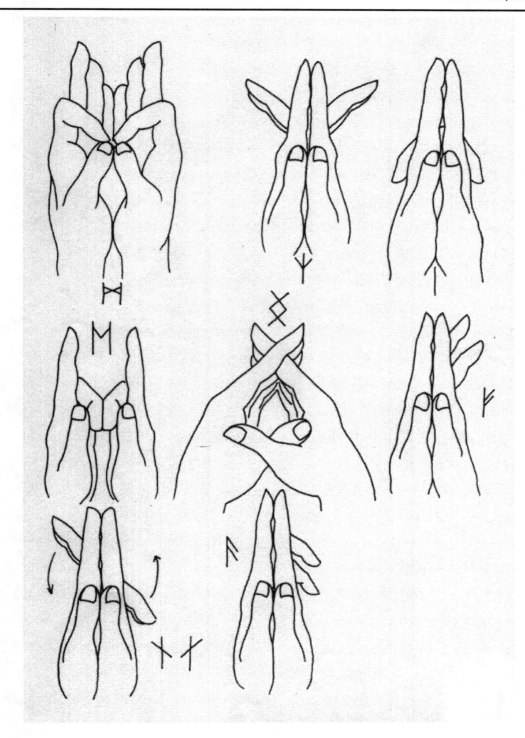

28 To rune with the deep

So far, I have tried to provide you with a set of new tools and techniques. These tools are the rune signs and similar symbols, the techniques are practices such as divination, sigil crafting, song, posture, astral projection and so on. The articles on history and ethnology should have given flesh and belief to the signs. The various experiments may have produced a few new experiences which, I hope, have enriched your patterns of ritual and festivity.

Now we come to a topic which is very dear to my heart. It is the exploration of new territory. Maybe these lines will make more sense to your subconscious mind than to you. Previously, I have dealt with particular methods and specific techniques. Now I would like to 'rune' about the patterns that are behind the technique, about the structures of consciousness and about the models that seem to describe them. This chapter will present several models. Like those in previous chapters, they are meant to organize experience. They cannot represent 'the truth', none of us is equipped to experience anything but a personal truth, nor do they describe an 'objective reality', whatever that may be. None of these models is strictly true or real, but if you put them into practice you will find that they produce results.

The 'true history' of the runes, for instance, matters very little compared to the question of what you may do with them. The 'real nature' of the subconscious mind is less important than the 'how do I get in touch with it?' Nor am I only speaking of runes, there are several magical currents (or world views) woven into this net. They have found earthing around the futhorc system, but then they could just as easily be applied to any other system of magical symbolism and practice.

With sufficient experience you may forget about the rune signs and replace them with any other magical symbolism that suits your fancy. There is a secret centre to all magick; the heart and tongue of Helruning, of speaking with the deep. Let us remember, hel is the realm and consciousness of the hidden, forgotten, repressed and unborn, the veiled land of in-between, the outland beyond the limits of our mind, the abyss of horror and dispersion, the earth of origin and innocence and the vastness that defies our comprehension. Hel[1] or Helja can also be seen as an entity, a personification of the deep realm, and this anthropomorphic representation gives us the opportunity of direct communication - we can talk with the sentience as though it were a friend. The Helrunar learn to be a friend of this entity, and to rune with it.

To rune is to talk, sing, chant, whisper, scream or keep silence. Hel and Helja, as you will understand, are metaphors that describe certain phenomena and permit certain modes of interaction. These are not the whole truth, but true enough for our purposes. Other metaphors for the deep realm offer different, and equally valid visions of the inexplicable. In psychology, the hidden reaches are often called 'the subconscious mind' or 'the

unconscious', meaning those parts of our selves of which we are unconscious most of the time. The unconscious mind is not unconscious at all, indeed it is far more conscious than we are, as it receives an immense amount of sensual information, far more than our conscious minds could cope with. Are you conscious of your heartbeat right now, of your breath rate, the chemistry of your gastric juices, your hormone production or the muscular tone in your left foot? Do you know how to laugh, how to walk, swim or ride a bicycle? How do you manage to go to sleep and how do you wake up? Can you remember how you learned to stand, to walk, to run? Your subconscious mind knows these things and does them for you. You do not even have to be aware of them, you can do them and they happen 'automatically'. Learning to walk was very difficult when you were young. Nowadays you do it without even noticing. In exactly the same fashion you have learned to do millions of difficult things, and you have learned them so well that you do not even have be conscious of them. This allows you to concentrate your attention on other activities.

The unconscious mind has a fantastic range of strategies, habits and routines which keep us in action and sustain our world-view, our concepts of reality. More so, it contains an immense store of memories of events and sensual impressions and has methods of using this material in a creative fashion. By night it creates entire dream worlds out of this material, by day it receives the overwhelming flood of sensual data, orders it according to belief,

---

[1] Spelt Hel in the *Edda*, Helja in the Old High German version

filters it according to priorities, providing the conscious identity with a small range of selected experiences and 'forgetting' (storing) the rest. The outcome of this selective and constructive process is what we consider 'reality'.

Reality functions by habit. There are also inner functions. Where do dream visions come from? How do thoughts arise? Do you think in pictures, in words or feelings? Where do these come from? Is it your ego, or some subconscious aspect of 'self' that creates your daily moods, your energy level, your spontaneous reactions, the impulses of desire and dread that motivate you? How does the unconscious mind create such notions like sympathy, antipathy, doubt, hope, belief, trust, confidence, regret, shame, weariness, eagerness, enthusiasm and so on? All of these create a climate, an atmosphere which gives substance to your reality. You may think that you make your own, conscious and reasonable decisions, but then your decision will only look, sound and feel good when the subconscious mind agrees. More often than not, it is the deep mind that provides impulse, choice and motivation, and it is the conscious 'I' that receives these, finds some reasons and explanations for them and thinks it has come to a sensible decision. Healing and wholeness depend on good communication with the deep realm. Reasonable people who fight unconscious beliefs become sick or worse yet, cut themselves off from their living core of joy, inspiration and vitality.

What then, is the nature and will of this 'subconscious mind?' As it takes place largely outside of our awareness, and all that we perceive is what it shows to us, this question is rather hard to answer. The curious thing is that the behaviour of the unconscious mind seems to accord with what we believe about it. Socrates called it his 'daemon' and was thankful for the inspiration it provided. Abra-Melin called it his 'Holy Guardian Angel' and offered prayer and thanksgiving to it. Crowley, who used Abra-Melin's method to make contact with his Holy Guardian Angel, considered it his artistic genius and named it as the source of his best poems and magical rituals. Quite typically, he explained the 'HGA' as a phenomena that can be seen as a personified expression of the unconscious mind, or as a distinct entity with super-human power and intelligence. Both of these explanations are quite true, and there are many others of equal validity. In this case, the magical description of the deep realm is much more efficient than the psychological. Too many psychologists see the subconscious aspects of self as a potential threat.

Now it may be true that the subconscious mind can cause troubles, but this is not what it is there for. Such troubles can arise from misunderstanding between the conscious mind and the deep realm, they can occur when the deep mind learns the wrong sort of strategies or clings to methods that are out of date. All of this can happen, but it is not what should happen. The deep mind tries to do its best for the whole system, and when if finds its methods inefficient it will do its best to change them. If you want to effect a healing you will have to ask the deep mind to do so.

The conscious mind, the reasonable identity can't do this job on its own. The real changes, the transformations of life and experience, come from the subconscious mind. You will find that your subconscious mind wants to heal and will work wonders to improve the situation. The system works on feedback. When the conscious and unconscious aspects learn to work in friendly cooperation healing happens naturally.

Shamanism offers another interesting model. A shaman will not speak of such things as a 'subconscious mind', which is a very abstract and obscure concept, but of a variety of 'spirits'. These spirits are considered definite entities. Usually, a shaman works with spirits that appear in natural forms. There are beast-spirits, plants, trees, fungi, stones, crystals, ancestral figures, archetypal figures (such as the 'first shaman') mythical beings, spirits of the scenery, star spirits and beings of the outer reach and so on. All of these represent parts of the subconscious mind but they are treated as if they were individual entities. These spirits have definite purposes. In many shamanic world views, the mind is viewed as an ecological system with many different life forms that depend on each other. In a healthy mind the system is in balance and all beings get what they require. What the psychologist calls the 'subconscious' is the sum of the whole ecological system. The shamans describe it as the great spirit that unites and harmonizes all life. When a person gets sick, the shaman often considers the disease as the work of an angry or unhappy spirit. This may seem crude if you have learned that you must find the 'real cause' of a disorder through years of psychoanalysis, but then we should remember that the weary task of analysis produces reasons, not healing. If we ask 'why' we will get any amount of justification and personal history.

The shaman says 'the spirits did it', and proceeds to do something about it. Often enough, the shaman finds that the so-called 'angry spirit' is not evil but simply trying to follow its essential nature. We can learn to come to terms with it, to find an agreement that is pleasant for all concerned. Some spirits are 'angry' as they feel that the conscious mind is restricting them. When I do not allow my beast spirits enough action, physical motion, body consciousness or sex they certainly get edgy, then angry. All parts of the self want to follow their nature, and if you ignore, restrict or deny them, they will find ways of telling you so. Some of these ways can be rather unpleasant, so why not ask them from time to time '*hey! subconscious mind, do you have a message for me? Does any part of you wish to tell me something?*'

Does this sound too simple? Do you have to make it more complicated, through the use of a consecrated circle, a prayer wand, a holy symbol, special incense, ritual, fasting, robes and what not so that you may believe in it? It is your belief that determines whether the rite works. If you believe in complicated procedures and serious occult study you will certainly get what you asked for.

The many spirits that populate the shaman's world are often coordinated by a greater spirit, who acts as a helper for the shaman. A shaman may live with several spirit-helpers, who work divination, exorcise unwanted influences, control ritual, heal disease, provide power, offer advice and so on. Such spirits possess a lot of sentience and individuality. They can be considered alternative identities of the shaman. In their own special function they are much more efficient than the conscious mind. Many magical traditions claim that it is difficult to make contact with such beings. This may occasionally be true, but is not always so. Some spirits, especially the more powerful ones like the Guardian Angel of the Abra Melin system may require months, if not years of intense ritual, prayer and purification. Others may come on their own accord when the time is ripe, and appear in dreams and visions to tell the shaman that they wish to be integrated.

This is one of the aspects of magick that is frequently ignored. The spirits and god forms want to be enacted, want to be integrated in ritual, want to be lived in living flesh. It is not enough to merely contemplate such things, the shaman must allow the spirits to act through his or her body, allows them to obsess, to take control. This takes a measure of trust and experience.

I have no intention of discussing whether 'spirits', 'Egos', 'Guardian Angels' or 'subconscious minds' exist or not. In themselves, these terms are meaningless. If we use them for practice, however, we will find that things happen. When we speak to the 'subconscious mind' we do not have to define what it may or may not be; the point is that something answers. Who answers? It depends on your belief.

Austin Spare pointed out that the more you are interested in yourself, the more will this self be interested in you. As Richard Bandler and John Grinder emphasized, there are no useless or troublesome parts in the minds. Each part of the mind, like every life form in an ecosystem, does its best to fulfill a useful function for the whole. Maybe it uses problematic strategies to do its job, but in essence its function is meant to be good for you. If we accept this point of view, change becomes a fairly easy matter; we simply have to find better strategies to improve the situation. Now one of the troubles in this process is the fact that very few of us bother to consider the deep realm. In growing up we all received a lot of negative conditioning, sad beliefs in the necessity of duty, suffering, pain, disappointment and so on. All of these reduce sensitivity. This is the barrier, the shell of armour that keeps the ego apart from self and the world around. If we want to make contact with the essentially life-embracing aspects of ourselves we have to get past the barrier, have to find ways to suspend the restrictive belief long enough for the deep mind to receive a stimulus to change. We have to speak a language that the deep mind understands. We also have to speak it in a way that does not make the ego throw up resistance.

Here arises the importance of trance, which suspends the limited beliefs of the ego and opens its reality for new choices, and of subtle suggestions which slip past the ego unnoticed. Trance is a phenomena that is frequently misunderstood, as many people tend to have firm and dramatic beliefs about it. Introverted or mystical trances are supposed to look like total paralysis in some holy posture, complete with total sensual withdrawal plus a generous measure of amnesia, while extroverted, or shamanic trances come in a package that includes violent twitches, rolling eyes, foaming mouth, a deplorable lack of manners and a full 'blackout' of the conscious identity. Of course such trances do happen on occasion, but on the whole they are rare and quite unnecessary (unless one indulges in show business as part of the job). Most trances are so common that they are not recognized as such. What happens when a friend tells you a story? All you get is a bare selection of words, symbols that mean one thing to your friend and quite another one to you. Nevertheless your mind clothed them in images, sounds and feelings until the experience was vivid and your reaction intense. In a sense a good story teller is a master in hypnosis.

One of my favourite games is to watch the people on the Underground. By the time they have come down the escalator and enter the platform a curious transformation comes over them. Their timing changes - when they enter the train their bodies show all sorts of trance symptoms (i.e. the switch from sympathetic to parasympathetic nervous system). Their muscle tone changes, which relaxes face and posture, and so does their skin colour and breath rate. Politeness requires that people do not look at each other and so everybody stares into some vague nothingness and waits. Soon enough people begin to hallucinate, i.e. to day-dream, to wallow in memories, to hold

inner dialogues, to doze or centre their attention on a book or newspaper which swiftly swallows their entire awareness. Some of them fall into their trance so deeply that they forget to get off and come 'awake' with a jolt. By the time they leave the station their faces are set in the usual, tensed mask again. These people experience a passive trance that is induced through boredom, waiting, lack of interest, monotonous experience etc., and do not even notice it. The same thing happens at boring lectures or classes, during long train or car rides and with any other repetitive, automatic activity. If you close your eyes, relax, calm down and focus your attention on a given word, picture, feeling etc, you get exactly the same effect.

'Becoming a tree', 'merging with the scenery', 'counting breath', 'contemplating a symbol' and other exercises from this book use the same method. These trances may be more intense than the everyday kind as they should capture more of your attention, but this is a difference in degree, not in nature. Awareness of inner activity reduces outside awareness and vice versa. Some trances, such as exhaustion, crisis or being in love, colour the entire vision of outside reality, provided reality is noticed at all.

'Active trances' are a similar phenomena. If you dance and sound a monotonous rhythm on a gong, bell, drum or rattle for long enough you will fall into a typical shamanistic trance state. Any word, gesture, motion or sound that is repeated for a period of sufficient length induces trance, and it matters very little whether it happens in dancing, chanting, prayer or in riding a bicycle, jogging through the park, washing clothes by hand or making love. Indeed, a good dance is also a natural trance.

These are 'active' or 'extroverted' trances in as far as they work by doing something in repetition in outside awareness. Rune song and dance are good examples of this sort of thing. Of course the distinction between 'active' and 'passive' trances is relative. Both methods can easily be combined and will effect much better results than a specialization.

What then, is 'trance' exactly? In a sense, the experience narrows your field of awareness (i.e. you forget all sorts of inessential things) but in another it intensifies it. Drawing pictures, making music, calculating maths, making love, going for a long walk, reading books (and writing them) are all trance states. The 'depth' of these trances depends on your involvement in them. Another aspect of this process is the change in awareness, which results in a different perception. A problem that seems hopeless to the everyday awareness may appear quite different in trance. Perhaps you will perceive in greater detail, or your intuition may work more easily. Compulsive drives may fade away and possibly you perceive new choices, new ways of sensing and doing your will. The subconscious mind is more easily contacted in these states and its answers are perceived with greater clarity.

Hypnotherapy uses trance to offer more freedom to the mind. The same happens in most systems of meditation and magick. Trance depth however, is not necessarily equal to efficiency. Psychologists have wasted decades in the attempt to measure trance depth with a couple of hare-brained performances that may or may not have anything to do with healing. The real miracle is that the subconscious mind of anybody is interested in playing such games at all. A deep trance is no guarantee for a healing or for the acceptance of suggestion, it is merely a state of consciousness. Sometimes we need deep trances to make contact with the subconscious mind and sometimes a few fitting words in everyday awareness will do the job just as well. What counts is the effect of the operation, not the measures we require to achieve it.

In Helruning you will notice that trance states are common, useful and natural phenomena that occur frequently. The trance, however, is but the gateway. Going into trance does not mean anything, the real question is what you make out of it. The answer will come from your subconscious mind. (On the topic of trance I heartily recommend *Tranceformations* by Richard Bandler and John Grinder, and *Hypnotic Realities* by Milton Erickson and Ernest Rossi.)

In a trance state, the mind may be free to accept changes in its belief structure, provided these changes are in accord with the subconscious will. The idea that people in trance will accept any sort of suggestion is a myth. In trance, people are usually much more in touch with their true self aspects and will recognize hostile suggestions quite easily. The suggestion which they accept are those that are in tune with their subconscious mind, which knows pretty well what is good for the whole. Conflict may arise when the conscious mind, the ego, tries to control the whole and pretends to know what is good for it. This gives a clue why magical suggestion if often quite abstract or veiled in the shape of symbols, words of power, sacred gestures etc. Symbolic belief, the rune shapes for instance, is easy to understand for the deep ranges of the mind while the ego cannot easily grasp its significance or meddle in the process. Thus, the runes have been called suggestions.

Suggestions are a pretty everyday matter. Everybody gives suggestions all of the time, clear suggestions, diffuse suggestions, indirect suggestions, conscious and unconscious suggestions and even suggestions that contradict themselves. We suggest what we experience and believe with all aspects of our being, be it in speech and silence, posture, motion, gesture, rhythm, sound level, energetic tone, smell, taste, emphasise and so on. All of these are understood as messages by the people (and other life forms) around us, consciously or not, so that even if we try to be silent this silence is a message. We are attuned to communication and cannot help communicating, as everything said and not said is a valid message. Now while every form of communication is suggestion, there seems to be different degrees of validity to our message. We accept easily all the suggestions that support the reality tunnel and our idea of ourselves (after all, they reinforce what we consider reality) but not so with suggestions that contradict our world view. Good suggestions are often those which do not contradict a given belief but improve it. The subconscious mind will produce the reality the ego believes in, and the ego will believe in its reality, thereby telling the deep mind to produce more of it. If you want to change reality, learn to believe that reality can be changed. If you can manage to believe that reality can be changed easily, with elegance and rapidity, and that such change is pleasant, you are well on your way to joining the Helrunar. The deep mind will learn that it gets more affection and joy supporting this sort of belief, and will make it come true.

When you practice rune song and posture you may perhaps notice that certain gestures stimulate certain forms of consciousness. Some rune shapes seem to lift the focus of attention, such as ᛁ ᚲ ᛦ ᛈ while others seem to lower it ᚠ ᛚ ᛏ ᚺ etc. Often this is accompanies by a sensation of power rushing up or down. Another group seems to centre it in the middle ranges such as; ᚺ ᚷ and those that move attention like, ✳ ᚷ etc. Moving the attention is one of the ways to change consciousness. An example. Moving attention outwards will reduce awareness of inner activities, it is easy to forget oneself when one watches, hears or feels something interesting outside, just as it is easy to forget the outside world when inner activity catches the attention. An interesting inner dialogue will reduce awareness of the outside world, and equally intent listening to outside world will shut the inner dialogue up. The conscious mind seems to have difficulties in being aware of inside and outside stimuli at the same time, and when we work both representations simultaneously (e.g. inner pictures and outside seeing, inner voice and outside words, inner feeling and outside touch etc) we may encounter some interesting states of confusion and/or magick.

Many magical practices move attention into a state of in-between-ness, when we are neither fully aware of the outside world nor of our inner realities. We embrace a fluid, third state that touches both ranges of sentience but goes beyond them. It should be emphasized that in-between awareness is a state (or none-state) in which consciousness (and reality) can be easily changed. Similar changes happen when we move attention in height. Attention at eye level (be it inside or outside awareness)is a very different thing than attention at heart, or groin level. In each of these cases we respond differently to the reality we perceive. What happens to your mood when you stare at the ground for half an hour? What happens when you go bird-watching and stare upwards for a while? Does it make a difference?

I hope that you will not take these words as gospel, it is much more rewarding to experiment. You will find that certain heights of attention are connected with certain moods and feelings. We find a similar model in Castaneda's *The Fire From Within*. In his system, the attention is described as a glowing point of awareness that 'assembles' reality in relation to its position. In Taoism, the same idea is symbolized by a dragon who dances through the oceans of infinity, playing with a fire pearl. This is much more than just a pretty picture. Dragon style Wu Shu contains a lot of movements that actually change the position of this fire pearl, and move attention under

will to change the world.

Spider cults use a similar model. The human aura is imagined as a cocoon or net, and the spider (the attention) crawls around in it. The position of the spider determines the nature of the reality believed. Do I have to add that Odin/Wodan rides an eight legged horse? I mention these matters in detail as I think that they are useful fields of research. The rune postures are not as specific as the model of the fire pearl, but on the whole they seem to produce similar effects. If you feel 'uplifted' or 'down to earth' after your practice you will know where your attention went.

By now you should have some experience in the use of rune shapes and sigils to communicate suggestions to the deep. Here are some other ways. Try rune dance for instance. You could spell out a short, positive key word in rune postures and repeat these until it becomes a proper dance. Another way would be to ask the deep mind for a few runes to create a good dance for some purpose. You select them through divination. Then you go through the motions repeatedly until the sequence becomes automatic and the whole thing induces pleasant a trance.

Dance, I think, is one of the fields of magick and self-exploration that has been badly neglected by the western occult tradition. Half of ordinary psychotherapy could be dispensed with if people treated themselves to fifteen minutes of dancing each day. The same goes for traditional ceremonial magick - if you want power, how about dancing until you get it? Rune dance, by the way, need not be specifically a 'rune dance'. Many of the gestures are so simple and natural that they happen anyway. If you dance wildly enough, quite a few of your guestures will resemble rune signs. The theme is also interesting for group sessions. Part of the group could sing/vibrate a given rune sign while the rest interprets it in dance. Perhaps you, personally, feel shy about dancing, or practising dance in private. Well, isn't this a marvellous chance to ask your deep mind for help? If you ask well, it will tell you how to do it. If you ask very well, you find yourself doing it. Seen this way, a difficulty is a lovely chance to learn something new.

Another useful tool is hand-gesture, or 'mudra', as it is called in some Indian systems. You will have seen the pages of pictures that show a variety of hand signs that more or less resemble the rune signs. Most rune signs can be done with one or two hands. On the whole, such hand gestures are not as intense as the practice of the full posture, but then they have advantages of their own. When you have done some practice and know your way with the runes, each of the symbols will carry an association. If you have worked well, each sign will be connected with certain images, inner words and body sensations, i.e. it will make sense in the three major sensual channels.

In NLP language, you would say that the signs are anchored to certain states of consciousness, and that you can find access to these states by the use of the signs. The hand gestures are just that; useful anchors to tap resources of energy and consciousness. They may not be as intense as the full posture and song evocation, but then they can be practised while waiting for a bus. Such anchors are useful for occasions of trouble and crisis, when mind feels upset and wants to change its consciousness. Of course you will have to work with the gestures for a while to ensure that they are effectively connected with their proper consciousness states, but once this connection is made the mind focused on the hand gesture will give a powerful suggestions to the deep realm.

I would like to add that most aspects of ritual magick work with such anchors. The wand is just a stick of wood or metal. Consecration and repeated practise connect it with the subconscious realm of will. Once this connection is made, the magician who wields the wand finds access to Will naturally. Ritual magick uses dozens of such anchors; robes, bells, incense, temple furniture, circle, crown, sword, wand, cup, pentacle, talismans, fetishes, signs of the gods, candles, words of power, gestures and even the pattern of their application are all anchors that touch and activate specific parts of the mind. A good magician can create and dissolve such anchors as s/he wills. A beginner usually depends on them and believes that the power resides in the objects, not in the associations that connect them to the deep mind. This is why beginners collect costly toys while experts can more readily improvise.

Well these are some ways of speaking or runing with the deep mind. They are of use in magick, but they equally work in everyday communication. When you communicate to someone consciously you are also speaking with her or his deep mind, and sometimes the deep mind gets the message while the conscious mind does not notice anything. Nema wrote; 'it does not matter to which mind one speaks the truth, speak it to the mind that listens.' Just as you can stimulate your subconscious mind by paying attention to it, asking it for help and thanking it for the things it does for you, you can also stimulate the deep mind of others.

Try this, pick some person who is not very much tune with the depth. When you notice that s/he has trouble, say 'why don't you ask your subconscious mind?' When you notice that s/he has a good idea, say 'hey! What a wonderful subconscious mind you have! Look at what great things it does for you!' Each time you do this, you give the subconscious mind a measure of affection. Soon enough you will find that it responds to you, and produces the sort of phenomena it gets recognition and affection for.

It does not matter whether your test person has any idea about the nature of the subconscious mind. You will be surprised how it likes to be remembered and accepted. Try this with several people and look out for the little signals, gestures, motions, ideas, spontaneous impulses etc that it may use as an answer. Above all, try it with yourself.

We have dealt with speaking. Listening is just as important. Your deep mind will give you plenty of feedback once you begin to watch for it. It will tell you many things, in images, words or feelings, and these forms or feedback are essential for communication. If you merely speak to it without listening for a response it may well happen that it will ignore you and rightly so. We deal with a living entity, not with a machine, so we should forget about 'ordering', 'commanding' or 'programming'. A good suggestion is a request, not a command, and it works as it strengthens the mutual will of the whole system. What we want is friendship and cooperation with the deep mind. We will not get this if we ignore its needs or try to boss it around. You will always get feedback, but sometimes it may be hard to recognize. If the feedback is subtle you will have to watch very carefully. Sometimes it happens that you cannot understand the message you receive. In this case you can ask the deep mind to make it clearer, and if it wants you to understand it will do so. With practice, you will learn to speak in a language the deep understands, and equally it will learn to answer in terms that are clear to you.

Another way of communication is astral projection. This technique allows you to experience a specific part of the subconscious mind by 'travelling in it'. Your presence poses the question, and your subconscious mind answers by producing scenery, persons, events and insights. This method is useful as it is so direct, it allows you to interact with any given part of the subconscious mind directly. The deep mind creates a dream in which you can move and act. In this way you may encounter material that is 'psycho-active' and deal with it on the spot. A good astral journey is 'real' in that it represents subconscious activity in clear vision, sound and feeling. Your job is not passive as it is in many forms of meditation but active, as the environment is fluid and can be changed just as you can change. Such event/experience causes transformation from within. Something very similar to astral projection happens when the Helrunar go for a walk in nature. In the wild and living world we encounter the group mind of all-life, and as we are part of this mutual self, we are dealing with ourselves in a variety of different aspects. When we go out into nature we enter a realm that is completely alive. In such surroundings, the mutual self, of the all-life can communicate with us quite easily. Perhaps our conscious minds will only perceive the more obvious messages, a bird in flight, a stone of curious colour, a twisted tree living the shape of an earth current, a spider in its web and other omens, but our deep minds will perceive and understand much more. For millennia the shamans of all cultures have learned from the natural world. Maatians believe in the vision that the mutual self, the planetary gestalt, will achieve consciousness through those people who manage to go beyond their humanity and tune into the sentience of all-life. As Nema put it: 'I experience the earth as a single living entity, and feel that those of us with neurosystems are the neurosystem of the planet.' Understanding the nature spirits within simultaneously opens the understanding of the nature-sentience around.

Some may scoff at the notion of an all-self that they cannot directly perceive, measure or analyze. Perhaps they may agree that the notion of this living all-self is a useful way to treat the earth and its life with more affection, respect and responsibility. In a time of ecological crisis such a belief, no matter whether it is scientific, religious or plain crazy, is of vital importance for the survival of us all. Personally I do not care whether this all-sentience really exists or whether I'm hallucinating it. The more of us believe in it the better for the health of the whole.

This leads to the topic of earthing. A vision, no matter how grand or refining, is useless as long as it does not effect change. It is the manifestation of our magick, be it in word, deed, picture, sound, art, action or whatever, that gives reality to it. If you wish to be a magus, then go ahead and speak your word. The magick is not worth much unless it makes life magical. Ultimately, there should be no difference between magick and everyday life. If we emphasize earthing, and manifest what flows through us, we give the current opportunity to transform the world.

Sometimes it does not even matter how 'good' or right' the earthing is - the act itself may be enough to stimulate a vital change. Through earthing, the vision is suggested to the world. When one has climbed to the top of the world-tree, the only way is down. The shaman climbs this tree frequently. In between climbs, s/he returns to the world of everyday awareness, to bring a tale of magick and healing to the living. Ritual is one of the ways of doing so. To most, ritual means something mysterious, artificial and strange. To magicians, who have learned some basic rituals, it means a series of symbolic acts, gestures and events that is performed in a specific and pre-arranged way. Such people memorize rituals and believe that power comes from performing them like a smooth running machine. In truth ritual is a natural activity.

We all practice ritual most of the time (any ethnologist could tell you so), rituals that are so common that we rarely notice our own and only recognize those which differ from ours. All customs are ritual, so are all habits, and ritual is in the way we speak, act, laugh, love, worry, enjoy, dream, eat, drink, sleep and so on. The ritual is not what we are doing, but the way we do it. We define our individuality by using our individual rituals. Rituals are behaviour patterns that keep our realities, and consequently your identities, intact. Change your rituals and you change your world view, which will mean that the world changes, and so will you. Magick offers rituals for exactly this purpose.

By integrating new rituals into your life you are changing it. How did rune posture practice feel when you began? If you have had previous experience with magick it will have been fairly easy, after all, you will be used to doing crazy things for no rational purpose. If you lacked this basic training in 'suspending belief' it was probably much harder. No doubt you needed any amount of reasonable arguments plus plenty of determination to get started at all, and when you did practice, it probably felt strange, if not 'unnatural'. Of course the most absurd practices of rune magick are by no means stranger than the way you set up the breakfast table or make love.

Ritual Magick, in its pure form, makes little sense to the conscious mind, but a great deal of sense to the deep mind. It is not surprise that many beginners dread to do 'unnatural', that is unfamiliar, rituals. How can we deal with this difficulty? For one thing, we can make magical ritual more natural by getting rid of memorized prayer, fixed roles, laws of tradition, and other issues that obstruct self expression. By the same mouth we can work on everyday activity and transform it into magical ritual. 'Doing the dishes' is a powerful ritual once you believe that, with each bit of waste removed, your soul is purified. When I tell myself 'I am going to walk up this mountain, it may be a little exhausting but with each step I gain more power and clarity, and when I arrive at the top I will be surprised with the fresh inspirations I will find.' This suggestion attaches a magical meaning to the reasonable activity 'going for a walk' and the doing makes the operation valid. Such associations work, and work well. Ritual magick is just like that, action that spells meaning to the deep mind. Waving a sharp bit of metal does not do anything. If you believe it to be a magick sword, however, your deep mind will be stimulated to banish unwanted influence. Lets take another example; having a shower makes excellent sense to the ego; it gets rid of physical waste. Defining your bathroom as the 'archetypal well of purification' will not make much sense to your ego but will speak strongly to the deep mind. The ego will shrug at this, but will go ahead and take a shower anyhow. And the ritual will work, on both levels of consciousness. 'Everyday life' is full of opportunities for highly efficient rituals.

In Helruning some of the best rites are so crazy that ego gets no reasons or explanations at all. If you are a flexible person who enjoys change and discovery, you can perform them

as a game, or as an 'art happening', but if you are the serious sort of fool who goes in for reasonable occultism and scientific cryptology you will need hundreds of sound reasons to do anything at all, and thousands to persist in it. As helrunar, you will know how often you are foolish, and will appreciate all the freedom that comes from it. Clowns have the complete freedom to do many wonderful and impossible things, rune magick is one of them. It is totally silly to vibrate ancient sound patterns in the woods, to carve suggestions into bone, to make decisions by throwing pieces of wood on the ground or to dance around a fire, snarling and leaping like a beast. On the other hand, everyday reality is quite as silly, but less enjoyable. You are free, to learn, to err and to learn anew. No doubt you will be silly much of the time, but then you will be free to appreciate and enjoy it. If this book has made your magick more flexible it will have achieved its purpose. Though the conscious mind (yours and mine) cannot comprehend all of it, the deep mind does. Like a mirror it will reflect the seer. Where this book ends, the deep mind begins with its instructions. To go beyond the pages, look into yourself. The dance of the helrunar begins now.

Love is the law, love under will.

To the future

Some sources

Adam, K.D., *Eiszeitkunst in Süddeutschland*, Kosmos, August 1978

Älteste deutsche Dichtungen, Insel Verlag, Leipzig, 1964

Amenophis, *Zur Praxis der Runenmagie*, Blätter für angewandte okkulte Lebenskunst, Fraternitas Saturni, Berlin, 1960

The American Heritage Dictionary of the English Language, Appendix: *Indo-European Roots*, Houghton Mifflin, Boston,1981

Anati, Emmanuel, *Capo di Ponte*, Camunian Studies Vol. 1, 1975

Andreas, Connirae & Steve, *Change your Mind and Keep the Change*, Real People Press, Utah, 1987

Anglo-Saxon Poetry, trans. Gordon, R. K., Everyman's Library Vol. 794, J. M. Dent, London, no year

Archaeologie in Deutschland, Schwerpunktthema *Neandertaler* 2,1998:

Conrad, Nicholas J. & Orschiedt, Jörg, *Archetyp des Urmenschen.*

Auffermann, Bärbel, *Mythos vom wilden Mann.*

Conrad, Nicholas J., *Meister ihrer Umwelt.*

Orschiedt, Jörg, *Robuste Typen.*

Richter, Jürgen, *Das Ende einer Menschenform.*

Archäologische Ausgrabungen in Baden-Württemberg, Theiss Verlag, Stuttgart, 1981

Arntz, *Handbuch der Runenkunde*, Niemeyer, Halle/Saale, 1944

Baker, *Man in the Trap: The Causes of Blocked Sexual Energy*, Avon, NY, 1976

Balfour, M., *Megalithic Mysteries*, Dragons World, Limpsfield, 1992

Bandler, Richard & Grinder, John, *Reframing*, 1982

Bandler, Richard & Grinder, John, *The Structure of Magic, 1 & 2*, 1975

Bandler, Richard & Grinder, John, *Trance-Formations*, Real People Press, Moab, 1981

Bandler, Richard, *Using your Brain, For a Change*, Real People Press, Moab,1985

Bauschatz, P.C. *The Well and the Tree*, Univ. of Massachusetts, 1982

Bertiaux, Michael, *The Voudon Gnostic Workbook*, Magickal Childe, NY, 1988

Biedermann, *Bildsymbole der Vorzeit*, Graz, 1977

Biedermann, *Höhlenkunst der Eiszeit*, Du Mont, Köln, 1984

Biel, Jörg, *Treasures from a Celtic Tomb*, National Geographic, March 1980

Boron, Robert de, *Merlin, Künder des Grals*, Stuttgart 1989

Brennan, Martin, *The Stones of Time, Calendars, Sundials, and Stone Chambers of Ancient Ireland*, Rochester, 1994

Busch, Ralf (ed.), *Opferplatz und Heiligtum, Kult der Vorzeit in Norddeutschland*, Catalogue, Wachholtz Verlag, Neumünster 2000

Caesar, Gaius Julius, *Bellum Gallicum*, Reclam, Stuttgart, 1980

I Camuni: Alle Radici della Civilta Europa, Jacla Books, Milano, 1980

Castaneda, Carlos, *Fire from Within*, 1984

Castaneda, Carlos, *The Power of Silence*, Pocket Books, NY, 1988

Chauvet, J.-M., *Grotte Chauvet*, Thorbecke Verlag, Sigmaringen, 1995

Chia, Mantak, *Awaken Healing Energy Through the Tao*, Aurora Press, NY, 1983

Crowley, Aleister, *Liber Al vel Legis*, 1993

Crowley, Aleister, *Magick*, ed. Symonds & Grant, 1993

Crowley, Aleister, *The Holy Books*, Weiser, 1993

Cunliffe, Barry, *The Celtic World*, Macgraw Hill, Maidenhead, 1979

Dickins, B., *Runic and Heroic Poems*, CUP, 1915

Diederichs, Ulf, (ed.) *Hessische Sagen*, Diederichs Verlag, Köln, 1978

Döbler, Hans F. *Die Germanen*, Prisma Verlag, 1975

Duden 7, *Herkunftswörterbuch Etymologie*, Dudenverlag, Mannheim, 1963

Dumézil, Georges, *Loki,* Wiss. Buchhandlung, Darmstadt, 1959

Düwel, Klaus, *Runenkunde,* Metzlerische Verlagsbuchhandlung, Stuttgart 1968

Edda, trans. Simrock, Cotta, Stuttgart, 1986; Phaidon, Essen 1987, edited by G. Neckel, Deutsche Buch Gemeinschaft, Berlin 1926.

Egils Saga, trans. Schier, Wiss. Buchhandlung, Darmstadt, 1978

Elliot, *Runes,* Manchester Univ. Press, 1982

Erickson, Milton H. *A Teaching Seminar with M. H. Erickson,* Bruner Mazel, NY, 1980

Erickson, Milton H., *Hypnotic Realities,* NY, 1976

Ettmüller, Ludwig, *Altnordischer Sagenschatz,* Magnus, Stuttgart, no year

Evers, Dietrich, *Jäger und Bauern,* Catalogue, 1982

Fischer-Fabian, S. *Die ersten Deutschen,* Knaur, München, 1975

Frazer, Sir G. *The Golden Bough,* Macmillan London, 1922

Friedrich, *Proto Indo-European Trees,* Univ. of Chicago Press, 1970

Fries, Jan, *Visual Magick, A Manual of Freestyle Shamanism,* Mandrake, 1992

Fries, Jan, *Seidways, Shaking, Swaying and Serpent Mysteries,* Mandrake of Oxford, 1996

Fries, Jan, *Cauldron of the Gods,* Mandrake, 2003

Ginethal, Charles, *Carl Sagan & Immanuel Velikovsky,* New Falcon Publications, Tempe, Arizona 1995

Golther, Wolfgang, *Handbuch der germanischen Mythologie,* Magnus, Kettwig, 1987

Graichen, Gisela, *Das Kultplatzbuch,* Hoffmann und Campe, Hamburg, 1988

Grant, Kenneth, *Images and Oracles of Austin Osman Spare,* Weiser, NY, 1975

Grant, Kenneth, *The Magical Revival,* Skoob, 1992

Gregorius (Eugen Grosche), *Die magische Erweckung der Chakren im Ätherkörper des Menschen,* Fraternitas Saturni, Berlin, no year

Grimm, Jacob, *Deutsche Mythologie, 1 & 2,* Dummlers, Berlin, 1975

Haack, *Wotans Wiederkehr,* Claudius, München, 1981

Haensch, W.G., *Die menschlichen Statuetten des mittleren Jungpaleolithikums,* Habelt, Bonn, 1982

Halifax, Joan, *Shamanic Voices,* Penguin, 1979

Halifax, Joan, *Shaman, the Wounded Healer,* London, 1982

Halsall, Maureen, *The Old English Rune Poem,* Toronto, 1981

Harner, Miachael, *The Way of the Shaman*, Bantam, NY, 1982

Helm, Karl, *Altgermanische Religionsgeschichte*, 1 & 2, Heidelberg, 1913

Helskog, Knut, *Helleristiningene I Alta*, Alta Museum, 1988

Herrmann, *Deutsche Mythologie*, Aufbau Verlag, Berlin, 1996

Heyne Schuckings, *Beowulf, Vol. 3*, Paderborn, 1961

Hutton, Ronald, *The Pagan Religions of the Ancient British Islands*, Oxford, 1991

Hutton, Ronald, *The Triumph of the Moon*, Oxford University Press, 1999

Jelinek, J. *Das große Bildlexicon des Menschen in der Vorzeit*, Artia, Prag, 1972

Jockenhövel & Kubach (ed) *Bronzezeit in Deutschland*, Theiss Verlag, Stuttgart, 1994

Kalevala, trans. Fromm, Reclam, Stuttgart, 1985

Die Kelten in Mitteleuropa, catalogue, Keltenmuseum Hallein, 1980

Koenigswald, Wieghart von & Hahn, Joachim, *Jagdtiere und Jäger der Eiszeit*. Theiss Verlag, Stuttgart, 1981.

Kossina, G. *Die deutsche Vorgeschichte*, Barth Verlag, Leipzig, 1912-1936

Krause, Wolfgang, *Was man in Runen ritzte*, Niemeyer, Halle/Saale, 1943

Krause, Wolfgang & H. Jankuhn; *Die Runeninschriften im älteren Futhark*, Vandenhoeck & Ruprecht, Göttingen 1966

Kuckenburg, Martin, *Lag Eden im Neandertal? Auf der Suche nach dem frühen Menschen*, Econ, München, 1999

Kuckenburg, Martin, *Vom Steinzeitlager zur Keltenstadt. Siedelungen der Vorgeschichte in Deutschland*. Theiss Verlag, Stuttgart, 2000

Kühn, Herbert, *Die Felsbilder Europas*, Kohlhammer, Stuttgart, 1971

Lange, I. & W. *Vineta, Atlantis des Nordens*, Urania, Leipzig, 1988

Lascaux, Höhle der Eiszeit, catalogue, Zabern, Mainz, 1982

Leuner, H. *Lehrbuch des katathymen Bilderlebens*, Stuttgart, 1985

Leroi-Gourhan, André, *Höhlenkust in Frankreich*, Lübbe Verlag, Bergisch Gladbach, 1981

Locmariaquer, Apecu de la Pensee megalithique dans le Golfe du Morbihan, Association Kergal, 1981

Lowen, Alexander, *Bioenergetik*, Rowohlt, 1979

Lucan, *The Civil War / Pharsalia*, trans. Rowe, Everyman, London, 1998

The Mabinogion, trans. Gantz, Penguin, 1976

MacKillip, Patricia, *The Riddlemaster of Hed*, 1976

MacKillip, Patricia, *Heir of Sea and Fire*, 1976

MacKillip, Patricia, *Harpist in the Wind*, 1979

Magnusson, Magnus, *The Hammer of the North*, Orbis, London, 1976

Malory, Sir Thomas, *Mort d'Arthur*, Insel, Leipzig, 1973

Mathews, John, *Taliesin, Shamanism and the Bardic Mysteries*, Aquarian Press, London, 1991

Momen, J.P., *The World of Megaliths*, Facts on File, NY, 1990

Mondfeld, W. *Wikingfahrt 2*, Koehlers, Herford, 1986

Much, Rudolf, (ed. Lange, Wolfgang), *Die Germania des Tacitus*, Carl Winter, Universitätsverlag, Heidelberg, 1967

Neckel, Gustav, (ed.), *Sagen aus dem germanischen Altertum*, Wiss. Buchgesellschaft Darmstadt, 1974

Nema, *The Cincinnati Journal of Ceremonial Magick, Vol.1, No.5*, Black Moon, 1983

Neuwald, Birgit (ed.) *Germanen und Germanien in römischen Quellen*, Phaidon, Kettwig, 1991

Oppitz, Michael, *Schamanen vom blinden Land*, Syndikat, Frankfurt, 1981

Oxenstierna, Eric Graf von, *Die Nordgermanen*, Stuttgart, 1957

Page, R. *An Introduction to English Runes*, Methuen, London, 1973

Pauels and Bergier, *The Dawn of Magic*, Gibbs & Phillips, London, 1963

Plutarch, *Große Griechen und Römer*, Propyläen Verlag, Berlin, no year

Pörtner, Rudolf, *Bevor die Römer kamen*, Econ, Düsseldorf, 1961

Priuli, *Incisioni Rupestri della Val Camonica*, Torino, 1985

Probst, Ernst (ed), *Deutschland in der Steinzeit*, Bertelsmann, München, 1991

Probst, Ernst (ed), *Deutschland in der Bronzezeit*, Bertelsmann, München, 1996

Pushong, Carlyle, *Rune Magic*, Regency Press, London, 1978

Reich, Wilhelm, *Die Entdeckung des Orgons, 1. Die Funktion des Orgasmus. 2. Der Krebs*, Fischer Verlag/Orgone Institute Press

Rig Veda, trans. Ralph Griffith, Motilal Banarsidass, 1992

Ross, A., *Pagan Celtic Britain*, Constable, London, 1992

Ruspoli, Mario, *Lascaux, un nouveau Refard*, Bordas, Paris, 1986

Schneider, Karl, *Die germanischen Runennamen*, Hain, Meisenheim, 1956

Schützeichel, R. *Althochdeutsches Wörterbuch*, Niemeyer, Tübingen, 1974

Scott, Arthur, (ed.), *The Saxon Age*, Scott & Finlay, London, 1979

Skinner, Stephen, *The Living Earth Manual of Feng Shui*, London, 1982

Spanuth, Jürgen, *Die Atlanter, Volk aus dem Bernsteinland,* Grabert, Türbingen, 1976

Spare, Austin Osman, *The Book of Pleasure*, 93 Publishing, Montreal, 1975

Der Spiegel, 29 / 2004, 131 *Rätselraten um den ersten Künstler.*

Der Spiegel, 34 / 2004, 128-131 *"Die Regeln mache ich".*

Der Spiegel, 48/ 2004, 206, *Pforte zum Himmel.*

Spiesberger, Karl, *Runenmagie*, Schickowsky Verlag, Berlin 1968

Squire, Charles, *Celtic Myth and Legend,* Newcastle, 1975

Stützer, Herbert, *Die Etrusker*, Du Mont Köln, 1975

Tacitus, *Germania*, Reclam, Stuttgart, 1971

Tacitus, *Sämtliche erhaltenen Werke*, trans. Bötticher & Schäfer, Phaidon, Essen, no year

Tannahill, R., *Sex in History*, Sphere Books, London, 1981

Thompson, C. W. *Studies in Upplandic Runography*, Univ. of Texas, 1975

Tohei, Koichi, *Ki in Daily Life*, Ki No Kenkyukai, Tokyo, 1978

Tolstoy, Nikolai, *The Quest for Merlin*, Hamilton, London, 1985

Torbrügge, Walter, *Europäische Vorzeit*, Holle, Baden-Baden, 1968

Erik Ulbrandson (ed.), *Der Wikinger Fahrten und Abenteuer*, Diederichs Verlag, Köln, 1980

Velikovsky, Immanuel, *Earth in Upheaval*, Doubleday, NY, 1956

Velikovsky, Immanuel, *Worlds in Collision*, Doubleday, NY, 1956

Verleger, A. *Taunus Sagen*, Hirschgraben Verlag, Frankfurt, no year

Wernick, Robert, *The Monument Builders*, Time-Life, NY, 1973

Wikinger, Waräger, Normannen, Catalogue, Staatl. Museen Berlin, 1992

Wilhelm R. & Jung, C.G., *Das Geheimnis der goldenen Blüte*, Köln, 1986

Wilson, D.M. and others, *The Northern World*, Thames, London, 1980

Wolf, Hans Jürgen, *Hexenwahn*, Gondrom, Bindlach, 1994

Wolf, J. W. *Hessische Sagen*, Leipzig, 1853

Zolbrod, Paul, *Diné Bahanè - The Navaho Creation Story*, Univ. of New Mexico Press, Albuquerque, 1984

Index

CPSIA information can be obtained
at www.ICGtesting.com
Printed in the USA
LVHW101158301220
675243LV00024B/130